CHAUCER AND THE BIBLE

GARLAND REFERENCE LIBRARY
OF THE HUMANITIES
(VOL. 839)

CHAUCER AND THE BIBLE
A Critical Review of
Research, Indexes,
and Bibliography

Lawrence Besserman

GARLAND PUBLISHING, INC. • NEW YORK & LONDON
1988

Library of Congress Cataloging-in-Publication Data

Besserman, Lawrence L., 1945–
  Chaucer and the Bible.

  (Garland reference library of the humanities ;
vol. 839)
  Bibliography: p.
  1. Chaucer, Geoffrey, d. 1400—Religion. 2. Bible
in literature. 3. Christianity in literature.
4. Bible—Influence—England. 5. Chaucer, Geoffrey,
d. 1400—Dictionaries, indexes, etc. 6. Chaucer,
Geoffrey, d. 1400—Bibliography. I. Title. II. Series.
PR1933.R4B47 1988   821'.1   88–5984
ISBN 0–8240–6340–6 (alk. paper)

Printed on acid-free, 250-year-life paper
Manufactured in the United States of America

For Judy

Strength and honour are her clothing; and she shall rejoice in time to come. She openeth her mouth with wisdom; and in her tongue is the law of kindness. She looketh well to the ways of her household, and eateth not the bread of idleness.

Proverbs 31:25-27

CONTENTS

Acknowledgments   xi

List of Abbreviations   xiii

Introduction   3

Research on Chaucer and the Bible: A Critical Review   15

A Guide to Index I   39

Index I: Chaucer's Biblical Allusions—An Annotated List
  The Canterbury Tales
    General Prologue   55
    Knight's Tale   62
    Miller's Prologue   65
    Miller's Tale   66
    Reeve's Prologue   71
    Reeve's Tale   71
    Cook's Prologue   72
    Man of Law's Prologue   72
    Man of Law's Tale   73
    Man of Law Endlink   80
    Wife of Bath's Prologue   80
    Wife of Bath's Tale   91
    Friar's Prologue   92
    Friar's Tale   92
    Summoner's Prologue   95
    Summoner's Tale   95

Clerk's Prologue	103
Clerk's Tale	103
Merchant's Tale	111
Squire's Tale	121
Franklin's Tale	122
Physician's Tale	123
Pardoner's Prologue	124
Pardoner's Tale	126
Shipman's Tale	134
Prioress's Prologue	136
Prioress's Tale	137
Tale of Sir Thopas	139
Thopas-Melibee Link	139
Tale of Melibee	140
Melibee-Monk Link	161
Monk's Tale	162
Nun's Priest's Prologue	174
Nun's Priest's Tale	174
Nun's Priest Endlink	178
Second Nun's Prologue	178
Second Nun's Tale	180
Second Nun-Canon's Yeoman Link	183
Cannon's Yeoman's Tale	183
Manciple's Prologue	184
Manciple's Tale	184
Parson's Prologue	187
Parson's Tale	188
Chaucer's Retraction	238
Book of the Duchess	238
House of Fame	243
Anelida and Arcite	247
Parliament of Fowls	247
Boece	249
Troilus and Criseyde	253
Legend of Good Women	
Prologue	276
Legend of Good Women	281
The Short Poems	
An ABC	284

The Complaint unto Pity   289
A Complaint to His Lady   289
The Complaint of Mars   289
Womanly Noblesse   290
Adam Scriveyn   290
The Former Age   290
Fortune   290
Truth   291
Gentilesse   292
Lak of Stedfastnesse   293
Lenvoy de Chaucer a Scogan   293
Lenvoy de Chaucer a Bukton   293
The Complaint of Chaucer to His Purse   294
Against Women Unconstant   294
The Romaunt of the Rose   295

Index II: Scriptural References   305

Bibliography   389

ACKNOWLEDGMENTS

I wish to thank those scholars who answered my queries on specific points or who were helpful in other ways: Robert Adams, John A. Alford, the late Judson Boyce Allen, Larry D. Benson, Robert M. Correale, David L. Jeffrey, R. E. Kaske, Robert J. Kiely, John Maynard, Siegfried Wenzel, and Chauncey Wood. The late Morton W. Bloomfield, my teacher and friend, was a source of constant encouragement and unerring wisdom. For help at an early stage in the compiling of the Indexes I am indebted to my research assistants, Jay Berman and Eugene Sotirescu, as well as to Peter Hirshberg, who very kindly aided me with his word-processing wizardry. My wife, Judith Burg Besserman, contributed directly and indirectly to the completion of this study; the extent of my debt of thanks to her is recorded in the dedication. During a sabbatical year in New York City and Cambridge, Massachusetts (1984-85), and at various times since, my work has been greatly facilitated by the gracious and generous hospitality of Charles and Valerie Diker; Dr. Gerald Epstein; my sister, Professor Perle Besserman; and my parents, Jacob and Lillian Besserman.

Lawrence Besserman
Jerusalem, 1988

ABBREVIATIONS

a. Books of the Bible (following the Douay-Rheims nomenclature and order, with King James Bible equivalents given in square brackets where there are differences; the apocryphal books, not included in the most recent King James editions, are indicated by ****):

Old Testament:

Gen.	= Genesis
Exod.	= Exodus
Lev.	= Leviticus
Num.	= Numbers
Deut.	= Deuteronomy
Jos.	= Josue [Joshua]
Judg.	= Judges
Ruth	= Book of Ruth
1 Kings	= First Book of Kings [I Samuel]
2 Kings	= Second Book of Kings [II Samuel]
3 Kings	= Third Book of Kings [I Kings]
4 Kings	= Fourth Book of Kings [II Kings]
1 Par.	= First Book of Paralipomenon [I Chronicles]
2 Par.	= Second Book of Paralipomenon [II Chronicles]
1 Esd.	= First Book of Esdras [Ezra]
2 Esd.	= Second Book of Esdras, alias Nehemias [Nehemiah]
Tob.	= Tobias [****]
Jud.	= Judith [****]
Esth.	= Esther

Job	= Book of Job
Ps.	= Psalms
Prov.	= Proverbs
Eccl.	= Ecclesiastes
Cant.	= Canticle of Canticles [Song of Solomon]
Wis.	= Wisdom [****]
Ecclus.	= Ecclesiasticus [****]
Isa.	= Prophecy of Isaias [Isaiah]
Jer.	= Prophecy of Jeremias [Jeremiah]
Lam.	= Lamentations of Jeremias [Lamentations of Jeremiah]
Bar.	= Prophecy of Baruch [****]
Ezech.	= Prophecy of Ezechiel [Ezekiel]
Dan.	= Prophecy of Daniel
Os.	= Prophecy of Osee [Hosea]
Joel	= Prophecy of Joel
Amos	= Prophecy of Amos
Abd.	= Prophecy of Abdias [Obadiah]
Jon.	= Prophecy of Jonas [Jonah]
Mich.	= Prophecy of Micheas [Micah]
Nah.	= Prophecy of Nahum
Hab.	= Prophecy of Habacuc [Habakkuk]
Soph.	= Prophecy of Sophonias [Zephaniah]
Ag.	= Prophecy of Aggeus [Haggai]
Zach.	= Prophecy of Zacharias [Zechariah]
Mal.	= Prophecy of Malachias [Malachi]
1 *Mach.*	= First Book of Machabees [****]
2 *Mach.*	= Second Book of Machabees [****]

New Testament:

Matt.	= Gospel according to St. Matthew
Mark	= Gospel according to St. Mark
Luke	= Gospel according to St. Luke
John	= Gospel according to St. John
Acts	= The Acts of the Apostles
Rom.	= Epistle of St. Paul to the Romans
1 *Cor.*	= First Epistle of St. Paul to the Corinthians
2 *Cor.*	= Second Epistle of St. Paul to the Corinthians
Gal.	= Epistle of St. Paul to the Galatians

Eph.	= Epistle of St. Paul to the Ephesians
Phil.	= Epistle of St. Paul to the Philippians
Col.	= Epistle of St. Paul to the Colossians
1 Thes.	= First Epistle of St. Paul to the Thessalonians
2 Thes.	= Second Epistle of St. Paul to the Thessalonians
1 Tim.	= First Epistle of St. Paul to Timothy
2 Tim.	= Second Epistle of St. Paul to Timothy
Titus	= Epistle of St. Paul to Titus
Philem.	= Epistle of St. Paul to Philemon
Heb.	= Epistle of St. Paul to the Hebrews
James	= Epistle of St. James
1 Pet.	= First Epistle of St. Peter
2 Pet.	= Second Epistle of St. Peter
1 John	= First Epistle of St. John
2 John	= Second Epistle of St. John
3 John	= Third Epistle of St. John
Jude	= Epistle of St. Jude
Apoc.	= Apocalypse of St. John [Revelation of St. John]

b. Chaucer's *Works* (following Benson, gen. ed., *The Riverside Chaucer*, with modifications adopted from the Variorum Chaucer, ed. Baker et al.):

ABC	= *An ABC*
Adam	= *Adam Scriveyn*
Anel	= *Anelida and Arcite*
Astr	= *A Treatise on the Astrolabe*
Bal Compl	= *A Balade of Complaint*
BD	= *The Book of the Duchess*
Bo	= *Boece*
Buk	= *Lenvoy de Chaucer a Bukton*
CkP, CkT	= *The Cook's Prologue, The Cook's Tale*
ClP, ClT, Cl-MerL	= *The Clerk's Prologue, The Clerk's Tale, Clerk-Merchant Link*
Compl d'Am	= *Complaynt d'Amours*
CT	= *The Canterbury Tales*
CYP, CYT	= *The Canon's Yeoman's Prologue, The Canon's Yeoman's Tale*

Form Age	= *The Former Age*
Fort	= *Fortune*
FranklP, FranklT	= *The Franklin's Prologue, The Franklin's Tale*
FrP, FrT, Fr-SumL	= *The Friar's Prologue, The Friar's Tale, Friar-Summoner Link*
Gent	= *Gentilesse*
GP	= *The General Prologue*
HF	= *The House of Fame*
KnT, Kn-MilL	= *The Knight's Tale, Knight-Miller Link*
Lady	= *A Complaint to his Lady*
LGWP, LGW	= *The Legend of Good Women Prologue, The Legend of Good Women*
MancP, MancT	= *The Manciple's Prologue, The Manciple's Tale*
Mars	= *The Complaint of Mars*
Mel, Mel-MkL	= *The Tale of Melibee, Melibee-Monk Link*
MercB	= *Merciles Beaute*
MerchT, MerchE-SqH	= *The Merchant's Tale, Merchant Endlink-Squire Headlink*
MilP, MilT, Mil-RvL	= *The Miller's Prologue, The Miller's Tale, Miller-Reeve Link*
MkP, MkT, Mk-NPL	= *The Monk's Prologue, The Monk's Tale, Monk-Nun's Priest Link*
MLH, MLP, MLT, MLE	= *Man of Law Headlink, The Man of Law's Prologue, The Man of Law's Tale, Man of Law Endlink*
NPP, NPT, NPE	= *The Nun's Priest's Prologue, The Nun's Priest's Tale, Nun's Priest Endlink*
PardP, PardT	= *The Pardoner's Prologue, The Pardoner's Tale*
ParsP, ParsT	= *The Parson's Prologue, The Parson's Tale*
PF	= *The Parliament of Fowls*

PhysT, Phys-PardL	= *The Physician's Tale, Physician-Pardoner Link*
Pity	= *The Complaint unto Pity*
Prov	= *Proverbs*
PrP, PrT, Pr-ThL	= *The Prioress's Prologue, The Prioress's Tale, Prioress-Thopas Link*
Purse	= *The Complaint of Chaucer to his Purse*
Ret	= *[Chaucer's] Retraction* (concluding *The Canterbury Tales*)
Rom	= *The Romaunt of the Rose*
Ros	= *To Rosemounde*
RvP, RvT, Rv-CkL	= *The Reeve's Prologue, The Reeve's Tale, Reeve-Cook Link*
Scog	= *Lenvoy de Chaucer a Scogan*
SecNP, SecNT, SecN-CYL	= *The Second Nun's Prologue, The Second Nun's Tale, Second Nun-Canon's Yeoman Link*
ShipT, Ship-PrL	= *The Shipman's Tale, Shipman-Prioress Link*
SqH, SqT, Sq-FranklL	= *Squire Headlink, The Squire's Tale, Squire-Franklin Link*
Sted	= *Lak of Stedfastnesse*
SumP, SumT	= *The Summoner's Prologue, The Summoner's Tale*
TC	= *Troilus and Criseyde*
Thop, Thop-MelL	= *The Tale of Sir Thopas, Sir Thopas-Melibee Link*
Ven	= *The Complaint of Venus*
WBP, WBT, WB-FrL	= *The Wife of Bath's Prologue, The Wife of Bath's Tale, Wife of Bath-Friar Link*
Wom Nob	= *Womanly Noblesse*
Wom Unc	= *Against Women Unconstant*

c. Other abbreviations (complete publication information for secondary sources and for selected primary sources listed below appears in the Bibliography, pp. 389–432; for editions of all other primary sources, see Guide to Index I, pp. 43–44):

B	Benson, Larry D., gen. ed., *The Riverside Chaucer*, 1987
CA	[John Gower,] *Confessio Amantis*
Cons.	[Boethius,] *De Consolatione Philosophiae*
DMCH	[Innocent III,] *De Miseria Condicionis Humane*
DCVI	[Boccaccio,] *De Casibus Virorum Illustrium*
DIOFU	[Petrarch,] *De Insigni Obedientia et Fide Uxoris*
DL	[Guillaume de Machaut,] *Le Dit dou Lyon*
EAJ	[Jerome,] *Epistola Adversus Jovinianum*
EETS	Early English Text Society
F	Fisher, John H., ed., *The Complete Poetry and Prose of Geoffrey Chaucer*, 1977
Fil.	[Boccaccio,] *Filostrato*
Inf.	[Dante,] *Inferno*
J	Dudley R. Johnson, "Chaucer and the Bible," 1941
JRB	[Guillaume de Machaut,] *Le Jugement dou Roy de Behaingne*
KJ	King James Bible
La	Landrum, Grace W. "Chaucer's Use of the Vulgate," 1921
La, 1924	Landrum, Grace W. "Chaucer's Use of the Vulgate," 1924
LCC	[Albertano of Brescia,] *Liber Consolationis et Consilii*
LDAD	[Albertano of Brescia,] *Liber De Amore et Dilectione Dei*
Liv. Gr.	[Anonymous,] *Le Livre Griseldis*
LMP	[Renaud de Louens,] *Le Livre de Mellibee et Prudence*
LRTC	[Beauvau,] *Le Roman de Troyle et de Criseida*
M	Manly, John M., ed., *The Canterbury Tales*, 1928
Mir.	[Eustache Deschamps,] *Miroir de Mariage*

N.S.	New Series
O.S.	Original Series
Par.	[Dante,] *Paradiso*
P	Pratt, Robert A., ed., *The Tales of Canterbury,* 1974
Purg.	[Dante,] *Purgatorio*
R	Robinson, F. N., ed., *The Works of Geoffrey Chaucer,* 1957
RF	[Guillaume de Machaut,] *Remede de Fortune*
Root	Root, ed., *The Book of Troilus and Criseyde,* 1926
RR	Guillaume de Lorris and Jean de Meun, *Le Roman de la Rose,* Félix Lecoy, ed.
S	Skeat, Walter W., ed., *The Complete Works of Geoffrey Chaucer,* 1894
S&A	Bryan and Dempster, eds., *Sources and Analogues of Chaucer's Canterbury Tales,* 1941 (rpt. 1958)
SCP	[Raymund of Pennaforte,] *Summa Casuum Poenitentiae*
SDOS	[Richard de Wetheringsett,] *Summa de Officio Sacerdotis*
SLS	[Robert Holkot,] *Super Libros Sapientiae*
SSS	[Robert Holkot,] *Super Sapientiam Solomonis*
S&T	Schoeck and Taylor, eds., *Chaucer Criticism,* 2 vols.,1960, 1961
SVV	[William Peraldus,] *Summa Virtutum et Vitiorum*
VC	[John Gower,] *Vox Clamantis*
Walther	Walther, *Proverbia Sententiaeque Latinitatis Medii Aevi,* 1963-69
Whi	Whiting, B. J., and Helen Wescott Whiting, *Proverbs, Sentences, and Proverbial Phrases from English Writings Mainly Before 1500,* 1968
Wi	Windeatt, B. A., ed., *Geoffrey Chaucer: Troilus & Criseyde,* 1984

Chaucer and the Bible

INTRODUCTION

Two of the most distinguished scholars and critics of
Chaucer have recently stated that the Bible seems to have
been the one book "continually present" to Chaucer's
imagination and "the source which Chaucer drew on more than
any other, and which he must have accepted completely."[1] Yet
these observations about Chaucer's relationship to the Bible,
which were meant to serve as non-contentious guideposts for the
beginning student or general reader, are actually fraught with
logical and literary-historical difficulties; at the very least
(as the Bibliography of the present book attests) they point to
one of the most exciting and controversial topics in the recent
interpretation and evaluation of medieval England's greatest
poet.

How are Chaucer's secular, literary adaptations of the
Bible colored by the unique status of the Bible in medieval
culture? What would "complete acceptance" of biblical
authority have meant to a writer of Chaucer's independence
and originality? And how cogent, after all, is the premise of
Chaucer's "complete acceptance" of biblical authority, given
that he was at work in late-fourteenth-century England, at a
time of material and intellectual crisis that reached to the
very heart of the matter of biblical authority itself? How
much did he in fact draw from the Bible? If it was "continually
present to his imagination," then how did the Bible impress
itself upon him? In precisely what ways? With what local as
well as wider structural and thematic effects on his poetry? To
what extent did the literary nature of the Bible—"alle the

bokes of Goddis storye," as one Middle English Bible manuscript refers to it—influence Chaucer's writing of fiction, especially his "boke of the tales of Caunterbury"?[2] Did he have a "biblical" period or is the influence of Scripture uniformly in evidence throughout his works? What are the broader implications of Chaucer's uses of the Bible for his poetics at large?

To begin by trying to assess the place of the Bible in medieval culture is like trying to apprehend the oxygen in the air we breathe. In the liturgy, in proverbs and idioms of common speech, in the language of the law and of political thought, through dramatic performances in churchyards and in village squares, in the art of the cathedrals and of parish churches, for high born and low born alike, the Bible was everywhere; it was a constant component of the mental life of medieval men and women.[3] Throughout the European Middle Ages it was regarded as the sole irrefutably true source of history, wisdom, and doctrine, a guide to proper actions and procedures in all the domains of human endeavor. If today a worldwide bestseller may still be touted as "second only to the Bible" in sales, we can trace the origin of this bromide to the Middle Ages; for even then, when producing a single copy of this preeminent text was a laborious procedure, it surpassed all other books—excepting the liturgical service books derived from it—in distribution and in the lavish expenditures that were regularly incurred to produce, to illustrate, and to bind it.[4] It was the book upon which a serf would swear his oath of fealty to his lord, a book whose mere physical presence could perform miracles.[5]

Claims for the Bible's absolute authority, necessary and sufficient truth, and preeminent beauty are commonplaces of medieval ecclesiastical literature. As Augustine wrote in his *De Doctrina Christiana*:

> . . . the knowledge collected from the books of the pagans, although some of it is useful, is also little as compared with that derived from Holy Scriptures. For whatever a man has learned

elsewhere is censured there if harmful; if it is useful, it is found there. And although anyone may find everything which he has usefully learned elsewhere there, he will also find very abundantly things which are found nowhere else at all except as they are taught with the wonderful nobility and remarkable humility of the Holy Scriptures.[6]

Augustine's words, or a reflex of them, lie behind these words in the seminal Rule of Saint Benedict: "For what page or word of the Bible is not a perfect rule for temporal life?"[7] And similar ideas appear in an influential formulation by the twelfth-century ecclesiastical author, Hugh of St. Victor, who said of the Bible: "It can never be absurd; it can never be false . . . it admits no contradiction; it is always appropriate, always true."[8]

In Chaucer's time and place, too, we feel safe in assuming, Augustine's, Benedict's, and Hugh of St. Victor's claims for the preeminence, inviolability, and stability of biblical authority and meaning and for the art and beauty of the Bible were automatically and unconditionally granted. In medieval library inventories the Bible is frequently listed as *Bibliotheca* or *Bibliotheca sacra*—a listing that invites us, as Cahn says, "to regard Scripture as a vast repository of wisdom, a library, a world" (1982, p. 11). But when Chaucer, at the beginning of the Canterbury pilgrimage, refers to Christ's "brode" speech in "hooly writ" to indemnify himself against charges of scurrility on account of any ribald stories he may be about to tell, and then doubles his indemnity with an appeal to a purported saying of Plato from the *Timaeus*: " . . . whoso that kan hym rede,/ The wordes moote be cosyn to the dede"—a saying that sounds more like a homely proverb than a deep platonism (see *CT,* I [A] 725-46)—we would be more than a little remiss not to recognize that his words constitute something other than simply another link in the catena of unquestioning deference and obeisance before the determinative power of the Bible that I have sketched.

At the end of the Canterbury pilgrimage, long after Chaucer's appeal in the *General Prologue* to Christ's "broad"

speech in the Bible, and after many ribald stories containing
scores of travestied biblical passages have been told, Chaucer's
Parson approaches the issue from another angle when he
explains why he is in no way troubled by the fact that the
Bible sometimes (as in Genesis 19) speaks of "horrible" things
like sodomy: " . . . but though that hooly writ speke of horrible
synne, certes hooly writ may nat been defouled, namoore than
the sonne that shyneth on the mixne ['dunghill']" (*CT*, X [I]
911). Chaucer's probable Latin source (identified by Siegfried
Wenzel [1974]) reads: "Ibi dicit expositor Radulphus quod non
vituperandus stilus Spiritus sancti etsi sordes scribit, sicut nec
radius solis cum immunda ['filthy' or 'foul (things)']
illustrat. . ."; but, as Wenzel illustrates, the image was
normally used to explain the stability of the sacraments and
Christian doctrine, even in the hands of "an evil preacher or a
sinful priest" (376, n. 117)—not to protect the Bible.[9]

The Parson's use of the sun-dunghill simile leads us to
another conjunction in the area of fiction and the Bible, a
conjunction between Chaucer and the older Italian
contemporary from whose works he borrowed (some would say
plagiarized) more major narrative subject matter than from
anywhere else, the Bible included (see Root [1912], McGrady
[1977-78], and Wallace [1985]). For in the "Conclusione
dell'Autore" of his *Decameron*, Boccaccio proposes an
extraordinary double analogy: it anticipates both Chaucer's use
of the Bible in the *General Prologue* to justify the telling of
"dirty" stories and Chaucer's use of the sun-dunghill simile in
the *Parson's Tale* to protect the Bible from pollution. Boccaccio
writes:

> No corrupt mind ever understood a word in a healthy way!
> And just as fitting words are of no use to a corrupt mind, so a
> healthy mind cannot be contaminated by words which are not
> so proper, *any more than mud can dirty the rays of the sun or
> earthly filth can mar the beauties of the skies. What books,
> what words, what letters are more holy and more revered than
> those of the Holy Scriptures? And yet there are many who have*

perversely interpreted them and have dragged themselves and others down to eternal damnation because of this. Everything is, in itself, good for some determined goal, but badly used it can also be harmful to many; and I can say the same of my stories."

(trans. and ed. Musa and Bondanella [1977], p. 145; my italics)

Placing his stories on the same plane as Scripture—"good for some determined goal" as Scripture is, and subject to the same kind of perverse mishandling as Scripture is—Boccaccio takes a stance that was unusually bold. More daring than Jean de Meun or any of his other predecessors, what he asserts in this passage is nevertheless recognizable in the context of the scholastic revolution in medieval literary theory to which, as A. J. Minnis has shown ([1984], pp. 190-209, et passim), both he and Chaucer were heirs.[10] This was a revolution in the light of which one major facet of Chaucer's individual artistic achievements can be seen for what it is: a bold and unrivaled extension of human, secular fiction into dialogue and debate with the sacred Word.

As a poet, then, Chaucer seems to have had something else in mind when using the Bible than merely demonstrating its inviolability, abiding by orthodox ecclesiastical procedures for its interpretation, or enunciating a pious churchman's awe for its status. The Parson, after all, is a figure in the *Canterbury Tales*, in a work of fiction. And in creating such biblical adepts as the Pardoner and the Wife of Bath—other figures in that same fiction—Chaucer problematized the orthodox claim advanced by the Parson in a way that is profoundly vexing.

The Pardoner, for example, urges his listeners to "read the Bible"—it will validate everything he has to say; but he makes that obviously fallacious claim border on the absurd by having first defined himself as a quintessentially anti-biblical man ("I wol noon of the apostles countrefete"), by slyly introducing the counter-example of Attila the Hun into his remarks about abstemious Old Testament warriors, and by taunting his audience with a quote from the wisdom of "Lamuel" in the Book of Proverbs, which they might mistake for something having to do with Samuel (see *CT*, VI [C] 447, 573-86)![11] His avaricious exploitation of the Bible turns it into a lethal weapon, like the "rasour sharp" carried up the sleeve of his literary ancestor, the figure of False-Seeming in the *Romance of the Rose*—a figure who bears a Bible "about his neck" (*RR* 7412-20). Perhaps the simplest (but not the only) way of understanding the Pardoner's uses of the Bible is in terms provided by Chaucer's contemporary, the conservative John Gower, who warns his reader, through the priestly figure Genius, that there are many men who "speke of Peter and John but think Judas in their hearts" (*CA* 1.655-57).

Gower's formula, applicable to the Pardoner, seems however to be a much less adequate way of explaining the textual strategies applied to the Bible by the Wife of Bath. To be sure, she too quotes the Bible in a selfish and self-interested way. But when she puzzles over what Jesus could possibly have meant when he told the Samaritan Woman " . . . 'that ilke man that now hath thee/ Is noght thyn housbonde,'" and when she authoritatively informs her listeners that *she* knows what St. Paul *must* have meant when he said it is good for a man "no womman for to touche" (see *CT*, III [D] 14-20, 8-88, etc.) she is broaching an issue—the problem of validity and authority in biblical interpretation—that obviously puzzled Chaucer and his contemporaries as well.[12]

All of the above instances of biblical allusion in Chaucer— and the many hundreds of others also listed in Index I—are uniquely important because they would have been more prominent, more immediately recognizable as derivative to his audience than any of the other sources he alludes to. Unlike Chaucer's borrowings from Dante or Boccaccio or St. Jerome, his biblical allusions (even the many that came to him at second hand) would surely have been heard and recognized as biblical by the educated members of his audience. These allusions would stand apart from and show through their proximate sources. And some members of Chaucer's audience, surely, would have noticed, and savored, Chaucer's frequently artful and dramatically pointed "mistakes" in biblical reference and quotation. There is evidence that with the growth of lay literacy in fourteenth-century England it was not unusual for the nobility to own vernacular Bibles; and illiterate laymen were not only well-versed in the text of the Bible, but were also capable of memorizing lengthy portions of it.[13] Orthodox devotional texts produced by secular and regular clergy alike usually included scores, and sometimes hundreds, of biblical verses translated into the vernacular. These verses are sometimes rendered or augmented with a freedom and originality that we, with our oversimplified notions of what was considered orthodox and what heterodox in Chaucer's time, may find shocking.[14] And all this aside from the explosion of vernacular biblical translation and commentary ignited by Chaucer's contemporary, John Wyclif (see pp. 31–35, below). It seems in fact reasonable to suspect that at least some members of Chaucer's original audience would have held their favorite poet and courtly maker in high esteem for his distinctive translations of Scripture—in addition, of course, to all the other reasons they would have had for admiring him. Chaucer's biblical diction and the substantial amount of original translation of Vulgate verses throughout his works are an aspect of his biblical poetics; together they constitute a chapter in the history of the English Bible that still remains to be written.[15] The significance of Chaucer's various kinds of biblical allusion—because they were so well known, so often recited and heard in prayers and sermons, and because they derive from a book that was held to be so fatefully authoritative—is clearly paramount.

In this book I have attempted to take stock of the past and present state of studies on Chaucer and the Bible, to provide data that will facilitate progress in the field, and to indicate what I believe to be the most fruitful avenues for future investigation. The section which immediately follows, entitled "Research on Chaucer and the Bible: A Critical

Review," outlines and evaluates the nearly one-hundred-year history of the subject. Index I comprises an annotated list of all the biblical allusions, quotations, and analogies in Chaucer. Index II lists all of the references from Index I in their biblical order. The problems and principles involved in compiling these indexes are discussed fully in "A Guide to Index I" and the prefatory "Note to Index II."

NOTES

1. Nevill Coghill, *The Poet Chaucer*, 2nd ed. (1967), p. 8; Derek Brewer, *Chaucer*, 3rd ed. (1973, rpt. 1977), p. 94. (Complete bibliographic information for all references in the notes of this study appears in the Bibliography, pp. 389–432, below).

2. For the former way of referring to the Bible, see the manuscript in *The Middle English Bible: Prefatory Epistles of Jerome*, ed. Conrad Linberg (1978), p. 60. As Pratt (1975) demonstrates, "the boke of the tales of Caunterbury" was until the sixteenth century the most frequent title for what since then has come to be called "The Canterbury Tales." Along these same lines, consider the following claim for an affinity between Chaucerian and biblical texts, advanced by James I. Wimsatt: " . . . next to the Bible *The Canterbury Tales* presents probably the most interesting study that literature offers of diversity in kinds" (1981, p. 129). On the multifaceted and vexed topic of "the Bible as literature" in the Middle Ages, see Allen (1971, 1982), Kugel (1983), and Minnis (1977, 1979-80, 1984).

3. Among a number of important individual and collaborative treatments of the vast topic of the Bible in the Middle Ages are: Margaret Deanesly, *The Lollard Bible and Other Medieval Biblical Versions* (1920); Hans Rost, *Die Bibel im Mittelalter* (1939); Jean Leclercq, *L'Amour des Lettres et le Désir de Dieu* (1957); Robert E. McNally, S.J., *The Bible in the Early Middle Ages* (1959); Henri De Lubac, *Exégèse Médiévale* (1959-64); the

various essays in *La Bibbia Nell'Alto Medoevo* (1963); D. W. Robertson, Jr.'s brief but cogent "The Medieval Bible," in *The Literature of Medieval England* (1970), pp. 24-27; the studies of biblical *distinctiones*, concordances, and formats by R. H. and M. A. Rouse (1974[a], 1974[b], 1982); Beryl Smalley's classic, *The Study of the Bible in the Middle Ages*, 3rd rev. ed. (1983), as well as Smalley's other studies in the field of medieval biblical exegesis (1981, 1985, 1986); Pierre Riché and Guy Lobrichon, eds., *Le Moyen Age et la Bible* (1984); and Katherine Walsh and Diana Wood, eds., *The Bible in the Medieval World* (1985). For a valuable discussion of the Bible and "popular religion" in the High Middle Ages, see R. and C. Brooke (1984), pp. 130-45; and for a recent treatment of "the idea of the book" in the Middle Ages which has much to say about the Bible, see Gellrich (1985).

4.   On the production and distribution of manuscripts of the Bible and Bible commentaries in the Middle Ages, see Berger (1893), Glunz (1933), Stegmüller (1950-80), and the essays by several hands (e.g., Raphael Loewe on the Vulgate) in G. W. H. Lampe, ed., *The Cambridge History of the Bible*, vol. 2: *The West from the Fathers to the Reformation* (1969). On the format, illustration, and binding of Bibles in the Middle Ages, see James Strachan, *Early Bible Illustrations* (1957); Wormald (1969); Boyd (1973), pp. 4, 98 (and references); Walter Cahn, *Romanesque Bible Illumination* (1982); and De Hamel (1984).

5.   For the instance of a serf swearing on the gospels, see Pantin (1955), p. 208, quoting from the *Memoriale Presbiterorum*. The spiritual power of the book itself is conveyed in the following anecdote which the historian Gerald of Wales tells, in his *Itinerarium Cambriae* (1.5), about a certain "Meilerius" who lived near Caerleon and had commerce with evil spirits, through whom he could predict the future, distinguish truth from falsehood, and, even though he was illiterate, pick out the false passages in a book. "It happened once, when he was being abused beyond measure by foul spirits, that the Gospel of John was placed on his breast; the spirits vanished completely, at once flying away like birds. . . . " But when, "by way of experiment," Geoffrey of Monmouth's *Historia Regum Brittaniae* was placed on Meilerius's chest the evil spirits

returned and "settled down again, not only on his entire body, but also on the book itself, for a longer time than they were accustomed to, in greater numbers, and more loathsomely" (quoted from R. S. Loomis [1959], pp. 87-88).

6.   Augustine, *De Doctrina Christiana* 2.42 (trans. D. W. Robertson, Jr. ([1958], p. 78).

7.   Benedict of Nursia, *Rule,* chapter 73 (trans. and ed. Meisel and del Matro, 1975, p. 106).

8.   Hugh of St. Victor, *Didascalicon* VI.x (quoted by Evans, 1984, p. 141).

9.   Cp. the Latin proverb cited by Walther (14a1): "Sol licet lustret cloacas, purus ac putus manet."

      Who was Radulphus? And in what work does he say what Chaucer here quotes about the invulnerability of the Bible? In a letter replying to the author's query, Siegfried Wenzel (1985) writes: "I do not know who the Radulphus quoted is. At least one MS reads 'Rabanus'—a possibility, but in the light of the other MSS of *Primo* and of *Quoniam* [i.e., the Latin source] not a strong one. The context suggests that the quoted Radulphus is a biblical commentator writing on Leviticus 20.13, which is quoted immediately before the remark and image, and connected with it by *ibi.* I suspect that Radulphus may be Radulphus of Laon, who worked on the *Glossa ordinaria.* . . . Since Radulphus is quoted and not a Father or other earlier theologian, I imagine Radulphus was considered the source of the comment. . . . Should Radulphus turn out to be an Englishman . . . a distinct possibility . . . then it is possible that he derived the idea from William de Montibus [quoted in Wenzel (1974), 376, n. 117] and applied it to Holy Scripture." Shortly before his sudden and untimely death, the late Judson B. Allen wrote, in a letter replying to the same author's query (1985[b]): "I have checked the exegesis on Genesis 19 in the *Glossa ordinaria,* Hugh of St. Cher, and Nicholas of Lyra, and find no quotation of Radulphus, nor, indeed, any mention at all of the appropriateness or inappropriateness of this sordid story in the Bible."

10.   For Jean de Meun's yoking of the Bible and obscene language in a passage which Chaucer used in the *Summoner's Tale* and *Pardoner's Tale,* and which he may also have had in mind in his

apology in the *General Prologue,* see *RR* 7079-92; cp. Burnley, 1986, pp. 211-13.

11. For these and other instances of the Pardoner's dexterous—or I should say sinister—manipulations of biblical allusion, see Besserman (1984[b]), pp. 43-50.

12. I have borrowed several sentences in this paragraph, as well as the Gower quotation, from my article entitled "Chaucer and the Bible: The Case of the *Merchant's Tale* " (1978), pp. 29-30.

13. See Coleman (1981), pp. 18-22, 170-72, 184-88, et passim (and references).

14. See, for example, *Aelred of Rievaulx's De Institutione Inclusarum: Two English Versions,* ed. Ayto and Barratt (1984); and on medieval English "Gospel harmonies" and orthodox religious prose translation in general, see Salter (1974). The standard work on medieval English Bibles is Margaret Deanesly's *The Lollard Bible* (1920); also valuable is Anna C. Paues's *A Fourteenth-Century English Biblical Version* (1902). On the church's attitude toward vernacular biblical translation, see the important essay by Boyle (1985), reinterpreting the evidence adduced by Deanesly to prove that Innocent III suppressed vernacular Bibles.

15. A major, first step was taken by W. Meredith Thompson (1962).

RESEARCH ON CHAUCER
AND THE BIBLE:
A CRITICAL REVIEW

The first major landmark in the history of studies of Chaucer and the Bible appeared almost one hundred years ago in the pages of Thomas R. Lounsbury's *Studies in Chaucer* (1892). Although many of Lounsbury's important observations about the extent and nature of Chaucer's biblical allusions still occupy Chaucer critics today, his investigation is marred by a curious bias. For a major reason he chose to look carefully at Chaucer's biblical allusions, as he forthrightly explained, was in order to judge whether or not "Chaucer possessed any of that accuracy of information which in modern times is looked upon as one essential, if not the most essential, characteristic of the man of learning" (2.189; and 2.186-89 for the quotations that follow).

On this score Lounsbury found Chaucer seriously wanting; nor was he about to allow any mitigation of guilt for Chaucer's having "borrowed inexact information from authors that were inexact." Claiming that his list of Chaucer's inaccuracies "could be enlarged with other instances," Lounsbury noted the following places where Chaucer erred: in the *Wife of Bath's Prologue* III (D) 145-46, where Mark rather than John is named as the Evangelist who tells how Christ refreshed men with barley bread; in the *Book of the Duchess,* lines 738-39, where Chaucer is guilty of "a somewhat strained interpretation of Scripture" in stating that Samson dies "for the love of

Delilah"; in the *Monk's Tale* VII (B^{2*}) 2165-66 (*3355-56), where Daniel's three companions, "well known to us all as Shadrach, Meshach, and Abednego, are reduced to two, and Daniel himself makes up the third"; in the *Legend of Good Women*, lines 1870-82 (in the legend of *Lucrece*), where the "person of whom our Lord uttered the remark" that "nowhere in all Israel had he found so much faith" was "not a woman, but the Roman centurion at Capernaum"; and finally, in *Anelida*, lines 149-54, where Chaucer speaks of Lamech "not only as the inventor of bigamy, but likewise of tents," when it was actually Lamech's son Jabel who is described in Genesis 4:20 as "the father of such as dwell in tents."

Lounsbury's calling of Chaucer to account for these errors made by characters such as the Wife of Bath, the Monk, the obtuse dreamer in the *Book of the Duchess*, and the ironic persona who writes under duress in the *Legend of Good Women* is to say the least highly questionable. In addition, Lounsbury's short list of errata—forgetting its irrelevance for the moment—can hardly sustain the charge that Chaucer was not as careful a reader of the Bible as he ought to have been as "a man of learning," given the fact that (as the Indexes to the present work testify) there are scores of places in his works where Chaucer recalls recondite biblical passages with complete accuracy.

On another aspect of Chaucer's uses of the Bible and his relationship to biblical authority, however, Lounsbury's observations were much more to the point. Taking the biblically based tirade that Proserpina unleashes against Solomon in the *Merchant's Tale* (IV [E] 2276-2310) as his major piece of evidence, Lounsbury concluded that Chaucer appplied a "critical spirit" to the Bible "as cooly as . . . the most cold-blooded of rationalists or the most scoffing of infidels" (2.509). Though once again he introduces specious criteria and overstates his conclusions, it seems to me that this time Lounsbury's view of the place of the Bible in Chaucer's imaginative life is much closer to the mark. (As we shall see, scholars such as W. Meredith Thompson, Ruth Ames, Judson Boyce Allen, A. J. Minnis, and others have recently come to similar, or at least related, conclusions.) Lounsbury's general assessment of the place of the Vulgate version of the Bible in the medieval cultural and literary landscape and of the frequency and manner of Chaucer's allusions to it was, as far as it went, entirely accurate: " . . . there was one work of which no scholar could well be ignorant. Not only must much of the information contained in it have been repeated again and again in church services, but the work itself must have always been accessible in its entirety in the monastic libraries. . . . There are numerous references to it and quotations from it in Chaucer's writings. Some of them were certainly taken at second-hand. Still, there are enough indisputably his own to show his familiarity with the book" (2.187; and cp. 2.389).

Despite the wrong-headedness of his remarks about Chaucer's errors in citing Scripture and his overheated way of describing Chaucer's "critical spirit," the fact remains that by raising these matters and also drawing attention to the simple fact that Chaucer so frequently alludes to the Bible, Lounsbury adumbrated three key and recurrent issues in much of the subsequent scholarship that sought, and still seeks, to grasp the stylistic and thematic import of the Bible for Chaucer's poetics.

Indeed, very soon after Lounsbury wrote, his claims regarding the extent of Chaucer's citation of Scripture found impressive support in the monumental edition of *The Complete Works of Geoffrey Chaucer* by W. W. Skeat (six volumes of which appeared in 1894, followed by a supplementary volume in 1897). In an Appendix (6.381-84), Skeat listed some 380 instances of biblical passages in Chaucer's works, and in his notes to individual works he drew attention to several hundred other putative Chaucerian allusions to the Bible. In many cases Skeat examined Chaucer's biblical borrowings in light of their most likely intermediate sources. What he provided, in short, was the first systematic and thorough consideration of the data relevant for all future inquiries into the subject.[1] What was still lacking, however, was a theoretical framework for evaluating what Chaucer the poet had made of his biblical materials. After Skeat, the question that still loomed largest—and the one to which the entire subject had in fact almost contracted— was, Did Chaucer go to the Bible directly or not?

In *The Development and Chronology of Chaucer's Works* (1907; volume 37 in the Second Series of the Chaucer Society's Publications), John S. P. Tatlock stated the consensus that had been reached by English and German source-hunting scholarship. In an oft-quoted footnote, Tatlock wrote: " . . . the more one investigates Chaucer's reading the more convinced one becomes that his familiarity with the Bible (and other quotable literature, like Cato and Seneca) was largely at second-hand" (p. 202, n. 4). Tatlock's opinion seems all the more surprising given his belief in the affinities between Chaucer and Wyclif, a subject which he briefly investigated in an article published in 1916. Though Tatlock did assume that Chaucer would have been aware of the Wycliffite Bible, he failed to consider that "first-hand acquaintance" with the Bible, a fundamental axiom of the Wycliffites, might also have attracted Chaucer, and might well have been a goal of the reformers that he would investigate or "problematize" in his poetry. Tatlock's failure to respond to this facet of Chaucer's religious sensibility was reinforced in Eleanor Prescott Hammond's extremely influential *Chaucer: A Bibliographical Manual* (1908), which treated the topic of Chaucer and the Bible by simply listing several new entries to supplement the extensive lists of allusions compiled by Skeat (Hammond, p. 86).

Grace Warren Landrum's Radcliffe College dissertation, "Chaucer's Use of the Vulgate" (1921), was the first comprehensive study of the biblical element in Chaucer's works after Skeat's notes and Index. Landrum sought to identify all the biblical passages in Chaucer and to determine whether they were taken by him from the Vulgate directly or from intermediate sources, such as Jerome's *Epistola adversus Jovinianum*, the *Roman de la Rose,* Dante's *Commedia,* Robert Holkot's commentary on the Book of Wisdom, and so forth. Of the more than 700 passages she identified, Landrum judged that 285 were "direct borrowings" (pp. 47-48). She further observed how "Chaucer does far more than repeat the commonest passages" (p. 52), and she posited the likelihood of Chaucer's owning a copy of the Vulgate to account for the extent and nature of his biblical borrowings ("No fine-spun allegory attracts him"; p. 63). Her results not only seemed to refute Tatlock's influential claim that Chaucer's biblical matter came to him second-hand, but also disallowed the suggestion by Ramsay (1882) that Chaucer had sometimes followed the Wycliffite Bible.

Landrum's dissertation has been extremely influential in Chaucer studies, but not so much directly, or even by way of the good précis of it that she published in *PMLA* in 1924, as by virtue of the fact that the notes on biblical allusions in F. N. Robinson's second edition of Chaucer's works (1957)—when not derived from Skeat—were based almost exclusively upon her findings. But Landrum's principal contention (against Tatlock), namely that Chaucer used the Vulgate and found in it one of his main sources of thematic and stylistic nourishment, was rejected by Robinson, as well as by J. Burke Severs (1935), Dudley R. Johnson (1941, 1951), and W. Meredith Thompson (1962).

In his 1941 Yale dissertation on "Chaucer and the Bible," Dudley R. Johnson set out to reconsider Landrum's data and reassess her conclusions. Johnson agreed with Landrum that Chaucer, on those occasions when he cited the Bible, was using an unglossed version: "For the most part, Chaucer tells a Bible story or uses a biblical quotation in a purely straightforward manner, that is, unadorned by any interpretation or expansion. Thus Chaucer, in all probability, did not use a Bible equipped with glosses or commentaries explaining the text according to patristic interpretation" (p. 83). Like Tatlock, however, Johnson concluded that Chaucer's biblical borrowings were almost always second-hand, by way of Innocent III's *De Miseria Conditionis Humanae*, the French translation of Albertano of Brescia's *Liber Consolationis et Consilii*, and so forth; and Johnson went on to advance the theory that on those rare occasions when Chaucer was not following an intermediate source, he was working not from the Vulgate itself but from a French Bible (a composite of earlier French Bibles that scholars refer to as the *Bible Historiale* and ascribe to Guyart Desmoulins). In 1951 Johnson published an article in *PMLA* focused on the *Monk's Tale.* He outlined his reasons for disagreeing with Landrum and showed why in several passages at least it was more likely that a French rather than a Latin Bible was Chaucer's source. Most often the evidence is hardly compelling, and in many instances, as Johnson himself admitted, either the Vulgate or the *Bible Historiale* could have been Chaucer's source. It seems likely that Chaucer had access to, and may occasionally have drawn upon, both the Vulgate and a French Bible. It is also likely, however, as Johnson asserted in 1951, that "the *Bible Historiale* is the prime source of the Biblical portions of the *Monk's Tale* " (p. 843).

F. N. Robinson never makes a decisive statement on the matter of Chaucer's uses of the Bible in his widely used *The Works of Geoffrey Chaucer* (1957). Although Robinson neglected to treat the subject in his Introduction, he nevertheless did offer important observations at several points in his notes. For example, after identifying a wonderfully misappropriated reference to Mark 1:7 ("There cometh after me one mightier than I, the latchet of whose shoes I am not worthy to stoop down and loose") in the bitter lament of the jilted falcon in *Squire's Tale* V (F) 555 (" . . . Ne were worthy unbokelen his galoche . . . "), Robinson had this to say about the "irreverence" of Chaucer's uses of the Bible here and at large: "Modern taste might impose a restraint in such use of a scriptural passage, though the comparison had become proverbial. . . . In Chaucer's age men spoke freely of sacred persons and things" (pp. 720-21, n. 555). The other key passages where Chaucer uses the Bible with particular audacity that Robinson cites are *LGW* 1038; *BD* 237, 679; *PF* 199 ff.; *Buk* 1 ff.; "the somewhat startling application of the proverb *God foryaf his deth* " in *TC* 3.1577; and "the illustration drawn from the Gospels" in the *Thop-MelL* VII (B^{2*}) 943-52 (*2133-42) which "would be less natural today." An example from Gower, two from the Welsh poet Dafydd ap Gwilym, and references to the frequent "irreverence" of the miracle plays briefly illustrate the hardly contentious claim that "examples from other writers might be indefinitely multiplied." For when Chaucer and other medieval writers make such seemingly "irreverent" references to the Bible, one reasonable way of reading them— instead of puzzling over their religious sensibility—is simply to recognize that " . . . such passages do not necessarily indicate lack of proper reverence. Sometimes they seem to show affectionate familiarity with objects of worship."

These remarks by Robinson are a good deal more sensible than Lounsbury's hasty conclusions in the opposite direction. But more recent scholarship has shown that the theory and practice of biblical authority and interpretation, of (mis)appropriation, self-interested translation, and the glossing of Scripture were clearly more problematic and of much greater concern to Chaucer than Robinson allowed.[2]

On the matter of Chaucer's direct borrowings from the Vulgate versus his reliance on intermediate sources, Robinson observes non-committally (in a note to *Prioress's Tale* VII 627, identifying a reference to Matthew 2:18, which Chaucer seems to have quoted from the liturgy): " . . . it is an interesting general question how far Chaucer's scriptural quotations were suggested by the services of the Church rather than the consecutive reading of the Bible" (pp. 735-36, n. 627). The very pertinent question of liturgical sources for Chaucer's biblical diction and imagery had indeed been raised by Mossé (1923), and it would figure again, at least implicitly, as the subject of Beverly Boyd's *Chaucer and the Liturgy* (1967); but in his

explanatory headnote to the *Parson's Tale* Robinson proclaims
his reliance on Skeat and Landrum and their predecessors and
seems to imply support for Landrum's thesis regarding
Chaucer's frequent, direct recourse to the Vulgate. He announces
that biblical references are provided:

> . . . where the editor found it possible, to the ultimate source of
> quotations from the Bible and other authors, and to significant
> parallel passages in Chaucer's other works. Most of this
> material was of course brought together by Skeat and his
> predecessors. Miss G. W. Landrum, in an unpublished
> Radcliffe dissertation on Chaucer's Use of the Vulgate, has
> pointed out a number of biblical quotations where Chaucer is
> closer to the original text than the intermediate sources he is
> supposed to have followed. In the following notes references
> are not always given for familiar biblical persons and events; of
> course such citations might be indefinitely multiplied. . . .
>
> (p. 766)

W. Meredith Thompson's essay on "Chaucer's Translation
of the Bible" (1962), like Dudley R. Johnson's dissertation, took
Landrum to task for over-emphasizing the extent of Chaucer's
direct indebtedness to the Vulgate. Thompson reaffirmed
Tatlock's belief that Chaucer's familiarity with biblical and
other sources was most often "at second-hand" and illustrated
how consistently Chaucer's biblical texts derive from
intermediate sources, citing as examples *An ABC*, the *Prologue*
to the *Man of Law's Tale*, and *Melibee*. Thompson further
suggested that the biblical translations in the *Parson's Tale*
may also have been derived from a yet to be discovered French
work. (Although the missing French source may indeed one day
be identified, Siegfried Wenzel [1984] has suggested that until
that time we should recognize that Chaucer may have been a
good deal more independent and innovative in his use of
biblical authority in the *Parson's Tale* than either Robinson or
Thompson believed.)
    Thompson addressed a number of other key issues. The most
original of these was the claim that Chaucer occupies an

important position in the history of English Bible translation, which Thompson supported by culling and briefly but cogently analyzing the stylistic qualities of Chaucer's translations of forty-eight verses from Proverbs—"the largest group of his quotations from any one book of the Bible" (p. 198)—that appear scattered throughout the *Canterbury Tales.* As Thompson says, this artificially constructed "Book of Proverbs as translated by Chaucer" and the many other renderings of the Bible in his works constitute "the finest biblical translation in English before the sixteenth and seventeenth centuries" (p. 195). Having found no sign of Chaucer's indebtedness to either the 1382 or the 1395 Wycliffite translations of the Bible, Thompson points out that the former was probably completed before Chaucer composed his most biblically enriched works. This Thompson considered—mistakenly, I think—"probably not significant" (p. 191). It may well be reasonable to discount the few slight correspondences between Chaucerian and Wycliffite biblical phraseology that Ramsay (1882) had noticed; however, Thompson overlooks the demonstrable influence on Chaucer's poetry exerted by the existence of English biblical versions and the controversy surrounding them.

Thompson also saw and explained very astutely how Chaucer frequently made use of the Bible in "comic and serio-comic ways," according to a "rhetorical principle of decorum" (p. 184)—which not only helps to explain why biblical authority is so prominent in the performances of the Wife of Bath, Pardoner, Merchant, and other Canterbury pilgrims, but also why Chaucer so often makes "errors" of the kind that exercised Lounsbury:

> . . . [Chaucer's] methods of translation reveal much concerning his attitude to holy scripture: and this, primarily, was not that of a scholar, theologian, or preacher, but that of a professional writer to whom all experience and all books, including the Bible, were grist for the mill. This will explain most of the occasional inaccuracies of quotation—of translation, attribution, and reference, or the frequent and free elaboration, or the blending

together of different citations; and it will explain passages
which, in a later writer, might seem irreverent or in questionable
taste. . . . In Chaucer's case, the sometimes incautious Biblist
was ever the careful artist.

(pp. 192-93)

As the Bibliography in the present book attests, in the years
that have elapsed since the appearance of Thompson's
relatively neglected essay, scores of articles have been
published in which critics have repeatedly demonstrated the
truth of the above well-chosen words. Yet it is interesting to
note how even before the great proliferation in the 1960s of
fine-tuned biblically and exegetically founded readings of
Chaucer's poetry, Thompson was beginning to suspect "the over-
zealousness of scholars in finding remoter (biblical)
reminiscences" in Chaucer (pp. 190-91).

The appearance of D. W. Robertson's *A Preface to Chaucer*
in 1962, the same year as Thompson's essay, seems now
fortuitous, for it ushered in a veritable explosion of that
tendency of scholars to display "over-zealousness" in finding
the "remoter" biblical allusions, parallels, and (most endemic
to the method) parodic inversions of biblical story, theme, or
image in Chaucerian texts. Since 1962 the tendency has
persisted, and in the past few years it has even gathered
strength. The fruitful controversy surrounding Robertson's
important book (and the influential articles by him that
preceded it ([1951a], [1951b], [1952]) has been written about at
great length.[3] For our present purposes there would be no point
in trying to reassess the many issues that these articles and *A
Preface to Chaucer* raised. Their impact on the awareness and
appreciation of Chaucer's indebtedness to the Bible as a source
was enormous. Almost equally important in this regard was
Ralph Baldwin's monograph, *The Unity of the* Canterbury
Tales (1955), which coincided in time and spirit with the
nascent Robertsonian movement. Baldwin proposed a sweeping
but powerfully suggestive analogy between the *Canterbury
Tales* and the Bible as a whole: the latter opening with the

Creation in Genesis and ending at the Apocalypse, the former opening with the "creation" of the first lines of the *General Prologue* and progressing to "a last judgment" in the *Parson's Tale*. This insight has become a kind of commonplace of criticism of the *Canterbury Tales*, and one not limited to "Robertsonians" (among the many scholars who have adduced the Genesis-Apocalypse paradigm in reading the *Canterbury Tales* are Nitzsche [1978] and Bloomfield [1983]).

Especially noteworthy for our present purpose is the section of Robertson's *A Preface to Chaucer* called "Chaucer's Exegetes" (pp. 317-36), in which Robertson discusses the uses of the Bible by the Wife of Bath, the Pardoner, and the Parson. Here for the first time the problems of biblical authority and interpretation and the use of biblical analogies and thematically rich allusions are accorded the full attention they deserve, in light of the weight that Chaucer has patently allowed them to carry in the framing of his fictions and the delineation of his characters. Robertson's assessment of the biblical element in Chaucer's poetics may be over-schematized and his conclusions forced, but he was the first scholar to bring this issue to the forefront of Chaucer studies. Still, the charge that his approach produces biblically based homilies on Chaucer instead of contextually sensitive criticism and analysis seems fundamentally correct. For example, Robertson claims to elucidate the nature of Troilus's love for Criseyde by quoting Ecclesiasticus 9:2, "Give not the power of thy soul to a woman, lest she enter upon thy strength and thou be confounded" (1952, p. 99 in rpt.)—but there is scant textual evidence, if any at all, to support the association of this verse with the love affair of Troilus and Criseyde.

Huppé and Robertson's *Fruyt and Chaf: Studies in Chaucer's Allegories* (1963) shows the method in full bloom, with both its ingenuity and its reductionist bias in full view, as applied particularly to the *Book of the Duchess* and the *Parliament of Fowls*. The authors unconvincingly claim that both of these poems are imaginative reworkings of Scriptural themes, indeed of the same theme (mediated by authoritative ecclesiastical texts, especially St. Augustine's *De Doctrina Christiana*): Charity, or Christ's love for mankind, and the comically depicted perversion of Charity into Cupidity which men stumble into when they exercise their will unchecked by reason and revelation. As it turns out, under this same thematic heading all of Chaucer's poetry can indeed be viewed as fundamentally "biblical" in reference. The thematic univocity that Robertson and Huppé's procedures posit is in fact the main deficiency of their method.

Still, their specific discoveries of biblical analogies and possible biblical reminiscences of various kinds are often impressive; at the very least they raise intriguing possibilities. Thus the walled garden that the dreamer enters in the *Parliament of Fowls* suggests to Huppé and Robertson "the *hortus conclusus* of Canticles 4:12"; while the gathering of the birds that is the central action of the poem "recalls the gathering of birds of all kinds in Apoc. 19.17, where the birds represent the faithful of all classes assembled by the Angel to put down carnal desires so as to be worthy of a place in the feast of the Lamb" (p. 123). In the *Book of the Duchess* the mysterious eight-year sickness that causes the dreamer's sleeplessness takes on new meaning, as Huppé and Robertson adduce the following passage from the Acts of the Apostles:

> And it came to pass that Peter, as he passed through, visiting all, came to the saints who dwelt at Lydda. And he found there a certain man named Eneas, who had kept his bed for eight years, who was ill of the palsy. And Peter said to him: Eneas, the Lord Jesus Christ healeth thee: arise, and make thy bed. And immediately he arose.
>
> (9:32-34)

The circumstantiality of the connections between the biblical and Chaucerian passages in the preceding examples will prove more or less off-putting to the reader as he is more or less favorably disposed to the allegorical interpretation of Chaucer's poetry at large.

Similar problems arise with the biblically grounded readings of Chaucer by scholars such as Huppé, in his *A Reading of the Canterbury Tales,* in the dissertation of Robert Ray Black (1974), in a number of important articles and books by Dahlberg, Delasanta (sometimes critical of Robertson, but fundamentally in accord with the univocally religious thrust of his approach), Fleming, R. P. Miller, Wood, and, most recently, in many of the contributions to the volume on *Chaucer and Scriptural Tradition* edited by David L. Jeffrey (1984). According to the criteria used by the majority of these and other scholars often referred to as the "Robertsonians," the list of Chaucer's biblical allusions approaches a limit defined only by the extent of the interpreter's biblically based understanding of Chaucer.

The strain that such biblical readings place upon the credulity of the uncommitted reader will vary, but in almost every case of this kind the underlying assumption of the critic seems to be that whether or not Chaucer *explicitly* cites the Bible is hardly to the point; indeed, it sometimes seems as if critics who make claims for biblical allusions of this sort are really asserting, somewhat perversely to say the least, that the absence of an explicit reference to the Bible actually strengthens their argument. Two illustrative instances of this approach will suffice. David C. Fowler, in his recent book on the *Bible in Middle English Literature* (1984), proposes that we are meant to read the *Parliament of Fowls* as an encoded retelling of hexameral tradition: "The influence of the hexameral tradition on the poem is present, but at a deep level; so deep that it governs its structure while scarcely ever showing itself on the 'surface' of the text" (p. 134). But Fowler's "scarcely" proves to be, in this reader's opinion, an understatement. John V. Fleming's *Reason and the Lover* (1984) sets out its main thesis—namely, that Reason in the *Roman de la Rose* stands for "the sapiential Christ in man, and the mirror of *sapientia* in the created world" (p. 30)—with many significant references to explicit as well as so-called implicit biblical references. Fleming for the most part shares Fowler's assumptions and methodology, but he adds some important nuances which are worth quoting at length. In the following passage Fleming defines his coinage of the term "supertext":

> . . . the operation within a poem of a secondary literary presence of a specifically, and often uniquely, powerful authority. A supertext is not a text, for it appears only by inference or implication; it is not a subtext because it does not infiltrate from below but commands from above. The concept is necessarily related to that of "intertextuality," and it has a particular vitality with regard to medieval literary culture which in many ways fostered real or feigned subservience of original genius to literary authority and encouraged complex patterns of literary dependence, appropriation, imitation, and what in our own day would be downright plagiarism.
>
> (pp. 69-70)

The Bible, appropriately implied but left unnamed, is of course Fleming's main example of a "supertext" in the *Roman*, but there are others (e.g., Augustine's *Confessions;* see pp. 83-96). Fleming goes on to point out that poet-translators such as Jean de Meun and Chaucer show "deference and servility on the one hand *and an assertive competitiveness* on the other" (my italics) in their handling of texts (p. 70). And the reader will observe that he does in fact acknowledge the possibility of "*feigned* subservience of original genius" (my italics) in its encounter with the "supertext." But when the Bible is at issue, he proves over and over again that the relationship of these writers toward their "supertexts"—Jean de Meun and Chaucer in the present context—was uniformly one of "deference and servility."

Fowler and Fleming, in the passages quoted above, demonstrate the fundamental bias in methodology that typifies biblically grounded readings of Chaucer of the kind that have come to be known as "Robertsonian." Their specific formulations explain why most readings of this kind— protected by what Karl Popper called "immunizing tactics or

stratagems" against refutation—are (at least to those who
have eyes yet see not) so unconvincing.

R. E. Kaske's important contributions, drawing on the
Vulgate and exegetical tradition to interpret crucial or obscure
passages in Chaucer, are related to those of Robertson and other
members of the allegorizing school. What sets them apart,
however, is a sharper and less reductive focus on controlling
literary context. In a major theoretical statement of the
problems involved, Kaske (1960) maintained that a biblical
allusion or image in Chaucer and other vernacular writers must
not be read as evangelic preaching but with the understanding
that "a civilized Christian writer will use it with objective
artistry, as a meaningful, evocative, and perhaps unique image
for what he is trying to express" (pp. 28-29). While
sympathetic to its focus on the Bible and exegesis, he pointedly
criticizes the Robertsonian methodology: "The interpreter of
[exegetical] imagery must not be content to reduce it
indiscriminately to the most inclusive and uniform terms, but
must analyze carefully its precise meanings in its particular
contexts. Not every exegetical image or allusion is most
fruitfully interpreted by direct recourse to *charitas* and
cupiditas, accurate though the formula may be as
universalizing commentary" (p. 29). Kaske's 1962 study of the
Miller's Tale and Canticles is the fullest illustration of his
contextual method; in addition, it is probably the most
extensive and detailed claim to date for the relevance of a
biblical text in the elucidation of the verbal and thematic
structure of a Chaucerian one. In an influential review-essay of
Robertson's *Preface to Chaucer*, Kaske (1963) offered a largely
favorable account of the Robertsonian methodology, while at
the same time providing several broad and theoretical
objections, corrections, and counter-interpretations on a number
of specific points, as well as further examples of his own
related approach. His subsequent essays have confirmed that
Kaske continues to view the Bible as a key to Chaucer's poetry.

Theodore Buermann's dissertation, "Chaucer's 'Book of Genesis' in *The Canterbury Tales*" (1967), argues ingeniously for a biblical paradigm in Chaucer's major literary effort. Like Baldwin (1955), Buermann starts out with the premise that "Chaucer intended the *schema* of the Bible to unify the *Canterbury Tales* so that the pilgrimage from the Tabard to its completion would mirror, suggest, and point to the sequence of biblical narrations from the story of creation to the apocalyptic vision of the end of the world in the book of Revelations" (pp. 1-2). But Buermann goes on to apply a biblical paradigm not merely to the whole of the *Canterbury Tales* in a general way, but to the *General Prologue* and the tales of the first Fragment in particular: "The spring time opening of the *General Prologue* appears as the creation of the world; the sworn brothers Palamon and Arcite in the *Knight's Tale* as Cain and Abel; Nicholas' 'Noees flood' in the *Miller's Tale* as Noe's flood in Genesis; and the vengeance the visiting clerks heap on the miller in the *Reeve's Tale* as the two visiting angels' avenging destruction of Sodom and Gomorrah" (p. 2).

The obvious question that arises is, Why would Chaucer have done this? And if he did compose the *Canterbury Tales* as a crypto-biblical poem, why did he feel compelled to offer a Retraction for it? Why has the true life and significance of the work seemed for so long and to so many to lie elsewhere? Buermann can provide no truly satisfactory answers to these questions, but he does make a number of ingenious and provocative suggestions about the ways in which Chaucer has alluded to a "unifying substratum" of biblical imagery. Despite what I find to be its fundamentally mistaken assumptions, his study deserves to be better known.

More recently, Ruth Ames (1977, 1982, 1984) has argued that Chaucer's biblical parody, frequently aimed at Old Testament figures like Noah and Solomon, is actually "as irreverent as it sounds," and that Chaucer generally avoided allegorizing interpretations of Scripture in favor of the literal sense: "Committed only to the basic moral teaching of the Old

Testament, Chaucer could safely laugh at both popular vulgarization and learned allegorization" (1977, pp. 87, 102). Ames contends that Chaucer's biblical parodies are as sincerely "irreverent" as they sound, but that his piety is sincere, too. While Chaucer may "raise an eyebrow" at Solomon and Noah, he also "bowed the head to true prototypes of virtue like Rebecca and Susannah" (1977, p. 87). Of Chaucer's parody of Canticles in the *Miller's Tale,* Ames writes: " . . . the joke is not on Christ but on Solomon and his Canticle, on both the literal and the spiritual signification" (1977, pp. 98-99). But Ames's attempt to localize and limit the sources of Chaucer's biblical humor is vexed. It overlooks the extent to which Chaucer was obviously concerned not only with humorous biblical motifs but with the problematics of interpreting the Bible as a whole, the Gospels, Epistles, and Apocalypse included.

In three articles (Besserman 1978, 1984[a], 1984[b]) I have tried to show how Chaucer used biblical diction, imagery, and story in variously original and audaciously independent ways. And it was not only the Old Testament that he appropriated for his literary purposes. In my view Chaucer's works, especially the *Canterbury Tales,* reflect an awareness of and deep interest in the controversy over biblical translation, interpretation, and authority that was exercising his contemporaries: Wyclif and his followers on the one hand and the friars and other opponents of the reform party on the other.[4] The satire in the *General Prologue* and elsewhere in the *Canterbury Tales* has more in common with the reform party's lists of contemporary abuses than is generally noted. For example, Wycliffites describe friars who, like Friar Huberd in the *General Prologue,* are adept at getting money and sexual favors from women by turning up at their doors as pedlars bearing "knives, purses, pins," and other "gifts"; and they write of clerks who, like Absolon in the *Miller's Tale,* are intent upon intoning and waving incense at the wives of the parish rather than preaching the Gospels.[5]

The Wycliffites also complain about the way "true men who teach the Gospels" are slandered by their wicked and corrupt antagonists—a complaint that is strikingly reflected in Chaucer's idealized portrait of the Parson in the *General Prologue* and his depiction of the slanderous treatment of the Parson by his fellow pilgrims.[6] Thus one of several scenes in the *Canterbury Tales* where a Lollard perspective can be detected is the Epilogue to the *Man of Law's Tale* (II[B^{1*}] 1170-71), in which the Parson objects to the Host's incessant cursing—an abuse repeatedly inveighed against by the Wycliffites—and is upbraided by Harry Bailey and the Shipman in the following terms:

> 'Now! goode men,' quod oure Hoste, 'herkeneth me;
> Abydeth, for Goddes digne passioun,
> For we schal han a predicacioun;
> This Lollere heer wil prechen us somwhat.'
> 'Nay, by my fader soule, that schal he nat!'
> Seyde the Shipman; 'heer schal he nat preche;
> He schal no gospel glosen here ne teche.
> We leven alle in the grete God,' quod he;
> 'He wolde sowen som difficulte,
> Or springen cokkel in our clene corn. . . .'

$$\text{(II [B}^{1*}\text{] 1174-83)}^{7}$$

Though the Parson may be an idealized figure without actually being a Wycliffite preacher, let alone a portrait of Wyclif himself, it certainly would be a mistake to argue that *because* he is an idealized figure he could not possibly stand for Wycliffite positions that were not also held by orthodox reformers and hence—so the fallacious argument goes—would not have been held by Chaucer.[8]

Chaucer and Wyclif were both revolutionaries, both great innovators in their respective fields. They were two of the greatest—perhaps *the* two greatest—original minds at work in *fin de siècle,* fourteenth-century England. Traditional histories of this period speak of the dissolution of the medieval outlook and stress other signs of breakdown and decay, but this was also a time when, with a surge of creativity and originality in many quarters, there was a breaking with the past and a push toward linguistic, philosophical, and religious reform and innovation that is hardly matched in any other century (see Utley [1961], Bloomfield [1973], and Coleman [1983]). Despite their different domains of work—and setting aside for a moment the preeminent difference between them, namely, that Chaucer was a creative artist and Wyclif a theologian and biblical scholar—both Chaucer and Wyclif faced a similar challenge of genius: to adapt and alter the European cultural monuments that they revered and to shape them into something new, something English.

Yet for all that Chaucer has in common with Wyclif, and however much he may have applauded the latter's reformist efforts, it must be stressed that he created the Parson as a character in a work of fiction and not as a sign of approbation of the reformer's enterprise. The ideality of the Parson is in fact too easily and too frequently exaggerated; there are comic dimensions to the portrayal of the Parson in the *Canterbury Tales,* just as there are comic dimensions to the other portraits. Chaucer comprehends and overreaches this character of his imaginative devising as much as he does all the others. The Wycliffite stylistic ideal of *plana locutio,* favoring simplicity of style and the avoidance of *titilans delectatio*—an ideal that the Parson propounds and illustrates in his treatise on penitence—is not the ideal of the *Canterbury Tales.* That work the Wycliffites would have found (just as the Parson in his *Prologue* indicates he found it) a frivolous fiction—too multi-layered, interlaced, ornate, maze-like, copious, inexhaustibly interpretable, and above all too often secular, and sometimes even downright vulgar in its concerns to merit the righteous man's attention. Chaucer and Wyclif part company: Wyclif on the road to Puritanism and Chaucer in the direction of Spenser, Milton, and the Christian humanist literary tradition.

Nevertheless the time is ripe for a reassessment of Chaucer's works in light of the Wycliffite controversy, at least with respect to the issue of biblical translation and interpretation. An important step in this direction has been taken by David L. Jeffrey, who addresses the question of Chaucer's relation to Wyclif on a more theoretical plane than it has been explored in the past (1984[c]). In the Introduction to the volume on *Chaucer and Scriptural Tradition* which he edited, Jeffrey writes: " . . . Chaucer is not interested in scriptural tradition merely as a repository of typologies, nor in using it merely to signal a kind of fideistic self-accrediting. He is interested in the largest questions of interpretation, in the reliability of text and textual tradition, and in the recovery of truth from the written word" (1984[b], p. XVI). And Judith Ferster (1985), using contemporary literary theory (especially the work of Wolfgang Iser) as her point of departure, has also drawn attention to the centrality of the problem of interpretation and its procedures and validating strategies throughout Chaucer's works.

For the future we can expect increasing attention to these two related areas of inquiry—Chaucer and Wyclif, Chaucer and interpretation—and the Bible should loom large in their investigation. As Derek Brewer (1984) writes of Chaucer: "It is not surprising that he was associated with the so-called Lollard Knights. . . . Lollard pietism was based upon a literalistic reading of the Bible. Literalism is powerfully iconoclastic and radical. It denies 'glosing.' The radicalism of Lollardy is too well known to need an illustration of it here, but it is fair to see it both as part of a new literalistic and modernistic movement and as [a] force well exemplified in Chaucer" (pp. 16-17). Brewer goes on to credit Chaucer with a skeptical and conservative outlook associated with his literalism. Although aspects of the nature of Chaucer's skepticism and conservatism have been studied (see Thomas, 1950; Delany, 1972; and Peck, 1978), much remains to be said. The history of the idea of skepticism itself, with special attention to late-fourteenth-century religion and the birth of humanism, needs further elucidation (see, among others:

Oberman, 1957; Popkin, 1968; Trinkaus and Oberman, eds., 1974; Leff, 1976; Trinkaus, 1983; and Boitani, ed., 1983).

Another potentially fruitful area of inquiry into Chaucer's uses of the Bible is his relationship, and the relationship of his upperclass audience, to fourteenth-century Carthusian spirituality (see Tuck, 1984). Chaucer and the so-called "Lollard knights" with whom he was associated at the court of Richard II were, Tuck asserts, "attracted to the pietistic and moralistic attitudes of the early Lollards rather than to their more specifically antisacramental and pacifist teachings" (Tuck, 1984, p. 153). And without invoking either the Lollards or Carthusian spirituality, Patterson (1978) and Dean (1985) have stressed the movement in Chaucer's works in the direction of conventional, biblically based piety, a movement evidenced most pointedly in the *Tale of Melibee* and *The Parson's Tale*.

As we have seen, much light has been cast on the problem of Chaucer and the Bible over the last century. Nevertheless, because we now have sharper and more nuanced notions of what the "problem" of Chaucer and the Bible entails, we are even further from a consensus on where, how, and to what extent Chaucer used the Bible than in the days of Skeat and Landrum. Though the present book will not bring about a consensus, the two Indexes which it includes do attempt to set before the reader a comprehensive analysis of the extent and patterning of Chaucer's indebtedness to the Bible. The principles upon which these Indexes are built are somewhat complicated. They are explained at length in the pages that follow. In addition to the immediate relevance of these principles for users of the Indexes, their elucidation may help to clarify further some of the issues that have been raised in the preceding discussion.

NOTES

1.   Dillon offers a list of Chaucer's biblical allusions (1974, pp. 27-
      39) which, as Chauncey Wood points out in a letter to the
      author (1984[a]), " . . . appears to be an augmented Skeat, with
      cross-reference by Chaucerian title rather than by footnote
      number. . . . Dillon's book, although it has been around for a
      decade, is so little used and known it is as though it was
      published in secret." A more recent reference work that lists
      books and articles dealing with allusions to the Bible in
      Chaucer is Lynn King Morris's *Chaucer Source and Analogue
      Criticism* (1985), pp. 335-45.

2.   Having said that what might seem "irreverent" to us in
      medieval literary treatment of religious themes is more often
      best understood as "affectionate familiarity," Robinson ends his
      note with the following: "But the examples cited from Provençal
      poets in Spec., XIII, 387 appear to involve real disrespect for
      sacred things" (p. 721-22, n. 555). This is curious, since the
      "irreverence" in the examples cited in the *Speculum* article to
      which Robinson refers is, so far as I can see, in no way
      distinguishable from the kind that Robinson illustrates in the
      Welsh quotations, or indeed in the passages he cites from
      Chaucer.

3.   For what are still the two most telling general critiques of the
      Robertsonian approach, see E. Talbot Donaldson (1960) and
      Donald R. Howard (1966), pp. 13-40. A more recent appraisal of
      Robertson's allegorical method and its shortcomings, especially
      with respect to the evaluation of medieval literary texts, is
      offered by William E. Rogers (1980). On Robertsonian readings
      of Chaucer's *Troilus and Criseyde*, see Kaminsky (1980), pp. 32-
      34, et passim; and for a recent, detailed "Robertsonian" reading
      of *Troilus and Criseyde*, see Chauncey Wood's *The Elements of
      Chaucer's* Troilus (1984), vigorously criticized by Ian Bishop
      (1985).

4.   On the controversy, see the studies and bibliographical essays
      by Deanesly (1920, 1951), Hargreaves (1961, 1965-66), Hudson
      (1975), Muir (1970), Paues (1902), Szittya (1977), and Talbert and
      Thomson (1970). Chaucer has been linked to the controversy
      and located on the pro-Wycliffite side in an important and

      rarely cited reading of the *Summoner's Tale* by Roy Peter Clark (1976).

5.   For these details see respectively: Matthew, ed., *English Works of Wyclif* (1902), p. 12; and Talbert and Thomson (1970), p. 364, entries 26 and 27; and cp. *GP* 221-34, 253-55 and *MilT* 3340-41.

6.   See Talbert and Thomson (1970), pp. 364-65, no. 28; and cp. *GP* 496-500, 525-28; *MLE* 1163-1183; and *ParsP* 22-29.

7.   On the textual problems surrounding the epilogue to the *Man of Law's Tale* as a whole, and the reading "Shipman" in line 1179 in particular, see Eberle and Hanna, in B, 1987, pp. 862-63 and 1126, respectively. For Wycliffite complaints about swearing see, inter alia, Matthew, ed., *English Works of Wyclif* (1902), pp. 60, 120, 139, et passim; and Hudson, ed., *Selections from English Wycliffite Writings* (1978), pp. 35, 101, et passim.

8.   See Besserman (1983).

A GUIDE TO INDEX I

Where in his works does Chaucer use the Bible?

The answer to this seemingly straightforward and simple question proves to be actually quite complex. For the question "where" also usually assumes or at least implicates the "how" and the "why" of Chaucer's biblically steeped poetics. Chaucer's works include a variety of types of biblical reference. These may be divided into seven main categories: 1) many general references to the Bible, Holy Writ, the Gospel, "the Book," etc. (*GP* 438, *PardT* 578, *SumT* 1935, *TC* 1265, etc.); references to "text" and "gloss" (which may not always be references to the Bible exclusively, but are most often likely to be; *SumT* 1919-20, *TC* 4.1409-10, etc.); and many references to individual biblical books and/or their authors (*PardT* 529-33, 633-34, 635-37; *SqT* 596; *Mel* 989, 995, 996; etc.); 2) a small number of direct quotations of biblical Latin (*RvT* 4287; *SumT* 1934; *ParsT* Headnote; etc.); 3) a very large number of commonplace biblical idioms, phrases, and expressions ("by God that made Adam," "Christ that died on the Cross," etc.) and direct allusions to scriptural characters, events, terms, and concepts; 4) an almost equally large number of accurate and original translations or paraphrasings of biblical verses or parts of verses (there are hundreds of these, concentrated in the *Tale of Melibee* and the *Parson's Tale*, but they appear throughout the *Canterbury Tales* and they occur in Chaucer's other works as well); 5) a smaller but significant number of what seem for the most part to be dramatically motivated and thematically apt misquotations, misattributions, misleadingly partial quotations of biblical verses or of a single verse out of several, or "errors" of other kinds (*WBP* 46-52, 145-46; *MerchT* 1311; *MkT* 2151-52; *LGW* 1879-82; etc.); 6) a number of allusions, or possible allusions, to non-canonical apocryphal traditions about biblical characters, events, and concepts, which presumably came to Chaucer (when they were not present in his intermediate sources) by way of popular ecclesiastical traditions—the liturgy, sermons, the plastic arts, legends of the saints, vernacular drama, etc.—rather than by way of the relatively inaccessible texts of the non-canonical works themselves (*MilT* 3539-40, 3712; *MerchT* 2355-67, 2414; etc.); and most problematic of all: 7) a very large number of allusions, or possible allusions, to biblical verses and what are perhaps oblique allusions ("analogies") to biblical characters, events, and concepts (*MilT* 3785; *RvP* 3876; *RvT* 4280; *WBP* 6-7; *ClT* 211-31; *PardT* 366-71; *TC* 2.1513-3.217, 4.194-96; etc.).

Chaucer and his contemporaries would have been intimately familiar with the narratives, diction, imagery, and themes of the Bible, even if they had not studied the Latin text itself (or a French or English translation of the Latin). The primer of Chaucer's day, used in elementary education as a child's first reader, included the Lord's Prayer, the Hail Mary, the Creed, the Ten Commandments, the Seven Deadly Sins, the Beatitudes, quotations from Matthew 25 , 1 Corinthians 13, and other biblical texts (see Plimpton, 1935). And if the reader checks the Index which follows against the Indexes in the Procter and Wordsworth edition of the *Breviarium ad Usum Insignis Ecclesiae Sarum* (vol. 3, pp. xxvii-cxvi) and the J. Wickham Legg and F. H. Dickinson editions of *The Sarum Missal*, he or she will discover that many, and perhaps even most, of the biblical allusions in Chaucer's works either derive from or are at least paralleled in the liturgy of the medieval English Church (cp. Robinson, 1957, pp. 735-36, n. 627; and Boyd, 1967). This is simply to say that the language of medieval Christian prayer, which is often the language that Chaucer's characters speak (*PrP* 453-72; *SecNP* 29-77; *TC* 1.29-

51, 3.1-49; etc.), was in essence the language of the Bible internalized, confirmed, and made new.

Because the Bible is the ultimate validating text in which God and all the visible and invisible elements of Christian cosmogony are first defined, there is a sense in which Chaucer's every mention of God, heaven or hell, angels, and so forth could be considered biblical. For the most part I have not done so; but when oaths, exclamations, and asseverations "By God who sits above," "the devil bound deep in hell," "By Mary," "Peter," "Saint John," "Christes mooder," etc., may have a contextually biblical significance, they are included and referred to a specific biblical verse. Thus even the mention of cherubim, in *GP* 642, is listed because (as Robinson's note implies) the biblical context of Ezechiel 10:2 ff. explains why the Summoner's face would recall the "fire-red" face of a "cherub." So too with oaths such as "God my soule save," "God that made Adam," "God y-heried be thy name," and other biblically based expressions or images: they are generally listed in Index I with reference to a pertinent biblical verse, followed by the notation "etc." To be sure, when these expressions are used colloquially by the likes of Harry Bailey, Pandarus, or other characters, they are hardly more "biblical" than simple mentionings of God, heaven and hell, and the like. Yet these expressions also exist at another level in the design of Chaucer's poetry. For when Chaucer the poet puts them in the mouths of characters in fictional contexts in which there are also more specifically biblical allusions with more pointedly and profoundly biblical themes, it seems plausible to argue—as many recent critics of Chaucer have argued—that they are semantically rejuvenated and their biblical origin, however slight or even obliterated it might have become in contemporary colloquial usage, becomes artistically relevant.

For example, *"benedicite"* or "bendiste"—an oath derived from Daniel 3:57, etc., by way of the liturgy, meaning literally "let us praise" but used to mean roughly "by God!"—occurs some eighteen times in Chaucer. Its proximate origin clearly liturgical, the biblical context of the expression—it is the first word of the canticle sung by the young men rescued from the fiery furnace in the Book of Daniel—may nevertheless be significant. For example, In line 1785 of the *Knight's Tale,* when Theseus speaks in mock praise of Cupid's power to make men—especially young men—miserable, he uses the expression *benedicite* in what becomes a pointedly ironic juxtaposition to his apostrophe to the God of Love. Similarly, if even more tenuously, Friday in Chaucer might seem to be innocent of biblical associations; but as Adams and Levy (1965-66) have argued, Friday as the biblical day of the Creation of Adam and Paradise, the day of the Fall (according to ecclesiastical tradition), and the day of man's redemption through Christ's crucifixion is also, at least potentially, a time-setting evocative of key biblical events and themes. Were these the only, or even the majority of the kinds of biblical matter in Chaucer's works their importance would be relatively slight. But in conjunction with the other kinds of biblical matter one finds, they take on greater importance.

Index I includes all seven of the types of allusions discussed above. Entries are listed according to the order of Chaucer's works in Larry D. Benson's third edition of *The Riverside Chaucer* (1987), beginning with the *General Prologue* to the *Canterbury Tales* and ending with *The Romaunt of the Rose* (excluding the *Treatise on the Astrolabe* and a work probably by Chaucer but not included in Benson's's edition, the *Equatorie of the Planetis*). The text of Chaucer and line references cited are also Benson's, except for *Troilus and Criseyde,* which is quoted from Barry A. Windeatt's *Troilus & Criseyde: A New Edition of "The Book of Troilus"* (1984). Line references to the *Prologue* of the *Legend of Good Women* refer to the F-version, unless they are marked "G." I have sometimes modified the spelling and punctuation of Benson's and Windeatt's editions in my quotations, adapting the latter to modern conventions in the use of capital and lower-case letters, "u" and "v," "i" and "y," etc. Lines cited generally include the biblical allusion and its immediate context of Chaucerian interpretation or elaboration; but the lengthier interpretative passages in the *Parson's Tale* are not included (*WBP* 63-68; *ParsT* 904-06, 1036-37, etc.). My decision to include *The Romaunt of the Rose,* a Middle English translation of less than a third of the French *Le Roman de la Rose*—even if only a small portion of it is likely to be Chaucer's work (see the discussion by Alfred David, in Benson's ed., pp. 1103-04)—is further justified, I think, by the fact that the work includes some important biblical passages and was a source that Chaucer frequently drew upon in his other works. For the same reason I include Chaucer's translation of Boethius's *Consolation of Philosophy* even though its "biblical allusions" are not original with Chaucer and are in themselves highly dubious (but see D'Alverny [1956], and De Vogel [1972]).

Biblical chapter and verse numbers are cited from the Douay-Rheims Bible, the modern English version which most closely follows Chaucer's Bible, the Vulgate Latin. Chapter and verse references for the Psalms are also from the Douay-Rheims version, with the King James numbering added in parentheses. References to New Testament apocrypha are to the texts in Hennecke-Schneemelcher, in the translation edited by R. McL. Wilson. In cases where two or more different biblical verses may be alluded to in a single passage their chapter and verse numbers, with relevant annotation, are listed on separate lines (i.e., vertically); in cases where two or more related biblical verses may be alluded to in a single passage their chapter and verse numbers, with relevant annotation, are listed on the same line (i.e., horizontally). The decision to present some passages of four or five lines as a cluster of allusions in a single entry, while other passages are divided into separate entries, was not an arbitrary one. Continuity of Chaucer's text, the relationship of the biblical allusions to Chaucer's text and to one another, and clarity of presentation were the goal; but in some cases a different format might be equally valid. Unless otherwise indicated, all manuscript, edition, and chapter or section numbers of intermediate sources are those cited by the contemporary scholar named immediately after the intermediate source.

Chaucer's allusions to non-canonical biblical themes—to characters and stories that he might have encountered in books outside of the medieval canon of the Old and New Testaments, such as the Gospel of Nicodemus, which treats of the Harrowing of Hell, to which Chaucer sometimes alludes (*MilT* 3512; *MLT* 634; *SumT* 2507; etc.), or to the Protevangelium of James and the Life of Saint Anne, which treat of Joseph and Mary and Mary's mother St. Anne, to whom Chaucer also sometimes alludes (*MLT* 640-42; *FrT* 1613; etc.)—are related to the closest biblical or apocryphal source (if there is one) and/or referred to what is usually a much more likely intermediate source or analogue, such as the *Legenda Aurea* or the vernacular biblical drama. Chaucer's uses of these and other non-canonical themes—themes that were very likely considered "biblical" in the popular medieval mind because of their presentation in drama, the plastic arts, and in sermon literature, as E.K. Chambers, Emile Mâle, G.R. Owst, and others have taught us to see—constitute a set of his "biblical" matter that deserves special attention. A synoptic view of the biblical sources and the apocryphal elaborations that Chaucer evokes in certain fictional contexts is often illuminating, for one of the most certain results of this study is to show that his level of familiarity with the Bible was such that he would have always been aware of the difference between a biblical story and its apocryphal elaboration, even if there were many in his audience who were not.

Following many biblical chapter and verse notations I have added a question mark to indicate those references which are most dubious; question marks also follow some of the suggested intermediate sources. I doubt that every reader will concur with my decisions in this matter. Reading Chaucer with the Bible always in mind, as some pious and biblically adept members of his original audience might have done, as certain single-minded modern critics do, and as I have done for the purposes of this study, one can begin, like Mr. Dick with the head of Charles the First, to see the Bible everywhere. What about Boethius, the *Romance of the Rose*, Dante, Boccaccio, Gower, and the fourteenth-century French love poets? Were these not the truly important literary models for Chaucer?

Of course they were. Chaucer's "biblical poetics" and seemingly "biblical" world view came to him in part by way of these writers and their works (especially Boethius, Dante, Boccaccio, and Gower)—or in reaction to and departure from, as much if not more than in emulation of their approaches to biblical form and content. But this does not invalidate the very obvious counter-proposition that Chaucer's poetry is steeped in biblical language, imagery, and ideas, and that the Bible, in sum, is the most important and most pervasive of all those works out of which he made original poetry and prose. It is when trying to assess the extent to which this proposition holds true, and when trying to weigh its implications, that different approaches divide sharply. Thus some of my readers—such as those committed to a realist Chaucer, or a Chaucer who is first and foremost a secular courtly maker in the French tradition, or a humanist poet in the Italian tradition— will find that, like Mr. Dick with the head of Charles the First, I have seen biblical allusions where they could not possibly be; while there may also be Mr. Dicks among my readers—such as those committed to a deeply religious, constantly allegorizing Chaucer—who will find that I have overlooked or mistakenly identified as many allusions as I have seen. The question mark together with the extensive Bibliography and annotations in Index I will give at least some satisfaction to both kinds of readers. They will also satisfy, I hope, a third kind of reader, for whom this book is especially intended: one interested in seeing how much of Chaucer's writing makes use of the Bible, how often and in what contexts its authority and exemplary power are invoked, with what effects, and with what larger implications for Chaucer's poetics.

A sample entry and annotation (somewhat lengthier than the average one) is the following from the *Pardoner's Tale* in the *Canterbury Tales* (p. 127, below):

485-87: Lo, how that dronken Looth, unkyndely,/ Lay by his doghtres two, unwityngly;/ So dronke he was, he nyste what he wroghte.

Cp. *Gen. 19:29-38* (Holkot, *SLS* 21; Petersen, 1898, p. 113; cp. John Bromyard, *Summa Praedicantium;* cp. Innocent III, *DMCH* 2.20; Gratian, *Decretum* 1.35.1.9; Johnson, 1941, pp. 165-66; John of Wales, *Communiloquium* 4.3.7; Pratt, 1966, 634-35; Peter Comestor, *Historia Scholastica;* Taitt, 1971; cp. Reiss, 1984, p. 59; R; P; F; cp. Hilary, in B, 1987, nn. 485, 488).

In this instance, as elsewhere in Index I, the first "Cp." precedes a phrase, or verse, or passage in the Bible that is comparable to but not quite the same as that in Chaucer. Sometimes the differences are a good deal more substantial than in the present case (*Mel* 997 [*2187]; *Mel* 1406-07 [*2596-97]; etc.). In many other instances, however, the notation "Cp." preceding a biblical citation points to an especially remarkable difference, or even to a sharp discrepancy, between Chaucer's text and the putative biblical allusion. When "cp." precedes a putative intermediate source or a reference to a modern critical discussion of the lines in question, it may point to a significant difference, or even to a sharp discrepancy between Chaucer's text and the putative biblical allusion in the intermediate source. It may point to a significant difference between the biblical or intermediate source proposed and that critical discussion—i.e., the putative source has one biblical reference and Chaucer has substituted another, or has expanded or altered his direct biblical source in an especially remarkable way, or has mistaken a non-biblical text for a biblical one; or the critical discussion proposes another biblical reference, or rejects the notion of a biblical allusion outright (for examples, see the entries under *Mel* 1676-77 [*2866-67]; *ParsT* 502, 521, 750-51; *TC* 4.1585, 5.543, inter alia; an illustration from the entry for *PardT* 485-87 follows shortly).

I have also noted in the annotations of Index I if Skeat ("S"), Robinson ("R"), Fisher ("F"), or Benson ("B")—or the various sub-editors in Benson—in the notes to their comprehensive editions of Chaucer's works, or Manly ("M") in his edition of selected *Canterbury Tales,* or Pratt ("P") in his complete edition of the *Canterbury Tales,* address the matter of the biblical allusion in question (in the case of *PardT* 485-87, Skeat and Manly do not and Robinson, Pratt, Fisher, and Hilary [in Benson] do). In some entries the notations "S," "M," "R," "P," and "B" lead the reader to notes in which an alternative biblical allusion is proposed, or the matter of the biblical allusion in question is raised but regarded as highly doubtful, or even rejected outright. My annotations from Skeat are complete for *Canterbury Tales,* but selective for other works. The notes in Pratt and Fisher identify many allusions but they generally do not include the full survey of critical opinion and documentation as to proximate sources that one finds in Skeat, Robinson, and Benson. Yet in a few instances Pratt and Fisher point out biblical echoes that all the other editions overlook.

All the annotations are intended to send the reader to the relevant primary and secondary texts. For example, as noted in Index I (p. 90, below), line 801 of the *Wife of Bath's Prologue* is interpreted with reference to Galatians 4:22 by D.W. Robertson (1979-80). But to make his case in this seventeen-page article, Robertson cites other passages in the *Wife of Bath's Prologue,* other biblical verses, and contemporary documents from English economic history. For the reader merely to consult *WBP* 801 and consider it in light of Galatians 4:22 would hardly be sufficient. Yet even after having consulted the article the reader may find that—like Pearsall (1986), also cited in the annotation to *WBP* 801—he or she is still not convinced of the relevance of Galatians 4:22. Similarly, the reader who turns to the article by Delasanta (1968-69) which adduces Luke 12:22-23, 16:19, and 19:35-36 with reference to *ParsT* 413 will find that these same verses are also adduced therein to explain a number of other passages in the *Canterbury Tales* which I have not annotated.

The annotations in Index I do not present a consensus of opinion, nor are they exhaustive. Furthermore, a few of the articles are included because even while not exclusively biblical in focus they suggestively place an actual or doubtful biblical allusion in a wider interpretative context (Kolve [1981] on the *Second Nun's Tale*, Patterson [1983] on *Wife of Bath's Prologue* and *Tale*, etc.). The reader who wishes to ascertain the extent and source of any specific allusion and to begin to fathom its literary function in its context should therefore, I repeat, consult all the authorities cited in the entry on that allusion. It would also be worth his or her while to check Index II, the Scriptural index that cross-references all of the biblical citations of Index I (see pp. 306-88 and the "Note to Index II" on pp. 305–06), for other instances of the allusion in question. Because Index II provides a comprehensive, synoptic view of which verses reappear in which works, I have kept cross-references in Index I to a minimum.

Returning now to the sample entry from *PardT* 485-87 (p. 46, above): when the reader follows up the references to medieval sources and contemporary scholarly discussions cited therein, he or she will find that Kate O. Petersen, in her book *On the Sources of the Nonne Prestes Tale* (1898), p. 113, points out that Robert Holkot's commentary on the Wisdom of Solomon includes the example of Lot as well as other examples of the dangers of drink that the Pardoner adduces. Citing other passages in Chaucer, mainly from the *Nun's Priest's Tale* which is the focus of her study, but also from *Troilus and Criseyde*, the *Summoner's Tale*, and the *Squire's Tale*, Petersen concludes rather non-commitally: "Granting, however, that in some cases the agreement between Chaucer and Holkot arises from an independent use of stock material, there still remain agreements between the two authors which are significant enough to make it more than probable that Chaucer knew Holkot" (p. 116).

The next scholar cited in the sample annotation is Dudley R. Johnson ("Chaucer and the Bible," Diss. Yale, 1941, pp. 165-66), who suggests that a passage in Gratian's *Decretum* was Chaucer's ultimate source for the Pardoner's biblical allusion to Lot's drunkenness and incest. Johnson also compares the lines in Chaucer with a brief allusion to the story of Lot and his daughters in Innocent III's *De Contemptu Mundi* (a work that figures prominently as the proximate source of Chaucer's biblical matter in the *Wife of Bath's Prologue* and elsewhere and has recently been edited for The Chaucer Library as *De Miseria Condicionis Humane*, by Robert E. Lewis); and he points to another brief allusion to the story in John Bromyard's *Summa Praedicantium*. Robert A. Pratt ("Chaucer and the Hand that Fed Him," 1966, 634-35) cites lines from John of Wales's *Communiloquium* that include not only the Pardoner's reference to Lot but a number of his other phrases and exemplary allusions on the subject of drunkenness. Peter Taitt ("In Defense of Lot," 1971) analyzes Genesis 19:30-36 and concludes that Lot in the biblical narrative is a much less guilty figure than the Pardoner makes him out to be; Taitt further suggests that the Pardoner's Lot and Herod exempla (*PardT* 485-91) came to Chaucer by way of Peter Comestor's *Historia Scholastica*. Edmund Reiss ("Biblical Parody: Chaucer's 'Distortions' of Scripture," 1984, p. 59) claims that the Pardoner's reading of Genesis 19:30 ff. is "garbled" in several ways: "First, the biblical passage explicitly states that Lot's daughters made their father drunk, and, moreover, that they 'lay with their father.' Though the Pardoner uses the adverb 'unwityngly' as a reinforcement of Lot's drunken state[?], the Bible in effect exonerates Lot. But the most serious misuse of Scripture here is the Pardoner's term 'unkyndely,' for in the Bible it is clear that Lot's daughters commit incest so 'that we may preserve offspring through our father.' That is, their action is wholly [?] in accord with nature, as well as with God's command to be fruitful and multiply, in contrast with the unnatural sexuality of the Sodomites."

Each of these discussions of the biblical allusion in lines 485-87 of the *Pardoner's Tale* raises interesting points. But the reader who diligently compares all of the relevant passages will conclude, I think, that although Chaucer might well have recalled the Lot story from the Bible directly, Pratt's suggestion that John of Wales's *Communlioquium* was the proximate source for the allusion, as well as for other elements in the Pardoner's sermonizing against drunkenness, has the most to recommend it; Petersen's citation of Holkot is similarly to the point, though a bit less striking. Taitt and Reiss (the latter especially, as I have already indicated by my question marks in square brackets) seem to me to go much too far in finding fault with the Pardoner's use of biblical authority in this instance. Lot's drunken stupor and the incest that follows from it are the Pardoner's obviously valid homiletical point. True, Lot's daughters mistakenly believe that "there is no man left on the earth" (Gen. 19:31) except for their father. But to say that the Bible exonerates Lot and to fault the Pardoner for condemning Lot for drunkenness and incest when orthodox authorities such as Gratian, Innocent III, Bromyard, and John of Wales all do the same is surely a mistake. As the annotations "R" and "Hilary, in B, 1987, nn. 485, 488" imply, some of the preceding information derives from or is duplicated in the notes to the *Pardoner's Tale* in F. N. Robinson's *The Works of Geoffrey Chaucer* (1957) or in Christine Ryan Hilary's notes to the *Pardoner's Tale* in Larry D. Benson's *The Riverside Chaucer* (1987). But some of what appears in the annotation is not duplicated in Robinson or Benson, and the notes in these editions include one or two additional suggested sources or analogues—again, the reader must turn to the secondary sources in the annotation for the complete picture.

I have passed over in silence the scores of mostly minor mechanical errors in biblical citation and reference that I have found in the various editions with which I have worked; readers following up on the annotations will encounter such minor discrepancies but will be able to correct for them without too much effort. It would probably be too sanguine of me—or worse (see Matthew 7:3)—to assert that I have been more careful than my predecessors in this regard. In the hope of making this book of the greatest possible use to all those lovers of Chaucer and the Bible into whose hands it will find its way, I shall be very grateful to receive and to ackowledge any information, corrections, or suggestions that might be incorporated in future editions. A final caution: the total number of Chaucer's biblical allusions (were there any significance to having this information in itself) is hard to come by because of the large number of doubtful cases and the wide range of types of allusion (from shadowy parallels, to echoes of phrasing, to sustained direct quotation), but the few hundred referred to by Thompson (1962), the 600-or-so references listed by Skeat (1894), and even the seven hundred-and-thirty cited by Landrum (1924, 98-99) are clearly on the low side.

[Mr. Eames:]	" . . . you talk too much that's what it is. If Eve hadn't've started off clacking the serpent wouldn't 'ave caught 'er in his trap."
[Mrs. Eames:]	"Oo began it, the serpent or her, tell me that."
[Mr. Eames:]	"Well I don't know if I remember for sure which of 'em it was."
[Mrs. Eames:]	"You don't know the Bible, that's what's the matter with you my man."
[Mr. Eames:]	"Well what if I don't know, where's the Bible come into it anyway?"

Henry Green, *Living*

INDEX I:
CHAUCER'S BIBLICAL
ALLUSIONS
AN ANNOTATED LIST

THE CANTERBURY TALES

General Prologue, I (A), lines 1-858:

1-18: Whan that Aprill with his shoures soote/ The droghte of
March hath perced to the roote/ . . . Thanne longen folk to goon
on pilgrimages/ . . . The hooly blisful martir for to seke,/ That
hem hath holpen whan that they were seeke.
> *Gen. 1* ? (Baldwin, 1955, pp. 19-28, et passim; Buermann,
> 1967, pp. 39-41, 57; Rudat, 1976; Nitzsche, 1978;
> Bloomfield, 1983; Lawler, 1980, pp. 162-63; cp. Miller,
> 1977, pp. 11-37; cp. B).
> *Gen. 7:11-24* ? (Wood, 1970, pp. 161-72).
> *Heb. 11:13; etc.* ? (cp. Baldwin, 1955, pp. 19-28, et passim;
> Robertson, 1962, pp. 373-74).

5-6: Whan Zephirus eek with his sweete breeth/ Inspired hath
in every holt and heeth . . .
> *Gen. 2:7* ? (Andrew, 1984).
> *Gen. 8:1* ? (Taylor, 1982).

26: . . . and pilgrimes were they alle . . .
   Heb. 11:13-16 ?

59: . . . and in the Grete See . . .
   Cp. *Num. 34:6-7, Jos. 1:4, etc.* (S).

133-35: Hir over-lippe wyped she so clene/ That in hir coppe
ther was no ferthyng sene/ Of grece, whan she dronken hadde
hir draughte.
   Matt. 23:25-26 ? (Knoepflmacher, 1969-70, 180-81).

142-50: But for to speken of hire conscience. . . . Of smale
houndes hadde she that she fedde/ With rosted flessh, or milk
and wastel-breed. . . . And al was conscience and tendre herte.
   Matt. 15:26-28 ? (Knoepflmacher, 1969-70, 181-82; cp.
   Ridley, in B, 1987, n. 142-50).

162: . . . *Amor vincit omnia.*
   1 Cor. 13:13 ? (cp. Virgil, *Eclogue* 10.69; P; Ridley, in B,
   1987, n. 162; cp. Robertson, 1962, pp. 246-47).
   2 Pet. 1:7 ? (Jacobs, 1980-81).

177-78: He yaf nat of that text a pulled hen,/ That seith that
hunters ben nat hooly men. . . .
   Gen. 10:8-9 ? (Cp. Jerome[?], *Breviarium in Psalmo*, Ps. xc;
   Augustine, *De Civitate Dei* 16.3-4 ?; Flügel, 1897, 126-133;
   Willard, 1947; S; R; F; cp. Fleming, 1984, pp. 189-94; cp.
   Ridley, in B, 1987, n. 177).

187: . . . How shal the world be served?
   Matt. 16:26, Mark 8:36 ? (Huppé, 1967, p. 22; cp.
   Cavanaugh, in B, 1987, n. 187).

214: Unto his ordre he was a noble post.
   Gal. 2:9 ? (S; Richardson, in B, 1987, n. 214).

240-45: He knew the tavernes wel in every toun/ And everich hostiler and tappestere/ Bet than a lazar or a beggestere,/ For unto swich a worthy man as he/ Acorded nat, as by his facultee,/ To have with sike lazars aqueyntaunce.

> *Matt. 10:8; etc.* (Miller, 1977, p. 241).
> *Luke 16:20; etc.* (S).

253-55: For thogh a wydwe hadde noght a sho,/ So plesaunt was his "*In principio,* "/ Yet wolde he have a ferthyng, er he wente.

> *Mark 12:42* ? (David, 1976, p. 70).
> *John 1:1(-14 ?)* (liturgy or charm?, Law, 1922; Bloomfield, 1955; S; M; R; P; F; Richardson, in B, 1987, n. 254).
> *Gen. 1:1* ? (ibid.).

256: His purchas was wel bettre than his rente.

> *Matt. 21:33-41; etc.* ? (Jeffrey, 1971; proverbial; Whi P438; cp. Richardson, in B, 1987, n. 256).

261: . . . But he was lyk a maister or a pope.

> Cp. *Matt. 23:10; James 3:1* (Miller, 1977, pp. 242-43; cp. Richardson, in B, 1987, n. 261).

301: And bisily gan for the soules preye . . .

> *2 Mach. 12:42-46; etc.* ? (liturgy; S; cp. Ginsberg, in B, 1987, n. 299-302).

410: His barge ycleped was the Maudelayne.

> *John 20:1-18* ? (Gibson, 1981, pp. 107-10; cp. pseudo-Origen, *De Maria Magdalena;* McCall, 1971; cp. Burrow and Scattergood, in B, 1987, n. 410).

435-38: Of his diete mesurable was he,/ For it was of no superfluitee,/ But of greet norissyng and digestible./ His studie was but litel on the Bible.

> *Matt. 4:4* ? (Wood, 1984[c], pp. 43-46; cp. P; C. D. Benson, in

B, 1987, nn. 435-37, 438).
G (R).

445-76: A good WIF was ther OF biside BATHE. . . . Of remedies of love she knew per chaunce,/ For she koude of that art the olde daunce.
> Cp. *Prov. 31:10-31* ? (Weissman, 1975, pp. 115-16; Miller, 1977, p. 391; Coletti, 1984, pp. 180-81; cp. Hilary, in B, 1987, nn. 445, 447-48).

446: . . . But she was somdel deef, and that was scathe.
> *Ps. 113(115):[6]; etc.* ? (Robertson, 1962, p. 320).
> *Matt. 13:9-16* ? (Levy, 1965, 372, n. 4).

449-52: In al the parisshe wif ne was ther noon/ That to the offrynge bifore hire sholde goon;/ And if ther dide, certeyn so wrooth was she/ That she was out of alle charitee.
> Cp. *Matt. 5:23-24* ? (liturgy; Hoffman, 1973-74; cp. Hilary, in B, 1987, nn. 449-51, 452).

453-55: Hir coverchiefs ful fyne weren of ground;/ I dorste swere they weyeden ten pound/ That on a Sonday weren upon hir heed.
> *Prov. 31:22* ? (Weissman, 1979; cp. Hilary, in B, 1987, n. 453).
> *1 Cor. 11:3-10* ? (Weissman, 1979; cp. Hilary, in B, 1987, n. 453).

460: Housbondes at chirche dore she hadde fyve . . .
> *John 4:5-19* ? (Robertson, 1962, pp. 317-31; cp. Hilary, in B, 1987, n. 460).

478-79: . . . And was a povre PERSOUN OF A TOUN,/ But riche he was of hooly thoght and werk.
> *Prov. 13:7* ? (R).

481: . . . That Cristes gospel trewely wolde preche.
   G (P).

496-98: This noble ensample to his sheep he yaf,/ That first he wroghte, and afterward he taughte./ Out of the gospel he tho wordes caughte. . . .
   Matt. 5:19 (cp. Gower, *CA* 5.1825; Wenzel, in B, 1987, n. 497-98; S; R).
   G

500: . . . if gold ruste, what shal iren do?
   Lam. 4:1 ? (Cp. Gregory, *Cura Pastoralis* 2.7; Renclus de Moiliens, *Roman de Carité* st. 62; Kittredge, 1897, 115; Bode, 1962; R; Wenzel, in B, 1987, n. 500).
   James 5:3 ? (Bode, 1962).

503-14: And shame it is, if a prest take keep,/ A shiten shepherde and a clene sheep. . . . He sette nat his benefice to hyre/ And leet his sheep encombred in the myre . . . But dwelte at hoom, and kepte wel his folde,/ So that the wolf ne made it nat myscarie;/ He was a shepherde and noght a mercenarie.
   John 10:1-30 (esp. vv. 11-13) (Cp. Renclus de Moiliens, *Roman de Carité* sts. 58, 71; Kittredge, 1897, 113-14; S; R; cp. Gower, *VC* 3.1063; Wenzel, in B, 1987, nn. 504, 514).

521-23: But it were any persone obstinat,/ What so he were, of heigh or lough estat,/ Hym wolde he snybben sharply for the nonys.
   Cp. *Matt. 18:15; etc.* (S; cp. Wenzel, in B, 1987, n. 523).

527-28: But Cristes loore and his apostles twelve/ He taughte; but first he folwed it hymselve.
   Acts 1:1 (S; Wenzel, in B, 1987, n. 528).
   Cp. *Matt. 5:19*

533-35: God loved he best with al his hoole herte/ At alle tymes, thogh him gamed or smerte,/ And thanne his neighebor right as hymselve.
> *Matt. 22:37-39; Mark 12:30-31; etc.* (R; F; B).

560: . . . and a goliardeys . . .
> *1 Kings 17:4, etc.* ? (S; cp. Gray, in B, 1987, n. 560).

624: . . . That hadde a fyr-reed cherubynnes face . . .
> *Ezech. 10:2, etc.* ? (S; R; P; cp. Richardson, in B, 1987, n. 624).

634: Wel loved he garleek, oynons, and eek lekes . . .
> *Num. 11:5* ? (Kaske, 1959; Biggins, 1964; Wood, 1970-71; F; cp. Richardson, in B, 1987, n. 634).

635-36: . . . And for to drynken strong wyn, reed as blood;/ Thanne wolde he speke and crie as he were wood.
> *Prov. 23:31-33* ? (cp. S; cp. Richardson, in B, 1987, n. 635).

637-38: And whan that he wel dronken hadde the wyn,/ Thanne wolde he speke no word but Latyn.
> *Acts 2:1-15* ? (R; cp. Richardson, in B, 1987, n. 637-38).

672: Ful loude he soong "Com hider, love, to me!"
> *Cant. 4:7-8* ? (S; R; cp. Hilary, in B, 1987, n. 672).
> *Cant. 2:10, etc.* ? (Kaske, 1962, 480, n. 3; ———, 1973, p. 95).

673-74: This Somonour bar to hym a stif burdoun;/ Was nevere trompe of half so greet a soun.
> *Exod. 4* ? (Fleming, 1985, pp. 161-63; cp. Hilary, in B, 1987, n. 673).

675-79: This Pardoner hadde heer as yelow as wex . . . And therwith he his shuldres overspradde. . . .
> *1 Cor. 11:14* ? (Weissman, 1979; cp. Hilary, in B, 1987, n. 675-79).

680-83: But hood, for jolitee, wered he noon . . . Hym thoughte
he rood al of the newe jet;/ Dischevelee, save his cappe, he
rood al bare.
   1 Cor. 11:3-10 ? (Weissman, 1979; cp. Hilary, in B, 1987, n.
   683).

686-87: His walet lay biforn hym in his lappe,/ Bretful of
pardoun comen from Rome al hoot.
   Cp. *John 12:6* ? (Fleming, 1978-79, 22-25; ———, 1984, pp.
   186-89).

689-91: No berd hadde he . . . I trowe he were a geldyng or a
mare.
   Cp. *Matt. 19:12* ? (Miller, 1955; Fleming, 1984, pp. 187-89;
   cp. Hilary, in B, 1987, nn. 688-89, 691).

696-98: He seyde he hadde a gobet of the seyl/ That Seint Peter
hadde, whan that he wente/ Upon the see, til Jhesu Crist hym
hente.
   Matt. 14:29-31; etc. (M; R; F; Hilary, in B, 1987, n. 696-98).

709: Wel koude he rede a lessoun or a storie. . . .
   G (Young, 1915, 97-99; M; R; Hilary, in B, 1987, n. 709).

712: . . . and wel affile his tonge . . .
   Ps. 139(140):4(3) ? (proverbial; Whi T378; Hilary, in B,
   1987, n. 712).

739: Crist spak hymself ful brode in hooly writ . . .
   G (Cp. Boccaccio, *Decameron,* "Author's Conclusion"; Root,
   1912; Besserman, 1984[b], pp. 45-46; cp. *RR* 7079-92; cp.
   Burnley, 1986, pp. 211-13; cp. Hilary, in B, 1987, n. 725-
   42).
   Cp. *Matt. 13:10-13* ? (Huppé, 1967, pp. 26-28).

Knight's Tale, I (A), lines 859-3108:

1051: And in the gardyn, at the sonne upriste,/ She walketh up and doun . . .
> *Gen. 3* ? (Robertson, 1962, p. 387; cp. Boccaccio, *Teseida* 3.1-14; Havely, 1980, pp. 111-12; cp. Pearsall and Salter, 1973, pp. 4, 9, 195, et passim).

1055: . . . And as an aungel hevenysshly she soong.
> Cp. *Apoc. 5:11; etc.* (Robertson, 1962, p. 387; cp. Boccaccio, *Teseida* 3.10-11; Havely, 1980, p. 112; Cummings, 1916, p. 137).

1073: That he was born, ful ofte he seyde, "allas!"
> Cp. *Job 3:3; Jer. 20:14*

1104-05: . . . Venus, if it be thy wil/ Yow in this gardyn thus to transfigure . . .
> Cp. *Matt. 17:2, Mark 9:1, Luke 9:29* ?

1260: We witen nat what thing we preyen heere. . . .
> Cp. *Rom. 8:26* (S; R; F; cp. DiMarco, in B, 1987, n. 1251-67).

1307-12: What is mankynde moore unto you holde/ Than is the sheep that rouketh in the folde?/ For slayn is man right as another beest,/ And dwelleth eek in prison and arreest,/ And hath siknesse and greet adversitee,/ And ofte tymes giltelees, pardee.
> Cp. *Eccl. 3:18-19* (Innocent III, *DMCH* 1.2; R; cp. DiMarco, in B, 1987, n. 1307-09).
> *Job* ?

1422: Wel koude he hewen wode, and water bere . . .
> Cp. *Jos. 9:21, 23, 27; etc.* (Hinckley, 1916-17, 317; Hoffman, 1966-67, 172-73; R; DiMarco, in B, 1987, n. 1422).

1542: Allas . . . that day that I was bore! . . .
    Cp. *Job 3:3; Jer. 20:14*

1599: . . . By God that sit above. . . .
    Deut. 4:39; etc.

1663-73: The destinee, ministre general,/ That executeth in the
world over al/ The purveiaunce that God hath seyn biforn. . . .
Al is this reuled by the sighte above./ This mene I now by
myghty Theseus. . . .
    Cp. *Matt. 10:29-30* ? (cp. Dante, *Inf.* 7.67-96 ?; Schless, 1984,
        p. 174; cp. R; cp. DiMarco, in B, 1987, n. 1663-72).

1785: The god of love, a benedicite!
    Dan. 3:57, etc. (liturgy; R; cp. DiMarco, in B, 1987, n. 1785).

1800: . . . for Goddes sake that sit above . . .
    Cp. *Deut. 4:39; etc.*

1942: Ne yet the folye of kyng Salomon . . .
    Cp. *3 Kings 11; etc.* (R; F; cp. DiMarco, in B, 1987, n. 1942; cp.
        Gower, *CA* 7.4469-4545).

2007: The nayl ydryven in the shode anyght . . .
    Cp. *Judg. 4:21* (S; R; F; DiMarco, in B, 1987, n. 2007).

2075-86: This goddesse on an hert ful hye seet . . . And
undernethe hir feet she hadde a moone. . . . A womman
travaillynge was hire biforn . . . And seyde, "Help, for thou
mayst best of alle!"
    Cp. *Apoc. 12:1-12* (cp. DiMarco, in B, 1987, n. 2085).

2115: To fighte for a lady, benedicitee!
    Dan. 3:57, etc. (liturgy; S; R; cp. *KtT*, I [A], 1785).

2160: . . . clooth of Tars . . .
> *Acts 9:11; etc.* ? (Hinckley, 1916-17, 318; Magoun, 1961, pp. 150-51; R).

2249: . . . Youre vertu is so greet in hevene above . . .
> Cp. *Deut. 4:39; etc.* (cp. Boccaccio, *Teseida* 7.48; Havely, 1980, p. 128).

2414-18: And eek to this avow I wol me bynde:/ My beerd, myn heer, that hongeth long adoun,/ That nevere yet ne felte offensioun/ Of rasour nor of shere, I wol thee yive,/ And ben thy trewe servant whil I lyve.
> *Num. 6:1-5; Judg. 16:17* (Boccaccio, *Teseida* 7.28.6-8; Hoffman, 1966-67, 173-75; Allen & Moritz, 1981, p. 28; R; cp. DiMarco, in B, 1987, n. 2410-17).

2439: . . . in the hevene above . . .
> Cp. *Deut. 4:39; etc.*

2466: I slow Sampsoun, shakynge the piler . . .
> *Judg. 16:29-30* (Hoffman, 1966-67, 173-75; Allen & Moritz, 1981, p. 28; DiMarco, in B, 1987, n. 2466).

2470: Now weep namoore; I shal doon diligence . . .
> *Apoc. 21:4* ? (Allen & Moritz, pp. 187-88).

2478: Weep now namoore; I wol thy lust fulfille.
> *Apoc. 21:4* ? (ibid.).

2561-62: The voys of peple touchede the hevene,/ So loude cride they with murie stevene.
> Cp. *Acts 4:24; etc.*

2809-10: His spirit chaunged hous and wente ther,/ As I cam nevere, I kan nat tellen wher.

Cp. *2 Cor. 5:1, 6-8* (La; Bennett, 1974, p. 132; cp. Boccaccio, *Teseida* 11.1-6; Havely, 1980, p. 144; cp. DiMarco, in B, 1987, n. 2809-15).

2847-48: This world nys but a thurghfare ful of wo,/ And we been pilgrymes, passynge to and fro.
   Cp. *Eccl. 7:1; Heb. 11:13-16; 1 Pet. 2:11; etc.* (cp. Dante, *Purg.* 13:95-96; La; R; cp. Smith, 1950; Herz, 1964, 221-22; cp. DiMarco, in B, 1987, n. 2847-49).

2987-3035: The Firste Moevere of the cause above. . . . .
What maketh this but Juppiter, the kyng . . .
   Cp. *Deut. 4:39; etc.*
   Cp. *Matt. 10:29-30; etc.* (cp. R; cp. DiMarco, in B, 1987, n. 2987-3089).

3089: . . . For gentil mercy oghte to passen right.
   Cp. *Ps. 84(85):11(10)* (Root, 1926, p. 485, n. 1282; Klinefelter, 1965; cp. DiMarco, in B, 1987, n. 3089).

Miller's Prologue, I (A), lines 3109-86:

3124: . . . But in Pilates voys he gan to crie . . .
   Cp. *Matt. 27:2; etc.* (vernacular biblical drama; S; R; P; F; Harder, 1956; cp. Gray, in B, 1987, n. 3124).

3141-42: For I wol telle a legende and a lyf/ Bothe of a carpenter and of his wyf . . .
   Luke 1:26-38 ? (cp. Protevangelium of James; Rowland, 1974, pp. 43-44; cp. Gray, in B, 1987, n. 3141).
   Matt. 13:55 ? (ibid.).

3154-55: Ther been ful goode wyves many oon,/ And evere a thousand goode ayeyns oon badde.
   Cp. *Eccl. 7:29* (Deschamps, *Mir.* 9097-100; R; cp. Gray, in B, 1987, n. 3154-56).

Miller's Tale, I (A), lines 3187-3854:

3189: . . . And of his craft he was a carpenter.
  Matt. 13:55 ? (Rowland, 1974, pp. 43-44; cp. Gray, in B, 1987, n. 3189).

3199: This clerk was cleped hende Nicholas.
  Cp. *Apoc. 2:14-15* ? (Bolton, 1962, 88; Buermann, 1967, p. 144; cp. Gray, in B, 1987, n. 3199).

3213-15: . . . And al above ther lay a gay sautrie,/ On which he made a-nyghtes melodie/ So swetely that al the chambre rong . . .
  Cp. *Ps. 149:5* ? (Gellrich, 1974, 180-81).

3216: And *Angelus ad virginem* he song . . .
  Luke 1:26-38 (anon. song; Stevens, 1981; Rowland, 1974; R; P; F; cp. Gray, in B, 1987, n. 3216).

3259: Therto she koude skippe and make game . . .
  Cp. *Cant. 7:1* (Kaske, 1960, p. 56).

3261-62: Hir mouth was sweete as bragot or the meeth,/ Or hoord of apples leyd in hey or heeth.
  Cp. *Cant. 7:8-9* (Kaske, 1960, p. 55).

3263: Wynsynge she was, as is a joly colt. . . .
  Cp. *Cant. 7:1* (Kaske, 1960, p. 56).

3265-66: A brooch she baar upon hir lowe coler,/ As brood as is the boos of a bokeler.
  Cp. *Cant. 4:4* (Kaske, 1960, pp. 55-56).

3267: Hir shoes were laced on hir legges hye.
  Cp. *Cant. 7:1* (Kaske, 1960, p. 56).

3305-06: . . . He kiste hire sweete and taketh his sawtrie,/ And pleyeth faste, and maketh melodie.
> Cp. *Ps. 148-50* ? (Gellrich, 1974).

3312-17: Now was ther of that chirche a parissh clerk,/ The which that was ycleped Absolon./ Crul was his heer, and as the gold it shoon,/ And strouted as a fanne large and brode;/ Ful streight and evene lay his joly shode./ His rode was reed, his eyen greye as goos.
> Cp. *2 Kings 14:25-26* (Beichner, 1950; Olson, 1963, 232-33; cp. Fleming, 1984, pp. 194-95; F; cp. Gray, in B, 1987, n. 3312-38).
> Cp. *Cant. 5:10-12* (Kaske, 1960, p. 56-57; cp. Ames, 1977, p. 100).

3384: . . . He pleyeth Herodes upon a scaffold hye.
> Cp. *Matt. 2; etc.* (vernacular biblical drama; S; R; P; F; Harder, 1956; cp. Gray, in B, 1987, n. 3384).

3451-54: This man is falle, with his astromye,/ In some woodnesse . . . Men sholde nat knowe of Goddes pryvetee.
> Cp. *Acts 1:7; etc.* (Gray, in B, 1987, n. 3451-54).

3464: . . . by Jhesus, hevene kyng!
> Cp. *Dan. 4:34; etc.*

3478: . . . thenk on Cristes passioun!
> *Matt. 27:2, 26, 35-50; etc.* (Gray, in B, 1987, n. 3478).

3485: . . . the white pater-noster!
> Cp. *Matt. 6:9-13, Luke 11:2-4* (charm; F; Gray, in B, 1987, nn. 3480-86, 3486).

3486: . . . Seinte Petres soster?
> *Matt. 4:18; etc.* (charm; F; Gray, in B, 1987, nn. 3480-86, 3486).

3512: . . . by hym that harwed helle!
> *Gospel of Nicodemus* (vernacular biblical drama; S; R; P; F; Gray, in B, 1987, n. 3512).

3517-82: . . . Shal falle a reyn, and that so wilde and wood,/ That half so greet was nevere Noes flood. . . . . And thanne shul we be lordes al oure lyf/ Of al the world, as Noe and his wyf.
> *Gen. 6-9* (R; F; Olson, 1962, 4-5, n. 9; Buermann, 1967, pp. 124-77; Wood, 1970, pp. 161-72; ———, 1984, p. 42; cp. Gray, in B, 1987, n. 3515).

3519-21: This world . . . in lasse than an hour/ Shal al be dreynt, so hidous is the shour./ Thus shal mankynde drenche, and lese hir lyf.
> Cp. *Gen. 6:17* (cp. Vaughan, 1981).

3529-30: For thus seith Salomon, that was ful trewe,/ "Werk al by conseil, and thou shalt nat rewe."
> 8
> *Ecclus. 32:24* (cp. Albertano of Brescia, *LCC;* Bühler, 1949; Bolton, 1962, 92-93; S; R; proverbial; Whi C470; cp. Gray, in B, 1987, n. 3530).

3534-36: Hastow nat herd hou saved was Noe,/ Whan that oure Lord hadde warned hym biforn/ That al the world with water sholde be lorn?
> *Gen. 6:17-19*

3539-40: . . . The sorwe of Noe with his felaweshipe,/ Er that he myghte gete his wyf to shipe?
> Cp. *Gen. 7:7* (vernacular biblical drama; S; R; P; F; Harder, 1956; cp. Gray, in B, 1987, n. 3538-43).

3560-61: . . . To han as greet a grace as Noe hadde./ Thy wyf shal I wel saven, out of doute.
> Cp. *Gen. 8:16*

3581-82: And thanne shul we be lordes al oure lyf/ Of al the world, as Noe and his wyf.
   Cp. *Gen. 8:16, 9:2-3*

3612: Men may dyen of ymaginacioun . . .
   Gen. 8:21 ?

3616: . . . Noees flood come walwynge as the see . . .
   Gen. 7:10-24

3638: Now, *Pater-noster,* clom! . . .
   Matt. 6:9-13; Luke 11:2-4 (liturgy; S; P).

3690-93: But first he cheweth greyn and lycorys,/ To smellen sweete, er he hadde kembd his heer,/ Under his tonge a trewe-love he beer,/ For therby wende he to ben gracious.
   Cp. *Cant. 5:13, 16* (Kaske, 1960, p. 57; Ames, 1977, pp. 94-95, 98-99).

3698-99: What do ye, hony-comb, sweete Alisoun,/ My faire bryd, my sweete cynamome?
   Cp. *Cant. 4:11, 14* (Kaske, 1960, p. 53; Ames, 1977, pp. 94-95, 98-99; cp. F; cp. Gray, in B, 1987, n. 3698-707).

3700: Awaketh, lemman myn, and speketh to me!
   Cp. *Cant. 2:13-14* (Kaske, 1960, p. 53; Ames, 1977, pp. 94-95, 98-99; cp. Gray, in B, 1987, n. 3698-707).

3702: . . . That for youre love I swete ther I go.
   Cp. *Cant. 5:2* (Kaske, 1960, p. 54; Ames, 1977, pp. 94-95, 98-99; cp. Gray, in B, 1987, n. 3698-707).

3705-06: Ywis, lemman, I have swich love-longynge/ That lik a turtel trewe is my moornynge.
   Cp. *Cant. 2:5, 5:8* (Kaske, 1960, p. 54; Ames, 1977, pp. 94-95, 98-99; cp. Gray, in B, 1987, n. 3698-707).

Cp. *Cant. 2:12* (Kaske, 1960, p. 54; Ames, 1977, pp. 94-95, 98-99).

3708: "Go fro the wyndow, Jakke fool," she sayde. . . .
Cp. *Cant. 5:5* ? (Kaske, 1960, p. 54; Ames, 1977, pp. 94-95, 98-99).

3710-11: I love another—and elles I were to blame—/ Wel bet than thee, by Jhesu, Absolon.
Cp. *Matt. 9:15; etc.* ? (Kaske, 1960, pp. 59-60; cp. Ames, 1977, pp. 94-95, 100).

3712-13: Go forth thy wey, or I wol caste a ston,/ And lat me slepe, a twenty devel wey!
Cp. *Num. 35:17* ?
Cp. *John 8:3-11* ? (Bolton, 1962, 93; Reiss, 1980, 397).
Cp. *Cant. 2:7, 3:5, 8:4* ? (Kaske, 1960, p. 55; Ames, 1977, pp. 98-99).

3716-17: Thanne kysse me, syn it may be no bet,/ For Jhesus love, and for the love of me.
Cp. *Matt. 9:15; etc.* ? (Kaske, 1960, pp. 59-60).

3734: . . . But with his mouth he kiste hir naked ers. . . .
Cp. *Cant. 1:1* ? (Kaske, 1960, p. 57; Ames, 1977, pp. 98-99).

3768: . . . Why rise ye so rathe? ey, benedicitee!
Dan. 3:57, etc. (liturgy; cp. *KtT* 1785).

3785: . . . And caughte the kultour by the colde stele.
Cp. *Isa. 2:4* ? (Bolton, 1962, 93).

3790-91: This Alison answerde, "Who is ther/ That knokketh so? I warante it a theef."
1 Thess. 5:2-8 ? (Delasanta, 1978, 245).

3818: . . . And thoughte, "Allas, now comth Nowelis flood!"
  Gen. 7:10-24 (S; R; F; cp. Gray, in B, 1987, n. 3818).

3834: He was agast so of Nowelis flood . . .
  Gen. 7:10-24
  Cp. *Gen. 9:15* (Robertson, 1962, 384-85).

Reeve's Prologue, I (A), lines 3855-920:

3876: We hoppen alwey whil that the world wol pype.
  Luke 7:31-32; Matt. 11:16-17 ? (La, 1924, 96; Wood, 1984[c],
    pp. 39-42; S; R; cp. Gray, in B, 1987, n. 3876).

3877: For in oure wyl ther stiketh evere a nayl. . . .
  2 Cor. 12:7 ? (F; Gray, in B, 1987, n. 3877).

3902: What shul we speke alday of hooly writ?
  G

3919-20: He kan wel in myn eye seen a stalke,/ But in his owene
he kan nat seen a balke.
  Matt. 7:3 (cp. Olson, 1962, 8-10; S; M; R; P; F; proverbial;
    Whi M710; Gray, in B, 1987, n. 3919).

Reeve's Tale, I (A), lines 3921-4324:

3941: His name was hoote deynous Symkyn.
  Acts 8:18; etc. ? (*Acts of Peter* ?; Herzman, 1982; F).

4084: . . . for Cristes peyne . . .
  Matt. 27:2, 26, 35-50; etc.

4233: . . . Til that the thridde cok bigan to synge.
  Cp. *Matt. 26:34; etc.* ? (cp. Gray, in B, 1987, n. 4233).

4280: . . . Til that the millere sporned at a stoon . . .
  Ps. 90(91):12 ? (liturgy; Buermann, 1967, pp. 234-35).

4287: *In manus tuas!* Lord, to thee I calle!
   Luke 23:46 (liturgy; Correale, 1966-67; Buermann, 1967, pp.
   234-35; S; R; P; F; cp. Gray, in B, 1987, n. 4287).

Cook's Prologue, I (A), lines 4325-64:

4327: . . . For Cristes passion . . .
   Matt. 27:2, 26, 35-50; etc. (cp. Gray, in B, 1987, n. 4327).

4330-32: Wel seyde Salomon in his langage,/ "Ne bryng nat
every man into thyn hous,"/ For herberwynge by nyghte is
perilous.
   g
   Ecclus. 11:31 (S; La; R; P: F; cp. Gray, in B, 1987, n. 4331).

Cook's Tale, I (A), lines 4365-4422:

Man of Law Headlink, II (B¹), lines 1-98:

Man of Law's Prologue, II (B¹), lines 99-133:

110-12: "Parfay," seistow, "somtyme he rekene shal,/ Whan
that his tayl shal brennen in the gleede,/ For he noght helpeth
needfulle in hir neede."
   Cp. *Luke 16:19-26* (Innocent III, *DMCH* 2.18, 37; Köppel,
      1890, 407; R; cp. Gower, *CA* 6.970-1109).

113-14: Herkne what is the sentence of the wise:/ "Bet is to
dyen than have indigence"; . . .
   g
   Ecclus. 40:29 (Innocent III, *DMCH* 1.15; Lewis, 1966, 486-87;
      cp. Köppel, 1890, 408; Ames, 1984, pp. 98-99; cp. Nicholas
      of Lyre, *Postillae;* Wurtele, 1984, pp. 99-100; S; R; cp.
      Eberle, in B, 1987, n. 114).
   Ecclus. 11:28 ? (cp. *RR 8178* ?; M).

115: "Thy selve neighebor wol thee despise."
  Prov. 14:20 (Innocent III, *DMCH* 1.15; Lewis, 1966, 486-87;
    Ames, 1984, pp. 98-99; cp. Eberle, in B, 1987, n. 115).

117-18: Yet of the wise man take this sentence:/ "Alle the
dayes of povre men been wikke."
    g
  Prov. 15:15 (Innocent III, *DMCH* 1.15; Lewis, 1966, 486-87;
    Ames, 1984, pp. 98-99; S; M; R; cp. Eberle, in B, 1987, n.
    118).

120-21: If thou be povre, thy brother hateth thee,/ And alle
thy freendes fleen from thee, allas!
  Prov. 19:7 (Innocent III, *DMCH* 1.15; Lewis, 1966, 486-87; cp.
    Köppel, 1890, 408; Ames, 1984, pp. 98-99; cp. Nicholas of
    Lyre, *Postillae;* Wurtele, 1984, p. 100; S; R; proverbial;
    Whi P295; Eberle, in B, 1987, n. 120-21).

127: Ye seken lond and see for yowre wynnynges . . .
  Matt. 23:15 ? (S).

The Man of Law's Tale, II (B^1), lines 134-1162:

201-02: Of Sampson . . ./ The deeth . . .
  Judg. 16:29-30 (cp. Eberle, in B, 1987, n. 190-203).

286-87: Wommen are born to thraldom and penance,/ And to
been under mannes governance.
  Gen. 3:16 (Wurtele, 1984, p. 100; R; cp. Eberle, in B, 1987, n.
    285-87).

358: . . . roote of iniquitee!
  1 Tim. 6:10 (La, p. 188; cp. Eberle, in B, 1987, n. 358).

360: O serpent under femynynytee . . .
>   Cp. *Gen. 3:1; etc.* (cp. Peter Comestor, *Historia Scholastica Libri Genesis* 21; S; M; R; P; F; cp. Eberle, in B, 1987, n. 360-61).

361: Lik to the serpent depe in helle ybounde!
>   Cp. *2 Peter 2:4; Jude 6; Apoc. 20:1-3* (Spencer, 1927, 187; Gospel of Nicodemus; vernacular biblical drama; R; S; cp. Nicholas of Lyre, *Postillae;* Wurtele, 1984, pp. 101-02; cp. Eberle, in B, 1987, n. 361).

365-66: O Sathan, envious syn thilke day/ That thou were chaced from oure heritage. . . .
>   Cp. *Wis. 2:24* (Bloomfield, 1952, p. 382, n. 16; Eberle, in B, 1987, n. 365).

368: Thou madest Eva brynge us in servage . . .
>   Cp. *Gen. 3*

421-23: O sodeyn wo, that evere art successour/ To worldly blisse, spreynd with bitternesse,/ The ende of the joye of oure worldly labour!
>   Cp. *Prov. 14:13* (Innocent III, *DMCH* 1.22; Lewis, 1966, 489-90; ——, 1967, 6-7; S; R; cp. Eberle, in B, 1987, n. 421).

424: Wo occupieth the fyn of oure gladnesse.
>   *Prov. 14:13* (Innocent III, *DMCH* 1.22; Lewis, 1966, 489-90; ——, 1967, 6-7; Köppel, 1890, 408-09; cp. Caie, 1984, pp. 83-85; S; R).

425-27: Herke this conseil for thy sikernesse:/ Upon thy glade day have in thy mynde/ The unwar wo or harm that comth bihynde.
>   *Ecclus. 11:27* (Innocent III, *DMCH* 1.22; Lewis, 1966, 489-90; ——, 1967, 6-7; S; R; cp. *TC* 4.836).

451-53: "O cleere, o welful auter, hooly croys,/ Reed of the Lambes blood ful of pitee,/ That wessh the world fro the olde iniquitee . . . "

John 1:29 (liturgy; La, p. 154; S; cp. Eberle, in B, 1987, n. 449-62).

456-58: Victorious tree, proteccioun of trewe,/ That . . . bere/ The Kyng of Hevene with his woundes newe . . .

Matt. 27:50; etc. (liturgy; cp. Eberle, in B, 1987, n. 449-62).

459: The white Lamb, that hurt was with a spere . . .

Apoc. 5:6 (cp. Eberle, in B, 1987, n. 449-62).

460: Flemere of feendes . . .

Matt. 10:1, etc. (cp. Eberle, in B, 1987, n. 449-62).

473-76: Who saved Danyel in the horrible cave/ Ther every wight save he, maister and knave,/ Was with the leon frete er he asterte?/ No wight but God that he bar in his herte.

Dan. 6:16-24, 14:30-42 (liturgy; Farrell, 1970; cp. Block, 1953, 585-86; Delasanta, 1970-71, 294-96; cp. Ames, 1977, 89-90; La; cp. Eberle, in B, 1987, n. 463-90).

479: Crist, which that is to every harm triacle . . .

Jer. 33:6; etc. ? (La).

486-87: Who kepte Jonas in the fisshes mawe/ Til he was spouted up at Nynyvee?

Jon. 2:1, 11; 3:2, etc. (liturgy; Farrell, 1970; cp. Block, 1953, 585-86; Delasanta, 1970-71, 294-96; Clark and Wasserman, 1978; cp. Ames, 1977, 89-90; La, 1924, 91; R; F; cp. Eberle, in B, 1987, n. 463-90; cp. Gower, *VC* 1.18.1819-20, 2.5.271-72).

488-90: Wel may men knowe it was no wight but he/ That kepte peple Ebrayk from hir drenchynge,/ With drye feet thurghout the see passynge.

Exod. 14:21-31 (liturgy; Farrell, 1970; cp. Block, 1953, 585-86; cp. Ames, 1977, 89-90; R; F; cp. Eberle, in B, 1987, n. 463-90).

491-94: Who bad the foure spirites of tempest/ That power han t'anoyen lond and see,/ Bothe north and south, and also west and est,/ "Anoyeth neither see, ne land, ne tree"?
  Apoc. 7:1-3 (Root, 1904; S; M; R; P; F; cp. Eberle, in B, 1987, n. 491-94).

502-04: Fyve thousand folk it was as greet mervaille/ With loves fyve and fisshes two to feede./ God sente his foyson at hir grete neede.
  Matt. 14:13-21, Mark 6:30-44, Luke 9:10-17, John 6:1-13 (liturgy; Farrell, 1970; cp. Ames, 1977, 89-90; La, 1924, 91; R; F; Eberle, in B, 1987, n. 502-03).

582: Sathan, that evere us waiteth to bigile . . .
  Cp. *1 Pet. 5:8*

617-18: For as the lomb toward his deeth is broght,/ So stant this innocent bifore the kyng.
  Cp. *Isa. 53:7*

633: But he that starf for our redempcioun . . .
  Rom. 5:9, Col. 1:20, etc.

634: . . . And boond Sathan (and yet lith ther he lay) . . .
  Cp. *2 Peter 2:4; Jude 6; Apoc. 20:1-3* (Spencer, 1927, 187; Gospel of Nicodemus; R; S; cp. Nicholas of Lyre, *Postillae;* Wurtele, 1984, pp. 101-02).

639-40: Immortal God, that savedest Susanne/ Fro false blame . . .
  Dan. 13:43-44 (Block, 1953, 585-86; S; R; P; F).

640-42: . . . merciful mayde,/ Marie I meene, doghter to Seint
Anne,/ Bifore whos child angeles synge Osanne. . . .
>   Cp. *Luke 2:13-14* (cp. Protevangelium of James; cp. Jacobus
>   de Voragine, *Legenda Aurea*, p. 50; cp. Dante, *Par.* 32.133-
>   35; Schless, 1984, p. 181; cp. Block, 1953, 585-86; S; R; cp.
>   Eberle, in B, 1987, nn. 641, 641-42).
>   Cp. *Matt. 21:9, 15; Mark 11:9; John 12:13; etc.* (cp. Dante,
>   *Par.* 32.133-35; Schless, 1984, p. 181; S; R).

666-67: A Britoun book, written with Evaungiles,/ Was fet, and
on this book he swoor anoon. . . .
>   G (cp. Nicholas Trivet, *Chronique;* Schlauch, in *S&A*, 1941,
>   p. 171; S; R; P; F).

674-76: . . . "Thou hast desclaundred, giltelees,/ The doghter of
hooly chirche in heigh presence;/ Thus hastou doon, and yet
holde I my pees!"
>   Cp. *Ps. 49(50):20-21* (cp. Nicholas Trivet, *Chronique;*
>   Schlauch, in *S&A*, 1941, p. 172; R; cp. Eberle, in B, 1987, n.
>   676).

701-02: Me list nat of the chaf, ne of the stree,/ Maken so long a
tale as of the corn.
>   *Matt. 3:12, Luke 3:17* ? (cp. Eberle, in B, 1987, n. 701-02).
>   *2 Cor. 3:6; Rom. 7:6* ?

762-63: Lord, welcome be thy lust and thy plesaunce;/ My lust I
putte al in thyn ordinaunce.
>   Cp. *Ps. 30(31):15-16(15)*

776-77: Ther dronkenesse regneth in any route,/ Ther is no
conseil hyd, withouten doute.
>   *Prov. 31:4* (proverbial; Whi D425; Innocent III, *DMCH* 2.19;
>   Lewis, 1966, 488-89; ———, 1967, 7-8; Köppel, 1890, 409;
>   S; R; cp. Eberle, in B, 1987, n. 771-77; cp. *PardT* 560-61 and
>   *Mel* 776-77).

783-84: . . . feendlych spirit . . ./ Thogh thou heere walke, thy spirit is in helle!

> Cp. *John 13:27; Ps. 54(55):16 (15)* (cp. Dante, *Inf.* 33:121-32 ?; Schless, 1984, pp. 181-82; R; cp. Eberle, in B, 1987, n. 784).

811-12: "Lord Crist . . . how may this world endure,/ So ful of synne is many a creature?"

> Cp. *Gen. 6:5-7*

813-16: "O myghty God, if that it be thy wille,/ Sith thou art rightful juge, how may it be/ That thou wolt suffren innocentz to spille,/ And wikked folk regne in prosperitee?

> Cp. *Ps. 93(94):2-6* (La; cp. *Bo* 1.m.5.34-46; S; R; cp. Eberle, in B, 1987, n. 813-16).
>
> *Job* ? (Clark and Wasserman, 1978).

837-38: With that hir coverchief of hir heed she breyde,/ And over his litel eyen she it leyde. . . .

> Cp. *Gen. 22:1-14* ? (vernacular biblical drama; Lancashire, 1974-75, 324; cp. Eberle, in B, 1987, n. 837-38).

842-43: Sooth is that thurgh wommanes eggement/ Mankynde was lorn, and damned ay to dye. . . .

> *1 Tim. 2:14; etc.* (S).

844-48: . . . For which thy child was on a croys yrent./ Thy blisful eyen sawe al his torment. . . ./ Thow sawe thy child yslayn bifore thyne yen. . . .

> *John 19:25*

852: . . . Thow haven of refut, brighte sterre of day . . .

> *Ps. 45(46):2(1), etc.* (liturgy; R; cp. Eberle, in B, 1987, n. 852).
> Cp. *Apoc. 22:16* (liturgy).

925-27: O foule lust of luxurie, lo, thyn ende!/ Nat oonly that thou feyntest mannes mynde,/ But verraily thou wolt his body shende.

Cp. *1 Cor. 6:18* (Innocent III, *DMCH* 2.21; Lewis, 1966, 489;
———, 1967, 8; S; La, p. 171; R; cp. Eberle, in B, 1987, n.
925-31).

934-38: O Golias, unmesurable of lengthe,/ Hou myghte David
make thee so maat,/ So yong and of armure so desolaat?/ Hou
dorste he looke upon thy dredful face?/ Wel may men seen, it
nas but Goddes grace.
  Cp. *1 Kings 17:4-51* (Block, 1953, 585-86; cp. Delasanta,
  1970-71, 294-96; S; R; F; Eberle, in B, 1987, n. 934).

939-42: Who yaf Judith corage or hardynesse/ To sleen hym
Olofernus in his tente,/ And to deliveren out of wrecchednesse/
The peple of God? . . .
  Jud. 13:1-10 (Block, 1953, 585-86; S; R; F; Eberle, in B, 1987,
  n. 940).

1109: It am I, fader. . . .
  Cp. *John 6:20* ? (S).

1132-33: But litel while it lasteth, I yow heete,/ Joye of this
world. . . .
  Cp. *Prov. 14:13* (Innocent III, *DMCH* 1.22; Lewis, 1966, 489-
  90; Köppel, 1890, 410; S; La; R; cp. Eberle, in B, 1987, n.
  1132-38).

1133-34: . . . for tyme wol nat abyde;/ Fro day to nyght it
changeth as the tyde.
  Ecclus. 18:26 (Innocent III, *DMCH* 1.21; Lewis, 1966, 489-90;
  ———, 1967, 8-9; Köppel, 1890, 410; S; R; cp. Eberle, in B,
  1987, n. 1132-38).

1135-38: Who lyved euere in swich delit o day/ That hym ne
moeved outher conscience,/ Or ire, or talent, or som kynnes
affray,/ Envye, or pride, or passion, or offence?
  Ecclus. 40:4 ? (cp. Innocent III, *DMCH* 1.21; Lewis, 1966, 489-

90; ———, 1967, 9-10; Köppel, 1890, 410).
Cp. *Job 21:12-15* ? (S; R; cp. Eberle, in B, 1987, n. 1132-38).

Man of Law Endlink, II (B¹), lines 1163-90:

1170: The Parson him answerde, "Benedicite! . . . "
Dan. 3:57, etc. (liturgy; S; M; cp. *KtT* 1785).

1180: He schal no gospel glosen here ne teche.
G (cp. Eberle, in B, 1987, n. 1180).

1183: . . . Or springen cokkel in our clene corn.
Cp. *Matt. 13:25* ? (S; R [n. to line 1173]; cp. Eberle, in B, 1987,
n. 1183).
Rom 15:4; 2 Cor. 3:6; Rom. 7:6 ? (Peck, 1984, p. 145).

Wife of Bath's Prologue, III (D), lines 1-856:

6-7: Housbondes at chirche dore I have had fyve--/ If I so ofte
myghte have ywedded bee . .
John 4:17-18 ? (Robertson, 1962, pp. 317-31; cp. Hilary, in B,
1987, n. 6).

10-11: . . . Crist ne wente nevere but onis/ To weddyng, in the
Cane of Galilee . . .
John 2:1-2 (Jerome, *EAJ* 1.14, 40; Whiting, in *S&A*, 1941, p.
209; S; R; P; F; Hilary, in B, 1987, nn. 11, 13; Robertson,
1962, pp. 317-31; Spisak, 1980, 154-55, 160).

14-23: Herkne eek, lo, which a sharp word for the nones,/
Biside a welle, Jhesus, God and man,/ Spak in repreeve of the
Samaritan:/ "Thou hast yhad fyve housbondes," quod he/ . . . . .
. . . . . How manye myghte she have in mariage?
John 4:5-19 (Jerome, *EAJ* 1.14; Whiting, in *S&A*, 1941, p. 209;
S; M; La, 1924, 95; R; P; F; Hilary, in B, 1987, n. 15;
Robertson, 1962, pp. 317-31; Spisak, 1980, 154-55, 160).

26-29: Men may devyne and glosen, up and doun,/ But wel I
woot, expres, withoute lye,/ God bad us for to wexe and
multiplye;/ That gentil text kan I wel understonde.
> G (cp. Gower, *VC* 4.567-72; Mann, 1975, pp. 176-78).
> *Gen 1:28* (Jerome, *EAJ* 1.3, 16; Whiting, In *S&A*, 1941, p. 210;
> S; R; P; F; Hilary, in B, 1987, n. 28; Robertson, 1962, pp.
> 317-31; Delasanta, 1977-78; Spisak, 1980, 155-56, 160;
> Lawler, 1980, pp. 17-18; cp. Gower, *VC* 3.27, 4.13; Miller,
> 1977, pp. 216, 226).

30-31: Eek wel I woot, he seyde myn housbonde/ Sholde lete
fader and mooder and take to me.
> *Gen. 2:24; Matt. 19:5; Eph. 5:32* (Jerome, *EAJ* 1.5; S; R; P; F;
> Hilary, in B, 1987, n. 30-31; Robertson, 1962, pp. 317-31).

35-43: Lo, heere the wise kyng, daun Salomon;/ I trowe he
hadde wyves mo than oon./ . . . . so wel was hym on lyve.
> *3 Kings 11:3* (Jerome, *EAJ* 1.24; Köppel, 1890, 414-15, n. 2; La;
> S; R; P; F; Hilary, in B, 1987, n. 35; liturgy ?; Higdon,
> 1972; cp. Gower, *CA* 7.4469-4545; cp. Matheolus,
> *Lamentations* II.4087-89; Thundy, 1979, p. 34).

39: Which yifte of God hadde he . . .
> *1 Cor. 7:7* ? (Robertson, 1962, pp. 323-24).

44: Yblessed be God that I have wedded fyve!
> *John 4:17-18* (see lines 6-7, above).

46: For sothe, I wol nat kepe me chaast in al.
> *1 Cor. 7:9* (Jcromc, *EAJ* 1.9; S; R; cp. Hilary, in B, 1987, n. 46-
> 51; cp. line 52, below).

47-50: Whan myn housbonde is fro the world ygon,/ Som Cristen
man shal wedde me anon,/ For thanne th'apostle seith that I
am free/ To wedde, a Goddes half, where it liketh me.

8

1 *Cor. 7:39; Rom 7:2-3* (Jerome, *EAJ* 1.10; Köppel, 1890, 414, n. 2; Holkot, *SLS* 45; Petersen, 1898, p. 111; S; R; P; F; cp. Hilary, in B, 1987, n. 46-51).

51: He seith that to be wedded is no synne. . . .

    g
1 *Cor. 7:28* (Jerome, *EAJ* 1.10; S; R; P; cp. Hilary, in B, 1987, n. 46-51).

52: Bet is to be wedded than to brynne.
    1 *Cor. 7:9* (Jerome, *EAJ* 1.9; cp. Innocent III, *DMCH* 1.18; Köppel, 1890, 414, n. 2; S; R; P; proverbial; Whi W162; Hilary, in B, 1987, n. 52; cp. line 46, above).

53-54: What rekketh me, thogh folk seye vileynye/ Of shrewed Lameth and his bigamye?
    Gen. 4:18-24 (Jerome, *EAJ* 1.14; Whiting, in *S&A*, 1941, p. 209; S; M; R; P; F; cp. Hilary, in B, 1987, n. 54-56; cp. Matheolus, *Lamentations* 161-65; Thundy, 1979, pp. 34-35).

55-57: I woot wel Abraham was an hooly man,/ And Jacob eek, as ferforth as I kan;/ And ech of hem hadde wyves mo than two . . .
    Gen. 16:2-3, 25:1, 30:1-13 (Jerome, *EAJ* 1.5; Whiting, In *S&A*, 1941, p. 208; S; M; cp. Hilary, in B, 1987, n. 54-56).

59-68: Wher can ye seye . . . That hye God defended mariage/ By expres word? . . . Th'apostel, whan he speketh of maydenhede,/ He seyde that precept therof hadde he noon./ Men may conseille a womman to been oon,/ But conseillyng is no comandement./ He putte it in oure owene juggement. . . .

    G
    g
1 *Cor. 7:25-26* (Jerome, *EAJ* 1.12; Whiting, In *S&A*, 1941, pp. 208-09; S; M; R; P; F; Hilary, in B, 1987, nn. 64-65, 67; Spisak, 1980, 153-54).

73-74: Poul dorste nat comanden, atte leeste,/ A thyng of which his maister yaf noon heeste.

    g
    1 Cor. 7:25 (ibid.; Hilary, in B, 1987, n. 73; cp. Mann, 1975, pp. 178-79).

75-76: The dart is set up for virginitee;/ Cacce whoso may, who renneth best lat see.

    1 Cor. 9:24 (Jerome, *EAJ* 1.12; Whiting, In *S&A*, 1941, p. 209; Caie, 1976-77, 354-55; ————, 1983, p. 338; S; R; proverbial; Whi C112; Hilary, in B, 1987, nn. 75, 76; cp. Mann, 1975, pp. 178-79; Matheolus, *Lamentations* II.1827-28; Thundy, 1979, p. 35).

77-78: But this word is nat taken of every wight,/ But ther as God lust gyve it of his myght.

    Matt. 19:11-12 (cp. Jerome, *EAJ* 1.12; Köppel, 1890, 414-15, n. 2; R; Hilary, in B, 1987, n. 77-78; cp. Nicholas of Lyre, *Postillae;* Wurtele, 1984, pp. 103-06).

    Cp. *Apoc. 14:4* ? (cp. Nicholas of Lyre, *Postillae;* Wurtele, 1984, pp. 103-06).

79-81: I woot wel that th'apostel was a mayde;/ But nathelees, thogh that he wroot and sayde/ He wolde that every wight were swich as he . . .

    g
    1 Cor. 7:7 (Jerome, *EAJ* 1.8; S; R; P; Hilary, in B, 1987, n. 81; Lawler, 1980, pp. 17-18).

82: Al nys but conseil to virginitee.

    1 Cor. 7:25 (cp. Jerome, *EAJ* 1.12; Whiting, In *S&A*, 1941, p. 209).

83-84: And for to been a wyf he yaf me leve/ Of indulgence . . .

    1 Cor. 7:6 (cp. Jerome, *EAJ* 1.12; cp. Whiting, In *S&A*, 1941, p. 209; S; R; P; F; Hilary, in B, 1987, n. 84).

84-86: . . . so nys it no repreve/ To wedde me, if that my make dye,/ Withouten excepcion of bigamye.

    1 Cor. 7:39

87: Al were it good no womman for to touche . . .

    1 Cor. 7:1 (La; Jerome, *EAJ* 2.22; S; R; P: F; cp. Hilary, in B, 1987, nn. 87, 89).

91-92: This is al and som, he heeld virginitee/ Moore parfit than weddyng in freletee.

    g

    1 Cor. 7:8-9 (Jerome, *EAJ* 2.22; S; R; Hilary, in B, 1987, n. 91).

99-101: . . . a lord in his houshold,/ He nath nat every vessel al of gold;/ Somme been of tree, and doon hir lord servyse.

    2 Tim. 2:20 (Jerome, *EAJ* 1.40; Whiting, In *S&A*, 1941, p. 210; S; R; P; F; Hilary, in B, 1987, n. 99-101; Robertson, 1962, pp. 326-27).

102-04: God clepeth folk to hym in sondry wyse,/ And everich hath of God a propre yifte—/ Som this, som that, as hym liketh shifte.

    1 Cor. 7:7 (Jerome, *EAJ* 1.8; S; R; P; F; cp. Hilary, in B, 1987, n. 103; Lawler, 1980, pp. 17-18).

105: Virginitee is greet perfeccion . . .

    Cp. *Apoc. 14:1-5* (Jerome, *EAJ* 1.40; S; M; R; P; F; Hilary, in B, 1987, n. 105; cp. Nicholas of Lyre, *Postillae;* Wurtele, 1984, pp.103-06).

107-11: But Crist, that of perfeccion is welle,/ Bad nat every wight he sholde go selle/ Al that he hadde, and gyve it to the poore/ And in swich wise folwe hym and his foore./ He spak to hem that wolde lyve parfitly . . .

    g

    Matt. 19:21 (cp. *RR* 11377-83; Jerome, *EAJ* 1.34-2.6; S; R; P; F; Hilary, in B, 1987, n. 107-12; Robertson, 1962, pp. 327-28).

129-30: Why sholde men elles in hir bookes sette/ That man shal yelde to his wyf hire dette?
G
1 Cor. 7:3 (S; R; P; F; cp. Hilary, in B, 1987, n. 129-30; Robertson, 1962, pp. 327-28; cp. *ParsT* 940; *MerchT* 2048).

145-46: And yet with barly-breed, Mark telle kan,/ Oure Lord Jhesu refresshed many a man.
g
Cp. *John 6:3-11* (cp. Jerome, *EAJ* 1.7; Köppel, 1890, 414, n. 2; La, 1924, 100, n. 66; S; R; P; F; cp. Hilary, in B, 1987, n. 144-45; Robertson, 1962, pp. 328-29; liturgy ?; Higdon, 1972).
Cp. *Mark 6:34-42* (La, 1924, 100, n. 66).

147-48: In swich estaat as God hath cleped us/ I wol persevere. . . .
1 Cor. 7:20 (Jerome, *EAJ* 1.11; La, 1924, 95; S; R; Hilary, in B, 1987, n. 147).

153: . . . Whan that hym list come forth and paye his dette.
1 Cor. 7:3 (cp. lines 129-30, above).

154-55: An housbonde I wol have—I wol nat lette—/ Which shal be bothe my dettour and my thral . . .
1 Cor. 7:3 (cp. Jerome, *EAJ* 1.11; Köppel, 1890, 414-15, n. 2; S).

156-57: . . . And have his tribulacion withal/ Upon his flessh, whil that I am his wyf.
1 Cor. 7:28 (cp. Jerome, *EAJ* 1.7, 13; Köppel, 1890, 414-15, n. 2; La; Harwood, 1972; Patterson, 1983; Robertson, 1962, p. 329; S; R; P; F; cp. Hilary, in B, 1987, n. 154-60, 155).

158-60: I have the power durynge al my lyf/ Upon his propre body, and noght he./ Right thus the Apostel tolde it unto me . . .

1 Cor. 7:4 (La, 1924, 95; S; R; P; F; cp. Hilary, in B, 1987, n. 158).

g

161-62: . . . And bad oure housbondes for to love us weel./ Al this sentence me liketh every deel. . . .

g

Eph. 5:25; Col. 3:19 (Holkot, *SLS* 45; Petersen, 1898, p. 111; S; R; P; F; cp. Hilary, in B, 1987, n. 158; Robertson, 1962, pp. 329-30; Wood, 1984[c], pp. 37-38).
Cp. *1 Cor. 7:3* (Caie, 1984, p. 76).

164: . . . by God and by seint John!

g ?

167: What sholde I bye it on my flessh so deere?
Cp. *1 Cor. 7:28* (cp. lines 156-57, above).

207: . . . by God above . . .
Cp. *Deut. 4:39; etc.*

274-75: . . . no wys man nedeth for to wedde,/ Ne no man that entendeth unto hevene.
Cp. *1 Cor. 7:32* (cp. Jerome, *EAJ* 1.47; Whiting, In *S&A*, 1941, p. 211; S).

278-80: Thow seyst that droppyng houses, and eek smoke,/ And chidyng wyves maken men to flee/ Out of hir owene houses. . . .
Prov. 19:13, 27:15 (Innocent III, *DMCH* 1.16.33; cp. Jerome, *EAJ* 1.28; Köppel, 1890, 414-15; Holkot, *SLS* 38; Petersen, 1898, p. 113; S; M; R; F; proverbial; Whi T187; cp. Hilary, in B, 1987, n. 278; cp. *ParsT* 631 and *Mel* 1086).

280: . . . a! benedicitee!
Dan. 3:57 (liturgy; cp. *KtT* 1785; etc.).

313-14: Thou shalt nat bothe, thogh that thou were wood,/ Be maister of my body and of my good. . . .
> *1 Cor. 7:4* (cp. lines 158-60, above; cp. Matheolus, *Lamentations* II.3167; Thundy, 1979, p. 40).

326-27: "Of alle men his wysdom is the hyeste/ That rekketh nevere who hath the world in honde."
> Cp. *1 Tim. 6:6, 8* (S; R; cp. Hilary, in B, 1987, n. 327).

341-45: And seye thise wordes in the Apostles name:/ "In habit maad with chastitee and shame/ Ye wommen shul apparaille yow," quod he,/ "And noght in tressed heer and gay perree,/ As perles, ne with gold, ne clothes riche."
> g
> *1 Tim. 2:9* (Jerome, *EAJ* 1.27; Köppel, 1890, 414-15, n. 2; S; M; R; P; F; Hilary, in B, 1987, n. 341).

346-47: After thy text, ne after thy rubriche,/ I wol nat wirche. . . .
> G

362-67: Thou seydest eek that ther been thynges thre,/ The whiche thynges troublen al this erthe,/ And that no wight may endure the ferthe. . . . and seyst an hateful wyf/ Yrekened is for oon of thise meschances.
> *Prov. 30:21-23* (Jerome, *EAJ* 1.28; Whiting, In *S&A*, 1941, p. 210; S; R; F; Hilary, in B, 1987, n. 362-64; Spisak, 1980, 154).

368-69: Been ther none othere maner resemblances/ That ye may likne youre parables to . . . ?
> g ? (Proverbs ?; cp. Jerome, *EAJ* 1.28; Whiting, In *S&A*, 1941, p. 210).

371-75: Thou liknest eek wommenes love to helle,/ To bareyne lond, ther water may nat dwelle./ Thou liknest it also to wilde fyr;/ The moore it brenneth, the moore it hath desir/ To consume every thyng that brent wole be.

> *Prov. 30:16* (Jerome, *EAJ* 1.28; Whiting, In *S&A*, 1941, p. 210; S; R; Hilary, in B, 1987, n. 371).

376-77: Thou seyest, right as wormes shende a tree,/ Right so a wyf destroyeth hire housbonde. . . .

> *Prov. 25:20* (Jerome, *EAJ* 1.28; S; R; Hilary, in B, 1987, n. 376).

399: Under that colour . . .

> *Acts 27:30* ? (S).

401-02: . . . spynnyng God hath yive/ To wommen kyndely. . . .

> *Prov. 31:13, etc.* ? (Lawler, 1980, pp. 58, 184-85, n. 3; proverbial; Walther, 8751 and Whi D120; Hilary, in B, 1987, n. 401).

436: Sith ye so preche of Jobes pacience . . .

> g
> Cp. *James 5:11* (cp. Matheolus, *Lamentations* II.1837-40; Thundy, 1979, p. 40).

446: Peter! . . .

> *Matt. 4:18; etc.* (cp. P; F).

469-70: But--Lord Christ!--Whan that it remembreth me/ Upon my yowthe, and on my jolitee . . .

> Cp. *2 Tim. 2:22* ? (*RR* 12932-48; Hilary, in B, 1987, n. 469-73; cp. Caie, 1984, p. 78).

534: For hadde myn housbonde pissed on a wal . . .

> *1 Kings 25:22, 34; etc.* (R. Cook, 1978; cp. Hilary, in B, 1987, n. 534-38).

650: And thanne wolde he upon his Bible seke . . .

> G

651-53: . . . That ilke proverbe of Ecclesiaste/ Where he comandeth, and forbedeth faste/ Man shal nat suffre his wyf go roule aboute.

g

Ecclus. 25:34 (John of Wales, *Communiloquium* 2.4.2; Pratt, 1966, 621-23; Johnson, 1941, pp. 188-89; S; R; P; F; cp. Hilary, in B, 1987, n. 651-57).

679: . . . And eek the Parables of Salomon . . .

g (P; F; cp. Hilary, in B, 1987, n. 679).

687: . . . Than been of goode wyves in the Bible.

G

688-89: For trusteth wel, it is an impossible/ That any clerk wol speke good of wyves. . . .

Cp. *Prov. 31:10-31* ? (cp. Caie, 1975-76, 353; Miller, 1977, p. 391; Coletti, 1984, pp. 180-81; cp. Hilary, in B, 1987, n. 688).

696: . . . Than al the mark of Adam may redresse.

Gen. 5:3, etc. (S; R; P).

713-20: Upon a nyght Jankyn, that was oure sire,/ Redde on his book, as he sat by the fire,/ Of Eva first, that for hir wikkednesse/ Was al mankynde broght to wrecchednesse . . . . Lo, heere expres of womman may ye fynde/ That womman was the los of al mankynde.

Gen. 3:1-16 (S; cp. Hilary, in B, 1987, n. 715-25; cp. Lawler, 1985).

717-18: . . . For which that Jhesu Crist hymself was slayn,/ That boghte us with his herte blood agayn.

1 Cor. 15:21-22, Rom. 3:25, etc.

721-23: Tho redde he me how Sampson loste his heres:/ Slepynge, his lemman kitte it with hir sheres;/ Thurgh which treson loste he bothe his yen.

> *Judg. 16:17-21* (Holkot, *SLS* 38; Petersen, 1898, p. 112; cp.
> *MkT* 2015-94 [*3205-84] and *RR* 9173-76; S; R; F; cp.
> Hilary, in B, 1987, n. 715-25).

769-70: And somme han dryve nayles in hir brayn,/ Whil that they slepte, and thus they had hem slayn.

> *Judg. 4:21* (S; R; Hilary, in B, 1987, n. 769-70).

775-77: "Bet is," quod he, "thyn habitacioun/ Be with a leon or a foul dragoun,/ Than with a womman usynge for to chyde."

> *Ecclus. 25:23* (S; M; R; cp. Hilary, in B, 1987, n. 775-77).

778-79: "Bet is," quod he, "hye in the roof abyde,/ Than with an angry wyf doun in the hous ... "

> *Prov. 21:9, 19; 25:24* (Jerome, *EAJ* 1.28; Köppel, 1890, 414-15,
> n. 2; Holkot, *SLS* 38; Petersen, 1898, pp. 112-13; S; M; R; P;
> Hilary, in B, 1987, n. 778-79).

780-81: " ... They been so wikked and contrarious,/ They haten that hir housbondes loven ay."

> *Ecclus. 25:30* (Holkot, *SLS* 38; Petersen, 1898, p. 113; cp. S; R;
> P).

784-85: "A fair womman, but she be chaast also,/ Is lyk a gold ryng in a sowes nose."

> *Prov. 11:22* (John of Wales, *Communiloquium* 3.3.4; Pratt,
> 1966, 623-24; Holkot, *SLS* 133; Petersen, 1898, p. 113, n. 3;
> cp. *ParsT* 155-56; Köppel, 1891, 44; S; R; P; Hilary, in B,
> 1987, n. 784-85).

801: "And for my land thus hastow mordred me? ... "

> *Gal. 4:22; etc.* ? (Robertson, 1979-80, 415-16, et passim; cp.
> Pearsall, 1986, p. 140, et passim).

The Wife of Bath's Tale, III (D), lines 857-1264:

1117-18: Crist wole we clayme of hym oure gentillesse,/ Nat of oure eldres for hire old richesse.
Cp. *Matt. 23:8-10* (cp. Dante, *Convivio* 4.3.21-37, et passim; Lowes, 1915-16, 20-21; R; Hilary, in B, 1987, n. 1109).

1129-31: . . . for God, of his goodnesse,/ Wole that of hym we clayme oure gentillesse;/ For of oure eldres may we no thyng clayme . . . .
Matt. 23:8-10 (ibid.).

1162-63: Thy gentillesse cometh fro God allone./ Thanne comth oure verray gentillesse of grace. . . .
Cp. *Matt. 23:8-10; etc.* (cp. Dante, *Convivio* 4.20.47-57, et passim; Lowes, 1915-16, 25; R).
Cp. *Heb. 1:3; etc.*
Cp. *James 2:5; etc.*

1178-79: The hye God, on whom that we bileeve,/ In wilful poverte chees to lyve his lyf.
2 Cor. 8:9 (John of Wales, *Communiloquium* 3.4.2; Pratt, 1966, 625-27; R; Hilary, in B, 1987, n. 1178-79).

1185-90: Whoso that halt hym payd of his poverte/ . . . . Is riche, although ye holde hym but a knave.
Cp. *Apoc. 3:17* (John of Wales, *Communiloquium* 3.4.2; Pratt, 1966, 625-27; Hilary, in B, 1987, n. 1186).

1208-10: . . . thogh noon auctoritee/ Were in no book, ye gentils of honour/ Seyn that men sholde an oold wight doon favour. . . .
G
Lev. 19:32 ? (S; R).

1211-12: . . . And clepe hym fader, for youre gentilesse;/ And auctours shal I fynden, as I gesse.
Matt. 23:9 ?

1251: . . . she so fair was, and so yong therto. . . .
  Cp. *Ps. 102 (103):1-5* ? (Allen & Moritz, 1981, pp. 153-54).

The Friar's Prologue, III (D), lines 1265-1300:

1300: . . . Tel forth your tale, leeve maister deere.
  Cp. *Matt. 23:10; James 3:1* (Miller, 1977, pp. 242-43).

The Friar's Tale, III (D), lines 1301-1664:

1309: . . . Of usure, and of symonye also.
  Cp. *Acts 8:9-24* (R; Richardson, in B, 1987, n. 1309).

1332: "Peter! . . . "
  Matt. 4:18; etc.

1350-51: And right as Judas hadde purses smale,/ And was a theef, right swich a theef was he. . . .
  John 12:6 (La, 1924, 96; Fleming, 1984, pp. 186-89; S; R; P; F; Richardson, in B, 1987, n. 1350-51).

1352: His maister hadde but half his duetee.
  Matt. 6:24; Luke 16:13

1390-91: . . . To ryden, for to reysen up a rente/ That longeth to my lordes duetee.
  Matt. 18:23-34 (cp. Jeffrey, 1971).

1413: . . . fer in the north contree . . .
  Isa. 14:13-14 ? (S; M; R; P; Richardson, in B, 1987, n. 1413).

1456: . . . "benedicite! . . . "
  Dan. 3:57; etc. (liturgy; cp. *KtT* 1785).

1465: . . . Or lyk an angel kan I ryde or go.
  2 Cor. 11:14 (Birney, 1959).

1475: . . . Seyde this feend, "but alle thyng hath tyme. . . . "
   Eccl. 3:1 (R; P; F; proverbial; Whi T88; Richardson, in B,
      1987, n. 1475).

1489-91: And somtyme, at oure prayere, han we leve/ Oonly the
body and nat the soule greve;/ Witnesse on Job, whom that we
diden wo.
   Job 1:12, 2:6 (S; R; F; Richardson, in B, 1987, n. 1491).

1496: . . . and al is for the beste.
   Cp. *Rom. 8:28* (proverbial; Whi A93.1).

1497-98: Whan he withstandeth oure temptacioun,/ It is a
cause of his savacioun. . . .
   James 1:12

1503: . . . And to the apostles servant eek was I.
   Luke 9:1, 10:17-19 ? (S; R; F; cp. Sister Mary Immaculate,
      1942).
   Acts 19:15 ? (S; R).

1507-12: Somtyme we feyne, and somtyme we aryse/ With dede
bodyes, in ful sondry wyse,/ And speke as renably and faire and
wel/ As to the Phitonissa dide Samuel./ (And yet wol som men
seye it was nat he;/ I do no fors of youre dyvynytee.)
   1 Kings 28:7-25; 1 Par. 10:13 (S; M; R; P; F; Richardson, in B,
      1987, n. 1503).

1573: . . . an old rebekke . . .
   Gen. 25:20, etc. ? (liturgy; S; R; Hatton, 1968; Richardson, in
      B, 1987, n. 1573).

1613: . . . or by the sweete seinte Anne . . .
   Cp. *Luke 2:36* (S; cp. Jacobus de Voragine, *Legenda Aurea*, p.
      50, et passim; cp. Richardson, in B, 1987, n. 1613).

1614-15: . . . I wol bere awey thy newe panne/ For dette which thou owest me of old.
> *Deut. 24:17* ?

1626: "Now, Mabely, myn owene mooder deere . . . "
> Cp. *Matt. 12:48-50* ? (Jacobs and Jungman, 1985).

1636: Thou shalt with me to helle yet tonyght . . .
> Cp. *Luke 23:43* (P, p. xxx; F; cp. Richardson, in B, 1987, n. 1636).

1642-43: And God, that maked after his ymage/ Mankynde . . .
> *Gen. 1:26-27* (Black, 1974, pp. 52-55).

1647:. . . After the text of Crist, Poul, and John . . .
> G (cp. Richardson, in B, 1987, n. 1647).
> *8, 8*

1651: . . . Thogh that I myghte a thousand wynter telle . . .
> *Apoc. 20:2* ?

1652: . . . The peynes of thilke cursed hous of helle.
> *Apoc. 14:10-11, etc.*

1653-55: But for to kepe us fro that cursed place,/ Waketh and preyeth Jhesu for his grace/ So kepe us fro the temptour Sathanas.
> *Matt. 26:41, Mark 14:38*

1657-58: "The leoun sit in his awayt alway/ To sle the innocent, if that he may."
> *Ps. 10:8-9 (Hebrew); 1 Pet. 5:8* (Jerome, *EAJ* 2.3; Correale, 1964-65; cp. John Bromyard, *Summa Praedicantium* ?; Johnson, 1941, pp. 159-60; Bugge, 1975-76; Reiss, 1984, p. 53; S; R; P; F; Richardson, in B, 1987, n. 1657-58).

1659-60: Disposeth ay youre hertes to withstonde/ The feend,
that yow wolde make thral and bonde.

  Ecclus. 2:1 (Jerome, *EAJ* 2.3; Correale, 1964-65; cp. John
   Bromyard, *Summa Praedicantium* ?; Johnson, 1941, pp.
   159-60; cp. Richardson, in B, 1987, n. 1659-60).

1661-62: He may nat tempte yow over youre myght,/ For Crist
wol be youre champion and knyght.

  1 Cor. 10:13 (Jerome *EAJ* 2.3; Correale, 1964-65; cp. La, 1924,
   96; cp. John Bromyard, *Summa Praedicantium* ?; Johnson,
   1941, pp. 159-60; S; R; cp. Richardson, in B, 1987, n. 1661).

The Summoner's Prologue, III (D), lines 1665-1708:

1675-79: For, pardee, ye han ofte tyme herd telle/ How that a
frere ravysshed was to helle/ In spirit ones by a visioun;/ And
as an angel ladde hym up and doun,/ To shewen hym the peynes
that ther were . . .

  2 Cor. 12:4 (S).

The Summoner's Tale, III (D), lines 1709-2294:

1734: . . . With *Qui cum patre* forth his wey he wente.

  Cp. *Eph. 4:30; etc.* (liturgy; cp. F; P; Richardson, in B, 1987,
   n. 1734).
  Cp. *Apoc.1:18; etc.* (liturgy; cp. F; P; Richardson, in B, 1987,
   n. 1734).

1737: With scrippe and tipped staf, ytukked hye . . .

  Cp. *Matt. 10:9-10; Luke 9:3, 10:4* (Kaske, 1972, 122-23;
   Miller, 1977, p. 241; Richardson, in B, 1987, n. 1737).

1740-45: His felawe hadde a staf tipped with horn,/ A peyre of
tables al of yvory,/ And a poyntel polysshed fetisly,/ And
wroot the names alwey, as he stood,/ Of alle folk that yaf hym
any good,/ Ascaunces that he wolde for hem preye.

  Cp. *Luke 10:1* (Richardson, in B, 1987, n. 1740).

Exod. 31:18, etc. (Kaske, 1972, 123-26; cp. Richardson, in B, 1987, n. 1741).
2 Cor. 3:3 (Kaske, 1972, 123-26).

1765-71: So longe he wentc, hous by hous, til he/ Cam til an hous ther he was wont to be/ Refresshed moore than in an hundred placis./ Syk lay the goode man whos that the place is;/ Bedrede upon a couche lowe he lay./ "*Deus hic!*" quod he, "O Thomas, freend, good day!"/ Seyde this frere, curteisly and softe.
Cp. *Matt. 10:8-14* (Miller, 1977, p. 241; P; F; cp. Richardson, in B, 1987, nn. 1768, 1770).

1781: "O deere maister," quod this sike man. . .
Cp. *Matt. 23:10; James 3:1* ? (Miller, 1977, pp. 242-43).

1789-93: . . . And seyd a sermon after my symple wit--/ Nat al after the text of hooly writ,/ For it is hard to yow, as I suppose,/ And therfore wol I teche yow al the glose./ Glosynge is a glorious thyng, certeyn . . .
G (Adams, 1962, 127-28; Besserman, 1984[a]; cp. Richardson, in B, 1987, n. 1792).

1794: . . . For lettre sleeth, so as we clerkes seyn.
G
Cp. *2 Cor. 3:6; Rom. 7:6* (La, 1924, 96-97, n. 58; Besserman, 1984[a]; S; R; P; F; Richardson, in B, 1987, n. 1794).

1819: . . . And studie in Petres wordes and in Poules.
8, 8

1820: I walke and fisshe Cristen mennes soules . . .
Matt. 4:19, Mark 1:17, Luke 5:10 (La, 1924, 96-97, n. 58; Kaske, 1972, 123; S; R; cp. *Rom* 7490-91; Richardson, in B, 1987, n. 1820).

1821-22: . . . To yelden Jhesu Crist his propre rente;/ To sprede his word is set al myn entente.
> *Col. 1:25* ? (La, 1924, 96-97, n. 58).
> *Matt. 21:33-41; etc.* ? (Jeffrey, 1971).

1832-33: "O Thomas . . . this moste ben amended."
> Cp. *Matt. 10:8* (Miller, 1977, p. 241).

1834: Ire is a thyng that hye God defended. . . .
> *Eph. 4:31* ? (La, 1924, 96-97, n. 58).

1836-45: "Now, maister," quod the wyf, "er that I go,/ What wol ye dyne? . . . . " "Now, dame," quod he, " . . . My spirit hath his fostryng in the Bible."
> Cp. *Luke 10:7-8* (La, 1924, 96-97, n. 58; Kaske, 1972, 122-23;
>   Miller, 1977, p. 241).

1844-45: I am a man of litel sustenaunce;/ My spirit hath his fostryng in the Bible.
> *Deut. 8:3, Matt. 4:4, Luke 4:4; John 4:34* (S; La, 1924, 96-97, n.
>   58; R; P; cp. La, 1921, p. 60; Wood, 1984[c], pp. 43-46).
> *Job 23:12* (S; R).
> G

1851-68: "Now sire," quod she, "but o word er I go./ My child is deed withinne thise wykes two. . . . "/ "His deeth saugh I by revelacioun,"/ Seide this frere, " . . . I saugh hym born to blisse/ In myn avision, so God me wisse!/ . . . to Christ I seyde an orison,/ Thankynge hym of his revelacion.
> Cp. *Matt. 10:8* (Miller, 1977, p. 241).

1866: *Te Deum* was oure song, and nothyng elles. . . .
> Cp. *Ps 21(22):24(23); etc.* (liturgy; Richardson, in B, 1987, n.
>   1866).

1876: We han this worldes lust al in despit.
> *1 John 2:15* ? (La).

1877-78: Lazar and Dives lyveden diversly,/ And divers gerdon hadden they therby.
>   *Luke 16:19-31* (cp. Jerome, *EAJ* 2.17; Tupper, 1915, 8-9; S; R; P; F; Richardson, in B, 1987, n. 1877; cp. Gower, *CA* 6.970-1109).

1879-80: Whoso wol preye, he moot faste and be clene,/ And fatte his soule, and make his body lene.
>   *Matt. 4:2, 17:20; etc.* (S; cp. Jerome, *EAJ* 2.6; Richardson, in B, 1987, n. 1880).

1881-82: We fare as seith th'apostle; clooth and foode/ Suffisen us, though they be nat ful goode.
>   g
>   *1 Tim. 6:8* (La, 1924, 96-97, n. 58; S; R; P; F; cp. Richardson, in B, 1987, n. 1881-82).

1883-84: The clennesse and the fastynge of us freres/ Maketh that Crist accepteth oure preyeres.
>   *Matt. 17:20, Mark 9:28; Luke 2:37* ? (La, 1924, 96-97, n. 58; cp. lines 1885-1917, below).

1885-90: Lo, Moyses fourty dayes and fourty nyght/ Fasted, er that the heighe God of myght/ Spak with hym in the mountayne of Synay./ With empty wombe, fastynge many a day,/ Receyved he the lawe that was writen/ With Goddes fynger . . .
>   *Exod. 34:28* (cp. Jerome, *EAJ* 2.15; Tupper, 1915, 8-9; S; R; P; F; Richardson, in B, 1987, n. 1885-90).
>   G

1890-93: . . . and Elye, wel ye witen,/ In mount Oreb, er he hadde any speche/ With hye God, . . ./ He fasted longe and was in contemplaunce.
>   Cp. *3 Kings 19:4-9* (cp. Jerome, *EAJ* 2.15; Tupper, 1915, 8-9; Reiss, 1984, pp. 58-59; S; R; P; F; Richardson, in B, 1987, n. 1890-93).

1892: . . . hye God, that is oure lyves leche . . .
    Cp. *Ps. 146(147):3; Matt. 9:12, Mark 2:17, Luke 5:31; etc.*

1894-1901: Aaron, that hadde the temple in governaunce,/ And
eek the othere preestes everichon,/ Into the temple whan they
sholde gon/ To preye for the peple and do servyse,/ They
nolden drynken in no maner wyse/ No drynke which that
myghte hem dronke make,/ But there in abstinence preye and
wake,/ Lest that they deyden. . . .
    Lev. 10:8-9 (cp. Jerome, *EAJ* 2.15; Tupper, 1915, 8-9; cp. Reiss,
    1984, p. 59; S; R; P; F; Richardson, in B, 1987, n. 1898).

1904-05: Oure Lord Jhesu, as hooly writ devyseth,/ Yaf us
ensample of fastynge and preyeres.
    G
    Cp. *Matt. 4:2, 17:20, etc.* (La).

1909: . . . To persecucioun for rightwisnesse . . .
    Cp. *Matt. 5:10; etc.* (La).

1915-17: Fro Paradys first, if I shal nat lye,/ Was man out
chaced for his glotonye;/ And chaast was man in Paradys,
certeyn.
    Cp. *Gen. 3:6-24* (cp. Jerome, *EAJ* 2.15; Tupper, 1915, 8-9; S; R;
    cp. Richardson, in B, 1987, n. 1915-16).

1919-24: I ne have no text of it, as I suppose,/ But I shal fynde it
in a maner glose,/ That specially oure sweete Lord Jhesus/ Spak
this by freres, whan he seyde thus:/ "Blessed be they that
povere in spirit been."/ And so forth al the gospel may ye
seen . . .
    G (Adams, 1962, 127-28; Besserman, 1984[a]).
    Matt. 5:3 (S; R; P; Richardson, in B, 1987, n. 1923).

1933-34: . . . Whan they for soules seye the psalm of Davit:/ Lo,
"buf!" they seye,*"cor meum eructavit!"*
    g

Ps. 44(45):2(1) (La, 1924, 96-97, n. 58; S; R; P; F; Hamilton,
    1942; Beichner, 1956; Adams, 1962, 129; Clark, 1976-77,
    175; Richardson, in B, 1987, n. 1934).

1935-36: Who folweth Cristes gospel and his foore,/ But we
that humble been, and chaast, and poore. . . .
    G
    Matt. 5:3-4 (La, 1924, 96-97, n. 58; cp. lines 1919-24, above;
        cp. Richardson, in B, 1987, n. 1935).

1937: . . . Werkeris of Goddes word, nat auditours?
    James 1:22 (Jerome, EAJ 2.3; Correale, 1964-65; La, 1924, 96-
        97, n. 58; S; R; Richardson, in B, 1987, n. 1937).

1956: What nedeth hym that hath a parfit leche . . .
    Cp. Ps. 146(147):3; Matt. 9:12, Mark 2:17, Luke 5:31; etc.

1972-73: The hye God, that al this world hath wroght,/ Seith
that the werkman worthy is his hyre.
    Gen. 1
    Matt. 10:10, Luke 10:7; 1 Tim 5:18 (La, 1924, 96-97, n. 58;
        Adams, 1962, 129; Kaske, 1972, 122-23; Miller, 1977, p.
        241; S; R; Richardson, in B, 1987, n. 1973).

1978-80: Thomas, if ye wol lernen for to wirche,/ Of buyldynge
up of chirches may ye fynde/ If it be good in Thomas lyf of Inde.
    Cp. John 20:26-30 ? (cp. Jacobus de Voragine, "Life of St.
        Thomas the Apostle," Legenda Aurea, pp. 39-46; Clark,
        1976-77; cp. Richardson, in B, 1987, n. 1980).

1981-82: Ye lye heere ful of anger and of ire,/ With which the
devel set youre herte afyre. . . .
    Cp. Ps. 88(89):47(46) (cp. John Bromyard, Summa
        Praedicantium; Johnson, 1941, p. 161).

1988-90: . . . lo, what the wise seith:/ "Withinne thyn hous ne
be thou no leon;/ To thy subgitz do noon oppression . . . "

8
Ecclus. 4:35 (La, 1924, 96-97, n. 58; cp. John Bromyard,
  Summa Praedicantium ?; Johnson, 1941, pp. 162-63; S; R; P;
  Richardson, in B, 1987, n. 1989-91).

1991: " . . . Ne make thyne acqueyntances nat to flee."
  Ecclus. 28:11 ? (cp. John Bromyard, *Summa Praedicantium* ?;
  Johnson, 1941, p. 162-63).

2001-04: Ther nys, ywys, no serpent so cruel,/ Whan man tret on
his tayl, ne half so fel,/ As womman is, whan she hath caught
an ire;/ Vengeance is thanne al that they desire.
  Ecclus. 25:21-23 ? (cp. *RR* 9800-804; cp. John Bromyard,
  Summa Praedicantium ?; Johnson, 1941, pp. 162-63; R; cp.
  Richardson, in B, 1987, n. 2001-03).

2075: Syngeth *Placebo* . . .
  Ps. 114:(116)9 (liturgy; S; R; P; F; Richardson, in B, 1987, n.
  2075; *Roman de Fauvel* ?; Fleming, 1965).

2085-88: Lo, what seyde he that so wel teche kan?/ "Ne be no
felawe to an irous man,/ Ne with no wood man walke by the
weye,/ Lest thee repente;" I wol no ferther seye.
  Prov. 22:24-25 (John of Wales, *Communiloquium* 2.8.2; Pratt,
  1966, 629-31; cp. La, 1924, 96-97, n. 58; cp. John Bromyard,
  Summa Praedicantium ?; Johnson, 1941, pp. 163-64; Burnley, 1986, pp. 211-13; S; R; Richardson, in B, 1987, n. 2085).

2107: . . . for hym that harwed helle!
  Gospel of Nicodemus (vernacular biblical drama; R; P;
  Richardson, in B, 1987, n. 2107).

2116-17: But syn Elye was, or Elise,/ Han freres been—that
fynde I of record. . . .
  3 Kings 18:19-20 (cp. La, 1924, 96-97, n. 58; S; R; P; F;
  Richardson, in B, 1987, n. 2116).
  4 Kings 2:2

2119-49: " . . . Now Thomas, help, for seinte charitee!"/ And doun anon he sette hym on his knee. . . . "Now thanne, put in thyn hand doun by my bak,"/ Seyde this man, "and grope wel bihynde./ Bynethe my buttok there shaltow fynde/ A thyng that I have hyd in pryvetee."/ . . . And doun his hand he launcheth to the clifte . . . Aboute his tuwel grope there and heere,/ Amydde his hand he leet the frere a fart. . . .

    Cp. *Acts 2:1-13* ? (Levy, 1966; Levitan, 1971; cp. Richardson, in B, 1987, nn. 2126-28, 2149).

    Cp. *John 20:26-30* ? (cp. Jacobus de Voragine, "Life of St. Thomas the Apostle," *Legenda Aurea,* pp. 39-46; Clark, 1976-77).

2170: This lord gan looke, and seide, "Benedicitee! . . . "

    Dan. 3:57, etc. (liturgy; cp. *KtT* 1785).

2185-88: . . . "No maister, sire," quod he, "but servitour,/ Thogh I have had in scole that honour./ God liketh nat that 'Raby' men us calle,/ Neither in market ne in your large halle."

    Matt. 23:10; James 3:1 (Miller, 1977, p. 243, n. 4; Adams, 1962, 126-27).

    Matt. 23:6-10, Mark 12:38-39; Luke 11:43, 20:46; etc. (cp. La, 1924, 90, 96-97, n. 58; S; R; P; F; cp. Richardson, in B, 1987, n. 2186-87).

    Mark 5:13 (S; R).

2196: Ye been the salt of the erthe and the savour.

    Matt. 5:13 (Kaske, 1972, 123; Reiss, 1984, p. 59; S; R; P; F; Richardson, in B, 1987, n. 2196; cp. Gower, *VC* 3.27; Miller, 1977, p. 216).

2262-74: Thanne shal they knele doun, by oon assent,/ And to every spokes ende, in this manere,/ Ful sadly leye his nose shal a frere. . . . Thanne shal this cherl, with bely stif and toght/ As any tabour, hyder been ybroght;/ And sette hym on the wheel right of this cart,/ Upon the nave, and make hym lete a fart./

. . . That equally the soun of it wol wende,/ And eke the stynk, unto the spokes ende. . . .
> *Acts 2:1-4* ? (Levy, 1966; Levitan, 1971; Szittya, 1974, 22-29; Clark, 1976; Richardson, in B, 1987, n. 2255).
> Cp. *John 20:22-23* ? (Clark, 1976-77, 174-75).

2275-77: . . . this worthy man . . . / By cause he is a man of greet honour,/ Shal have the firste fruyt, as resoun is.
> Cp. *Exod. 23:19, 34:26; Lev. 23:10, 20; Num. 18:26* ? (cp. Szittya, ibid.).
> Cp. *2 Tim. 2:6* ? (cp. William of St. Amour, *De Periculis* 14; Miller, 1977, p. 248 and p. 250, n. 19).
> Cp. *Gal. 5:22-23* ? (Clark, 1976).

2284: . . . He hadde the firste smel of fartes thre. . . .
> Cp. *Exod. 23:19, 34:26, Lev. 23:10, 20, Num. 18:26* ? (cp. Szittya, ibid.).

Clerk's Prologue, IV (E), lines 1-56:

6: But Salomon seith "every thyng hath tyme."
> *Eccl. 3:1* (cp. Albertano of Brescia, *De Arte Loquendi et Tacendi;* Olson, 1984; S; R; F; Ginsberg, in B, 1987, n. 6).

Clerk's Tale, IV (E), lines 57-1212:

120-26: And thogh youre grene youthe floure as yit,/ In crepeth age alwey, as stille as stoon,/ And deeth manaceth every age, and smyt/ In ech estaat, for ther escapeth noon;/ And al so certein as we knowe echoon/ That we shul deye, as uncerteyn we alle/ Been of that day whan deeth shal on us falle.
> *James 4:14-15* ? (McNamara, 1972-73, 190; Petrarch, *DIOFU* 1.39-44 and *Liv. Gr.* 1.25-29; Severs, in *S&A*, 1941[a], pp. 298-99).

206-07: But hye God somtyme senden kan/ His grace into a litel
oxes stalle. . . .

> *Luke 2:7* (La, 1924, 91-92; Kellogg, 1972, pp. 298-99; Utley,
> 1971-72, pp. 218-19; cp. Petrarch, *DIOFU* 2.3-4 and *Liv.*
> *Gr.* 2.5-6; Severs, in *S&A*, 1941[a], pp. 302-03; cp. Ames,
> 1984, pp. 170-78; R; F; Ginsberg, in B, 1987, nn. 207, 291-
> 94).
> *Isa. 1:3* (Utley, 1971-72, 218-19).
> *Gospel of Ps.-Matt.* (Utley, 1971-72, 218-19).

211-31: But for to speke of vertuous beautee,/ Thanne was she
oon the faireste under sonne. . . ./ She wolde noght been ydel til
she slepte./ . . . And ay she kepte hir fadres lyf on-lofte/ With
everich obeisaunce and diligence/ That child may doon to
fadres reverence.

> *Prov. 31:10-31* ? (Kellogg, 1972, pp. 286-88, 298; Petrarch,
> *DIOFU* 2.5-14 and *Liv. Gr.* 2.18-19; Severs, in *S&A*,
> 1941[a], pp. 302-03; Ginsberg, in B, 1987, nn. 207, 291-94).
> *Gospel of Ps.-Matt.* ? (Utley, 1971-72, 220-21; Ginsberg, in B,
> 1987, n. 223).

274-76: Grisilde . . . To fecchen water at a welle is went . . .

> *Gen 24:15-67; 29:1-12; John 4:7; etc* ? (Utley, 1971-72, 224, n.
> 76; Alter, 1981, pp. 52-62; cp. Petrarch, *DIOFU* 2.32-33;
> Severs, in *S&A*, 1941[a], p. 304; F; Ginsberg, in B, 1987, n.
> 276-94).

290: And she set doun hir water pot anon . . .

> *John 4:28* ? (cp. Ginsberg, in B, 1987, n. 276-94).

291: . . . Biside the thresshfold, in an oxes stalle . . .

> *Luke 2:7* (La, 1924, 91-92; Kellogg, 1972, pp. 298-99; Utley,
> 1971-72, 224; Ames, 1984, pp. 170-78; F; cp. Ginsberg, in B,
> 1987, n. 276-94).
> *Isa 1:3* ? (Utley, 1971-72, 218-19).
> *Gospel of Ps.-Matt.* ? (Utley, 1971-72, 218-19).

351-54: I seye this: be ye redy with good herte/ To al my lust, and that I frely may,/ As me best thynketh, do yow laughe or smerte,/ And nevere ye to grucche it, nyght ne day?
  Gen. 22 (cp. *Sacrifice of Isaac* vv. 79-80, 190-93, 441-42; Kellogg, 1972, pp. 301-02; cp. Petrarch, *DIOFU* 2.52-57 and *Liv. Gr.* 2.61-66; Severs, in *S&A*, 1941[a], pp. 306-07).

361: . . . But as ye wole youreself, right so wol I.
  Luke 1:38 ? (Kean, 1972, 2.127).

362-63: And heere I swere that nevere willyngly,/ In werk ne thoght, I nyl yow disobeye. . . .
  Cp. *Gen.* 22 (liturgy, *Confiteor* ?; cp. Ames, 1984, pp. 170-78; cp. Ginsberg, in B, 1987, n. 362-64).

365: "This is ynogh, Grisilde myn," quod he.
  Matt. 4:10, Luke 4:13 ? (Kellogg, 1972, pp. 285-86, 294-95; Petrarch, *DIOFU* 2.62 and *Liv. Gr.* 2.73; Severs, in *S&A*, 1941[a], pp. 306-07; cp. line 1051, below; cp. Ginsberg, in B, 1987, n. 365).

398: . . . or in an oxe-stalle . . .
  Luke 2:7 (Kellogg, 1972, pp. 298-99; Utley, 1971-72, 218-19; cp. Ames, 1984, pp. 170-78).
  Isa. 1:3? (Utley, 1971-72, 218-19).
  Gospel of Ps.-Matt. ? (Utley, 1971-72, 218-19).

428-29: . . . this Grisildis thurgh hir wit/ Koude al the feet of wyfly hoomlinesse . . .
  Prov. 31:10-31 ? (Kellogg, 1972, pp. 286-88; *Liv. Gr.* 2.101-03; Severs, in *S&A*, 1941[a], p. 309; cp. lines 211-31, above).

440-41: . . . That she from hevene sent was, as men wende,/ Peple to save and every wrong t'amende.
  Cp. *Matt. 18:11, Luke 19:10; Rom. 5:11; etc.* (*Liv. Gr.* 2.108-09; Severs, in *S&A*, 1941[a], p. 311; cp. Ames, 1984, pp. 170-78; cp. Cook, 1918; cp. Ginsberg, in B, 1987, n. 441).

451-52: This markys in his herte longeth so/ To tempte his wyf, hir sadnesse for to knowe . . .

> *Gen. 22:1* (Kellogg, 1972, pp. 301-02; Utley, 1971-72, 223;
> *Liv. Gr.* 3.1-2; Severs, in *S&A*, 1941[a], p. 311; cp. lines
> 351-54, above; cp. Ginsberg, in B, 1987, n. 452).

456-58: He hadde assayed hire ynogh bifore,/ And foond hire evere good; what neded it/ Hire for to tempte, and alwey moore and moore. . . .

> Cp. *Job 2:3*
> *Gen. 22* (Kellogg, 1972, pp. 301-02; Utley, 1971-72, 223; cp.
> Petrarch, *DIOFU* 3.1-4 and *Liv. Gr.* 3.3-7; Severs, in *S&A*,
> 1941[a], pp. 310-11; cp. lines 351-54, above).

493-94: . . . but this wol I . . . That ye to me assente as in this thyng.

> *Gen. 22* ? (Kellogg, 1972, pp. 301-02; cp. Petrarch *DIOFU*
> 3.13-14 and *Liv. Gr.* 3.18-19; Severs, in *S&A*, 1941[a], pp.
> 310-11; cp. lines 351-54, above).

538-39: . . . And as a lamb she sitteth meke and stille,/ And leet this crueel sergeant doon his wille.

> *Isa. 53:7* ? (Kellogg, 1972, pp. 300-01; Ginsberg, in B, 1987, n.
> 538-39).

554-60: And thus she seyde in hire benigne voys,/ "Fareweel my child! I shal thee nevere see. . . ./ For this nyght shaltow dyen for my sake."

> *John 19:25* ? (Utley, 1971-72, 218-25).

556-58: But sith I thee have marked with the croys/ Of thilke Fader—blessed moote he be!—/ That for us deyde upon a croys of tree . . .

> *Rom. 5:9; Col. 1:20; etc.* (cp. Petrarch *DIOFU* 3.37 and *Liv.
> Gr.* 3.45-46; Severs, in *S&A*, 1941[a], pp. 312-13).

559: . . . Thy soule, litel child, I hym bitake . . .
  Luke 23:46 ?

560: For this nyght shaltow dyen for my sake.
  Cp. *John 13:37-38* ?
  Cp. *Rom. 5:9; Col. 1:20; etc.*

619-20: This markys caughte yet another lest/ To tempte his wyf yet ofter, if he may.
  Gen. 22:1 (Kellogg, 1972, pp. 301-02; cp. lines 351-54, above).

654-55: For as I lefte at hoom al my clothyng,/ Whan I first cam to yow . . .
  Job 1:21 ? (Petrarch, *DIOFU* 4.19-20 and *Liv. Gr.* 3.85-87;
  Severs, in *S&A*, 1941[a], pp. 316-17; cp. lines 871-72, and
  901-03, below).

666-67: Deth may noght make no comparisoun/ Unto youre love. . . .
  Cant. 8:6 ? (Kellogg, 1972, p. 287; ps.-Origen, ibid., p. 322, n.
  42; Petrarch, *DIOFU* 4.25-26 and *Liv. Gr.* 3.92; Severs, in
  S&A, 1941[a], pp. 316-17; Ginsberg, in B, 1987, n. 666-67).

704: . . . But, right as they were bounden to that stake . . .
  Gen. 22:9 ? (McNamara, 1972-73, 190-91).

706-07: Right so this markys fulliche hath purposed/ To tempte his wyf as he was first disposed.
  Gen. 22:1 (Kellogg, 1972, pp. 301-02; cp. lines 351-54, above).

735: To tempte his wyf was set al his entente.
  Gen. 22:1 (ibid.; cp. *Liv. Gr.* 4.38-39, ibid., p. 319).

785-91: Among al this, after his wikke usage,/ This markys, yet his wyf to tempte moore/ To the outtreste preeve of hir corage,/ Fully to han experience and loore/ If that she were as stidefast

as bifoore,/ He on a day in open audience/ Ful boistously hath
seyd hire this sentence ...
> *Job 2:1-6* ? (McNamara, 1972-73, 190-91).

786: This markys, yet his wyf to tempte moore ...
> *Gen. 22:1* (Kellogg, 1972, pp. 301-02; Petrarch, *DIOFU* 5.1
> and *Liv. Gr.* 5.6-7; Severs, in *S&A*, 1941[a], pp. 320-21).

871-72: ". . . Naked out of my fadres hous," quod she,/ "I cam,
and naked moot I turne agayn. . . . "
> *Job 1:21* (Kellogg, 1972, pp. 305-08; Petrarch, *DIOFU* 5.29
> and *Liv. Gr.* 5.42-43; Severs, in *S&A*, 1941[a], pp. 322-23;
> Besserman, 1979, pp. 111-13; S; R; cp. lines 654-55, above,
> and lines 901-03, below; Ginsberg, in B, 1987, n. 871).

880: Lat me nat lyk a worm go by the weye.
> *Ps. 21(22):7(6)* ? (Kean, 1972, 2.127; cp. *Rom* 455; S; R;
> proverbial; Whi W672; Ginsberg, in B, 1987, n. 880-82).

897-900: The folk hire folwe, wepynge in hir weye,/ And
Fortune ay they cursen as they goon;/ But she fro wepyng kepte
hire eyen dreye,/ Ne in this tyme word ne spak she noon.
> *Luke 23:9, 27* ? (Salter, 1963, p. 47).

901-03: Hir fader, that this tidynge herde anoon,/ Curseth the
day and tyme that Nature/ Shoop hym to been a lyves
creature.
> *Job 3:3* (La, 1924, 92; Kellogg, 1972, pp. 305-08; Besserman,
> 1979, pp. 111-13; S; R; F; Ginsberg, in B, 1987, n. 902-03).

932: Men speke of Job, and moost for his humblesse ...
> Cp. *Job 39:33-35, 42:1-6* (Severs, 1934; Utley, 1971-72, 223;
> Besserman, 1979, pp. 111-13; S; R; Ginsberg, in B, 1987, n.
> 932-38).
> *James 5:11* (McNamara, 1972-73, 191).

967-70: "Nat oonly, lord, that I am glad," quod she,/ "To doon youre lust, but I desire also/ Yow for to serve and plese in my degree/ Withouten feyntyng, and shal evermo. . . .
    Cp. *Heb. 12:5-7* ? (Peck, 1984, p. 163).

1051: "This is ynogh, Grisilde myn," quod he . . .
    Matt. 4:10, Luke 4:13 ? (Kellogg, 1972, pp. 285-86, 294-95; Petrarch, *DIOFU* 6.44-45 and *Liv. Gr.* 6.6; Severs, in *S&A,* 1941[a], pp. 328-29; cp. line 365, above).

1056: Now knowe I, dere wyf, thy stedfastnesse . . .
    Gen. 22:12 (Kellogg, 1972, pp. 301-02; Utley, 1971-72, 223; Petrarch, *DIOFU* 6.45 and *Liv. Gr.* 6.7; Severs, in *S&A,* 1941[a], pp. 328-29; cp. lines 451-52, above).
    Cp. *Job 2:3, 42:7*

1062: . . . by God, that for us deyde . . .
    Cp. *Rom. 5:9, Col. 1:20, etc.*

1064: . . . as God my soule save!
    Cp. *James 5:20; etc.*

1117-19: . . . And in a clooth of gold that brighte shoon,/ With a coroune of many a riche stoon/ Upon hire heed . . .
    Apoc. 12:1, 19:7, 9 ? (Kellogg, 1972, p. 312).

1121-37: Thus hath this pitous day a blisful ende. . . . For moore solempne in every mannes syght/ This feste was, and gretter of costage,/ Than was the revel of hire mariage./ Ful many a yeer in heigh prosperitee/ Lyven thise two in concord and in reste. . . . His sone succedeth in his heritage/ In reste and pees, after his fader day,/ And fortunat was eek in mariage . . .
    Job 42:10-16 ? (cp. Petrarch, *DIOFU* 6.61-68 and *Liv. Gr.* 6.23-31; Severs, in *S&A,* 1941[a], pp. 328-31).

1145-47: . . . But for that every wight, in his degree,/ Sholde be constant in adversitee/ As was Grisilde. . . .

Cp. *Rom 13:1-6; 1 Pet. 2:13-16* ? (cp. Ginsberg, in B, 1987, nn. 1141-62, 1153-55).

1150-51: . . . wel moore us oghte/ Receyven al in gree that God us sent . . .
   Cp. *Job 1:21; James 5:7; etc.* (cp. Petrarch, *DIOFU* 6.73 and *Liv. Gr.* 6.36-37; Severs, in *S&A*, 1941[a], pp. 330-31; cp. Ginsberg, in B, 1987, nn. 1141-62, 1153-55).

1152: For greet skile is he preeve that he wroghte . . .
   Cp. *Prov. 3:11-12; James 1:12; etc.* (Ginsberg, in B, 1987, nn. 1141-62, 1153-55).

1153-54: But he ne tempteth no man that he boghte,/ As seith Seint Jame, if ye his pistel rede . . .
   James 1:13 (cp. Petrarch, *DIOFU* 6.74-75 and *Liv. Gr.* 6.37-38; Severs, in *S&A*, 1941[a], pp. 330-31; Jerome, *EAJ* 2.3?; Correale, 1964-65; S; R; F; Ginsberg, in B, 1987, nn. 1141-62, 1153-55).

   g

1155-62: He preeveth folk al day, it is no drede,/ And suffreth us, as for our exercise,/ With sharpe scourges of adversitee/ Ful ofte to be bete in sondry wise/ . . . . Lat us thanne lyve in vertuous suffraunce.
   Cp. *Job; Prov. 3:11-12; James 1:12; etc.* (Petrarch, *DIOFU* 6.75-80 and *Liv. Gr.* 6.39-44; Severs, in *S&A*, 1941[a], pp. 330-31; Ginsberg, in B, 1987, nn. 1141-62, 1153-55).
   1 Cor. 13:4 ? (Pearsall, 1985, pp. 159-60).

1164-65: It were ful hard to fynde now-a-dayes/ In al a toun Grisildis thre or two. . . .
   Prov. 31:10 ? (Kellogg, 1972, p. 314; cp. Ginsberg, in B, 1987, n. 1164-69).

1167-69: . . . The gold of hem hath now so badde alayes/ With bras, that thogh the coyne be fair at ye,/ It wolde rather breste a-two than plye.
>   Cp. *James 5:3* ?
>   Cp. *Job 23:10* ? (cp. lines 211-31, above).

1170-71: For which heere, for the Wyves love of Bathe—/ Whos lyf and al hire secte God mayntene . . .
>   *Gal. 4:22; etc.* ? (Robertson, 1979-80, 415-16, et passim; cp.
>   Pearsall, 1986, p. 140, et passim; cp. Ginsberg, in B, 1987,
>   n. 1171).

1177-1212: Grisilde is deed, and eek hire pacience. . . . O noble wyves, ful of heigh prudence,/ Lat noon humylitee youre tonge naille. . . . . If thou be fair, ther folk been in presence,/ Shewe thou thy visage and thyn apparaille;/ If thou be foul, be fre of thy dispence;/ To gete thee freendes ay do thy travaille;/ Be ay of chiere as light as leef on lynde,/ And lat hym care, and wepe, and wrynge, and waille!
>   Cp. *Prov. 31:10-31* ? (Coletti, 1984).

The Merchant's Prologue, IV (E), 1213-1244:

The Merchant's Tale, IV (E), lines 1245-2418:

1258-60: . . . Preyinge oure Lord to graunten him that he/ Mighte ones knowe of thilke blisful lyf/ That is bitwixe an housbonde and his wyf. . . .
>   Cp. *Ruth 1:9* (cp. Deschamps, *Mir.* 217-20; Dempster, in
>   *S&A*, 1941, p. 334)

1261-62: . . . And for to lyve under that hooly boond/ With which that first God man and womman bond.
>   *Gen. 2:24* (S; R; cp. Deschamps, *Mir.* 217-20; Dempster, in
>   *S&A*, 1941, p. 334).

1264-65: " . . . For wedlok is so esy and so clene,/ That in this world it is a paradys."
>   Cp. *Gen. 2:8-3:24* (Kaske, 1973, pp. 55-56; cp. Deschamps, *Mir.* 217-20; Dempster, in *S&A*, 1941, p. 334).
>   Cp. *Prov. 19:14*

1267: . . . as sooth as God is kyng . . .
>   *Ps. 23(24):8, 10; etc.*

1277-80: And trewely it sit wel to be so,/ That bacheleris have often peyne and wo;/ On brotel ground they buylde, and brotelnesse/ They fynde whan they wene sikernesse.
>   *Ecclus. 36:27* ?

1288-92: Who is so trewe, and eek so ententyf/ To kepe hym, syk and hool, as is his make?/ For wele or wo she wole hym nat forsake;/ She nys nat wery hym to love and serve,/ Thogh that he lye bedrede til he sterve.
>   *Tob.* ? (cp. Deschamps, *Mir.* 252-56, 425-26; Dempster, in *S&A*, 1941, p. 335).

1311: A wyf is Goddes yifte verraily.
>   Cp. *Prov. 19:14* (Albertano, *LDAD* ; Köppel, 1891[a]; S; R; cp. Besserman, 1978, 16-17; Tavormina, in B, 1987, n. 1311-14).
>   *Ecclus. 26:1-3, 14*

1315: . . . That passen as a shadwe upon a wal.
>   Cp. *1 Par. 29:15; Wis. 2:5, 5:9; Job 14:2; etc.* (proverbial; Whi S185; cp. R; see *ShipT* 9 and *ParsT* 1068, below; Tavormina, in B, 1987, n. 1315).

1319: Mariage is a ful greet sacrement.
>   *Eph. 5:32* (S; R; Tavormina, in B, 1987, n. 1319).

1325-32: The hye God, whan he hadde Adam maked,/ And saugh him al allone, bely-naked,/ God of his grete goodnesse

seyde than,/ "Lat us now make an helpe unto this man/ Lyk to
hymself"; and thanne he made him Eve./ Heere may ye se, and
heerby may ye preve,/ That wyf is mannes helpe and his
confort,/ His paradys terrestre, and his disport.

> Gen. 2:18, 21-22, 25; 2:8-3:24 (Albertano, *LDAD*; Köppel,
> 1891[a]; S; R; Tavormina, in B, 1987, nn. 1325-29, 1332;
> Kaske, 1973, pp. 55-56).

1334-36: . . . They moste nedes lyve in unitee./ O flessh they
been, and o flessh, as I gesse,/ Hath but oon herte, in wele and
in distresse.

> Gen. 2:18, 23-24; Matt. 19:5; etc. (Albertano, *LDAD*; Köppel,
> 1891[a]; cp. Deschamps, *Mir.* 217-20; Dempster, in *S&A*,
> 1941, p. 334; S; R; F; Tavormina, in B, 1987, n. 1334-36).

1362-65: Lo, how that Jacob, as thise clerkes rede,/ By good
conseil of his mooder Rebekke,/ Boond the kydes skyn aboute
his nekke,/ For which his fadres benyson he wan.

> Gen. 27:5-29 (cp. Albertano, *LDAD*; La, 1924, 91; S; R; F; cp.
> E. Brown, 1974; ———, 1986, pp. 68-73; Besserman, 1978,
> 19-20; cp. *Mel* 2288-91; Tavormina, in B, 1987, n. 1362-74).

1366-68: Lo Judith, as the storie eek telle kan,/ By wys conseil
she Goddes peple kepte,/ And slow hym Olofernus, whil he
slepte.

> Jud. 13:1-10 (Albertano; cp. Deschamps, *Mir.* 9107-10;
> Dempster, in *S&A*, 1941, p. 338; Lowes, 1910, 182-83; S; R;
> F; cp. E. Brown, 1974; Besserman, ibid.; Tavormina, ibid.).

1369-71: Lo Abigayl, by good conseil how she/ Saved hir
housbonde Nabal whan that he/ Sholde han be slayn . . .

> 1 Kings 25:2-35 (Albertano; S; R; F; cp. E. Brown, 1974;
> Besserman, ibid.; Tavormina, ibid.).

1371-74: . . . and looke, Ester also/ By good conseil delyvered out
of wo/ The peple of God, and made hym Mardochee/ Of
Assuere enhaunced for to be.

Esth. 7-8 (Albertano; cp. Deschamps, *Mir.* 9124-25, 9135-38, 9143-44; Dempster, in *S&A*, 1941, p. 338; Lowes, 1910, 181-82; S; R; F; cp. E. Brown, 1974; ———, 1986, pp. 68-73; Besserman, ibid.; Tavormina, ibid.).

1381-82: Wel may the sike man biwaille and wepe,/ Ther as ther nys no wyf the hous to kepe.
> *Ecclus. 36:27* (Albertano, *LDAD*; Köppel, 1891[a], 42; S; R; Tavormina, in B, 1987, n. 1381-82).

1384-88: . . . Love wel thy wyf, as Crist loved his chirche./ If thou lovest thyself, thou lovest thy wyf;/ No man hateth his flessh, but in his lyf/ He fostreth it, and therfore bidde I thee/ Cherisse thy wyf, or thou shalt nevere thee.
> *Eph. 5:25, 28, 29* (Albertano, *LDAD*, fol. 39; Köppel, 1891[a]; cp. *ParsT* 929; Köppel, 1891[b], 42; S; R; F; Tavormina, in B, 1987, n. 1384-88).

1400-01: Freendes, I am hoor and oold,/ And almoost, God woot, on my pittes brynke . . .
> *Ps. 29(30):4(3); etc.* (S; R; cp. Tavormina, in B, 1987, n. 1401).

1435-36: . . . Thanne sholde I lede my lyf in avoutrye/ And go streight to the devel whan I dye.
> Cp. *Apoc. 2:22, etc.*

1438: Yet were me levere houndes had me eten . . .
> Cp. *3 Kings 21:19, etc.; 4 Kings 9:30-37* ? (Besserman, 1978, 20-21).

1446-47: If he ne may nat lyven chaast his lyf,/ Take hym a wyf with greet devocioun . . .
> Cp. *1 Cor. 7:2* (S; cp. Deschamps, *Mir.* 106-16; Dempster, in *S&A*, 1941, p. 334).

1448-49: . . . By cause of leveful procreacioun/ Of children . . .
   Gen. 1:28; etc. (cp. Deschamps, *Mir.* 106-16; Dempster, in
   S&A, 1941, p. 334).

1449: . . . of God above . . .
   Cp. *Deut. 4:39; etc.*

1451-52: And for they sholde leccherye eschue,/ And yelde hir
dette whan that it is due . . .
   1 Cor. 7:2-3 (cp. Deschamps, *Mir.* 106-16; Dempster, in *S&A*,
   1941, p. 334; Lowes, 1910, 174; cp. *ParsT* 941; Köppel,
   1891[b], 42; F; cp. Tavormina, in B, 1987, n. 1441-55).

1461-66: Though I be hoor, I fare as dooth a tree/ That blosmeth
er that fruyt ywoxen be. . . . Myn herte and alle my lymes been
as grene/ As laurer thurgh the yeer is for to sene.
   Cp. *Protevangelium of James* (vernacular biblical drama?;
   Burchmore, 1982; Bleeth, 1986, 60; cp. Tavormina, in B,
   1987, n. 1461).

1476: . . . Of whiche that oon was cleped Placebo . . .
   Ps. 114(116):9 (liturgy; S; R; *Roman de Fauvel* ?; Fleming,
   1965; F; Tavormina, in B, 1987, n. 1476).

1478: As in line 1476, above.

1483-87: . . . To weyven fro the word of Salomon./ This word
seyde he unto us everychon:/ "Wirk alle thyng by conseil," thus
seyde he,/ "And thanne shaltow nat repente thee."/ But
though that Salomon spak swich a word . . .
   8
   Ecclus. 32:24 (cp. Albertano of Brescia, *LCC*; Bühler, 1949;
   cp. Deschamps, *Mir.* 495-504; Dempster, in *S&A*, 1941, p.
   336; S; R; F; Besserman, 1978, 24-25; cp. Tavormina, in B,
   1987, n. 1485-86).

1520: As in line 1476, above.

1571: As in line 1476, above.

1617: As in line 1476, above.

1704-05: . . . And bad hire be lyk Sarra and Rebekke/ In wysdom and in trouthe of mariage. . . .
> Cp. *Gen. 11, 24* (liturgy; Sister Mary Immaculate, 1941, 62-64; S; R; cp. Deschamps, *Mir.* 275-77; Dempster, in *S&A*, 1941, p. 335; F; Tavormina, in B, 1987, n. 1704).

1719: . . . That nevere tromped Joab for to heere . . .
> *2 Kings 2:28; etc.* (S; R; F; Tavormina, in B, 1987, n. 1719).

1744-45: Queene Ester looked nevere with swich an ye/ On Assuer, so meke a look hath she.
> *Esth. 2, 5-7* (cp. Deschamps, *Mir.;* as in 1371-74, above; S; R; F; Lowes, 1910, 182; Besserman, 1978, 21-22; Tavormina, in B, 1987, n. 1744-45).
> *Esth. 14:15-16; 15:8, 10* ? (E. Brown, 1986, pp. 68-73).

1781-82: . . . But there I lete hym wepe ynogh and pleyne/ Til fresshe May wol rewen on his peyne.
> *Esth. 2:7* ? (E. Brown, 1986, pp. 68-73).

1822: . . . His fresshe May, his paradys, his make.
> Cp. *Gen 2:8-3:24* (Kaske, 1973, pp. 55-56).

1964: . . . Or wheither hire thoughte it paradys or helle.
> Cp. *Gen. 2:8-3:24* (Kaske, 1973, pp. 55-56).

1972: For alle thyng hath tyme, as seyn thise clerkes. . . .
> *Eccl. 3:1* (S; R; Tavormina, in B, 1987, n. 1972).

1974: . . . but grete God above . . .
> Cp. *Deut. 4:39; etc.*

2048: And whan he wolde paye his wyf hir dette . . .
   1 Cor. 7:3 (R; F; Tavormina, in B, 1987, n. 2048).

2055: But worldly joye may nat alwey dure . . .
   Cp. *Prov. 14:13; Ecclus. 11:27, 18:25* (R).

2058-60: Lyk to the scorpion so deceyvable/ . . . Thy tayl is
deeth. . . .
   Cp. *Apoc. 9:10; etc.* (cp. Tavormina, in B, 1987, n. 2058-68).

2134-36: . . . Januarie hath caught so greet a wil,/ . . . hym for to
pleye/ In his gardyn . . .
   Gen. 2:3-8, 2:8-3:24 ? (Burrow, 1957; Olson, 1961, 206-08, 210-
      11; Robertson, 1962, p. 387; Kaske, 1973, pp. 55-56;
      Pearsall and Salter, 1973, pp. 76-101, et passim; Bleeth,
      1974; F, n. 2043).
   Dan. 13:20, etc. (Kellogg, 1960, 275-79).
   Cant. 4:12-13, 5:1; etc. (Olson, 1961; Wimsatt, 1973, pp. 84-
      88; Kaske, 1973, pp. 55-56).

2138-40: Rys up, my wyf, my love, my lady free!/ The turtles
voys is herd, my dowve sweete;/ The wynter is goon with alle
his reynes weete.
   Cant. 2:10-12 (Jerome, *EAJ* 1.30-31; Köppel, 1891[c], 179-80;
      cp. Johnson, 1941, pp. 182-85; Rosenberg, 1970-71, 268-70;
      Besserman, 1978, 22-23; Kaske, 1962, 479, n. 2; Wimsatt,
      1973, pp. 84-88; S; R; F; cp. Tavormina, in B, 1987, n. 2138-
      48).

2141: Com forth now, with thyne eyen columbyn!
   Cant. 1:14, 2:13, etc. (cp. Jerome, *EAJ*; Köppel, 1891[c], 179;
      La, 1924, 95; cp. Johnson, 1941, pp. 182-85; S; F; cp.
      Tavormina, ibid.).

2142: How fairer been thy brestes than is wyn!
   Cant. 4:10 (cp. Jerome, *EAJ*; Köppel, 1891[c], 179; La, 1924,
      95; cp. Johnson, 1941, pp. 182-85; cp. Tavormina, ibid.).

2143: The gardyn is enclosed al aboute . . .
    Gen. 2:8-3:24 ? (Olson, 1961, 206-08, 210-11; cp. Pearsall and
    Salter, 1973, pp. 76-101, et passim; cp. Tavormina, ibid.).
    Cant. 4:12, 16 ? (ibid.; cp. Jerome, *EAJ;* Köppel, 1891[c],
    179-80).
    Dan. 13:20 ? (see lines 2134-36, above).

2144-45: Com forth, my white spouse! Out of doute/ Thou hast
me wounded in myn herte, O wyf!
    Cant. 4:8-9 (see lines 2138-40, above; S, 4:9-10; cp. Jerome,
    EAJ; Köppel, 1891[c], 179; cp. Johnson, 1941, p. 185, n. 4; cp.
    Tavormina, ibid.).

2146: No spot of thee ne knew I al my lyf.
    Cant. 4:7 (Johnson, 1941, p. 186; F; cp. Tavormina, ibid.).

2147-48: Com forth, and lat us taken oure disport;/ I chees thee
for my wyf and my confort.
    Cant. 2:13-14, 5:1, etc. (Johnson, 1941, p. 186; cp. Tavormina,
    ibid.).

2242-49: O Salomon . . . ./ . . . . . . Thus preiseth he yet the
bountee of man:/ "Amonges a thousand men yet foond I oon,/ But
of wommen alle foond I noon."/ Thus seith the kyng that
knoweth youre wikkednesse.
    g
    Eccl. 7:29 (S; R; F; Tavormina, in B, 1987, nn. 2242, 2247-48;
    cp. Gates, 1976; Besserman, 1978, 23-27).

2250-51: And Jhesus, *filius Syrak,* as I gesse,/ Ne speketh of
yow but seelde reverence.
    g
    Ecclus. 25:17-26, etc. (S; R; F; cp. Tavormina, in B, 1987, n.
    2250-51; Besserman, ibid.).

2276-79: What rekketh me of youre auctoritees?/ I woot wel
that this Jew, this Salomon,/ Foond of us wommen fooles many
oon./ But though that he ne foond no good womman ...
g
Eccl. 7:29 (cp. Deschamps, *Mir.* 9051-57, 9063-70; Jerome,
EAJ 1.46; R; Tavormina, in B, 1987, n. 2277-90; cp. Gates,
1976; Besserman, 1978, 23-27).

2282-83: Witnesse on hem that dwelle in Cristes hous;/ With
martirdom they preved hire constance.
Cp. *2 Cor. 5:1, 6-8; Apoc. 7:14-15; etc.* (cp. Tavormina, ibid.).

2287-90: ... Though that he seyde he foond no good womman,/ I
prey yow take the sentence of the man;/ He mente thus, that in
sovereyn bontee/ Nis noon but God, but neither he ne she.
g
Eccl. 7:29 (cp. *Glossa ordinaria;* Besserman, 1978, 26).
Cp. *Matt. 19:17; Mark 10:18; Luke 18:19; Gal. 3:28* (Black,
1974, p. 289; S; R; Tavormina, in B, 1987, n. 2290).

2291: ... for verray God that nys but oon ...
Deut. 6:4, Mark 12:29, etc.

2292-93: ... What make ye so muche of Salomon?/ What
though he made a temple, Goddes hous?
3 Kings 6 (Gates, 1976; Besserman, 1978, 23-27).

2294: What though he were riche and glorious?
3 Kings 3:13, etc. (ibid.; cp. Gower, *CA* 7.3891-3912).

2295-96: So made he eek a temple of false goddis./ How myghte
he do a thyng that moore forbode is?
3 Kings 11:7-8 (ibid.; F; cp. Gower, *CA* 7.4469-4545).

2298-99: ... He was a lecchour and an ydolastre,/ And in his
elde he verray God forsook.

3 *Kings 11:1-4* (Robertson, 1962, pp. 323-24; Gates, 1976; Besserman, 1978; Tavormina, in B, 1987, n. 2298-2302; cp. Gower, *CA* 7.4469-4545).

2300-02: And if that God ne hadde, as seith the book,/ Yspared him for his fadres sake, he sholde/ Have lost his regne rather than he wolde.
G
3 *Kings 11:11-12* (S; R; Robertson, 1962, pp. 323-24; Gates, 1976; Besserman, 1978; Tavormina, in B, 1987, n. 2298-2302; cp. Gower, *CA* 7.4469-4545).

2307: For sithen he seyde that we been jangleresses . . .
Prov. 19:13, 27:15; etc. ? (ibid.).

2335-36: I telle yow wel, a womman in my plit/ May han to fruyt so greet an appetit . . .
Cp. *Gen. 2:8-3:24* (Bleeth, 1974).
Cp. *Gospel of Ps.-Matt. 20* ("Cherry Tree Carol"; Rosenberg, 1970-71; cp. Tavormina, in B, 1987, n. 2330-37).

2355-67: . . . To Januarie he gaf agayn his sighte./ . . . . But on his wyf his thoght was everemo./ Up to the tree he caste his eyen two. . . . / And up he yaf a roryng and a cry. . . ./ "Out! help! Allas! Harrow! . . . what dostow?"
Tob. 11 ? (cp. Deschamps, *Mir.* 252-56; Dempster, in *S&A,* 1941, p. 335; cp. Tavormina, in B, 1987, n. 2367).
Matt. 1:19-25; Gospel of Ps.-Matt. ("Cherry Tree Carol"; Rosenberg, 1970-71; Bleeth, 1986).

2414: . . . And on hire wombe he stroketh hire ful softe. . . .
Luke 1:39-45 ? (iconography; Bleeth, 1986, 64; cp. Tavormina, in B, 1987, n. 2414).

Merchant Endlink, IV (D), lines 2419-40:

Squire Headlink, V (F), lines 1-8:

The Squire's Tale, V (F), lines 9-672:

249-51: . . . Of craft of rynges herde they nevere noon,/ Save that he Moyses and kyng Salomon/ Hadde a name of konnyng in swich art.

> *Exod. 7:10-11* ? (S; cp. R; F; cp. DiMarco, in B, 1987, n. 250-51).
>
> *Acts 7:22* ? (S; cp. R).

499: "Ther I was bred—allas, that ilke day! . . . "

> Cp. *Job 3:3, Jer. 20:14*

512-13: Right as a serpent hit hym under floures/ Til he may seen his tyme for to byte . . .

> *Matt. 23:33* ? (Allen & Moritz, 1980, p. 145; cp. S; R; cp. DiMarco, in B, 1987, n. 512).

518-20: As in a toumbe is al the faire above,/ And under is the corps, swich as ye woot,/ Swich was this ypocrite, bothe coold and hoot.

> Cp. *Matt. 23:27* (La, 1924, 90; S; R; DiMarco, in B, 1987, n. 514-19).

550-51: . . . Syn Lameth was, that alderfirst bigan/ To loven two, as writen folk biforn . . .

> *Gen. 4:19-23* (cp. Jerome *EAJ* 1.14; S; R; F; DiMarco, in B, 1987, n. 550).

552: Ne nevere, syn the firste man was born . . .

> *Gen. 1:26-27, 2:7*

555: . . . Ne were worthy unbokelen his galoche . . .

> *Mark 1:7; etc.* (S; R; cp. DiMarco, in B, 1987, n. 555).

596: . . . Seint John to borwe . . .

> *g* (S; F; DiMarco, in B, 1987, n. 596).

Squire-Franklin Link, V (F), lines 673-708:

The Franklin's Prologue, V (F), lines 709-28:

The Franklin's Tale, V (F), lines 729-1624:

777: Lerneth to suffre . . .
1 Cor. 13:4 ? (Pearsall, 1985, pp. 159-60).

779-80: For in this world, certein, ther no wight is/ That he ne dooth or seith somtyme amys.
Rom. 3:23 ? (La).

879-80: . . . Which mankynde is so fair part of thy werk/ That thou it madest lyk to thyn owene merk.
Gen. 1:26-27 (S; R; cp. Rice, in B, 1987, nn. 879, 880).

885-86: I woot wel clerkes wol seyn as hem leste,/ By argumentz, that al is for the beste . . .
Cp. *Rom. 8:28* (S; R; proverbial; Whi A93.1; Rice, in B, 1987, n. 886).

888: But thilke God that made wynd to blowe . . .
Gen. 8:1 ?

911-12: . . . That nevere was ther gardyn of swich prys/ But if it were the verray paradys.
Gen. 2:8-3:24 (La; Robertson, 1962, p. 387; cp. Boccaccio, *Il Filocolo;* Havely, 1980, pp. 157-58; cp. Pearsall and Salter, 1973, pp. 76-101, 99-100, et passim; cp. Rice, in B, 1987, n. 902-19).

983: . . . By thilke God that yaf me soule and lyf . . .
Cp. *Gen. 2:7*

989: . . . by heighe God above . . .
Cp. *Deut. 4:39; etc.*

1321: . . . for thilke God above . . .
  Cp. *Deut. 4:39; etc.*

1487-92: And forth he cleped a squier and a mayde:/ "Gooth
forth anon with Dorigen," he sayde,/ "And bryngeth hire to
swich a place anon."/ They take hir leve, and on hir wey they
gon,/ But they ne wiste why she thider wente./ He nolde no
wight tellen his entente.
  Gen. 22:3-5 ?

1558: . . . Curseth the tyme that evere he was born . . .
  Job 3:3, Jer. 20:14

The Physician's Tale, VI (C), lines 1-286:

5-6: This knyght a doghter hadde by his wyf;/ No children
hadde he mo in al his lyf.
  Cp. *Judg. 11:34* (R; cp. C. D. Benson, in B, 1987, n. 6).

93-100: Ye fadres and ye moodres eek also,/ Though ye han
children, be it oon or mo,/ . . . . Beth war, if . . . by youre
necligence in chastisynge,/ That they ne perisse; for I dar wel
seye/ If that they doon, ye shul it deere abeye.
  Prov. 13:24, 23:13-14 (S; R; proverbial; Whi Y1; C. D.
    Benson, in B, 1987, n. 98).

101-02: Under a shepherde softe and necligent/ The wolf hath
many a sheep and lamb torent.
  Cp. *John 10:11-12, etc.* (proverbial; Whi S242; Walther
    30542; C. D. Benson, in B, 1987, n. 101-02).

107-09: . . . For in hir lyvyng maydens myghten rede,/ As in a
book, every good word or dede/ That longeth to a mayden
vertuous. . . .
  2 Cor. 3:2 ? (R; cp. Ambrose, *De Virginitate;* Tupper, 1915, 5-
    7; C. D. Benson, in B, 1987, n. 107-08).

154: This false juge . . .
   Cp. *Wis. 1:1; etc. ?* (Allen & Moritz, 1981, p. 159).

215: . . . allas, that I was bore!
   Job 3:3, Jer. 20:14

221-26: O doghter, which that art my laste wo,/ And in my lyf
my laste joye also,/ . . . . thou most be deed;/ My pitous hand
moot smyten of thyn heed.
   Judg. 11:35 (cp. *RR* 5624-39; Shannon, in *S&A*, 1941, pp. 400-
   01).

231-55: "O mercy, deere fader!" quod this mayde,/ . . . . "Goode
fader, shal I dye?/ Is ther no grace, is ther no remedye?"/ . . . .
"Thanne yif me leyser, fader myn," quod she,/ My deeth for to
compleyene a litel space;/ For, pardee, Jepte yaf his doghter
grace/ For to compleyne, er he hir slow, allas!/ And, God it
woot, no thyng was hir trespas,/ But for she ran hir fader first
to see,/ To welcome hym with greet solempnitee."/ . . . "Blissed
be God that I shal dye a mayde!/ Yif me my deeth. . . . " Hir
fader, with ful sorweful herte and wil,/ Hir heed of smoot. . . .
   Judg. 11:34-39 (Ambrose, *De Virginitate* cap. i-iii ?; Tupper,
   1915, 7; cp. *RR* 5624-39; Shannon, in *S&A*, 1941, pp. 400-
   01; S; R; F; Middleton, 1973, 22-23, 27; cp. C. D. Benson, in
   B, 1987, n. 240; cp. Gower, *CA* 4.1505-95).

Physician-Pardoner Link, VI (C), lines 287-328:

The Pardoner's Prologue, VI (C), lines 329-462:

Headnote: *Radix malorum est Cupiditas. Ad Thimotheum, 6.*
   1 Tim. 6:10 (S).

333-34: My theme is alwey oon, and evere was—/*Radix
malorum est Cupiditas.*
   1 Tim. 6:10 (S; R; Hilary, in B, 1987, nn. 333, 334).

348: . . . Ycrammed ful of cloutes and of bones . . .
    Cp. *Acts 19:12* (S).

351: . . . Which that was of an hooly Jewes sheep.
    Gen. 30:31-43 ? (cp. *ParsT* 603-05; Köppel, 1891[b], 40; S; M;
      R; cp. Henkin, 1940; cp. Hilary, in B, 1987, n. 351).
    Judg. 6:36-40 ? (cp. Henkin, 1940).
    Deut. 18:3 ? (Rowland, 1971, pp. 150-52).

364: . . . As thilke hooly Jew oure eldres taughte . . .
    Gen. 30:31-43 ? (cp. line 351, above).
    Num. 7:13-20 ? (Rowland, 1971, pp. 150-52).

366-71: And, sires, also it heeleth jalousie;/ For though a man
be falle in jalous rage,/ Lat maken with this water his potage,/
And nevere shal he moore his wyf mystriste,/ Though he the
soothe of hir defaute wiste,/ Al had she taken prestes two or
thre.
    Num. 5:11-31 (Besserman, 1984[b], pp. 49-50).

407-08: For certes, many a predicacioun/ Comth ofte tyme of
yvel entencioun. . . .
    Phil. 1:15 ? (cp. *Rom* 5763-64; S; cp. Hilary, in B, 1987, n.
      407-08).

413: . . . Thanne wol I stynge hym with my tonge smerte . . .
    Cp. *Rom. 3:13-14; Ps. 139(140):4(3); etc.* (S).

425-26: Therfore my theme is yet, and evere was,/ *Radix
malorum est Cupiditas.*
    1 Tim. 6:10 (see lines 333-34, above; F).

429-31: But though myself be gilty in that synne,/ Yet kan I
maken oother folk to twynne/ From avarice, and soore to
repente.
    Cp. *Rom. 3:7-8* ? (Peck, 1984, pp. 166-67).

444-48: I wol nat do no labour with myne handes,/ Ne make baskettes, and lyve therby,/ By cause I wol nat beggen ydelly./ I wol noon of the apostles countrefete;/ I wol have moneie, wolle, chese, and whete. . . .

>   Cp. *Acts 18:3, 20:33-35* ? (cp. Fleming, 1978-79, 21-22; ——,
>   1984, pp. 186-89; Besserman, 1984[b], p. 48; S; La; R; cp.
>   *Rom* 6679-84, below).
>   Cp. *Mark 6:7-10* (Hilary, in B, 1987, n. 447-48).

The Pardoner's Tale, VI (C), lines 463-968:

467-68: . . . They daunce and pleyen at dees bothe day and nyght,/ And eten also and drynken over hir myght. . . .

>   Cp. *Exod. 32:6; 1 Cor. 10:7* ? (cp. John of Wales,
>   *Communiloquium* 1.10.7; Pratt, 1966, 631-32; cp. Hilary, in
>   B, 1987, nn. 468-71, 470).

469-71: . . . Thurgh which they doon the devel sacrifise/ Withinne that develes temple in cursed wise/ By superfluytee abhomynable.

>   Cp. *Col. 3:5* (cp. Gower, *CA* 5.1952-55).
>   Cp. *1 Cor. 10:20-21* (cp. Hilary, in B, 1987, nn. 468-71, 470).

472-75: Hir othes been so grete and so dampnable/ That it is grisly for to heere hem swere./ Oure blissed Lordes body they totere—/ Hem thoughte that Jewes rente hym noght ynough. . . .

>   *Exod. 20:7, etc.* (S).
>   *Heb. 6:6* ? (cp. *ParsT* 588-93; Köppel, 1891[b], 40; La; cp.
>   Hilary, in B, 1987, n. 474-75).

483-84: The hooly writ take I to my witnesse/ That luxurie is in wyn and dronkenesse.
>   G
>   Cp. *Eph. 5:18* (John of Wales, *Communiloquium* 4.3.7; Pratt,
>   1966, 634-35; cp. Innocent III, *DMCH* 2.19; Köppel, 1890,

411; Holkot, *SLS* 21; Petersen, 1898, p. 113; S; R; cp.
Hilary, in B, 1987, n. 483).

485-87: Lo, how that dronken Looth, unkyndely,/ Lay by his
doghtres two, unwityngly;/ So dronke he was, he nyste what he
wroghte.
  Cp. *Gen. 19:29-38* (Holkot, *SLS* 21; Petersen, 1898, p. 113; cp.
  John Bromyard, *Summa Praedicantium;* cp. Innocent III,
  DMCH 2.20; Gratian, *Decretum* 1.35.1.9; Johnson, 1941,
  pp. 165-66; John of Wales, *Communiloquium* 4.3.7; Pratt,
  1966, 634-35; Peter Comestor, *Historia Scholastica;* Taitt,
  1971; cp. Reiss, 1984, p. 59; R; P; F; cp. Hilary, in B, 1987,
  nn. 485, 488).

488-91: Herodes, whoso wel the stories soghte,/ Whan he of
wyn was repleet at his feeste,/ Right at his owene table he yaf
his heeste/ To sleen the Baptist John, ful giltelees.
  Cp. *Matt. 14:6-11, Mark 6:21-28* (cp. Innocent III, *DMCH*
  2.18; Köppel, 1890, 411; cp. John Bromyard, *Summa
  Praedicantium* ?; Johnson, 1941, pp. 166-67; La; cp. Taitt,
  1971; cp. Reiss, 1984, p. 60; S; M; R; F; cp. Hilary, in B,
  1987, n. 488).

498-511: O glotonye . . . . cause first of oure confusioun!/ . . . .
Adam oure fader, and his wyf also,/ Fro Paradys to labour and
to wo/ Were dryven for that vice, it is no drede./ For whil that
Adam fasted, as I rede,/ He was in Paradys; and whan that
he/ Eet of the fruyt deffended on the tree,/ Anon he was out
cast to wo and peyne.
  Gen. 3:6-24 (cp. Jerome, *EAJ* 2.15; Tupper, 1915, 8-9; cp.
  Innocent III, *DMCH* 2.18; Köppel, 1890, 411; cp. Gratian,
  Decretum; Johnson, 1941, p. 168; S; R; F; Hilary, in B, 1987,
  nn. 498, etc.; cp. Gower, *VC* 5.11.835-36).

501: . . . Til Crist hadde boght us with his blood agayn!
  1 Cor. 6:20, Rom. 5:9, Col. 1:20; etc. (S).

505-11: Adam oure fader, and his wyf also,/ Fro Paradys . . ./
. . . . Anon he was out cast to wo and peyne.
  Gen. 3
  Gen. 3:23-24; etc. (see *ParsT* 819; cp. Gratian, *Decretum* ?;
    Johnson, 1941, p. 168; Jerome, *EAJ* 2.15; Hilary, in B, 1987,
    nn. 505, 508-11).

512-16: O glotonye, on thee wel oghte us pleyne!/ O, wiste a
man how manye maladyes/ Folwen of excesse and of glotonyes,/
He wolde been the moore mesurable/ Of his diete, sittynge at
his table.
  Ecclus. 37:32-34 (Innocent III, *DMCH* 2.17; Köppel, 1890,
    412; S; R; cp. Hilary, in B, 1987, n. 512-16).

521-23: Of this matiere, O Paul, wel kanstow trete:/ "Mete unto
wombe, and wombe eek unto mete,/ Shal God destroyen bothe,"
as Paulus seith.
  g
  1 Cor. 6:13; Phil. 3:18-19 (Innocent III, *DMCH* 2.17; Köppel,
    1890, 412; cp. *ParsT* 818-20; Köppel, 1891[b], 41; Coletti,
    1979; Reiss, 1984, p. 60; Peck, 1984, pp. 167-68; S; M; R; F;
    Hilary, in B, 1987, n. 522-23).

529-33: The apostel wepyng seith ful pitously,/ "Ther walken
manye of whiche yow toold have I—/ I seye it now wepyng,
with pitous voys—/ They been enemys of Cristes croys,/ Of
whiche the ende is deeth; wombe is hir god!"
  g
  Phil. 3:18-19 (see *ParsT* 819-20; cp. John Bromyard, *Summa
    Praedicantium* ?; Johnson, 1941, p. 169; Reiss, 1984, p. 60;
    Peck, 1984, p. 168; S; M; R; F; cp. Hilary, in B, 1987, n. 529-
    35).

547-48: But, certes, he that haunteth swiche delices/ Is deed,
whil that he lyveth in tho vices.

1 Tim. 5:6 (Jerome, *EAJ* 2.9; Köppel, 1890, 416, n. 1; cp. John
of Wales, *Communiloquium* 4.3.7; Pratt, 1967, 635, n. 46;
S; M; R; cp. Hilary, in B, 1987, n. 547-48).
Cp. *Rom. 8:6* ? (Peck, 1984, p. 167).

549-50: A lecherous thyng is wyn, and dronkenesse/ Is ful of
stryvyng and of wrecchednesse.
Prov. 20:1 (Jerome, *EAJ* 2.10; cp. Innocent III, *DMCH* 2.19;
Köppel, 1890, 416, n. 1; cp. Holkot, *SLS* 21; Petersen, 1898,
p. 114; S; M; R; cp. lines 483-84, above; cp. Hilary, in B,
1987, n. 549-50).

554-55: . . . As though thou seydest ay "Sampsoun, Sampsoun!"/
And yet, God woot, Sampsoun drank nevere no wyn.
Judg. 13:7, 14, etc.; Num. 6:3-4 (cp. Geoffrey de la Tour
Landry, *Enseignements*, p. 175; Grennen, 1966; S; R;
Hilary, in B, 1987, n. 554-55).

558: . . . For dronkenesse is verray sepulture. . . .
Cp. *1 Tim. 5:6* ? (John of Wales, *Communiloquium* 4.3.7;
Pratt, 1966, 635; cp. *ParsT* 823; Köppel, 1891[b], 41; cp.
Hilary, in B, 1987, n. 558-59).
Cp. *Rom. 3:13-14; etc.* ? (Peck, 1984, pp. 166-67; cp. *ParsT*
823; Köppel, 1891[b], 41).

560-61: In whom that drynke hath dominacioun/ He kan no
conseil kepe; it is no drede.
Cp. *Prov. 31:4* (proverbial; Whi D425; cp. Innocent III,
DMCH 2.19; Köppel, 1890, 413; Lewis, 1967, 7; John of
Wales, *Communiloquium* 1.3.3; Pratt, 1967, 634; S; M; see
MLT 776-77 and *Mel* 1194; Hilary, in B, 1987, n. 560-61).

573-78: But herkneth, lordynges, o word, I yow preye,/ That
alle the sovereyn actes, dar I seye,/ Of victories in the Olde
Testament,/ Thurgh verray God, that is omnipotent,/ Were
doon in abstinence and in preyere./ Looketh the Bible, and ther
ye may it leere.

G
Cp. *Judg. 20:26, etc.* (John of Wales, *Communiloquium* 1.3.3;
  ibid.; Johnson, 1941, pp. 188-89; Besserman, 1984[b], pp.
  48-49).

G
583-87: And over al this, avyseth yow right wel/ What was
comaunded unto Lamuel—/ Nat Samuel, but Lamuel, seye I;/
Redeth the Bible, and fynde it expresly/ Of wyn-yevyng to
hem that han justise.
  Prov. 31:4-5 (John of Wales, *Communiloquium* 1.3.3; ibid.;
    cp. Holkot, *SLS* 21, 122; Petersen, 1898, pp. 114, 115, nn. 4-
    5; Besserman, 1984[b], p. 48; S; M; R; F; cp. Hilary, in B,
    1987, n. 584).
  1 Kings 1:20, etc. (John of Wales, *Communiloquium* 1.3.3;
    ibid., n. 42).

G

633-34: The heighe God forbad sweryng at al,/ Witnesse on
Mathew. . . .
  Matt. 5:34 (cp. *ParsT* 588-89; Köppel, 1891[b], 39-40; cp. John
    Bromyard, *Summa Praedicantium*; Johnson, 1941, p. 171;
    cp. Holkot, *SLS* 152; Petersen, 1898, p. 114, n. 3; S; M; R; F;
    cp. Hilary, in B, 1987, n. 633-34).
g
Cp. *James 5:12* (S; M; R).

635-37: Of sweryng seith the hooly Jeremye,/ "Thou shalt
swere sooth thyne othes, and nat lye,/ And swere in doom and
eek in rightwisnesse."
g
Jer. 4:2 (cp. *ParsT* 592; Köppel, 1891[b], 39-40; cp. John
    Bromyard, *Summa Praedicantium*; ibid.; Holkot, *SLS* 152;
    ibid.; Reiss, 1984, p. 61; S; M; R; cp. Hilary, in B, 1987, n.
    635).

639-47: Bihoold and se that in the firste table/ Of heighe
Goddes heestes honurable,/ Hou that the seconde heeste of

hym is this:/ "Take nat my name in ydel or amys."/ Lo . . . ./
This knoweth, that his heestes understondeth,/ How that the
seconde heeste of God is that.

> *Exod. 20:7, Deut. 5:11* (cp. *ParsT* 588; cp. John Bromyard,
> *Summa Praedicantium;* Johnson, 1941, p. 171; Sister Mary
> Immaculate, 1941, 64; S; R; F; Hilary, in B, 1987, nn. 639,
> 641).

648-50: . . . I wol thee telle al plat/ That vengeance shal nat
parten from his hous/ That of his othes is to outrageous.

> *Ecclus. 23:12* (cp. *ParsT* 588-93; Köppel, 1891[b], 40; cp. John
> Bromyard, *Summa Praedicantium;* Johnson, 1941, p. 171;
> S; M; R; Hilary, in B, 1987, n. 649-50).

658: Now, for the love of Crist, that for us dyde . . .

> *Rom. 5:9, Col. 1:20; etc.*

708-09: And many a grisly ooth thanne han they sworn,/ And
Cristes blessed body al torente. . . .

> *Heb. 6:6* ? (La; cp. lines 472-75, above).

710: Deeth shal be deed, if that they may hym hente!

> *1 Cor. 15:26; etc.*

713: . . . An oold man and a povre with hem mette.

> Cp. *Rom. 6:1-6; Eph. 4:17-24; Col. 3:1-10* ? (Miller, 1955; R;
> cp. Hilary, in B, 1987, n. 713).

721-24: . . . "For I ne kan nat fynde/ A man . . . That wolde
chaunge his youthe for myn age. . . . "

> Cp. *John 15:12-13* ? (cp. Black, 1974, p. 136; cp. *Rom* 4964-65;
> Hilary, in B, 1987, n. 721-24).

727-28: . . . Ne Deeth, allas, ne wol nat han my lyf./ Thus
walke I, lyk a restelees kaityf . . .

> Cp. *Rom. 7:24; Apoc. 9:6* (Miller, 1977, p. 490; Pearsall,
> 1985, pp. 102-03; cp. Hilary, in B, 1987, n. 727-36).

729: . . . And on the ground, which is my moodres gate . . .
   Ecclus. 40:1 ? (La; cp. S; R; cp. Hilary, in B, 1987, n. 730).
   John 3:4 ? (Pearsall, 1985, p. 103; cp. Hilary, in B, 1987, n.
   730).

742-44: In Hooly Writ ye may yourself wel rede:/ "Agayns an
oold man, hoor upon his heed,/ Ye sholde arise." . . .
   G
   Lev. 19:32 (cp. John Bromyard, *Summa Praedicantium;*
   Johnson, 1941, p. 172; Holkot, *SLS* 49; Petersen, 1898, p.
   115; S; M; R; F; cp. Hilary, in B, 1987, n. 743-44).

745-47: . . . Ne dooth unto an oold man noon harm now,/
Namoore than that ye wolde men did to yow/ In age, if that ye
so longe abyde.
   Ecclus. 8:7 (cp. John Bromyard, *Summa Praedicantium;*
   Johnson, 1941, p. 171; Holkot, *SLS* 49; ibid.; R; Hilary, in
   B, 1987, n. 745).

748: And God be with yow, where ye go or ryde!
   Cp. *1 Cor. 1:2; etc.*

766: God save yow, that boghte agayn mankynde . . .
   1 Cor. 6:20, Rom. 5:9, Col. 1:20; etc.

825: . . . And two of us shul strenger be than oon.
   Cp. *Eccl. 4:9-12*

847-48: . . . For-why the feend foond hym in swich lyvynge/
That he hadde leve him to sorwe brynge.
   Job 1:12, 2:6 ? (R; Hilary, in B, 1987, n. 848).

859-64: The pothecarie answerde, "And thou shalt have/ A
thyng that, also God my soule save,/ In al this world ther is no
creature/ That eten or dronken hath of this confiture/ Nought
but the montance of a corn of whete,/ That he ne shal his lif
anon forlete. . . .

John 12:24 ? (Leicester, 1982, p. 40).

871: . . . And borwed [of] hym large botelles thre . . .
Mark 2:22; etc. ? (ibid., pp. 40-41).

876-77: And whan this riotour, with sory grace,/ Hadde filled
with wyn his grete botels thre . . .
Mark 2:22; etc. ? (ibid.).

901: . . . thy creatour, which that the wroghte . . .
Gen. 1:26-27; 2:7, 21-22

902: . . . And with his precious herte-blood thee boghte . . .
1 Cor. 6:20, Rom. 5:9, Col. 1:20; etc.

906-09: Myn hooly pardoun may yow alle warice,/ So that ye
offre nobles or sterlynges,/ Or elles silver broches, spoones,
rynges./ Boweth youre heed under this hooly bulle!
Exod. 32:1-6 ? (Fleming, 1985, p. 163).

916: And Jhesu Crist, that is oure soules leche . . .
Cp. *Ps. 146(147):3; Matt. 9:12, Mark 2:17, Luke 5:31; etc.* (R;
Hilary, in B, 1987, n. 916).

946: "Nay, nay!" quod he, "thanne have I Cristes curs! . . . "
Cp. *Matt. 25:41; etc.*

952-55: " . . . I wolde I hadde thy coillons in myn hond . . . They
shul be shryned in an hogges toord!"
Cp. *Matt. 19:12* ? (Miller, 1955; Fleming, 1984, pp. 186-89;
cp. *RR* 7079-92; Burnley, 1986, pp. 211-13; Hilary, in B,
1987, n. 952-53).

958-59: "Now," quod oure Hoost, "I wol no lenger pleye/ With
thee, ne with noon oother angry man."
Cp. *Prov. 22:24-25* (Burnley, 1986, pp. 211-13).

The Shipman's Tale, VII (B²*), lines 1-434 (*1191-1624):

3-7 (*1193-97): A wyf hc hadde of excellent beautee;/ And compaignable and revelous was she,/ Which is a thyng that causeth more dispence/ Than worth is al the chiere and reverence/ That men hem doon at festes and at daunces.
    Cp. *Prov. 31:10-31* ? (Coletti, 1984, pp. 176-77, et passim).

9 (*1199): . . . Passen as dooth a shadwe upon the wal . . .
    Cp. *1 Par. 29:15; Wis. 2:5, 5:9; Job 14:2; etc.* (cp. R; see *MerchT* 1315 and *ParsT* 1068; proverbial; Whi S185; Burrow and Scattergood, in B, 1987, n. 9).

75 (*1265): The thridde day, this marchant up ariseth . . .
    Cp. *Matt. 16:21, 17:22; etc.* ?

76-79 (*1266-69): . . . And on his nedes sadly hym avyseth,/ And up into his countour-hous gooth he/ To rekene with hymself, as wel may be,/ Of thilke yeer how that it with hym stood. . . .
    Cp. *Matt. 18, 23; Luke 7, 13* ? (Adams, 1984, pp. 91-92).

85-87 (*1275-77): . . . For which ful faste his countour-dore he shette;/ And eek he nolde that no man sholde hym lette/ Of his acountes. . . .
    Cp. *Matt. 6:6* ? (Adams, 1984, p. 95).

91 (*1281): . . . And hath his thynges seyd ful curteisly.
    G (liturgy; S; Burrow and Scattergood, in B, 1987, n. 91).

113 (*1303): . . . "Ye, God woot al," quod she.
    Cp. *Ps. 43(44):22(21), 1 John 3:20; etc.*

131 (*1321): For on my porthors here I make an ooth . . .
    G (liturgy; S; Burrow and Scattergood, in B, 1987, n. 131).

178-79 (*1368-69): But by that ilke Lord that for us bledde,/ For his honour, myself for to arraye . . .
  Rom. 5:9, Col. 1:20; etc.
  John 20:1-15 ? (Gibson, 1981, pp. 107-10).

214 (*1404): . . . "Peter! . . . "
  Matt. 4:18; etc. (F; cp. Burrow and Scattergood, in B, 1987, n. 214).

375-76 (*1565-66): . . . And al that nyght in myrthe they bisette;/ For he was riche and cleerly out of dette.
  Cp. *1 Cor. 7:3, etc.* ? (Adams, 1984, pp. 88-89).

393 (*1583): But nathelees, by God, oure hevene kyng . . .
  Dan. 4:34; etc.

397-98 (*1587-88): . . . If any dettour hath in myn absence/ Ypayed thee . . .
  Cp. *1 Cor. 7:3*

413-17 (*1603-07): Ye han mo slakkere dettours than am I!/ For I wol paye yow wel and redily/ Fro day to day, and if so be I faille,/ I am youre wyf; score it upon my taille,/ And I shal paye as soone as ever I may.
  Cp. *1 Cor. 7:3* (Burrow and Scattergood, in B, 1987, n. 413-17).

423-24 (*1613-14): Ye shal my joly body have to wedde;/ By God, I wol nat paye yow but abedde!
  Cp. *1 Cor. 7:3*

Shipman-Prioress Link, VII (B²*), lines 435-52 (*1625-42):

The Prioress's Prologue, VII (B^{2*}), lines 453-87 (*1643-77):

Headnote: *Domine dominus noster.*
   Ps. 8:2(1) (liturgy; S; R; P).

453-59 (*1643-49): O Lord, oure Lord, thy name how
merveillous/ Is in this large world ysprad . . ./ For noght oonly
thy laude precious/ Parfourned is by men of dignitee,/ But by
the mouth of children . . . Somtyme shewen they thyn
heriynge. . . .
   Ps. 8:2-3(1-2) (liturgy; Tupper, 1915, 9-11; Sister Madeleva,
      1925, pp. 30-33; Hawkins, 1964; Bugge, 1975-76; S; R; P; F;
      Ridley, in B, 1987, nn. 453-59, etc.).
   Matt. 21:15-17 (Hawkins, 1964, 606-07).

461-62 (*1651-52): . . . Of thee and of the white lylye flour/
Which that the bar . . .
   Cant. 2:2 ? (R; liturgy; Sister Madeleva, 1925, pp. 30-33; P;
      Ridley, in B, 1987, n. 461).

467-71 (*1657-61): O mooder Mayde, O mayde Mooder free!/ . . .
That ravyshedest doun fro the Deitee,/ Thurgh thyn
humblesse, the Goost that in th'alighte,/ Of whos vertu, whan
he thyn herte lighte . . .
   Cp. *Luke 1:35, 48* (liturgy; Tupper, 1915, 9-11; Sister Made-
      leva, 1925, pp. 30-33; J; cp. Ridley, in B, 1987, n. 467-72).

468 (*1658): O bussh unbrent, brennynge in Moyses sighte . . .
   Exod. 3:2 (liturgy; Tupper, 1915, 9-11; Sister Madeleva,
      1925, pp. 30-33; Ames, 1977, p. 88; S; M; R; P; F; Ridley, in
      B, 1987, n. 461).

472 (*1662): . . . Conceyved was the Fadres sapience . . .
   1 Cor. 1:24 (liturgy; Tupper, 1915, 9-11; Sister Madeleva,
      1925, pp. 30-33; R; F; cp. Ridley, in B, 1987, n. 469-72).

484 (*1674): But as a child of twelf month oold, or lesse . . .
Cp. *Matt.* 2:16 (Hawkins, 1964, 600; cp. Ridley, in B, 1987, n.
481-86).

The Prioress's Tale, VII (B²*), lines 488-690 (*1678-1880):

491 (*1681): . . . For foule usure and lucre of vileynye . . .
1 Tim. 3:8 (R; Ridley, in B, 1987, n. 490-91).

506 (*1696): . . . Of Cristes mooder . . .
Luke 1:28, 42; etc. (liturgy).

508 (*1698): . . . His *Ave Marie* . . .
Luke 1:28, 42; etc. (liturgy; F; Ridley, in B, 1987, n. 508).

510 (*1700): . . . Oure blisful Lady, Cristes mooder deere . . .
Luke 1:28, 42; etc. (liturgy).

558 (*1748): Oure firste foo, the serpent Sathanas . . .
Cp. *Gen. 3:1* (cp. Ridley, in B, 1987, n. 558-64).

560-64 (*1750-54): . . . "O Hebrayk peple, allas!/ . . . . That
swich a boy shal walken as hym lest/ In youre despit, and
synge of swich sentence,/ Which is agayn youre lawes
reverence?"
Gen. 3:1 ? (La; cp. Ridley, in B, 1987, nn. 558-64, 564).

561 (*1751): Is this to yow a thyng that is honest . . .
Cp. *Rom. 12:17, etc.* (S).

571 (*1761): . . . And kitte his throte, and in a pit hym caste.
Ps. 39(40) ? (Hawkins, 1964, 613).

574 (*1764): O cursed folk of Herodes al newe . . .
Matt. 2:16, etc. (La; F).

578 (*1768): The blood out crieth on youre cursed dede.
   Gen. 4:10 (R; Ridley, in B, 1987, n. 578).

579-85 (*1769-75): O martir, sowded to virginitee,/ Now
maystow syngen, folwynge evere in oon/ The white Lamb
celestial—quod she—/ Of which the grete evaungelist, Seint
John,/ In Pathmos wroot, which seith that they that goon/
Biforn this Lamb and synge a song al newe,/ That nevere,
flesshly, wommen they ne knewe.
   8
   Apoc. 14:3-4 (S; R; P; F; cp. Ridley, in B, 1987, n. 580-85).

607-08 (*1797-98): O grete God, that parfounest thy laude/ By
mouth of innocentz, lo, heere thy myght!
   Ps. 8:3(2) (liturgy; Ridley, in B, 1987, n. 607-08).

618 (*1808): . . . And herieth Crist that is of hevene kyng . . .
   Dan. 4:34; etc.

627 (*1817): . . . This newe Rachel brynge fro his beere.
   Matt. 2:18 (liturgy; Ames, 1977, p. 88; S; R; P; F; cp. Ridley,
   in B, 1987, n. 627).

652-53 (*1842-43): But Jesu Crist, as ye in bookes fynde,/ Wil
that his glorie laste and be in mynde . . .
   Matt. 28:18-20, Mark 16:15; etc.

656 (*1846): This welle of mercy, Cristes mooder sweete . . .
   Zach. 13:1 ? (liturgy; La).

662-63 (*1852-53): . . . Me thoughte she leyde a greyn upon my
tonge./ Wherfore I synge, and synge moot certeyn . . .
   Matt. 13 ? (Hawkins, 1964, 614-15; cp. Ridley, in B, 1987, n.
   662).
   Jer. 1:6, 9 ? (Hawkins, 1964, 619).

669 (*1859): . . . Be nat agast, I wol thee nat forsake.
Cp. *John 14:18; Heb. 13:5; etc.* (R).

Prioress-Thopas Link, VII (B²*), lines 691-711 (*1881-1901):

The Tale of Sir Thopas, VII (B²*), lines 712-918 (*1902-2108):

784 (*1974): O Seinte Marie, benedicite!
Luke 1-2 (liturgy)
Dan. 3:57, etc. (liturgy; S; La; cp. *KtT* 1785).

827-32 (*2017-22): Sire Thopas drow abak ful faste;/ This geant
at hym stones caste/ Out of a fel staf-slynge./ But faire
escapeth child Thopas,/ And al it was thurgh Goddes gras,/
And thurgh his fair berynge.
Cp. *1 Kings 17:40-50* (Loomis, 1936; S; R; F; Burrow, in B,
1987, n. 829).

Thopas-Melibee Link, VII (B²*), lines 919-66 (*2109-56):

943-52 (*2133-42): As thus: ye woot that every Evaungelist/
That telleth us the peyne of Jhesu Crist/ Ne seith nat alle
thyng as his felawe dooth;/ But nathelees hir sentence is al
sooth,/ And alle acorden as in hire sentence,/ Al be ther in hir
tellyng difference./ For somme of hem seyn moore, and somme
seyn lesse,/ Whan they his pitous passioun expresse—/ I meene
of Mark, Mathew, Luc, and John—/ But doutelees hir sentence is
al oon.
G (cp. Robertson, 1962, pp. 367-38; Lawler, 1980, pp. 21-23;
Besserman, 1984[b], pp. 46-47; R; DeLong, in B, 1987, n.
943-52).
Matt.27:2, 26, 35-50; etc.
8, 8, 8, 8

The Tale of Melibee, VII (B^{2*}), lines 967-1888 (*2157-3078):

967 (*2157): A yong man called Melibeus, myghty and riche, bigat upon his wyf, that called was Prudence, a doghter which that called was Sophie.

> Cp. *Prov. 3:13-20, 31:10* ? (cp. Renaud, *LMP* 8-9; Severs, in *S&A*, 1941[b], p. 568; cp. Ames, 1984, p. 170; R; DeLong, in B, 1987, n. 967).

970 (*2160): Thre of his olde foes . . .

> *1 John 2:16* (Renaud, *LMP* 11; ibid.; DeLong, in B, 1987, n. 970).

987 (*2177): Jhesu Crist, oure Lord, hymself wepte for the deeth of Lazarus hys freend.

> *John 11:35* (Renaud, *LMP* 35-36; ibid., p. 569; S; R; P; F).

989 (*2179): The Apostle Paul unto the Romayns writeth, "Man shal rejoyse with hem that maken joye and wepen with swich folk as wepen."

> g
> *Rom. 12:15* (Renaud, *LMP* 38-41; ibid.; cp. Johnson, 1941, pp. 90-91; S; R; P; F; DeLong, in B, 1987, n. 989).

995 (*2185): Remembre yow that Jhesus Syrak seith, 'A man that is joyous and glad in herte, it hym conserveth florissynge in his age; but soothly sorweful herte maketh his bones drye.'

> g
> *Prov. 17:22* (Renaud, *LMP* 48-50; ibid., pp. 569-70; S; R; P; F; DeLong, in B, 1987, n. 995).

996 (*2186): He seith eek thus, that sorwe in herte sleeth ful many a man.

> g
> *Ecclus. 30:25* (Renaud, *LMP* 50-51; ibid., p. 570; S; R; P; F; DeLong, in B, 1987, n. 996).

997 (*2187): Salomon seith that right as motthes in the shepes
flees anoyeth to the clothes, and the smale wormes to the tree,
right so anoyeth sorwe to the herte.

g
Cp. *Prov. 25:20* (Renaud, *LMP* 51-53; ibid.; S; R; P; DeLong,
in B, 1987, n. 997).

999-1000 (*2189-90): Remembre yow upon the pacient Job. Whan
he hadde lost his children and his temporeel substance, and in
his body endured and receyved ful many a grevous tribulacion,
yet seyde he thus:/ 'Oure Lord hath yeve it me; oure Lord hath
biraft it me; right as oure Lord hath wold, right so it is doon;
blessed be the name of oure Lord!'
Job 1-2 (Renaud, *LMP* 53-58; ibid.; S; R; P; F; DeLong, in B,
1987, n. 1000).
Job 1:21 (Renaud, *LMP* 53-58; ibid.; S; R; P; F; DeLong, in B,
1987, n. 1000).

1003 (*2193): Salomon seith, "Werk alle thy thynges by conseil,
and thou shalt never repente."

g
Ecclus. 32:24 (Renaud, *LMP* 64-65; ibid.; cp. Albertano of
Brescia, *LCC*; Bühler, 1949; S; R; P; F; proverbial; Whi
C470; DeLong, in B, 1987, n. 1003).

1033 (*2223): And that shewed oure Lord Jhesu Crist by
ensample, for whan that the womman that was taken in
avowtrie was broght in his presence to knowen what sholde be
doon with hire persone, al be it so that he wiste wel hymself
what that he wolde answere, yet ne wolde he nat answere
sodeynly, but he wolde have deliberacion, and in the ground he
wroot twies.
Cp. *John 8:3-8* (Renaud, *LMP* 110-15; ibid., p. 572; S; F;
DeLong, in B, 1987, n. 1033).

1039 (*2229): Werre at his bigynnyng hath so greet an entryng
and so large that every wight may entre whan hym liketh and
lightly fynde werre. . . .
   Prov. 17:14 ? (Renaud, *LMP* 125-27; ibid.; S).

1045 (*2235): For Jhesus Syrak seith that "musik in wepynge is
a noyous thyng." . . .
   g
   Ecclus. 22:6 (Renaud, *LMP* 136-37; ibid.; cp. Johnson, 1941,
      pp. 89-90; S; R; P; F; DeLong, in B, 1987, n. 1045).

1047 (*2237): For Salomon seith: "Ther as thou ne mayst have
noon audience, enforce thee nat to speke."
   g
   Ecclus. 32:6 (Renaud, *LMP* 140-41; ibid., p. 573; cp. Johnson,
      1941, pp. 89-90; S; R; P; F; DeLong, in B, 1987, n. 1047).

1057 (*2247): . . . I seye that alle wommen been wikke, and noon
good of hem alle. For "of a thousand men,' seith Salomon, "I
foond o good man, but certes, of alle wommen, good womman
foond I nevere."
   g
   Eccl. 7:29 (Renaud, *LMP* 158-61; ibid.; S; R; P; F; DeLong, in
      B, 1987, n. 1057).

1059 (*2249): For Jhesus Syrak seith that "if the wyf have
maistrie, she is contrarious to hir housbonde."
   g
   Ecclus. 25:30 (Renaud, *LMP* 163-64; ibid., p. 574; cp. Johnson,
      1941, p. 90; S; R; P; F; DeLong, in B, 1987, n. 1059).

1060 (*2250): And Salomon seith: "Nevere in thy lyf to thy
wyf, ne to thy child, ne to thy freend ne yeve no power over
thyself, for bettre it were that thy children aske of thy persone
thynges that hem nedeth than thou see thyself in the handes
of thy children."
   g

Ecclus. 33:20-22 (Renaud, *LMP* 164-67; ibid.; S; R; P; F; DeLong, in B, 1987, n. 1060).

1074 (*2264): . . . oure Lord Jhesu Crist wolde nevere have descended to be born of a womman, if alle wommen hadden been wikke.
Luke 1-2, etc. (Renaud, *LMP* 196-97; ibid., p. 575).

1075 (*2265): . . . for the grete bountee that is in wommen, oure Lord Jhesu Crist, whan he was risen fro deeth to lyve, appeered rather to a womman than to his Apostles.
Mark 16:9, John 20:14 (Renaud, *LMP* 198-200; ibid.; S; R; DeLong, in B, 1987, n. 1075-79).

1076-79 (*2266-69): And though that Salomon seith that he ne foond nevere womman good . . . . this is to seyn, that ther is no wight that hath sovereyn bountee save God allone . . .
g
Eccl. 7:29 (Renaud, *LMP* 201, 205-06; ibid.; R; cp. *MerchT* 2287-90, above; cp. DeLong, in B, 1987, n. 1076).

1079-80 (*2269-70): . . . as [H]e hymself recordeth in hys Evaungelie./ For ther nys no creature so good that hym ne wanteth somwhat of the perfeccioun of God, that is his makere.
G
Cp. *Matt. 19:17, Mark 10:18, Luke 18:19, etc.* (Renaud, *LMP* 206-08; ibid.; S; R; P; F; DeLong, in B, 1987, n. 1079).

1086 (*2276): . . . thre thynges dryven a man out of his hous— that is to seyn, smoke, droppyng of reyn, and wikked wyves.
Cp. *Prov. 10:26, 19:13, 27:15* (Renaud, *LMP* 217-18; ibid.; S; R; F; proverbial; Whi T187; DeLong, in B, 1987, n. 1086).

1087 (*2277): . . . of swiche wommen seith Salomon that "it were bettre dwelle in desert than with a woman that is riotous."
g

Prov. 21:9, 25:24 (Renaud, *LMP* 218-20; ibid., pp. 575-76; S; R; P; F; cp. DeLong, in B, 1987, n. 1087).

1098 (*2288): Loo, Jacob by good conseil of his mooder Rebekka wan the benysoun of Ysaak his fader and the lordshipe over alle his bretheren.
  Gen. 27:5-29 (Renaud, *LMP* 237-39; ibid., p. 576; S; R; P; F; DeLong, in B, 1987, n. 1098-1102).

1099 (*2289): Judith by hire good conseil delivered the citee of Bethulie, in which she dwelled, out of the handes of Olofernus, that hadde it biseged and wolde have al destroyed it.
  Jud. 8-13 (Renaud, *LMP* 239-41; ibid.; S; R; P; F; DeLong, in B, 1987, n. 1098-1102).

1100 (*2290): Abygail delivered Nabal hir housbonde fro David the kyng, that wolde have slayn hym, and apaysed the ire of the kyng by hir wit and by hir good conseillyng.
  1 Kings 25:2-35 (S; R; P; F; DeLong, in B, 1987, n. 1098-1102).

1101 (*2291): Hester by hir good conseil enhaunced greetly the peple of God in the regne of Assuerus the kyng.
  Esth. 7 (Renaud, *LMP* 243-44; ibid.; S; R; P; F; DeLong, in B, 1987, n. 1098-1102).

1103-04 (*2293-94): . . . whan oure Lord hadde creat Adam, oure forme fader, he seyde in this wise:/ "It is nat good to been a man alloone; make we to hym an helpe semblable to hymself."
  Gen. 1:26-27, 2:7
  Gen. 2:18 (Renaud, *LMP* 245-47; ibid., pp. 576-77; S; R; DeLong, in B, 1987, n. 1104).

1113 (*2303): I se wel that the word of Salomon is sooth. He seith that "wordes that been spoken discreetly by ordinaunce been honycombes, for they yeven swetnesse to the soule and hoolsomnesse to the body."
  8

Prov. 16:24 (Renaud, *LMP* 257-59; ibid., p. 577; S; R; P; F; DeLong, in B, 1987, n. 1113).

1117-18 (*2307-08): . . . as taughte Thobie his sone:/ "At alle tymes thou shalt blesse God, and praye hym to dresse thy weyes, and looke that alle thy conseils been in hym for everemoore."
Tob. 4:20 (Renaud, *LMP* 266-68; ibid.; S; R; P; F).

1119 (*2309): Seint Jame eek seith: "If any of yow have nede of sapience, axe it of God."
    g
James 1:5 (Renaud, *LMP* 268-69; ibid.; cp. La, 1924, 91, n. 44; Johnson, 1941, pp. 87-89; S; R; P; F).

1130 (*2320): For the Apostle seith that coveitise is roote of alle harmes.
    g
1 Tim. 6:10 (Renaud, *LMP* 281-82; ibid., p. 578; cp. Johnson, 1941, pp. 92-93; S; R; P; F; DeLong, in B, 1987, n. 1130).

1141-42 (*2331-32): For Jhesus Syrak seith, "Neither to thy foo ne to thy frend discovere nat thy secree ne thy folie,/ for they wol yeve yow audience and lookynge and supportacioun in thy presence and scorne thee in thyn absence."
    g
Ecclus. 19:8-9 (Renaud, *LMP* 294-96; ibid.; S; R; P; F; DeLong, in B, 1987, n. 1141-42).

1144-45 (*2334-35): The book seith, "Whil that thou kepest thy conseil in thyn herte, thou kepest it in thy prisoun,/ and whan thou biwreyest thy conseil to any wight, he holdeth thee in his snare."
    G
Ecclus. 8:22 (Renaud, *LMP* 298-99; ibid.; S; R; DeLong, in B, 1987, n. 1144).

1158 (*2348): For Salomon seith that "right as the herte of a man deliteth in savour that is soote, right so the conseil of trewe freendes yeveth swetnesse to the soule."
g
Prov. 27:9 (Renaud, *LMP* 315-16; ibid., p. 579; S; R; P; F; DeLong, in B, 1987, n. 1158).

1159-60 (*2349-50): He seith also, "Ther may no thyng be likned to the trewe freend,/ for certes gold ne silver ben nat so muche worth as the goode wyl of a trewe freend."
g
Ecclus. 6:15 (Renaud, *LMP* 316-18; ibid.; S; R; P; F; DeLong, in B, 1987, n. 1159).

1161 (*2351): And eek he seith that "a trewe freend is a strong deffense; who so that it fyndeth, certes he fyndeth a greet tresour."
g
Ecclus. 6:14 (Renaud, *LMP* 318-19; ibid.; S; R; P; F; DeLong, in B, 1987, n. 1161).

1162 (*2352): Thanne shul ye eek considere if that youre trewe freendes been discrete and wise. For the book seith, "Axe alwey thy conseil of hem that been wise."
G
Tob. 4:19, Prov. 22:17, etc. (cp. Renaud, *LMP* 321; ibid.; S; R; P; F; cp. DeLong, in B, 1987, n. 1162).

1164 (*2354): For the book seith that "in olde men is the sapience, and in longe tyme the prudence."
G
Job 12:12 (Renaud, *LMP* 323-24; ibid.; S; R; P; F; DeLong, in B, 1987, n. 1164).

1167 (*2357): . . . for Salomon seith, "Manye freendes have thou, but among a thousand chese thee oon to be thy conseillour."
g

Ecclus. 6:6 (Renaud, *LMP* 330-31; ibid.; S; R; P; F; DeLong, in B, 1987, n. 1167).

1171 (*2361): For Salomon seith, "Salvacion of thynges is where as ther been manye conseillours."
g
Prov. 11:14, 15:22 (Renaud, *LMP* 335-36; ibid., p. 580; S; R; P; F; DeLong, in B, 1987, n. 1171).

1173 (*2363): . . . for Salomon seith, "Taak no conseil of a fool, for he ne kan noght conseille but after his owene lust and his affeccioun."
g
Ecclus. 8:20 (Renaud, *LMP* 339-41; ibid.; S; R; P; cp. DeLong, in B, 1987, n. 1173).

1177 (*2367): The book seith, "Thou shalt rather drede and flee fro the sweete wordes of flaterynge preiseres than fro the egre wordes of thy freend that seith thee thy sothes."
G
Prov. 28:23 (Renaud, *LMP* 346-47; ibid.; S; R; cp. DeLong, in B, 1987, n. 1177).

1178 (*2368): Salomon seith that "the wordes of a flaterere is a snare to cacche with innocentz."
g
Prov. 29:5 (Renaud, *LMP* 348-49; ibid.; S; R; P; F; DeLong, in B, 1987, n. 1178-79).

1179 (*2369): He seith also that "he that speketh to his freend wordes of swetnesse and of plesaunce setteth a net biforn his feet to cacche hym."
g
Prov. 29:5 (Renaud, *LMP* 349-51; ibid.; S; R; P; DeLong, in B, 1987, n. 1178-79).

1186 (*2376): And therfore seith Salomon, "In thyn olde foo trust nevere."

g
Ecclus. 12:10 (Renaud, *LMP* 360-61; ibid.; S; R; P; F; DeLong, in B, 1987, n. 1186).

1187-88 (*2377-78): For sikerly, though thyn enemy be reconsiled, and maketh thee chiere of humylitee, and lowteth to thee with his heed, ne trust hym nevere./ For certes he maketh thilke feyned humilitee moore for his profit than for any love of thy persone, by cause that he deemeth to have victorie over thy persone by swich feyned contenance, the which victorie he myghte nat have by strif or werre.
    Cp. *Ecclus. 12:11-12* (Renaud, *LMP* 361-65; ibid., pp. 580-81).

1194 (*2384): For Salomon seith, "Ther is no privetee ther as regneth dronkenesse."

g
Prov. 31:4 (proverbial; Whi D425; Renaud, *LMP* 373; ibid., p. 581; S; R; P; F; see *MLT* 776-77 and *PardT* 560-61; DeLong, in B, 1987, n. 1194).

1197 (*2387): For the book seith, "The conseillyng of wikked folk is alwey ful of fraude."
G
Prov. 12:5 (Renaud, *LMP* 378-79; ibid.; cp. Johnson, 1941, pp. 91-92; S; R; P; F; cp. DeLong, in B, 1987, n. 1197).

1198 (*2388): And David seith, "Blisful is that man that hath nat folwed the conseilyng of shrewes."

g
Ps. 1:1 (Renaud, *LMP* 379-80; ibid.; S; R; P; F).

1290-94 (*2480-84): . . . but certes, wikkednesse shal be warisshed by goodnesse, discord by accord, werre by pees, and so forth of othere thynges./ And heerto accordeth Seint Paul the Apostle in manye places./ He seith, "Ne yeldeth nat harm for harm, ne wikked speche for wikked speche,/ but do wel to hym that dooth thee harm, and blesse hym that seith to thee harm."/ And in manye othere places he amonesteth pees and accord.

g
Rom. 12:17; 1 Pet. 3:9; 1 Thess. 5:15, 1 Cor. 4:12; etc. (Renaud, *LMP* 501-07; ibid., p. 586; S; R; P; F; Lawler, 1980, pp. 105-06; DeLong, in B, 1987, n. 1292).

1303-04 ((*2493-94): To this sentence accordeth the prophete David, that seith,/ "If God ne kepe the citee, in ydel waketh he that it kepeth."

g
Ps. 126(127):1 (Renaud, *LMP* 515-16; ibid.; S; R; P; F; DeLong, in B, 1987, n. 1304).

1317-18 (*2507-08): And Salomon seith, "Weleful is he that of alle hath drede,/ for certes, he that thurgh the hardynesse of his herte and thurgh the hardynesse of hymself hath to greet presumpcioun, hym shal yvel bityde."

g
Prov. 28:14 (Renaud, *LMP* 531-33; ibid., p. 587; S; R; P; F; DeLong, in B, 1987, n. 1316-17).

1406-07 (*2596-97): For th'apostle seith that "the sciences and the juggementz of oure Lord God almyghty been ful depe;/ ther may no man comprehende ne serchen hem suffisantly."

g
Rom. 11:33 (Renaud, *LMP* 642-44; ibid., p. 592; cp. Johnson, 1941, p. 91; S; R; DeLong, in B, 1987, n. 1406).
Cp. *1 Cor. 4:5; etc.*

1416-17 (*2606-07): And Salomon seith, "If thou hast founden hony, ete of it that suffiseth,/ for if thou ete of it out of mesure, thou shalt spewe," and be nedy and povre.

g

Prov. 25:16 (Renaud, *LMP* 654-56; ibid.; S; R; P; F; DeLong,
   in B, 1987, n. 1416).

1418-19 (*2608-09): And peraventure Crist hath thee in despit,
and hath turned awey fro thee his face and his eeris of
misericorde . . . in the manere that thow hast ytrespassed.
   2 Par. 30:9 ? (Renaud, *LMP* 656-58; ibid.; La).

1420 (*2610): Thou hast doon synne agayn oure Lord Crist. . . .
   Cp. *Exod. 10:16; etc.* (Renaud, *LMP* 658-59; ibid., pp. 592-
   93).

1421-24 (*2611-14): . . . for certes, the three enemys of
mankynde—that is to seyn, the flessh, the feend, and the
world—/ thou hast suffred hem entre in to thyn herte wilfully
by the wyndowes of thy body,/ and hast nat defended thyself
suffisantly agayns hire assautes and hire temptaciouns,
so that they han wounded thy soule in fyve places;/ this is to
seyn, the deedly synnes that been entred into thyn herte by thy
fyve wittes.
   1 John 2:16 (Renaud, *LMP* 659-60; ibid., p. 593; DeLong, in B,
   1987, n. 1421).

1440-41 (*2630-31): And Seint Paul the Apostle seith in his
Epistle, whan he writeth unto the Romayns, that "the juges
beren nat the spere withouten cause,/ but they beren it to
punysse the shrewes and mysdoers and for to defende the goode
men."
   8
   Rom. 13:4 (Renaud, *LMP* 686-88; ibid., p. 594; S; R; P; F;
   DeLong, in B, 1987, n. 1440-43).

1458 (*2648): . . . the sovereyn Juge that vengeth alle vileynyes
and wronges.
   Exod. 34:7; etc. (Renaud, *LMP* 710-11; ibid., p. 595).

1459-60 (*2649-50): . . . where as he seith,/ "Leveth the vengeance to me, and I shal do it."
   G
   Rom. 12:19, etc. (Renaud, *LMP* 711-12; ibid.; S; R; P; F; DeLong, in B, 1987, n. 1460).

1485 (*2675): For Salomon seith, "It is a greet worshipe to a man to kepen hym fro noyse and stryf."
   g
   Prov. 20:3 (Renaud, *LMP* 743-44; ibid., p. 596; S; R; P; F; Lawler, 1980, pp. 105-06; DeLong, in B, 1987, n. 1485).

1495-96 (*2685-86): . . . for whiche defautes God hath suffred yow have this tribulacioun, as I have seyd yow heer-biforn./ For the poete seith that "we oghte paciently taken the tribulacions that comen to us, whan we thynken and consideren that we han disserved to have hem."
   Luke 23:41 ? (Renaud, *LMP* 752-56; ibid.; S; R; Kreuzer, 1948; Lawler, 1980, pp. 105-06; DeLong, in B, 1987, n. 1496).

1501 (*2691): Also ye owen to enclyne and bowe youre herte . . .
   Prov. 2:2, etc. (Renaud, *LMP* 760-61; ibid., p. 597; Lawler, 1980, pp. 105-06).

1501-04 (*2691-94): . . . to take the pacience of oure Lord Jhesu Crist, as seith seint Peter in his Epistles./ "Jhesu Crist," he seith, "hath suffred for us and yeven ensample to every man to folwe and sewe hym;/ for he dide nevere synne, ne nevere cam ther a vileyns word out of his mouth./ Whan men cursed hym, he cursed hem noght, and whan men betten hym, he manaced hem noght."
   g
   1 Pet. 2:21-23 (Renaud, *LMP* 761-65; ibid.; S; R; P; F; Lawler, 1980, pp. 105-06; DeLong, in B, 1987, n. 1502-04).

1509-10 (*2699-2700): . . . and the joye that a man seketh to have by pacience in tribulaciouns is perdurable, after that the

Apostle seith in his epistle./ "The joye of God," he seith, "is perdurable," that is to seyn, everlastynge.

g
2 *Cor. 4:17* (Renaud, *LMP* 770-72; ibid.; S; R; P; F; Lawler, 1980, pp. 105-06; DeLong, in B, 1987, nn. 1509, 1510).

1512 (*2702): For Salomon seith that "the doctrine and the wit of a man is knowen by pacience."

g
Prov. 19:11 (Renaud, *LMP* 773-74; ibid.; S; R; P; F; Lawler, 1980, pp. 105-06; DeLong, in B, 1987, n. 1512).

1513 (*2703): And in another place he seith that "he that is pacient governeth hym by greet prudence."

g
Prov. 14:29 (Renaud, *LMP* 774-75; ibid.; S; R; P; F; Lawler, 1980, pp. 105-06; DeLong, in B, 1987, n. 1513).

1514 (*2704): And the same Salomon seith, "The angry and wrathful man maketh noyses, and the pacient man atempreth hem and stilleth."

g
Prov. 15:18 (Renaud, *LMP* 775-76; ibid.; S; R; P; F; Lawler, 1980, pp. 105-06; DeLong, in B, 1987, n. 1514).

1515-16 (*2705-06): He seith also, "It is moore worth to be pacient than for to be right strong;/ and he that may have the lordshipe of his owene herte is moore to preyse than he that by his force or strengthe taketh grete citees."

g
Prov. 16:32 (Renaaud, *LMP* 776-79; ibid.; S; R; P; F; Lawler, 1980, pp. 105-06; DeLong, in B, 1987, n. 1515-16).

1517 (*2707): And therfore seith Seint Jame in his Epistle that "pacience is a greet vertu of perfeccioun."

g

James 1:4 (Renaud, *LMP* 779-80; ibid.; S; R; P; F; Lawler,
1980, pp. 105-06; DeLong, in B, 1987, n. 1517).

1539 (*2729): And therfore me thynketh that pacience is good.
For Salomon seith that "he that is nat pacient shal have greet
harm."
   g
   Prov. 19:19 (Renaud, *LMP* 811; ibid., p. 599; S; R; P; F;
   DeLong, in B, 1987, n. 1539).

1542-44 (*2732-34): And Salomon seith that "he that
entremetteth hym of the noyse or strif of another man is lyk to
hym that taketh an hound by the eris."/ For right as he . . . .
wheras it aperteneth nat unto hym.
   g
   Prov. 26:17 (Renaud, *LMP* 816-20; ibid.; cp. Johnson, 1941,
   pp. 92-93; S; R; P; F; DeLong, in B, 1987, n. 1542).

1550 (*2740): And Salomon seith that "alle thynges obeyen to
moneye."
   g
   Eccl. 10:19 (Renaud, *LMP* 826; ibid., p. 600; S; R; P; F;
   DeLong, in B, 1987, n. 1550).

1553 (*2743): . . . and that the richesses been goode to hem that
han wel ygeten hem and wel konne usen hem.
   1 Tim. 4:4 ? (Renaud, *LMP* 829-31; ibid.; S; DeLong, in B,
   1987, n. 1553).

1558-60 (*2748-50): And this Pamphilles seith also, "If thow be
right happy —that is to seyn, if thou be right riche—thou
shalt fynde a greet nombre of felawes and freendes./ And if thy
fortune change that thou wexe povre, farewel freendshipe and
felaweshipe,/ for thou shalt be alloone withouten any
compaignye, but if it be the compaignye of povre folk."
   Prov. 19:6-7 ? (Renaud, *LMP* 835-38; ibid.; S; R; proverbial;
   Whi F667; cp. DeLong, in B, 1987, n. 1558).

1571 (*2761): And seith Salomon that "bet it is to dye than for to have swich poverte."

g
Ecclus. 40:29 (Renaud, *LMP* 849-50; ibid., p. 601; S; R; P; F; DeLong, in B, 1987, n. 1571).

1572 (*2762): And as the same Salomon seith, "Bettre it is to dye of bitter deeth than for to lyven in swich wise."

g
Ecclus. 30:17 (Renaud, *LMP* 850-51; ibid.; S; R; P; F; DeLong, in B, 1987, n. 1572).

1578 (*2768): . . . and therfore seith Salomon, "He that hasteth hym to bisily to wexe riche shal be noon innocent."

g
Cp. *Prov. 28:20* (Renaud, *LMP* 859-60; ibid.; S; R; P; F; DeLong, in B, 1987, n. 1578).

1579-80 (*2769-70): He seith also that "the richesse that hastily cometh to a man soone and lightly gooth and passeth fro a man,/ but that richesse that cometh litel and litel wexeth alwey and multiplieth."

g
Prov. 13:11 (Renaud, *LMP* 860-62; ibid.; S; R; P; F; DeLong, in B, 1987, n. 1579).

1583 (*2773): For the lawe seith that "ther maketh no man himselven riche, if he do harm to another wight."

G
Cp. *Ecclus. 13:30* ? (cp. DeLong, in B, 1987, n. 1583).

1589 (*2779): For Salomon seith that "ydelnesse techeth a man to do manye yveles."

g
Ecclus. 33:29 (Renaud, *LMP* 871-72; ibid., p. 602; S; R; P; F; DeLong, in B, 1987, n. 1589).

1590-91 (*2780-81): And the same Salomon seith that "he that travailleth and bisieth hym to tilien his land shal eten breed,/ but he that is ydel and casteth hym to no bisynesse ne occupacioun shal falle into poverte and dye for hunger."

§
Prov. 28:19, 12:11 (Renaud, *LMP* 872-74; ibid.; S; R; P; F; DeLong, in B, 1987, n. 1590-91).

1593 (*2783): For ther is a versifiour seith that "the ydel man excuseth hym in wynter by cause of the grete coold, and in somer by enchesoun of the greete heete."

Prov. 20:4 ? (Renaud, *LMP* 875-77; ibid.; S; R; DeLong, in B, 1987, n. 1593).

1609 (*2799): . . . usynge youre richesses in swich manere that men seye nat that youre richesses been yburyed . . .

Cp. *Matt. 25:14-30, Luke 19:12-27* (Renaud, *LMP* 892-94; ibid.; F; cp. Gower, *CA* 5.1929-31).

1617-18 (*2807-08): And therfore seith Seint Austyn that "the avaricious man is likned unto helle,/ that the moore it swelweth the moore desir it hath to swelwe and devoure."

Prov. 27:20 (Renaud, *LMP* 898-900; ibid., p. 603; S; R; F; DeLong, in B, 1987, n. 1617).

1626-27 (*2816-17): First, ye shul have God in youre herte,/ and for no richesse ye shullen do no thyng which may in any manere displese God, that is youre creatour and makere.

Cp. *Deut. 11:1; etc.*
Gen. 1:27; etc.

1628-29 (*2818-19): For after the word of Salomon, "It is bettre to have a litel good with the love of God,/ than to have muchel good and tresour, and lese the love of his Lord God."

§
Prov. 15:16 (Renaud, *LMP* 909-10; ibid.; S; R; P; F; DeLong, in B, 1987, n. 1628).

1630-31 (*2820-21): And the prophete seith that "bettre it is to been a good man and have litel good and tresour/ than to been holden a shrewe and have grete richesses."

§

Ps. 36(37):16 (Renaud, *LMP* 911-12; ibid.; S; R; P; F; DeLong, in B, 1987, n. 1630).

1634 (*2824): And th'Apostle seith that "ther nys thyng in this world of which we sholden have so greet joye as whan oure conscience bereth us good witnesse."

§

2 *Cor. 1:12* (Renaud, *LMP* 913-15; ibid., p. 604; S; R; P; F; DeLong, in B, 1987, n. 1634).

1635 (*2825): And the wise man seith, "The substance of a man is ful good, whan synne is nat in mannes conscience."

§

Ecclus. 13:30 (Renaud, *LMP* 915-17; ibid.; S; R; P; F; DeLong, in B, 1987, n. 1635).

1638 (*2828): For Salomon seith that "bettre it is and moore it availeth a man to have a good name than for to have grete richesses."

§

Prov. 22:1 (Renaud, *LMP* 920-21; ibid.; S; R; P; F; DeLong, in B, 1987, n. 1638).

1639-40 (*2829-30): And therfore he seith in another place, "Do greet diligence," seith Salomon, "in kepyng of thy freend and of thy goode name;/ for it shal lenger abide with thee than any tresour, be it never so precious."

§

Ecclus. 41:15 (Renaud, *LMP* 921-23; ibid.; R; F; DeLong, in B, 1987, n. 1639-40).

Prov. 25:10 ? (S).

1653 (*2843): And Salomon seith that "the gretter richesses that a man hath, the mo despendours he hath."
> 𝓰
> *Eccl. 5:10* (Renaud, *LMP* 940; ibid., p. 605; S; R; P; F; DeLong, in B, 1987, n. 1653).

1656-57 (*2846-47): For the victorie of batailles that been in this world lyth nat in greet nombre or multitude of the peple, ne in the vertu of man,/ but it lith in the wyl and in the hand of oure Lord God Almyghty.
> *1 Mach. 3:18-19* (Renaud, *LMP* 944-46; ibid.).

1658-63 (*2848-53): And therfore Judas Machabeus . . . seyde right in this wise:/ "Als lightly . . . may oure Lord God Almyghty yeve victorie to a fewe folk as to many folk,/ for the victorie of a bataile comth nat by the grete nombre of peple,/ but it cometh from oure Lord God of hevene."
> *1 Mach. 3:18-19* (Renaud, *LMP* 946-51; ibid.; S; R; P; F; DeLong, in B, 1987, n. 1661-63).

1664 (*2854): . . . for as muchel as ther is no man certein if he be worthy that God yeve hym victorie, [*ne plus que il est certain se il est digne de l'amour de Dieu*], or naught . . .
> *Eccl. 9:1* (Renaud, *LMP* 952-54; ibid.; S; R; P; F; DeLong, in B, 1987, n. 1664).

1664-67 (*2854-57): . . . after that Salomon seith,/ therfore every man sholde greetly drede werres to bigynne./ And by cause that in batailles fallen manye perils,/ and happeth outher while that as soone is the grete man slayn as the litel man.
> 𝓰
> *Eccl. 9:13-15* ? (Renaud, *LMP* 954-57; ibid.; cp. DeLong, in B, 1987, n. 1666).

1668-69 (*2858-59): . . . and as it is writen in the seconde Book of
Kynges, "The dedes of batailles been aventurouse and nothyng
certeyne,/ for as lightly is oon hurt with a spere as another."
§
  2 *Kings 11:25* (Renaud, *LMP* 957-59; ibid.; cp. Johnson, 1941,
    pp. 87-89; S; R; P; F; DeLong, in B, 1987, n. 1668).

1671 (*2861): For Salomon seith, "He that loveth peril shal
falle in peril."
§
Ecclus. 3:27 (Renaud, *LMP* 961-62; ibid., p. 606; S; R; P; F;
    DeLong, in B, 1987, n. 1671).

1676-77 (*2866-67): For Seint Jame seith in his Epistles that "by
concord and pees the smale richesses wexen grete,/ and by
debaat and discord the grete richesses fallen doun."
§
Cp. *James 3:16-18* ? (Seneca, *Epistles* 94.46; Renaud, *LMP*
    968-70; ibid.; S; R; P; F; DeLong, in B, 1987, n. 1676).

1679-80 (*2869-70): And therfore seyde oure Lord Jhesu Crist to
his apostles in this wise:/ "Wel happy and blessed been they
that loven and purchacen pees, for they been called children of
God."
Matt. 5:9 (Renaud, *LMP* 971-73; ibid.; S; R; P; F; DeLong, in
    B, 1987, n. 1680).

1692-93 (*2882-83): And the prophete seith, "Flee
shrewednesse and do goodnesse;/ seke pees and folwe it, as
muchel as in thee is."
§
Ps. 33(34):15(14) (Renaud, *LMP* 987-88; ibid.; S; R; P; F;
    DeLong, in B, 1987, n. 1692).

1696 (*2886): And Salomon seith, "He that hath over-hard an
herte, atte laste he shal myshappe and mystyde."
§

Prov. 28:14 (Renaud, *LMP* 991-92; ibid.; S; R; P; F; DeLong,
  in B, 1987, n. 1696).

1704-05 (*2894-95): For Salomon seith that "he that repreveth
hym that dooth folye,/ he shal fynde gretter grace than he
that deceyveth hym by sweete wordes."
  g
  Prov. 28:23 (Renaud, *LMP* 1000-02; ibid., p. 607; S; R; P; F;
    cp. DeLong, in B, 1987, n. 1704).

1707-08 (*2897-98): For Salomon seith, "He is moore worth that
repreveth or chideth a fool for his folye, shewynge hym
semblant of wratthe,/ than he that supporteth hym and
preyseth hym in his mysdoynge and laugheth at his folye."
  g
  Eccl. 7:6 (Renaud, *LMP* 1004-06; ibid.; S; R; P; F; DeLong, in
    B, 1987, n. 1707-08).

1709-10 (*2899-2900): And this same Salomon seith afterward
that "by the sorweful visage of a man" (that is to seyn by the
sory and hevy contenaunce of a man)/ "the fool correcteth and
amendeth hymself."
  g
  Eccl. 7:4 (Renaud, *LMP* 1006-07; ibid.; S; R; P; cp. DeLong, in
    B, 1987, n. 1707-08).

1719-20 (*2909-10): For Salomon seith, "Whan the condicioun of
man is plesaunt and likynge to God,/ he chaungeth the hertes
of the mannes adversaries and constreyneth hem to biseken
hym of pees and of grace."
  g
  Prov. 16:7 (Renaud, *LMP* 1016-18; ibid.; S; R; P; F; DeLong,
    in B, 1987, n. 1719).

1735 (*2925): " . . . ye han shewed unto us the blessynge of
swetnesse," after the sawe of David the prophete.

Ps. 20(21):4(3) (Renaud, *LMP* 1033-34; ibid., p. 608; S; R; P; F; DeLong, in B, 1987, n. 1735).

g

1739-40 (*2929-30): Now se we wel that the science and the konnynge of Salomon is ful trewe./ For he seith that "sweete wordes multiplien and encreescen freendes and maken shrewes to be debonaire and meeke."

g
Ecclus. 6:5 (Renaud, *LMP* 1037-39; ibid.; S; R; P; F; DeLong, in B, 1987, n. 1740).

1754-58 (*2944-48): For Salomon seith, "Leeveth me, and yeveth credence to that I shal seyn: I seye . . . ye peple, folk and governours of hooly chirche,/ to thy sone, to thy wyf, to thy freend, ne to thy broother,/ ne yeve thou nevere myght ne maistrie of thy body whil thou lyvest."/ Now sithen he deffendeth . . . by a strenger resoun he deffendeth and forbedeth a man to yeven hymself to his enemy.

g
Ecclus. 33:19-20 (Renaud, *LMP* 1054-58; ibid., p. 609; S; R; P; F; DeLong, in B, 1987, n. 1753-56).

1840 (*3030): For after the sawe of the word of the Apostle, "Coveitise is roote of alle harmes."

g
1 Tim. 6:10 (Renaud, *LMP* 1138-39; ibid., pp. 612-13; S; R; P; F; DeLong, in B, 1987, n. 1840).

1867-68 (*3057-58): Wherfore I pray yow, lat mercy been in youre herte,/ to th'effect and entente that God Almighty have mercy on yow in his laste juggement.
Cp. *James 2:13* (Renaud, *LMP* 1165-67; ibid., p. 614).

1869 (*3059): For Seint Jame seith in his Epistle: "Juggement withouten mercy shal be doon to hym that hath no mercy of another wight."

g
James 2:13 (Renaud, *LMP* 1167-68; ibid.; S; R; P; F; DeLong, in B, 1987, n. 1869).

1881-84 (*3071-74): Wherfore I receyve yow to my grace/ and foryeve yow outrely alle the offenses, injuries, and wronges that ye have doon agayn me and myne,/ to this effect and to this ende that God of his endelees mercy/ wole at the tyme of oure diynge foryeven us oure giltes that we han trespassed to hym in this wrecched world.
James 2:13 (Renaud, *LMP* 1175-79; ibid.).
Matt. 6:14-15, etc.

1885-87 (*3075-77): For doutelees, if we be sory and repentant of the synnes and giltes which we han trespassed in the sighte of oure Lord God,/ he is so free and so merciable/ that he wole foryeven us oure giltes . . .
Cp. *1 John 1:9* (Tatlock, 1907, p. 191, n. 2; La, 1924, 91; Severs, 1941[b], p. 614; R; DeLong, in B, 1987, n. 1884-88).

1888 (*3078): . . . and bryngen us to the blisse that nevere hath ende. Amen.
Eph. 3:21, Matt. 25:46, etc.

Melibee-Monk Link, VII (B^{2*}), lines 1889-1990 (*3079-3180):

1951-53 (*3141-43): Nat oonly thou, but every myghty man,/ Though he were shorn ful hye upon his pan,/ Sholde have a wyf; for al the world is lorn!
Judg. 13-16 ? (cp. Geoffrey de la Tour Landry, *Enseignements*, p. 175; Grennen, 1966).

The Monk's Tale, VII (B²*), lines 1991-2766 (*3181-3956):

1999-2006 (*3189-96): At Lucifer . . . wol I bigynne. . . . From heigh degree yet fel he for his synne/ Doun into helle, where he yet is inne./ O Lucifer, brightest of angels alle,/ Now artow Sathanas, that mayst nat twynne/ Out of miserie, in which that thou art falle.

> *Isa. 14:12-15* (S; R; P; Cavanaugh, in B, 1987, n. 1999).
> *Luke 10:18, Apoc. 12:7-9* ? (S).

2007-14 (*3197-3204): Loo Adam, in the feeld of Damyssene/ With Goddes owene fynger wroght was he . . . And welte al paradys savynge o tree. . . . til he for mysgovernaunce/ Was dryven out of hys hye prosperitee/ To labour, and to helle, and to meschaunce.

> *Gen. 1-3, esp. 1:29, 2:7, 2:16-17, 3:23-24* (cp. Boccaccio, *DCVI* 1.1; Root, in *S&A*, 1941, p. 625; cp. Guyart Desmoulins, *Bible Historiale;* Johnson, 1941, pp. 130-32; ————, 1951, 829; cp. Innocent III, *DMCH* 1.1; Köppel, 1890, 416-17; cp. Vincent of Beauvais, *Speculum Historiale;* Aiken, 1942; S; R; P; Cavanaugh, in B, 1987, nn. 2007, 2009).

2015-46 (*3205-36): Loo Sampsoun . . . . as *Judicum* can telle.

> *Judg. 13-16* (cp. Boccaccio, *DCVI* 1.17; Root, in *S&A*, 1941, pp. 625-28; cp. Guyart Desmoulins, *Bible Historiale;* Johnson, 1941, pp. 132-37; ————, 1951, 830-32; cp. Vincent of Beauvais, *Speculum Historiale;* Aiken, 1942; La, 1924, 89-91; cp. Nicholas of Lyre, *Postillae* ?; Wurtele, 1984, pp. 103-07; cp. Geoffrey de la Tour Landry, *Enseignements,* p. 175; Grennen, 1966; S; R; P; F; Cavanaugh, in B, 1987, n. 2015).

8

2015-17 (*3205-07): Loo Sampsoun, which that was annunciat/
By th' angel, longe er his nativitee,/ And was to God Almyghty
consecrat . . .
> *Judg. 13:3-5* (cp. Boccaccio, *DCVI* 1.17; Root, in *S&A*, 1941,
> p. 626; cp. Guyart Desmoulins, *Bible Historiale;* Johnson,
> 1941, pp. 132-33; R).

2019-20 (*3209-10): Was nevere swich another as was hee,/ To
speke of strengthe, and therwith hardynesse. . . .
> *Judg. 14-16*

2021 (*3211): But to his wyves toolde he his secree . . .
> *Judg. 14:17, 16:17* (cp. La, 1924, 92; cp. Boccaccio, *DCVI* 1.17;
> Root, in *S&A*, 1941, pp. 626-27; S).

2022 (*3212): . . . Thurgh which he slow hymself for
wrecchednesse.
> *Judg. 16:4-30*

2023-26 (*3213-16): Sampsoun, this noble almyghty
champioun,/ Withouten wepen save his handes tweye,/ He
slow and al torente the leoun,/ Toward his weddyng walkynge
by the weye.
> *Judg. 14:5-7* (cp. Boccaccio, *DCVI* 1.17; Root, in *S&A*, 1941,
> p. 626; cp. Guyart Desmoulins, *Bible Historiale;* Johnson,
> 1941, p. 133; ———, 1951, 831; F).

2027-30 (*3217-20): His false wyf koude hym so plese and
preye/ Til she his conseil knew; and she, untrewe,/ Unto his
foos his conseil gan biwreye,/ And hym forsook, and took
another newe.
> *Judg. 14:16-17, 20* (cp. Boccaccio, *DCVI* 1.17; Root, in *S&A*,
> 1941, pp. 626-27; cp. Guyart Desmoulins, *Bible Historiale;*
> Johnson, 1941, p. 133; ———, 1951, 831; F).

2031-36 (*3221-26): Thre hundred foxes took Sampsoun for ire,/
And alle hir tayles he togydre bond,/ And sette the foxes

tayles alle on fire,/ For he on every tayl had knyt a brond;/
And they brende alle the cornes in that lond,/ And alle hire
olyveres, and vynes eke.

> *Judg. 15:4-5* (cp. Boccaccio, *DCVI* 1.17; Root, in *S&A*, 1941,
> p. 627; cp. Guyart Desmoulins, *Bible Historiale;* Johnson,
> 1941, pp. 134-35; ———, 1951, 831-32; S; R).

2037-38 (*3227-28): A thousand men he slow eek with his
hond,/ And hadde no wepen but an asses cheke.

> *Judg. 15:15* (cp. La, 1924, 92-93; cp. Boccaccio, *DCVI* 1.17;
> Root, in *S&A*, 1941, p. 627; cp. Guyart Desmoulins, *Bible
> Historiale;* Johnson, 1941, p. 135; ———, 1951, 832).

2039-46 (*3229-36): Whan they were slayn, so thursted hym
that he/ Was wel ny lorn, for which he gan to preye . . . . And of
this asses cheke, that was dreye,/ Out of a wang-tooth sprang
anon a welle,/ Of which he drank ynogh, shortly to seye;/ Thus
heelp hym God, as *Judicum* can telle.

> *Judg. 15:18-19* (cp. Guyart Desmoulins, *Bible Historiale;*
> Johnson, 1941, pp. 135-36; ———, 1951, 832; S;
> Cavanaugh, in B, 1987, nn. 2044, 2046).
>
> *g* (F).

2047-51 (*3237-41): By verray force at Gazan on a nyght,/
Maugree Philistiens of that citee,/ The gates of the toun he
hath up plyght,/ And on his bak ycaryed hem hath hee/ Hye
on an hill whereas men myghte hem see.

> *Judg. 16:1, 3* (cp. Boccaccio, *DCVI* 1.17; Root, in *S&A*, 1941,
> p. 627; cp. Guyart Desmoulins, *Bible Historiale;* Johnson,
> 1941, p. 136; ———, 1951, 830; S; R; Cavanaugh, in B,
> 1987, n. 2047).

2053 (*3243): . . . Had thou nat toold to wommen thy secree . . .

> *Judg. 14:17, 16:17* (cp. Boccaccio, *DCVI* 1.17; Root, in *S&A*,
> 1941, p. 627; cp. Johnson, 1951, 830).

2055-57 (*3245-47): This Sampson nevere ciser drank ne wyn,/ Ne on his heed cam rasour noon ne sheere,/ By precept of the messager divyn . . .

> *Judg.* 13:5, 7, 14 (cp. Boccaccio, *DCVI* 1.17; Root, in *S&A*, 1941, p. 626; cp. Guyart Desmoulins, *Bible Historiale;* Johnson, 1941, p. 136; ———, 1951, 832; cp. *KtT* 2414-17; Hoffman, 1966-67, 173-75).
> *Num.* 6:2-5

2058 (*3248): . . . For alle his strengthes in his heeres weere.
> *Judg.* 16:17 (cp. Guyart Desmoulins, *Bible Historiale;* Johnson, 1941, p. 136; ———, 1951, 832).

2059-60 (*3249-50): And fully twenty wynter, yeer by yeere,/ He hadde of Israel the governaunce.
> *Judg.* 15:20

2062 (*3252): . . . For wommen shal hym bryngen to meschaunce!
> *Judg.* 14, 16 (cp. Boccaccio, *DCVI* 1.17; Root, in *S&A*, 1941, pp. 627-28).

2063-70 (*3253-60): Unto his lemman Dalida he tolde/ That in his heeris al his strengthe lay,/ And falsly to his foomen she hym solde. . . . She made to clippe or shere his heres away . . . They bounde hym faste and putten out his yen.
> *Judg.* 16:17-21 (cp. Boccaccio, *DCVI* 1.17; Root, in *S&A*, 1941, pp. 627-28; cp. Wyclif, *Middle English Bible* ?; Ramsay, 1882; R; cp. Cavanaugh, in B, 1987, n. 2063).

2071-72 (*3261-62): But er his heer were clipped or yshave,/ Ther was no boond with which men myghte him bynde.
> *Judg.* 16:6, 10, 13, 17 (cp. Boccaccio, *DCVI* 1.17; Root, in *S&A*, 1941, p. 628).

2073-74 (*3263-64): But now is he in prison in a cave,/ Where-as they made hym at the queerne grynde.

Judg. 16:21 (cp. Boccaccio, *DCVI* 1.17; Root, in *S&A*, 1941, p.
628; cp. Guyart Desmoulins, *Bible Historiale;* Johnson,
1941, p. 137; ———, 1951, 830-31; S).

2079-86 (*3269-76): The ende of this caytyf was . . ./ His foomen
made a feeste upon a day,/ And made hym as hire fool biforn
hem pleye;/ And this was in a temple of greet array./ But atte
laste he made a foul affray,/ For he two pilers shook and made
hem falle,/ And doun fil temple and al, and ther it lay—/ And
slow hymself, and eek his foomen alle.
    Judg. 16:23-30 (cp. Boccaccio, *DCVI* 1.17; Root, in *S&A*, 1941,
    p. 628; S).

2087-89 (*3277-79): This is to seyn, the prynces everichoon,/
And eek thre thousand bodyes, were ther slayn/ With fallynge
of the grete temple of stoon.
    Judg. 16:27, 30 (cp. Guyart Desmoulins, *Bible Historiale;*
    Johnson, 1941, pp. 137-38; cp. La, 1924, 92-93).

2091-94 (*3281-84): Beth war by this ensample oold and playn/
That no men telle hir conseil til hir wyves/ Of swich thyng as
they wolde han secree fayn,/ If that it touche hir lymes or hir
lyves.
    Cp. *Judg. 14:17, 16:17-21* (cp. Geoffrey de la Tour Landry,
    Enseignements, pp. 151-52; Grennen, 1966; Cavanaugh, in
    B, 1987, n. 2091-94).

2142a (*3332a) (headnote): *Nabugodonosor*
    Dan. 1-4 (Wyclif, *Middle English Bible* ?; Ramsay, 1882;
    cp. Dante, *Par.* 4.14 ?; P; Schless, 1984, p. 209).

2143-2238 (*3333-3428): The myghty trone, the precious tresor,/
The glorious ceptre, and roial magestee/ That hadde the kyng
Nabugodonosor/ With tonge unnethe may discryved bee. . . . . . .
. . . . His sone, which that highte Balthasar,/
That heeld the regne after his fader day . . . Fortune caste hym

doun . . . ./ And Darius occupieth his degree,/ Thogh he therto
hadde neither right ne lawe.

> *Dan. 1-5* (cp. Boccaccio, *DCVI* 2.15; Root, in *S&A*, 1941, p.
> 632; cp. La, 1924, 93; cp. Vincent of Beauvais, *Speculum*
> *Historiale;* Aiken, 1942; cp. Peter Comestor, *Historia*
> *Scholastica;* Guyart Desmoulins, *Bible Historiale;*
> Johnson, 1951, 832-35, 838-39; S; R; F; Cavanaugh, in B,
> 1987, n. 2143-2246; cp. Gower, *CA* 1.2785-3042).

2147-48 (*3337-38): He twyes wan Jerusalem the citee;/ The
vessel of the temple he with hym ladde.

> *4 Kings 24:11-16, 25:1-9* (cp. Guyart Desmoulins, *Bible*
> *Historiale;* Johnson, 1951, 834-35; R; Cavanaugh, in B,
> 1987, n. 2147).
> *2 Par. 36:6-20*
> *Dan. 1:2*

2149-50 (*3339-40): At Babiloigne was his sovereyn see,/ In
which his glorie and his delit he hadde.

> *Dan. 1:1-2*

2151-53 (*3341-43): The faireste children of the blood roial/ Of
Israel he leet do gelde anoon,/ And maked ech of hem to been
his thral.

> *Dan. 1:3-5* (cp. Guyart Desmoulins, *Bible Historiale;*
> Johnson, 1941, pp. 139-40; cp. Vincent of Beauvais,
> *Speculum Historiale* 2.121; Aiken, 1942; cp. Jospehus,
> *Jewish Antiquities;* Peter Comestor, *Historia*
> *Scholastica;* Johnson, 1951, 832-34; R; F; Cavanaugh, in B,
> 1987, n. 2152).

2154 (*3344): Amonges othere Daniel was oon . . .

> *Dan. 1:6*

2155 (*3345): . . . That was the wiseste child of everychon . . .

> *Dan. 1:17* (Cavanaugh, in B, 1987, n. 2155).

2156-58 (*3346-48): . . . For he the dremes of the kyng
expowned,/ Whereas in Chaldeye clerk ne was ther noon/ That
wiste to what fyn his dremes sowned.
> *Dan. 2, 5* (cp. Guyart Desmoulins, *Bible Historiale;* Johnson,
> 1941, p. 140; cp. Peter Comestor, *Historia Scholastica;*
> Vincent of Beauvais, *Speculum Historiale;* ———, 1951,
> 835-36).

2159-60 (*3349-50): This proude kyng leet maken a statue of
gold,/ Sixty cubites long and sevene in brede . . .
> *Dan. 3:1* (cp. Guyart Desmoulins, *Bible Historiale;* Johnson,
> 1941, pp. 140-41; ———, 1951, 836).

2161-64 (*3351-54): . . . To which ymage bothe yong and oold/
Comanded he to loute, and have in drede,/ Or in a fourneys, ful
of flambes rede,/ He shal be brent that wolde noght obeye.
> *Dan. 3:4-6* (cp. Guyart Desmoulins, *Bible Historiale;*
> Johnson, 1941, pp. 140-42; ———, 1951, 837).

2165-66 (*3355-56): But nevere wolde assente to that dede/
Daniel ne his yonge felawes tweye.
> Cp. *Dan. 3:18* (cp. Guyart Desmoulins, *Bible Historiale;*
> Johnson, 1941, pp. 140-42; ———, 1951, 836; R;
> Cavanaugh, in B, 1987, n. 2166; cp. Gower, *VC* 2.5.257-58).

2167 (*3357): This kyng of kynges . . .
> *Dan. 2:37*

2167-82 (*3357-72): . . . proud was and elaat. . . . But sodeynly he
loste his dignytee,/ And lyk a beest hym semed for to bee,/ And
eet hey as an oxe. . . . And lik an egles fetheres wax his heres;/
His nayles lyk a briddes clawes weere;/ Til God relessed hym a
certeyn yeres. . . . And til that tyme he leyd was on his beere/
He knew that God was ful of myght and grace.
> *Dan. 4:27-34* (cp. Guyart Desmoulins, *Bible Historiale;*
> Johnson, 1941, pp. 142-43; ———, 1951, 837; cp. Wyclif,
> *Middle English Bible* ?; Ramsay, 1882).

2183a (*3372a) (headnote): *Balthasar*
    Dan. 5 :1, etc.

2183-90 (*3373-80): His sone, which that highte Balthasar . . .
proud he was of herte and of array,/ And eek an ydolastre was
he ay./ His hye estaat assured hym in pryde;/ But Fortune
caste hym doun, and ther he lay,/ And sodeynly his regne gan
divide.
    Dan. 5:22-31 (cp. Peter Comestor, *Historia Scholastica;*
        Guyart Desmoulins, *Bible Historiale;* Johnson, 1941, pp.
        144-46; ———, 1951, 838-39; cp. Boccaccio, *DCVI* 2.19;
        Root, in *S&A,* 1941, p. 632; cp. Vincent of Beauvais,
        Speculum Historiale; Aiken, 1942; S; R).

2191-2204 (*3381-94): A feeste he made unto his lordes alle . . . .
And saugh an hand, armlees, that wroot ful faste,/ For feere of
which he quook and siked soore.
    Dan. 5:1-6

2205-06 (*3395-96): This hand that Balthasar so soore agaste/
Wroot *Mane, techel, phares,* and namoore.
    Dan. 5:24-25

2207-08 (*3397-98): In all that land magicien was noon/ That
koude expoune what this lettre mente . . .
    Dan. 5:8

2209-30 (*3399-3420): . . . But Daniel expowned it anoon,/ And
seyde, "Kyng, God to thy fader lente/ Glorie and honour, regne,
tresour, rente;/ And he was proud and nothyng God ne dradde,/
And therfore God greet wreche upon hym sente,/ And hym
birafte the regne that he hadde./ . . . Eek thou, that art his
sone, art proud also . . . And art rebel to God, and art his foo./
. . . Therfore to thee yshapen ful greet pyne ys.
    Dan. 5:17-23 (cp. La, 1924, 93).

2231-32 (*3421-22): This hand was sent from God that on the
wal/ Wroot *Mane, techel, phares,* truste me . . .
>   *Dan. 5:24-25*

2233 (*3423): . . . Thy regne is doon; thou weyest noght at al.
>   *Dan. 5:26-27* (Guyart Desmoulins, *Bible Historiale;*
>   Johnson, 1951, 838).

2234-35 (*3424-25): Dyvyded is thy regne, and it shal be/ To
Medes and to Perses yeven . . .
>   *Dan. 5:28*

2236-37 (*3426-27): And thilke same nyght this kyng was
slawe,/ And Darius occupieth his degree . . .
>   *Dan. 5:30-31* (cp. Peter Comestor, *Historia Scholastica;*
>   Guyart Desmoulins, *Bible Historiale;* Johnson, 1951, 837-
>   38).

2244-46 (*3434-36): For what man that hath freendes thurgh
Fortune,/ Mishap wol maken hem enemys, I gesse;/ This
proverbe is ful sooth and ful commune.
>   Cp. *Prov. 19:4; Ecclus. 6:8-10* (proverbial; Whi F667; cp. S;
>   R; cp. Cavanaugh, in B, 1987, n. 2244-45).

2550a (*3740a) (headnote): *De Oloferno*
>   *Jud. 2-13* (cp. Peter Comestor, *Historia Scholastica;* Guyart
>   Desmoulins, *Bible Historiale;* Johnson, 1941, pp. 147-48;
>   ———, 1951, 838-39; P; Cavanaugh, in B, 1987, n. 2550).

2551-57 (*3741-47): Was nevere capitayn under a kyng/ That
regnes mo putte in subjeccioun,/ Ne strenger was in feeld of alle
thyng,/ As in his tyme, ne gretter of renoun,/ Ne moore pompous
in heigh presumpcioun/ Than Oloferne, which Fortune ay
kiste/ So likerously, and ladde hym up and doun . . .
>   *Jud. 2-3* (S; R; F; Cavanaugh, in B, 1987, n. 2553).

2558 (*3748): . . . Til that his heed was of, er that he wiste.
    Jud. 13:10

2559-64 (*3749-54): Nat oonly that this world hadde hym in
awe/ For lesynge of richesse or libertee,/ But he made every
man reneyen his lawe./ "Nabugodonosor was god," seyde hee;/
"Noon oother god sholde adoured bee."/ Agayns his heeste no
wight dar trespace . . .
    Jud. 3:1-13 (R).

2565-66 (*3755-56): . . . Save in Bethulia, a strong citee,/ Where
Eliachim a preest was of that place.
    Jud. 4:5, 6:10, etc. (R; Cavanaugh, in B, 1987, nn. 2565, 2566).

2567-74 (*3757-64): But taak kep of the deth of Oloferne:/
Amydde his hoost he dronke lay a-nyght,/ Withinne his tente
. . . And . . . Judith . . . his heed of smoot . . . And with his heed
unto hir toun she wente.
    Jud. 13:1-12

2574a (*3764a) (headnote): *De Rege Antiocho illustri*
    2 *Mach.* 8-9 (cp. Peter Comestor, *Historia Scholastica*;
    Guyart Desmoulins, *Bible Historiale*; Johnson, 1941, pp.
    147-51; ———, 1951, 838-39; S).

2575-82 (*3765-72): What nedeth it of kyng Antiochus/ To telle
his hye roial magestee,/ His hye pride, his werkes venymus?
. . . Rede which that he was in Machabee . . . And in an hill
how wrecchedly he deyde.
    2 *Mach.* 9 (S; R; P; F; Cavanaugh, in B, 1987, n. 2575-2630).
    g

2583-87 (*3773-77): Fortune hym hadde enhaunced so in pride/
That verraily he wende he myghte attayne/ Unto the sterres
upon every syde,/ And in balance weyen ech montayne,/ And
alle the floodes of the see restrayne.

2 *Mach.* 9:8, 10 (cp. La, 1924, 93; cp. Guyart Desmoulins,
Bible Historiale; Johnson, 1951, 840-41).

2588-90 (*3778-80): And Goddes peple hadde he moost in hate;/
Hem wolde he sleen in torment and in payne,/ Wenynge that
God ne myghte his pride abate.
   2 *Mach.* 9:4

2591-92 (*3781-82): And for that Nichanore and Thymothee/
Of Jewes weren vanquysshed myghtily . . .
   2 *Mach.* 8:24, 30; 9:3; 10:32-37 (F; Cavanaugh, in B, 1987, n.
   2591).

2593-97 (*3783-87): . . . Unto the Jewes swich an hate hadde he/
That he bad greithen his chaar ful hastily,/ And swoor, and
seyde ful despitously/ Unto Jerusalem he wolde eftsoone/ To
wreken his ire on it ful cruelly.
   2 *Mach.* 9:4

2598-606 (*3788-96): But of his purpos he was let ful soone./ God
for his manace hym so soore smoot/ With invisible wounde, ay
incurable. . . . And certeinly the wreche was resonable,/ For
many a mannes guttes dide he peyne./ But from his purpos
cursed and dampnable,/ For al his smert, he wolde hym nat
restreyne . . .
   2 *Mach.* 9:5-6 (cp. La, 1924, 93; Johnson, 1951, 840).

2607-09 (*3797-99): . . . But bad anon apparaillen his hoost;/
And sodeynly, er he was of it war,/ God daunted al his pride
and al his boost.
   2 *Mach.* 9:7, 11

2610-14 (*3800-04): For he so soore fil out of his char/ That it
his limes and his skyn totar,/ So that he neyther myghte go ne
ryde,/ But in a chayer men aboute hym bar,/ Al forbrused,
bothe bak and syde.
   2 *Mach.* 9:7-8

2615-22 (*3805-12): The wreche of God hym smoot so cruelly/ That thurgh his body wikked wormes crepte,/ And therwithal he stank so horribly/ That noon of al his meynee that hym kepte,/ Wheither so he wook or ellis slepte,/ Ne myghte noght the stynk of hym endure./ In this meschief he wayled and eek wepte,/ And knew God lord of every creature.
    2 Mach. 9:9-13 (cp. La, 1924, 93; Johnson, 1951, 840).

2623-25 (*3813-15): To al his hoost and to hymself also/ Ful wlatsom was the stynk of his careyne;/ No man ne myghte hym bere to ne fro.
    2 Mach. 9:10, 12

2626-30 (*3816-20): And in this stynk and this horrible peyne,/ He starf ful wrecchedly in a monteyne./ Thus hath this robbour and this homycide,/ That many a man made to wepe and pleyne,/ Swich gerdoun as bilongeth unto pryde.
    2 Mach. 9:9-11, 28

2631-41 (*3821-31): The storie of Alisaundre is so commune. . . . For al this world for drede of hym hath quaked.
    Cp. *1 Mach. 1:3* (cp. Peter Comestor, *Historia Scholastica;* Guyart Desmoulins, *Bible Historiale;* Johnson, 1951, 838-39, 841; cp. Cavanaugh, in B, 1987, n. 2631).

2655 (*3845): Twelf yeer he regned, as seith Machabee.
    1 Mach. 1:8 (cp. Guyart Desmoulins, *Bible Historiale;* Johnson, 1941, pp. 151-53; S; R; F; Cavanaugh, in B, 1987, n. 2655).
    8

2656-57 (*3846-47): Philippes sone of Macidoyne he was,/ That first was kyng in Grece the contree.
    1 Mach. 1:1 (cp. Guyart Desmoulins, *Bible Historiale;* Johnson, 1951, 841).

The Nun's Priest's Prologue, VII (B²*), lines 2767-820 (*3957-4010):

2796 (*3986): By hevene kyng that for us alle dyde . . .
  Dan. 4:34, etc.
  Rom. 5:9, Col. 1:20, etc.

2800-02 (*3990-92): For certeinly, as that thise clerkes seyn,/ Whereas a man may have noon audience,/ Noght helpeth it to tellen his sentence.
  Ecclus. 32:6 (S; R; Cavanaugh, in B, 1987, n. 2801-02).

The Nun's Priest's Tale, VII (B²*), lines 2821-3446 (*4011-4636):

2847-48 (*4037-38): A yeerd she hadde, enclosed al aboute/ With stikkes, and a drye dych withoute. . . .
  Cant. 4:12 ? (Dahlberg, 1954, 285-86).

2849 (*4039): . . . a cok, hight Chauntecleer.
  Cp. *Matt. 26:34; etc.* ? (Donovan, 1953; cp. Dahlberg, 1954; cp. Allen, 1969; cp. *Le Roman de Renart;* Hulbert, in *S&A,* 1941, pp. 645-58; cp. Pearsall, ed., 1984, pp. 57-62).

2867 (*4057): . . . his sustres and his paramours . . .
  Cant. 4:9-12 ? (Dahlberg, 1954, 285-86).

2909 (*4099): . . . "for, by that God above . . . "
  Cp. *Deut. 4:39; etc.*

2917 (*4107): " . . . by that God above!"
  Cp. *Deut. 4:39; etc.*

2987-97 (*4177-87): . . . And happed so, they coomen in a toun/ Wher as ther was swich congregacioun/ Of peple, and eek so streit of herbergage,/ That they ne founde as muche as o cotage/

In which they bothe myghte ylogged bee./ Wherfore . . . . That
oon of hem was logged in a stalle . . . with oxen of the plough.
  Luke 2:7 (cp. Valerius Maximus, *Factorum et Dictorum
    Memorabilium* 1.7.10; Hulbert, in *S&A*, 1941, p. 662; cp.
    Pratt, 1977, 561).

3004 (*4194): . . . for in an oxes stalle . . .
  Luke 2:7 (Pratt, 1977, 561).

3015 (*4205): Bihoold my bloody woundes depe and wyde!
  Luke 24:39 ? (Pearsall, ed., 1984, n. 4205; cp. Pratt, 1977,
    552).
  Matt. 26:34 ? (Dahlberg, 1954, 286-87).

3127-29 (*4317-19): And forthermoore, I pray yow, looketh wel/
In the olde testament, of Daniel,/ If he heeld dremes any
vanitee.
  G
  Dan. 1:17; 2; 4; 7-9; 10 (R; P; Pratt, 1977, 559; F; cp.
    Cavanaugh, in B, 1987, n. 3128).

3130-32 (*4320-22): Reed eek of Joseph, and ther shul ye see/
Wher dremes be somtyme—I sey nat alle—/ Warnynge of
thynges that shul after falle.
  Gen. 37, 40, 41 (cp. Holkot, *SLS* 202; Petersen, 1898, p. 108;
    Pratt, 1977, 559; R; P; F; Cavanaugh, in B, 1987, n. 3130-
    35).

3133 (*4323): Looke of Egipte the kyng, daun Pharao . . .
  Gen. 41 (cp. Holkot, *SLS* 202 and cp. 132; Petersen, 1898, p.
    108; Pratt, 1977, 560; R; P; Cavanaugh, in B, 1987, n. 3130-
    35).

3134-35 (*4324-25): . . . His bakere and his butiller also,/ Wher
they ne felte noon effect in dremes.
  Gen. 40 (R; P; Cavanaugh, in B, 1987, n. 3130-35).

3163 (*4353): For al so siker as *In principio* . . .
> *John 1:1(-14)* (liturgy ? charm ?; Law, 1922; Bloomfield,
> 1955; S; M; R; P; F; see *GP* 254; Cavanaugh, in B, 1987, n.
> 3163).
> *Gen. 1:1* ? (R; Cavanaugh, in B, 1987, n. 3163).

3179-84 (*4369-74): He looketh as it were a grym leoun. . . . Thus
roial, as a prince is in his halle . . .
> Cp. *Prov. 30:29-32* (cp. Hugh of St. Cher, *Opera Omnia;*
> Allen, 1969, 28-29).

3187-88 (*4377-78): Whan that the month in which the world
bigan,/ That highte March, whan God first maked man . . .
> *Gen. 1* (P; Cavanaugh, in B, 1987, n. 3187).

3205 (*4395): For evere the latter ende of joye is wo.
> Cp. *Prov. 14:13; Ecclus. 11:27* (S; R; Cavanaugh, in B, 1987, n.
> 3205-06).

3206 (*4396): God woot that worldly joye is soone ago.
> *Ecclus. 11:27* (R; Cavanaugh, in B, 1987, n. 3205-06).

3215 (*4405): A col-fox, ful of sly iniquitee . . .
> *Luke 13:31-32, etc.* ? (Cp. Pearsall, ed., 1984, pp. 57-62; cp.
> Cavanaugh, in B, 1987, n. 3215).

3227 (*4417): O newe Scariot . . .
> *Matt. 26:14-16, 47-49; etc.* (La; R; P; F).

3257-59 (*4447-49): Wommannes conseil broghte us first to wo/
And made Adam fro Paradys to go,/ Ther as he was ful myrie
and wel at ese.
> *Gen. 3* (cp. Holkot, *SLS* 38; Petersen, 1898, p. 110).

3322-24 (*4512-14): This Chauntecleer his wynges gan to
bete . . . So was he ravysshed with his flaterie.

Cp. *1 Cor. 9:26-27* ? (Hugh of St. Cher, *Opera Omnia;* Allen, 1969, 32).

3329 (*4519): Redeth Ecclesiaste of flaterye.
g
Ecclus. 12:10-16, etc. ? (Holkot, *SLS* 131; Petersen, 1898, p. 111; S; R; P; F; cp. Cavanaugh, in B, 1987, n. 3329).
Prov. 27:6, 29:5 ? (R).

3341 (*4531): And on a Friday fil al this meschaunce . . .
Cp. *Gen. 1:26-31; John 19:25-30* ? (Adams and Levy, 1965-66;
———, 1967; P; F; Cavanaugh, in B, 1987, n. 3341).

3393 (*4583): . . . benedicitee!
Dan. 3:57, etc. (liturgy; R).

3438 (*4628): But ye that holden this tale a folye . . .
1 Tim. 1:4, 4:7; 2 Tim. 4:4 ? (R; Cavanaugh, in B, 1987, n. 3438).

3441-42 (*4631-32): For seint Paul seith that al that writen is,/ To oure doctrine it is ywrite . . .
g
Rom. 15:4 (*Ovide Moralisé*; Minnis, 1979; Robertson, 1962, pp. 272, 367, et passim; Peck, 1984, p. 143; R; cp. Pearsall, ed., 1984, n. 4631; P; F; Cavanaugh, in B, 1987, n. 3441).

3443 (*4633): . . . Taketh the fruyt, and lat the chaf be stille.
2 Cor. 3:6; Rom. 7:6 ? (cp. Augustine, *De Doctrina Christiana* 3.5; Robertson, 1962, pp. 272, 367, et passim; Miller, 1977, pp. 57, n. 3 and 76, n. 1; Peck, 1984, p. 145; cp. Pearsall, ed., 1984, n. 4633; R; Cavanaugh, in B, 1987, n. 3443).
Cp. *Matt. 3:12, Luke 3:17* ?

3444-45 (*4634-35): Now, goode God, if that it be thy wille,/ As seith my lord, so make us alle goode men . . .

Matt. 26:39, 42 ? (liturgy; R; cp. P; Cavanaugh, in B, 1987, n. 3445; cp. Pearsall, ed., 1984, nn. 4634, 4635).
1 Thess. 4:3 ? (Correale, 1980).

3446 (*4636): And brynge us to his heighe blisse! Amen.
Dan. 7:18, etc. (liturgy; as in lines 3444-45, above).

Nun's Priest Endlink, VII (B²*), lines 3447-62 (*4637-52):

3454 (*4644): . . . Ya, moo than seven tymes seventene.
Matt. 18:22 ?

The Second Nun's Prologue, VIII (G), lines 1-119:

29-77: And thow that flour of virgines art alle,/ Of whom that Bernard list so wel to write. . . . Thow Mayde and Mooder, doghter of thy Sone. . . . . Now help, for to my werk I wol me dresse.
  Cp. *Luke 1-2; etc.* (liturgy; Tupper, 1915, 9-11; Sister Madeleva, 1925, pp. 33-35; Dante, *Par.* 33.1-39; cp. Gerould, in *S&A*, 1941, pp. 664-65; R; P; F; cp. Ridley, in B, 1987, nn. 29-77, 29-30).

56: . . . Thou goost biforn and art hir lyves leche.
  Cp. *Ps. 146(147):3; Matt. 9:12, Mark 2:17, Luke 5:31; etc.* (liturgy; Tupper, 1915, 9-11; Sister Madeleva, 1925, pp. 33-35; Dante, *Par.* 33.16-18; Gerould, in *S&A*, 1941, p. 664; Ridley, in B, 1987, n. 53-56).

58: . . . in this desert of galle.
  Exod. 15:23; Ruth 1:20; etc. (S; R; Ridley, in B, 1987, n. 58).

59-61: Thynk on the womman Cananee, that sayde/ That whelpes eten somme of the crommes alle/ That from hir lordes table been yfalle.

Matt. 15:22-28 (La, 1924, 100; S; R; P; F; Ridley, in B, 1987, n. 59).

62: . . . unworthy sone of Eve . . .
  Cp. *Rom. 8:13-17; etc.* (liturgy; Gardner, 1947; Gerould, in *S&A*, 1941, pp. 665-66; R; P; F; Ridley, in B, 1987, n. 62).

64: And, for that feith is deed withouten werkis . . .
  James 2:17, 20 (S; R; Ridley, in B, 1987, n. 64).

67: O thou, that art so fair and ful of grace . . .
  Luke 1:28 (S; R).

68: . . . Be myn advocat in that heighe place . . .
  1 John 2:1 (Jerome, *EAJ*; La).

69-70: . . . Theras withouten ende is songe "Osanne,"/ Thow Cristes mooder, doghter deere of Anne!
  Cp. *Luke 2:13-14* (liturgy; cp. Jacobus de Voragine, *Legenda Aurea*, p. 50; cp. Dante, *Par.* 32.133-35; Schless, 1984, p. 181; S; R; Ridley, in B, 1987, nn. 69-70, 70).
  Cp. *Matt. 21:9, 15; Mark 11:9; John 12:13; etc.* (cp. Dante, *Par.* 32.133-35; Gerould, in *S&A*, 1941, p. 665; Schless, 1984, p. 181; S; R).

72-74: . . . troubled . . . by the contagioun/ Of my body, and also by the wighte/ Of erthely lust and fals affeccioun. . . .
  Cp. *Rom. 7:24* (cp. Macrobius, *Commentaria in Somnium Scipionis* 1.8.8-9, etc.; Gerould, in *S&A*, 1941, pp. 666-67; cp. Ridley, in B, 1987, n. 71-74).

75-76: O havene of refut, O salvacioun/ Of hem that been in sorwe and in distresse . . .
  Ps. 45(46):2(1); etc. (liturgy; R; cp. Ridley, in B, 1987, n. 75).

96-98: . . . Of "hevene" and "Lia"; and heere, in figurynge,/ The "hevene" is set for thoght of hoolynesse,/ And "Lia" for hir lastynge bisynesse.
>   Cp. *Gen. 29:32-35; 30:16-21* ? (cp. Jacobus de Voragine, *Legenda Aurea*, p. 689; cp. S; R; P; F; Ridley, in B, 1987, n. 96-98).

118: . . . And brennynge evere in charite ful brighte.
>   *1 Cor. 13:3* ? (Kolve, 1981; cp. Ridley, in B, 1987, nn. 114, 118).

The Second Nun's Tale, VIII (G), lines 120-553:

122-23: . . . And from hir cradel up fostred in the feith/ Of Crist, and bar his gospel in hir mynde.
>   G (Jacobus de Voragine, *Legenda Aurea*; Gerould, in *S&A*, 1941, p. 671).

125: . . . and God to love and drede . . .
>   *Deut. 6:2, 5; etc.*

135-37: To God allone in herte thus sang she:/ "O Lord, my soule and eek my body gye/ Unwemmed, lest that it confounded be."
>   *Ps. 34(35):4, 10; 39(40):15(14); Thess. 5:23; etc.* (Jacobus de Voragine, *Legenda Aurea*; Gerould, in *S&A*, 1941, pp. 671-72; cp. Ridley, in B, 1987, nn. 134-38, 134-35).

138: And, for his love that dyde upon a tree . . .
>   *Rom. 5:8-9, Col. 1:20, etc.*

139-40: . . . Every seconde and thridde day she faste,/ Ay biddynge in hire orisons ful faste.
>   *Luke 18:1, 2 Cor. 6:5; etc.* (cp. Ridley, in B, 1987, n. 139).

152-55: I have an aungel which that loveth me,/ That with greet love, wher so I wake or sleepe,/ Is redy ay my body for to kepe.

Ps. 90(91):11, Matt. 4:6, Luke 4:10 ? (J; R; cp. Sister
Madeleva, 1925, pp. 40-41; Jacobus de Voragine, *Legenda
Aurea;* Gerould, in *S&A*, 1941, p. 672; cp. Ridley, in B,
1987, n. 152).

201-16: An oold man, clad in white clothes cleere,/ That hadde
a book with lettre of gold in honde . . . . And on his book right
thus he gan to rede:/ "O Lord, o feith, o God, withouten mo,/ O
Cristendom, and Fader of alle also,/ Aboven alle and over alle
everywhere."/ Thise wordes al with gold ywriten were. . . .
Tho vanysshed this olde man . . .
   G (Jacobus de Voragine, *Legenda Aurea;* Gerould, in *S&A*,
      1941, pp. 672-73; F).
   Eph. 4:5-6 (Jacobus de Voragine, *Legenda Aurea;* Gerould, in
      S&A, 1941, pp. 672-73; Peck, 1984, p. 169; S; R; P; F;
      Ridley, in B, 1987, nn. 201, 207-09, 208).

212: . . . Sey ye or nay.
   Matt. 5:37; etc. ? (cp. Jacobus de Voragine, *Legenda Aurea;*
      Gerould, in *S&A,* 1941, p. 672).

221: . . . Corones two . . .
   Cp. *Prov. 4:9, 1 Cor. 9:25, 2 Tim. 4:8; etc.* ? (Ridley, in B,
      1987, n. 221; cp. *TC* 2.1733-36).

239-41: The angel seyde, "God liketh thy requeste,/ And bothe
with the palm of martirdom/ Ye shullen come unto his blisful
feste."
   Cp. *Apoc. 3:20, 19:9; etc.* (Jacobus de Voragine, *Legenda
      Aurea;* Gerould, in *S&A*, 1941, p. 673; Delasanta, 1978;
      Ridley, in B, 1987, n. 240).

246-47: . . . I wondre, this tyme of the yeer,/ Whennes that soote
savour cometh so. . . .
   Cp. *2 Cor. 2:14-16* ? (Jacobus de Voragine, *Legenda Aurea;*
      Gerould, in *S&A,* 1941, p. 673; Peck, 1984, p. 169).

383: Now, Cristes owene knyghtes leeve and deere . . .
   2 Tim. 2:3-4 (Jacobus de Voragine, *Legenda Aurea;* Gerould, in *S&A*, 1941, p. 675).

384-85: . . . Cast alle awey the werkes of derknesse,/ And armeth yow in armure of brightnesse.
   Rom. 13:12 (Jacobus de Voragine, *Legenda Aurea;* Gerould, in *S&A*, 1941, p. 675; S; Ridley, in B, 1987, n. 384-85).

386-90: Ye han for sothe ydoon a greet bataille,/ Youre cours is doon, youre feith han ye conserved./ Gooth to the corone of lif that may nat faille;/ The rightful Juge, which that ye han served,/ Shal yeve it yow, as ye han it deserved.
   2 Tim. 4:7-8 (S; R; P; F; cp. Jacobus de Voragine, *Legenda Aurea;* Gerould, in *S&A*, 1941, p. 675; Ridley, in B, 1987, n. 386-88).

417-18: . . . Crist, Goddes Sone, withouten difference,/ Is verray God. . .
   Phil. 2:5-6; etc.

420: . . . This with o voys we trowen, thogh we sterve!
   Cp. *Job 13:15* (R; cp. Jacobus de Voragine, *Legenda Aurea;* Gerould, in *S&A*, 1941, p. 676; cp. *Passio;* Gerould, in *S&A*, 1941, p. 682).

421-512: Almachius . . . Bad fecchen Cecile . . . . Thise wordes and swiche othere seyde she. . . .
   John 18:33-38, 19:9-11 ? (Ridley, in B, 1987, n. 421-512).

434: . . . Of conscience and of good feith unfeyned.
   Cp. *1 Tim. 1:5* (La; Jacobus de Voragine, *Legenda Aurea;* Gerould, in *S&A*, 1941, p. 676; cp. *Passio;* Gerould, in *S&A*, 1941, p. 682).

437: "Youre myght," quod she, "ful litel is to drede . . . "
   Cp. *Prov. 31:17* ? (Ridley, in B, 1987, n. 437).

Second Nun-Canon's Yeoman Link, VIII (G), lines 554-719:

628: . . . *"Benedicitee! . . . "*
  Dan. 3:57; etc. (liturgy).

665: "Peter! . . . "
  Matt. 4:18; etc. (F).

The Canon's Yeoman's Tale, VIII (G), lines 720-1481:

857-58: . . . To tellen al wolde passen any bible/ That owher
is. . . .
  G

916-18: Though that the feend noght in oure sighte hym
shewe,/ I trowe he with us be, that ilke shrewe!/ In helle,
where that he is lord and sire. . . .
  Cp. *2 John 7; 2 Thess. 2; etc.* ? (Rosenberg, 1962, 575-78;
    Reidy, in B, 1987, n. 916-19).

960-61: And whan we been togidres everichoon,/ Every man
semeth a Salomon.
  Cp. *3 Kings 3:12; etc.* (cp. Spargo, in *S&A*, 1941, p. 697).

1001-05: . . . ye woot wel how/ That among Cristes apostelles
twelve/ Ther nas no traytour but Judas hymselve./ Thanne why
sholde al the remenant have a blame/ That giltlees were?
  Cp. *Matt. 10:4, etc.* (Ames, 1984, pp. 59-60).

1007: If any Judas in youre covent be . . .
  Cp. *Matt. 10:4; etc.*

1089: Sir hoost, in feith, and by the hevenes queene . . .
  Cp. *Jer. 44:17, 25* (liturgy).

1447: . . . the secree of secretes . . .
> Cp. *Cant., Eccl. 1:2; etc.* (pseudo-Aristotle, *Secreta
> Secretorum;* R; F; cp. Reidy, in B, 1987, n. 1441-47).

1476-78: For whoso maketh God his adversarie,/ As for to
werken any thyng in contrarie/ Of his wil, certes, never shal he
thryve. . . .
> *2 Par. 24:20* ? (La; cp. Spargo, in *S&A,* 1941, p. 698).

The Manciple's Prologue, IX (H), lines 1-104:

37-38: Hoold cloos thy mouth, man, by thy fader kyn!/ The
devel of helle sette his foot therin!
> *Isa. 5:11, 14; Job 41:5-22; 1 Cor. 15:52* ? (Gospel of Nicodemus;
> vernacular biblical drama; Pearcy, 1973-74, 168, n. 3, 169-
> 70; cp. Scattergood, in B, 1987, n. 38).
> *Apoc. 20:2-3; etc.*

60: . . . moysty ale . . .
> *Acts 2:13* ? (Jerome, *EAJ* 1.47; Baker, 1984, p. 90, n. 60; cp.
> Scattergood, in B, 1987, n. 60).

96-98: . . . good drynke . . ./ wol turne rancour and disese/ T'acord
and love . . .
> *Ps. 103(104):15; etc.* (cp. Cowgill, 1985, 176-77; cp.
> Scattergood, in B, 1987, n. 97-99).

99: O thou Bacus, yblessed be thy name . . .
> Cp. *Job 1:21; etc.* (cp. Cowgill, 1985, 176-77).

101: Worshipe and thank be to thy deitee!
> Cp. *Apoc. 7:12, etc.* (cp. Cowgill, 1985, 176-77).

The Manciple's Tale, IX (H), lines 105-362:

273: Allas, that I was wroght!
> Cp. *Job 3:3, Jer. 20:14*

314-15: Daun Salomon, as wise clerkes seyn,/ Techeth a man to kepen his tonge weel.

    8

    Prov. 21:23; Ps. 33(34):14(13) (S; R; F; Scattergood, in B, 1987, n. 314).

318: My sone . . .

    Cp. *Prov. 2:1; 3:1; 5:1; 6:1, 20; 7:1; and esp. 23:15, 19, 26, etc.* (R; cp. Gower, *CA* 768, etc.; Work, in *S&A,* 1941, pp. 709-11; Scattergood, in B, 1987, n. 318).

319: As in line 318, above.

319-24: My sone, keep wel thy tonge . . . . For man sholde hym avyse what he speeke.

    Cp. *James 3:3-10* (Delany, 1982-83; cp. Gower, *CA* 768, etc.; Work, in *S&A,* 1941, pp. 709-11; cp. Scattergood, in B, 1987, nn. 319, 320, 322-24; proverbial; cp. Whi T373, etc.).

321: As in line 318, above.

322: As in line 318, above.

325: As in line 318, above.

329: As in line 318, above.

329-34: My sone, thy tonge sholdestow restreyne. . . . Thus lerne children whan that they been yonge.

    Cp. *James 3:3-10* (Delany, 1982-83; cp. Gower, *CA* 768, etc.; Work, in *S&A,* 1941, pp. 709-11; cp. Scattergood, in B, 1987, n. 329-31; proverbial; cp. Whi T373, etc.).

335: As in line 318, above.

335-38: . . . of muchel spekyng yvele avysed,/ Ther lasse spekyng hadde ynough suffised,/ Comth muchel harm; thus

was me toold and taught./ In muchel speche synne wanteth
naught.

> *Prov. 10:19* (Albertano of Brescia, *De Arte Loquendi et
> Tacendi* 115; Baker, 1984, p. 124, n. 335-38; S; R;
> proverbial; Whi S608; Scattergood, in B, 1987, n. 338; cp.
> Delany, 1982-83).

339-42: Wostow wherof a rakel tonge serveth?/ Right as a
swerd forkutteth and forkerveth/ An arm a-two, my deere sone,
right so/ A tonge kutteth freendshipe al a-two.

> Cp. *Ps. 11(12):4(3), 51(52):4(2), 56(57):5(4), 63(64):4-9(3-8);
> etc.* (S; R; proverbial; Whi T385, 388; cp. Scattergood, in
> B, 1987, nn. 340-42, 344-45).
> Cp. *James 3:3-10* (Delany, 1982-83).

343-44: A jangler is to God abhomynable./ Reed Salomon, so wys
and honurable. . . .

> *Prov. 6:16-17* ? (S; R; cp. Scattergood, in B, 1987, nn. 343, 344-
> 45).
> *g*

345: Reed David in his psalmes . . .

> *g* (cp. Scattergood, in B, 1987, n. 344-45).

346: As in line 318, above.

351: As in line 318, above.

355-60: Thyng that is seyd is seyd. . . . be war, and be noon
auctour newe/ Of tidynges, wheither they been false or trewe.

> Cp. *James 3:3-10* (Delany, 1982-83; cp. Scattergood, in B,
> 1987, nn. 355-56, 357-58, 359-60).

359: As in line 318, above.

The Parson's Prologue, X (I), lines 1-74:

11: . . . I meene Libra--alwey gan ascende. . .
    Cp. *Dan. 5:27* ? (Delasanta, 1970, 303-07).

31-34: . . . Thou getest fable noon ytoold for me,/ For Paul, that
writeth unto Thymothee,/ Repreveth hem that weyven
soothfastnesse/ And tellen fables and swich wrecchednesse.
    g
    2 Tim. 4:4, 1 Tim 1:4, 4:7 (Patterson, 1978, 370-72; Delasanta,
        1978, 245; Wood, 1984, p. 36; Peck, 1984, p. 143; C. V.
        Kaske, 1975, p. 165; R; F; Wenzel, in B, 1987, n. 32-34).
    John 16:25 ? (Delasanta, 1978, 245).

35-36: Why sholde I sowen draf out of my fest,/ Whan I may
sowen whete, if that me lest?
    Matt. 3:12, Luke 3:17 ? (Lawler, 1980, pp. 162-63; Wenzel, in
      B, 1987, n. 35-36).

48-50: And Jhesu, for his grace, wit me sende/ To shewe yow the
wey, in this viage,/ Of thilke parfit glorious pilgrymage . . .
    Heb. 11:13-16, 1 Pet. 2:11; etc. (cp. Patterson, 1978, 370-72).

51: . . . That highte Jerusalem celestial.
    Apoc. 21:2 (cp. Miller, 1977, pp. 475-98; cp. Lawler, 1980,
      pp. 162-63; R; P; F; Wenzel, in B, 1987, n. 51).

61-66: Upon this word we han assented soone,/ . . . . And bade
oure Hoost he sholde to hym seye/ That alle we to telle his
tale hym preye.
    Cp. *Heb. 13* ? (Peck, 1984, pp. 150-51).

70-71: But hasteth yow; the sonne wole adoun;/ Beth fructuous,
and that in litel space. . . .
    John 12:35-36 ? (Delasanta, 1978, 244).

The Parson's Tale, X (I), lines 75-1092:

Headnote: *Jer. 6 . State super vias . . . animabus vestris, etc.*
  Jer. 6:16 (Baldwin, 1955, pp. 95-105; R; P; F; Wenzel, in B,
  1987, n. *State super vias*).

75: Oure sweete Lord God of hevene, that no man wole perisse
but wole that we comen alle to the knoweleche of hym and to
the blisful lif that is perdurable . . .
  Cp. *2 Pet. 3:9, 1 Tim. 2:4; Ezech. 18:23, 32; 33:11* (R; P;
    Wenzel, in B, 1987, n. 75).

76-78: . . . amonesteth us by the prophete Jeremie, that seith in
thys wyse:/ "Stondeth upon the weyes . . . and ye shal fynde
refresshynge for youre soules, etc."
  8
  Jer. 6:16 (cp. Holkot, *SLS* 62; Petersen, 1901, p. 4, n. 2; cp.
    Johnson, 1941, p. 120; Wood, 1970, pp. 289-90; ———, 1984,
    p. 36; Allen, 1973; ——— and Moritz, 1981, p. 227).
  Cp. *John 14:6* (Wood, 1970, pp. 290-91).

115: For which Crist seith in his gospel: "Dooth digne fruyt of
Penitence"; for by this fruyt may men knowe this tree . . .
  G (Patterson, 1978, 351).
  Cp. *Matt. 3:8* (cp. Petersen, 1901, p. 9, n. 2; cp. Johnson, 1941,
    pp. 115-16; R; P; F; Wenzel, in B, 1987, n. 115).
  Matt. 12:33

116: And therfore oure Lord Jhesu Crist seith thus: "By the fruyt
of hem shul ye knowen hem."
  G
  Matt. 7:20 (R; P; F; Wenzel, in B, 1987, n. 116).

117: . . . a seed of grace, the which seed is mooder of
sikernesse . . .
  Cp. *1 Pet. 1:23; etc.*

118: ... thurgh remembrance of the day of doom and on the peynes of helle.
Cp. *Matt. 10:28, Apoc. 14:10-13, etc.*

119: Of this matere seith Salomon that in the drede of God man forleteth his synne.
g
Prov. 16:6 (R; P; F; Wenzel, in B, 1987, n. 119).

120: ... the desiryng of the joye perdurable.
Cp. *Titus 1:2; etc.*

121: This heete draweth the herte of a man to God and dooth hym haten his synne.
Cp. *Ps. 44(45):8(7), Heb 1:9; etc.*

124: ... and desireth the lif perdurable. ...
Cp. *Titus 1:2; etc.* (cp. Lawler, 1980, pp. 162-63).

125: ... for which David the prophete seith: "I have loved thy lawe, and hated wikkednesse and hate"; he that loveth God kepeth his lawe and his word.
g
Ps. 118(119):113 (R; P; F; Wenzel, in B, 1987, n. 125).
John 14:15

126: This tree saugh the prophete Daniel in spirit, upon the avysioun of the kyng Nabugodonosor, whan he conseiled hym to do penitence.
g
Dan. 4:7-24 (R; P; F; Wenzel, in B, 1987, n. 126).

127: Penaunce is the tree of lyf to hem that it receyven, and he that holdeth hym in verray penitence is blessed, after the sentence of Salomon.
g

Prov. 3:18
Prov. 28:13 (R; P; F; Wenzel, in B, 1987, n. 127).

132: . . . for he hath wrathed and agilt hym that boghte hym, that with his precious blood hath delivered us fro the bondes of synne, and fro the crueltee of the devel, and fro the peynes of helle.
    Cp. *1 Cor. 6:20, Rom. 5:9, Col. 1:20, etc.* (Pennaforte, *SCP;* Petersen, 1901, p. 10; Dempster, in *S&A,* 1941, p. 733; Correale, 1981; S; Wenzel, in B, 1987, n. 130-32).
    Cp. *1 Pet. 5:8*
    Cp. *Matt. 10:28, Apoc. 14:10-13, etc.*

134: . . . For Job seith, "Synful men doon werkes worthy of confusioun."
    g
    Cp. *Prov. 12:4* (Pennaforte, *SCP;* Dempster, in *S&A,* 1941, p. 733; cp. Petersen, 1901, pp. 10-11; cp. Johnson, 1941, p. 114; R; P; F; Wenzel, in B, 1987, n. 134).

135: And therfore seith Ezechie, "I wol remembre me alle the yeres of my lyf in bitternesse of myn herte."
    g
    Isa. 38:15 (Pennaforte, *SCP;* Petersen, 1901, pp. 10, 19; Dempster, in *S&A,* 1941, p. 733; cp. Johnson, 1941, p. 111; R; P; F; Wenzel, in B, 1987, n. 135).

136: And God seith in the Apocalipse, "Remembreth yow fro whennes that ye been falle" . . .
    g
    Apoc. 2:5 (R; F; Wenzel, in B, 1987, n. 136).

138: . . . for ye trespassen so ofte tyme as dooth the hound that retourneth to eten his spewyng.
    2 Pet. 2:22 (R; P; F; cp. Wenzel, in B, 1987, n. 138).

140-41: . . . as God seith by the prophete Ezechiel,/ "Ye shal remembre yow of youre weyes, and they shuln displese yow." Soothly synnes been the weyes that leden folk to helle.

g
Ezech. 20:43; cp. Jer. 2:36 (Pennaforte, *SCP*; Petersen, 1901, p. 11; R; P; F; Wenzel, in B, 1987, n. 141).
Cp. *Isa. 59:7, Rom. 3:16; etc.*

142: . . . as seith Seint Peter, "whoso that dooth synne is thral of synne"; and synne put a man in greet thraldom.

g
Cp. *2 Pet. 2:19* (Pennaforte, *SCP*; Petersen, 1901, p. 11; Dempster, in *S&A*, 1941, p. 733; R; P; Patterson, 1978, 362).
John 8:34 (Pennaforte, *SCP*; Petersen, 1901, p. 11; R; cp. Johnson, 1941, pp. 113-14; F; Wenzel, in B, 1987, n. 142).

143: And therfore seith the prophete Ezechiel: "I wente sorweful in desdayn of myself."

g
Ezech. 20:43 (cp. Pennaforte, *SCP*; Petersen, 1901, p. 11; cp. Wenzel, in B, 1987, n. 143).
Job 42:6 ? (R; F).

149: . . . sith that thurgh synne ther he was free now is he maked bonde.
Cp. *John 8:34*

155-57: . . . remembreth yow of the proverbe of Salomon. He seith,/ "Likneth a fair womman that is a fool of hire body lyk to a ryng of gold that were in the groyn of a soughe."/ For right as a soughe wroteth in everich ordure, so wroteth she hire beautee in the stynkynge ordure of synne.

g
Prov. 11:22 (R; cp. Johnson, 1941, pp. 121-22; P; F; Wenzel, in B, 1987, n. 155-57).

158: . . . drede of the day of doom and of the horrible peynes of helle.

>   Cp. *Matt. 5:22; etc.* (Pennaforte, *SCP;* Petersen, 1901, p. 12).

159: For as Seint Jerome seith, "At every tyme that me remembreth of the day of doom I quake. . . . "

>   Cp. *Apoc. 14:7; etc.*
>   *Os. 7* ? (Pennaforte, *SCP;* Petersen, 1901, p. 12; pseudo-Jerome, *Regula Monachorum;* S; R; cp. Wenzel, in B, 1987, n. 159-60).

160-61: " . . . evere semeth me that the trompe sowneth in myn ere:/ 'Riseth up, ye that been dede, and cometh to the juggement.'"

>   Cp. *Apoc. 1:10, 20:12; etc.* (Pennaforte, *SCP;* Petersen, 1901, p. 12; Wenzel, in B, 1987, n. 159-60).

162-63: . . . "ther as we shullen been alle," as Seint Poul seith, "biforn the seete of oure Lord Jhesu Crist";/ whereas he shal make a general congregacioun, whereas no man may been absent.

>   *g*
>   *Rom. 14:10-12* (cp. Peraldus, *SVV* 1.4 [*De Donis*], 4.4; Petersen, 1901, p. 12, n. 3; R; P; F; Wenzel, in B, 1987, n. 162).

166: And, as seith Seint Bernard, "Ther ne shal no pledynge availle, ne no sleighte; we shullen yeven rekenynge of everich ydel word."

>   Cp. *Matt. 12:36* (pseudo-Bernard, *Sermo ad Prelatos in Concilio* 5; Wenzel, in B, 1987, n. 166; cp. Innocent III, *DMCH* 3.17; Köppel, 1890, 417; cp. Peraldus, ibid.; Petersen, 1901, p. 12, n. 4).

168: And therfore seith Salomon, "The wratthe of God ne wol nat spare no wight, for preyere ne for yifte" . . .

>   *g*

Cp. *Prov. 6:34-35* (cp. Peraldus, ibid.; Petersen, 1901, p. 12, n. 5; R; cp. Johnson, 1941, pp. 109-110; Wenzel, in B, 1987, n. 168).
Cp. *Prov. 1:28* ? (P; F).

169-73: Wherfore, as seith Seint Anselm, "Ful greet angwyssh shul the synful folk have at that tyme. . . . Whider shal thanne the wrecched synful man flee to hiden hym? Certes, he may nat hyden hym; he moste come forth and shewen hym."
    Cp. *Apoc. 6:9-17; etc.* (Anselm, *Meditatio* 1; Wenzel, in B, 1987, n. 169-73; R; cp. Peraldus, ibid.; Petersen, 1901, p. 12 and p. 13, n. 1).

174: For certes, as seith Seint Jerome, "the erthe shal casten hym out of hym, and the see also, and the eyr also, that shal be ful of thonder-clappes and lightnynges."
    Cp. *Ps. 96(97):3-4* (R; F; cp. Wenzel, in B, 1987, n. 174).

176-78: And therfore seith Job to God: "Suffre, Lord, that I may a while biwaille and wepe, er I go withoute returnyng to the derke lond, covered with the derknesse of deeth,/ to the lond of mysese and of derknesse, whereas is the shadwe of deeth whereas ther is noon ordre or ordinaunce, but grisly drede that evere shal laste."/ Loo, heere may ye seen that Job preyde respit a while to biwepe and waille his trespas. . . .
    8
    Job 10:20-22 (cp. Gregory, *Moralia* 9.63-66; Peraldus, ibid., *De Penis Infernis;* Petersen, 1901, p. 13, n. 2; cp. Innocent III, *DMCH* 3.8; Köppel, 1890, 417; Wyclif, *Middle English Bible* ?; Ramsay, 1882; cp. Johnson, 1941, p. 119; R; P; F; Wenzel, in B, 1987, n. 175-230; Patterson, 1978, 355).

181-86: The cause why that Job clepeth helle the "lond of derknesse":/ understondeth that he clepeth it "lond" or erthe, for it is stable. . . . "derk" . . . For certes, the derke light that shal come out of the fyr that evere shal brenne shal turne hym al to peyne that is in helle, for it sheweth him to the horrible

develes that hym tormenten. . . . "Lond of misese," by cause that
ther been three maneres of defautes, agayn three thynges that
folk of this world han in this present lyf . . .
g
Job 10:21-22 (cp. Gregory, *Moralia* 9.63-66; Petersen, 1901, p.
    13, n. 2; cp. Innocent III, *DMCH* 3.4; Köppel, 1890, 417-18).

186: . . . that is to seyn, honours, delices, and richesses.
    Cp. *1 John 2:16*

189: For which God seith by the prophete Jeremye, "Thilke
folk that me despisen shul been in despit."
g
1 Kings 2:30 (cp. Johnson, 1941, p. 122; R; P; F; Wenzel, in B,
    1987, n. 189).

191: And God seith, "The horrible develes shulle goon and
comen upon the hevedes of the dampned folk." . . .
G
Job 20:25 ? (Peraldus, ibid., *De Penis Infernis*; Petersen, 1901,
    p. 13, n. 2; S; R; P; F; Wenzel, in B, 1987, n. 191).

193: . . . of which that David seith, "The riche folk, that
embraceden and oneden al hire herte to tresor of this world,
shul slepe in the slepynge of deeth; and nothyng ne shal they
fynden in hir handes of al hir tresor."
g
Ps. 75(76):6(5) (cp. Johnson, 1941, p. 121; R; P; F; Wenzel, in
    B, 1987, n. 193).

195: For God seith thus by Moyses: "They shul been wasted
with hunger, and the briddes of helle shul devouren hem with
bitter deeth, and the galle of the dragon shal been hire drynke,
and the venym of the dragon hire morsels."
G
Deut. 32:24, 33 (Wyclif, *Middle English Bible* ?; Ramsay,
    1882; R; P; F; Wenzel, in B, 1987, n. 195).

198: Loo, what seith God of hem by the prophete Ysaye: that "under hem shul been strawed motthes, and hire covertures shulle been of wormes of helle."

Isa. 14:11 (R; P; F; Wenzel, in B, 1987, n. 198).

201: "The sones and the doghtren shullen rebellen agayns fader and mooder, and kynrede agayns kynrede, and chiden and despisen everich of hem oother bothe day and nyght," as God seith by the prophete Michias.

Mich. 7:6 (R; P; F; Wenzel, in B, 1987, n. 201).

204: . . . as seith the prophete David: "Whoso that loveth wikkednesse, he hateth his soule."

Ps. 10(11):6(5) (R; P; F; Wenzel, in B, 1987, n. 204).

208: But in helle hir sighte shal be ful of derknesse and of smoke, and therfore ful of teeres; and hir herynge ful of waymentynge and of gryntynge of teeth, as seith Jhesu Crist.

G

Matt. 8:12, 13:42, 25:30 (R; P; F; Wenzel, in B, 1987, n. 208).

209: Hir nosethirles shullen be ful of stynkynge stynk; and, as seith Ysaye the prophete, "hir savoryng shal be ful of bitter galle"; . . .

Isa. 24:9 (R; P; F; Wenzel, in B, 1987, n. 209).

210: . . . and touchynge of al hir body ycovered with "fir that nevere shal quenche and with wormes that nevere shul dyen," as God seith by the mouth of Ysaye.

Isa. 66:24 (cp. Peraldus, ibid., *De Penis Infernis;* Petersen, 1901, p. 13, n. 2; cp. Innocent III, *DMCH* 3.2, 4 and 1.19; Köppel, 1890, 417; R; P; F; Wenzel, in B, 1987, n. 210).

211: . . . by the word of Job, that seith, "ther as is the shadwe of deeth."

g
Job 10:22 (R; P; F).

216: And therfore seith Seint John the Evaungelist, "They shullen folwe deeth, and they shul nat fynde hym; and they shul desiren to dye, and deeth shal flee fro hem."

g
Apoc. 9:6 (cp. Peraldus, ibid., De Penis Infernis; Petersen, 1901, p. 13, n. 2; cp. Innocent III, DMCH 3.9; Köppel, 1890, 417; R; P; Miller, 1977, p. 490; F; Wenzel, in B, 1987, n. 216).

217: And eek Job seith that in helle is noon ordre of rule.

g
Job 10:22 (cp. Gregory, Moralia 9.63-66; cp. Peraldus, ibid., De Penis Infernis; Petersen, 1901, p. 13, n. 2; R; P; F).

220: For, as the prophete David seith, "God shal destroie the fruyt of the erthe as fro hem; ne water ne shal yeve hem no moisture, ne the eyr no refresshyng, ne fyr no light."

g
Ps. 106(107):33-34 (S; R; P; F; Wenzel, in B, 1987, n. 220).

221-22: For, as seith Seint Basilie, "The brennynge of the fyr of this world shal God yeven in helle to hem that been dampned,/ but the light and the cleernesse shal be yeven in hevene to his children" . . .
    Cp. Matt. 13:41-43 (cp. S; P; Wenzel, in B, 1987, n. 221).

223: . . . seith Seint Job atte laste that "ther shal horrour and grisly drede dwellen withouten ende."

g
Job 10:22 (cp. Peraldus, ibid., De Penis Infernis; Petersen, 1901, p. 13, n. 2; R; P; F).

225: . . . ne they ne may yeve no thyng for hir raunsoun . . .
  Job 7:9 ? (S).

227: And therfore seith Salomon: "The wikked man dyeth, and
whan he is deed, he shal have noon hope to escape fro peyne."
  g
  Prov. 11:7 (R; P; F; Wenzel, in B, 1987, n. 227).

229: For, as that seith Salomon, "Whoso that hadde the science
to knowe the peynes that been establissed and ordeyned for
synne, he wolde make sorwe."
  g
  Eccl. 1:18 ? (S; R).
  Ecclus. 1:17-18 ? (Wenzel, in B, 1987, n. 229).

236: And therof seith God by the mouth of Ezechiel, that "if
the rightful man returne agayn from his rightwisnesse and
werke wikkednesse, shal he lyve?"
  g
  Ezech. 18:24 (Correale, 1981-82; R; P; F; Wenzel, in B, 1987,
    n. 236-37).

237: Nay, for alle the goode werkes that he hath wroght ne
shul nevere been in remembraunce, for he shal dyen in his synne.
  Ezech. 3:20 (Correale, 1981-82; Wenzel, in B, 1987, n. 236-
    37).

253-54: For trust wel, "He shal yeven acountes," as seith Seint
Bernard, "of alle the goodes that han be yeven hym in this
present lyf, and how he hath hem despended,/ [in] so muche
that ther shal nat perisse an heer of his heed, ne a moment of
an houre ne shal nat perisse of his tyme, that he ne shal yeve of
it a rekenyng."
  Cp. *Luke 16:2* (Pennaforte, *SCP*; Petersen, 1901, p. 13, n. 3
    and p. 14, n. 1; cp. Wenzel, in B, 1987, n. 253-54).
  Cp. *Luke 21:18*

255: . . . remembrance of the passioun that oure Lord Jhesu Crist
suffred for oure synnes.
> *Rom. 5:8-9, Col. 1:20, etc.* (cp. Wenzel, in B, 1987, n. 255-82).

256-59: For, as seith Seint Bernard, "Whil that I lyve I shal
have remembrance of the travailles that oure Lord Crist
suffred in prechyng:/ his werynesse in travaillyng, his
temptaciouns whan he fasted, his longe wakynges whan he
preyde, hise teeres whan that he weep for pitee of good peple,/
the wo and the shame and the filthe that men seyden to hym,
of the foule spittyng that men spitte in his face, of the buffettes
that men yaven hym, of the foule mowes, and of the repreves
that men to hym seyden,/ of the nayles with whiche he was
nayled to the croys, and of al the remenant of his passioun that
he suffred for my synnes, and no thyng for his gilt."
> *Matt. 4:1-11, 9:34, 26:36-46, 26:67, 27:50, etc.* (Bernard,
> *Sermo in Quarta Feria Hebd. Sanctae* 11; Wenzel, in B,
> 1987, n. 256-59).
> *John 11:35, 20:25, etc.*
> *Rom. 4:25, 5:8-9, Col.1:20, etc.*

270: . . . and this suffred oure Lord Jhesu Crist for man, whan
they spetten in his visage.
> *Matt. 26:67, etc.*

272: And this suffred oure Lord Jhesu Crist for man upon the
croys, where as ther was no part of his body free withouten
greet peyne and bitter passioun.
> *Matt. 27:35-50; etc.*

273: And al this suffred Jhesu Crist, that nevere forfeted. And
therfore resonably may be seyd of Jhesu in this manere: "To
muchel am I peyned for the thynges that I nevere deserved, and
to muche defouled for shendshipe that man is worthy to have."
> *1 Pet. 3:18; etc.*
> Cp. *Ps. 68(69):5(4)* (cp. P; Wenzel, in B, 1987, n. 273).

277-80: For this disordinaunce of synful man was Jhesu Crist
first bitraysed, and after that was he bounde. . . . Thanne was
he byscorned. . . . Thanne was his visage . . . vileynsly bispet./
Thanne was he scourged . . . and finally, thanne was he
crucified and slayn.
>*Rom. 5:8-9, Col. 1:20, etc.*
>*Matt. 26:48-49, 67-68; 27:2, 26, 35-50, etc.*

281: Thanne was acompliced the word of Ysaye,/ "He was
wounded for oure mysdedes and defouled for oure felonies."
>*g*
>*Isa. 53:5* (R; P; F; Wenzel, in B, 1987, n. 281).

284: . . . therefore is he cleped *Jhesus Nazarenus rex Judeorum.*
>*John 19:19* (R; P; Wenzel, in B, 1987, n. 284).

285: *Jhesus* is to seyn "saveour" or "salvacioun," on whom men
shul hope to have foryifnesse of synnes, which that is proprely
salvacioun of synnes.
>Cp. *Acts 13:23, etc.* (cp. Wenzel, in B, 1987, n. 285).
>Cp. *Matt. 1:21, Eph. 1:7, etc.*

286: And therfore seyde the aungel to Joseph, "Thou shalt
clepen his name Jhesus, that shal saven his peple of hir
synnes."
>*Matt. 1:21* (R; P; F; Wenzel, in B, 1987, n. 286).

287: And heerof seith Seint Peter: "Ther is noon oother name
under hevene that is yeve to any man, by which a man may be
saved, but oonly Jhesus."
>*g*
>*Acts 4:12* (cp. Lawler, 1980, pp. 162-63; R; P; F; Wenzel, in B,
> 1987, n. 287).

288: *Nazarenus* is as muche for to seye as "florisshynge." . . . For
in the flour is hope of fruyt in tyme comynge, and in foryifnesse
of synnes hope of grace wel for to do.

Cp. *John 19:19* (cp. Wenzel, in B, 1987, n. 288; cp. Petersen, 1901, p. 14, n. 4).

Isa. 11:1 etc. ? (La; R; cp. Lawler, 1980, pp. 162-63).

289-90: "I was atte dore of thyn herte," seith Jhesus, "and cleped for to entre. He that openeth to me shal have foryifnesse of synne./ I wol entre into hym by my grace and soupe with hym . . . and he shal soupe with me. . . . "

G

Apoc. 3:20 (Pennaforte, *SCP;* Petersen, 1901, p. 14; cp. Johnson, 1941, p. 108; Delasanta, 1978; Lawler, 1980, pp. 162-63; R; P; F; Wenzel, in B, 1987, n. 289-90).

291: Thus shal man hope, for his werkes of penaunce that God shal yeven hym his regne, as he bihooteth hym in the gospel.

Cp. *Matt. 3:8, Luke 15:7* (Pennaforte, *SCP;* Petersen, 1901, p. 14; Wenzel, in B, 1987, n. 291).

G

294: . . . it is synne agayns the lawe of God . . .

G

301: For certes, God almyghty is al good. . . .

Cp. *Mark 10:18* (cp. line 1007, below).

304: . . . and therfore, whan my soule was angwissous withinne me, I hadde remembrance of God that my preyere myghte come to hym.

Jon. 2:8 (Wenzel, in B, 1987, n. 304; cp. Gower, *VC* 1.18.1819-20, 2.5.271-72).

307: For which seith David: "Ye that loven God, hateth wikkednesse."

g

Ps. 96(97):10; Amos 5:15; Rom. 12:9 (R; P; F; Wenzel, in B, 1987, n. 307).

309: . . . of which that David seith, "I seye," quod David (that is to seyn, I purposed fermely) "to shryve me, and thow, Lord, relessedest my synne."

§

Ps. 31(32):5 (Pennaforte, *SCP*; Petersen, 1901, pp. 15-16; cp. Johnson, 1941, pp. 114-15; R; P; F; Wenzel, in B, 1987, n. 309).

313: And forther over, it maketh hym that whilom was sone of ire to be sone of grace; and alle thise thynges been preved by hooly writ.

Eph. 2:3 (R; P; Wenzel, in B, 1987, n. 313).

G (Petersen, 1901, p. 16, n. 2).

322: Of the spryngynge of synnes seith Seint Paul in this wise: that "Right as by a man synne entred first into this world, and thurgh that synne deeth, right so thilke deeth entred into alle men that synneden."

§

Rom. 5:12 (Richard de Wetheringsett, *SDOS* ?; Kellogg, 1952, p. 346; R; P; Wenzel, in B, 1987, nn. 322-49, 322).

323: And this man was Adam, by whom synne entred into this world, whan he brak the comaundementz of God.

Cp. *Rom. 5:14* (Richard de Wetheringsett, *SDOS* ?; Kellogg, 1952, p. 346).

G

324: And therfore, he that first was so myghty that he sholde nat have dyed, bicam swich oon that he moste nedes dye, wheither he wolde or noon, and al his progenye in this world, that in thilke man synneden.

Rom. 5:12 (ibid.).

325: . . . whan Adam and Eve naked weren in Paradys, and nothyng ne hadden shame of hir nakednesse . . .

Gen. 2:25 (Kellogg, 1952, 351, n.16).

Cp. *Gen. 3:1-7* (cp. Johnson, 1941, pp. 119-20; R; P; F; Wenzel, in B, 1987, n. 325-30).

326: . . . how that the serpent, that was moost wily of alle othere beestes that God hadde maked, seyde to the womman, "Why comaunded God to yow ye sholde nat eten of every tree in Paradys?"
  Gen. 3:1 (Kellogg, 1952, 351, n. 16; cp. Johnson, 1941, pp. 119-20; Wenzel, in B, 1987, n. 325-30).

327: The womman answerde: "Of the fruyt," quod she, "of the trees in Paradys we feden us, but soothly, of the fruyt of the tree that is in the myddel of Paradys, God forbad us for to ete, ne nat touchen it, lest per aventure we sholde dyen."
  Gen. 3:2-3 (ibid.).

328: The serpent seyde to the womman, "Nay, nay, ye shul nat dyen of deeth; for sothe, God woot that what day that ye eten therof, youre eyen shul opene and ye shul been as goddes, knowynge good and harm."
  Gen. 3:4-5 (ibid.).

329: The womman thanne saugh that the tree was good to feedyng, and fair to the eyen, and delitable to the sighte. She took of the fruyt of the tree, and eet it, and yaf to hire housbonde, and he eet, and anoon the eyen of hem bothe openeden.
  Gen. 3:6 (ibid.).

330: And whan that they knewe that they were naked, they sowed of fige leves a maner of breches to hiden hire membres.
  Gen. 3:7 (ibid.).

331-32: . . . suggestion of the feend, as sheweth heere by the naddre . . . delit of the flessh, as sheweth heere by Eve . . . consentynge of resoun, as sheweth heere by Adam./ . . . the feend tempted Eve . . . the beautee of the fruyt . . . Adam . . . consented to the etynge of the fruyt. . . .

> Gen. 3:1-6 (Richard de Wetheringsett, *SDOS* ?; Kellogg, 1952, pp. 346-47; cp. F; Wenzel, in B, 1987, n. 331-32).

333: Of thilke Adam tooke we thilke synne original, for of hym flesshly descended be we alle. . . .

> Cp. *Rom. 5:12, 15-19; etc.* (Richard de Wetheringsett, *SDOS* ?; Kellogg, 1952, p. 347; cp. F; Wenzel, in B, 1987, n. 333-49).

334: And whan the soule is put in oure body, right anon is contract original synne. . . .

> Cp. *Rom. 5:12, 15-19; etc.* (ibid.).

335: And therfore be we alle born sones of wratthe and of dampnacioun perdurable, if it nere baptesme. . . . But for sothe, the peyne dwelleth with us, as to temptacioun, which peyne highte concupiscence.

> Cp. *Eph. 2:3; etc.* (ibid.).
> Cp. *1 Pet. 3:21; etc.* (ibid.).

336: And this concupiscence, whan it is wrongfully disposed or ordeyned in man, it maketh hym coveite, by coveitise of flessh, flesshly synne, by sighte of his eyen as to erthely thynges, and eek coveitise of hynesse by pride of herte.

> *1 John 2:16* (ibid.; R; Wenzel, in B, 1987, n. 336).

342: For lo, what seith Seint Paul: "The flessh coveiteth agayn the spirit, and the spirit agayn the flessh; they been so contrarie and so stryven that a man may nat alway doon as he wolde."

> g
> *Gal. 5:17* (Wyclif, *Middle English Bible* ?; Ramsay, 1882; R; P; F; Wenzel, in B, 1987, n. 342).

343: The same Seint Paul, after his grete penaunce in water and in lond--in water by nyght and by day in greet peril and in greet peyne; in lond, in famyne and thurst, in coold and cloothlees, and ones stoned almoost to the deeth . . .

g
2 Cor. 11:25-27 (R; P; F; Wenzel, in B, 1987, n. 343).

344: . . . yet seyde he, "Allas, I caytyf man! Who shal delivere me fro the prisoun of my caytyf body?"

g
Rom. 7:24 (R; P; F; Wenzel, in B, 1987, n. 344).

348: Witnesse on Seint Jame the Apostel, that seith that "every wight is tempted in his owene concupiscence." . . .

g
James 1:14 (Patterson, 1978, 341-42; R; P; F; Wenzel, in B, 1987, n. 348).

349: And therfore seith Seint John the Evaungelist, "If that we seyn that we be withoute synne, we deceyve us selve, and trouthe is nat in us."

g
1 John 1:8 (R; P; F; Wenzel, in B, 1987, n. 349).

355-56: And of this matere seith Moyses by the devel in this manere: "The feend seith, 'I wole chace and pursue the man by wikked suggestioun, and I wole hente hym by moevynge or stirynge of synne. And I wol departe my prise or my praye by deliberacioun, and my lust shal been acompliced in delit. I wol drawe my swerd in consentynge'"—/ for certes, right as a swerd departeth a thyng in two peces, right so consentynge departeth God fro man—"'and thanne wol I sleen hym with myn hand in dede of synne'; thus seith the feend."

G
Exod. 15:9 ? (Kellogg, 1953; P; F; cp. Wenzel, in B, 1987, nn. 350-56, 351, 355-56).

375: ... to yelde to his wyf the dette of his body. ...
    Cp. *1 Cor. 7:3* (F).

376: ... eke whan he wol nat visite the sike and the prisoner, if
he may; eke if he love wyf or child, or oother worldly thyng,
moore than resoun requireth; eke if he flatere or blandise moore
than hym oghte for any necessitee ...
    Cp. *Matt. 25:36, 43* (R; P; Wenzel, in B, 1987, n. 376).

386: ... by general confessioun of *Confiteor* at masse and at
complyn ...
    Cp. *Job 42:6; Matt. 11:25; etc.* (cp. Pennaforte, *SCP*; Petersen,
        1901, p. 30; liturgy, *Confiteor*; F; Wenzel, in B, 1987, n.
        386; cp. *TC* 2.525).

388: Of the roote of thise sevene synnes, thanne, is Pride the
general roote of alle harmes. ...
    Cp. *Ecclus. 10:15* (Peraldus, *SVV*; Petersen, 1901, p. 36; R; P;
        cp. Wenzel, in B, 1987, n. 388).

392: ... to the comandementz of God ...
    G

413: For certes, if ther ne hadde be no synne in clothyng, Crist
wolde nat so soone have noted and spoken of the clothyng of
thilke riche man in the gospel.
    G
    Luke 16:19 (Peraldus, *SVV*; Petersen, 1901, p. 38; Delasanta,
        1968-69, 33-36; R; P; F; Wenzel, in B, 1987, n. 413).
    Luke 12:22-23, 19:35-36; etc. ? (Delasanta, 1968-69, 33-36).

434: For which God seith by Zakarie the prophete, "I wol
confounde the rideres of swiche horses."
    g
    Zach.10:5, 12:4 (Peraldus, *SVV*; Petersen, 1901, p. 40; cp.
        Johnson, 1941, pp. 112-13; R; P; F; Wenzel, in B, 1987, n.
        434).

Zach. 9:9-10 ? (Delasanta, 1968-69, 29-33).

435: This folk taken litel reward of the ridynge of Goddes sone of hevene, and of his harneys whan he rood upon the asse, and ne hadde noon oother harneys but the povre clothes of his disciples; ne we ne rede nat that evere he rood on oother beest.

> *Matt. 21:7* (cp. Peraldus, *SVV*; Petersen, 1901, p. 40; La, 1924, 94; cp. Johnson, 1941, p. 100; R; P; F; Wenzel, in B, 1987, n. 435).

442: . . . for which thus seith David the prophete: "Wikked deeth moote come upon thilke lordshipes, and God yeve that they moote descenden into helle al doun; for in hire houses been iniquitees and shrewednesses, and nat God of hevene."

> 8
> *Ps. 54(55):16(15)* (cp. Johnson, 1941, p. 121; R; P; F; Wenzel, in B, 1987, n. 442).

443: . . . right as God yaf his benysoun to [Laban] by the service of Jacob, and to [Pharao] by the service of Joseph . . .

> *Gen. 30:27, 30; 41:47-49, 53-57* (cp. R; P; Wenzel, in B, 1987, n. 443).

459: . . . For certes, the flessh coveiteth agayn the spirit, and ay the moore strong that the flessh is, the sorier may the soule be.

> *Gal. 5:17* (cp. Peraldus, *SVV*; Petersen, 1901, p. 43; cp. Johnson, 1941, p. 115; R; P; Wenzel, in B, 1987, n. 459).

461-62: . . . and eek we ben alle of o fader and of o mooder; and alle we been of o nature, roten and corrupt, bothe riche and povre./ For sothe, o manere gentrie is for to preise, that apparailleth mannes corage with vertues and moralitees, and maketh hym Cristes child.

> *1 Cor. 15:45-50* (cp. Peraldus, *SVV*; Petersen, 1901, p. 43; cp. Wenzel, in B, 1987, n. 461).
> *Gal. 3:26*
> *Gen. 4:1; 1 Tim. 2:13-14*

463: For truste wel that over what man that synne hath maistrie, he is a verray cherl to synne.
John 8:34, etc. (cp. Peraldus, *SVV;* Petersen, 1901, p. 44).

482: Humilitee eek in werkes is in foure maneres. The firste is whan he putteth othere men biforn hym. . . .
Cp. *Rom.12:10* (cp. *Postquam* 73; Wenzel, 1984, p. 14).

483: The ferthe is to stonde gladly to the award of his sovereyns, or of hym that is in hyer degree. . . .
Cp. *1 Pet. 2:13-14, etc.* (cp. *Postquam* 79; ibid.).

485: This foule synne is platly agayns the Hooly Goost.. . . and Envye comth proprely of malice, therfore it is proprely agayn the bountee of the Hooly Goost.
Matt. 12:32, etc. (cp. *Quoniam;* Wenzel, 1974, 356; cp. Peraldus, *SVV;* Petersen, 1901, p. 46; R).

492: The seconde spece of Envye is joye of oother mannes harm, and that is proprely lyk to the devel, that evere rejoyseth hym of mannes harm.
Cp. *Prov. 2:14* (cp. *Quoniam;* ibid., 358; cp. Peraldus, *SVV;* Petersen, 1901, p. 47).
Cp. *1 Pet. 5:8*

500-01: Agayn God it is whan a man . . . gruccheth that shrewes han prosperitee, or elles for that goode men han adversitee./ And alle thise thynges sholde man suffre paciently, for they comen by the rightful juggement and ordinaunce of God.
Cp. *Ps. 36(37):1, 7, 28* (cp. *Quoniam;* ibid., 360; cp. Peraldus, *SVV;* Petersen, 1901, pp. 47-48; R; P).

502: Somtyme comth grucching of avarice; as Judas grucched agayns the Magdaleyne, whan she enoynted the heved of oure Lord Jhesu Crist with hir precious oynement.
John 12:3-6 (cp. Peraldus, *SVV;* Petersen, 1901, p. 48; La, 1924, 94; cp. Johnson, 1941, pp. 100-01; cp. *Quoniam;*

Wenzel, 1974, 360; cp. McCall, 1971; R; P; F; Wenzel, in B,
1987, n. 502).

504: Somtyme comth murmure of Pride, as whan Simon the
Pharisee gruchched agayn the Magdaleyne whan she
approched to Jhesu Crist and weep at his feet for hire synnes.
   Luke 7:39-40 (cp. Peraldus, *SVV*; Petersen, 1901, p. 48; cp.
   Quoniam; Wenzel, 1974, 360; cp. Johnson, 1941, pp. 102-03;
   cp. McCall, 1971; R; P; F; Wenzel, in B, 1987, n. 504).

506: Murmure eek is ofte amonges servauntz that grucchen whan
hir sovereyns bidden hem doon leveful thynges . . .
   Cp. *Matt. 20:11* ? (cp. *Quoniam;* Wenzel, 1974, 360; cp.
   Peraldus, *SVV;* Petersen, 1901, p. 48; R).

508: . . . whiche wordes men clepen the develes *Pater noster,*
though so be that the devel ne hadde nevere *Pater noster* . . .
   Matt. 6:9-13, Luke 11:2-4 (liturgy; cp. *Quoniam;* Wenzel,
   1974, 360; F; Wenzel, in B, 1987, n. 508).

512: . . . lyk the craft of the devel, that waiteth bothe nyght
and day to accusen us alle.
   Cp. *1 Pet. 5:8*
   Cp. *Ps. 10:9(Hebrew); Apoc. 12:10* (Cp. *Quoniam;* Wenzel,
   1974, 361; Wenzel, in B, 1987, n. 512).

515: . . . First is the love of God principal and lovyng of his
neighebor as hymself . . .
   Matt. 22:37-39, Mark 12:30-31; etc. (*Postquam* 67; Wenzel,
   1984, p. 14; R; Wenzel, in B, 1987, n. 515-32).

516: . . . for certes alle we have o fader flesshly and o mooder--
that is to seyn, Adam and Eve--and eek o fader espiritueel, and
that is God of hevene.
   Cp. *Gen. 4:1*
   Cp. *Matt. 6:9, Luke 11:2* (*Postquam* 839; ibid., p. 15).

517: . . . and therfore seith God, "Love thy neighebor as thyselve." . . .
> G
> *Matt. 22:39, etc.* (*Postquam* 816; ibid.; Wenzel, in B, 1987, n. 517).

518: And mooreover thou shalt love hym in word, and in benigne amonestynge and chastisynge, and conforten hym in his anoyes, and preye for hym with al thyn herte.
> *Mark 12:33* ? (*Postquam* 829; ibid.).

519: . . . thou shalt doon to hym in charitee as thou woldest that it were doon to thyn owene persone.
> *Matt. 22:39, Gal. 5:13-14, James 2:8; etc.* (*Postquam* 818; ibid.).

520: And therfore thou ne shalt doon hym no damage in wikked word, ne harm in his body, ne in his catel . . .
> *Lev. 19:13* (*Postquam* 845, 847-48, 850; ibid.; cp. F).

521: Thou shalt nat desiren his wyf ne none of his thynges. . . .
> *Exod. 20:17, Deut. 5:21; etc.* (Wenzel, 1984, p. 27; cp. Dolan, 1986, p. 262).

522-23: Certes, man shal loven his enemy, by the comandement of God; and soothly thy freend shaltow love in God./ I seye, thyn enemy shaltow love for Goddes sake, by his comandement.
> *Matt. 5:44, Luke 6:32-35; etc.* (*Postquam* 860, 862, 865, 939; ibid., pp. 15-16).
> G

526-30: For Crist seith: "Loveth youre enemys, and preyeth for hem that speke yow harm, and eek for hem that yow chacen and pursewen, and dooth bountee to hem that yow haten." Loo, thus comaundeth us oure Lord Jhesu Crist to do to oure enemys./ For soothly, nature dryveth us to loven oure freendes. . . . the lovynge of oure enemy hath confounded the venym of the

devel./ For . . . the devel . . . is . . . wounded to the deeth by love
of oure enemy.
G
Matt. 5:44, Luke 6:32-35; etc. (Postquam 880, 906, 909-10,
913, 919, 933, 935; ibid., p. 16; R; P; F; Wenzel, in B, 1987,
n. 526).

528: . . . in thilke dede have we remembraunce of the love of
Jhesu Crist that deyde for his enemys.
Cp. Rom. 5:10 (cp. Postquam 913; ibid.).

539: . . . and therfore seith a wys man that Ire is bet than pley.
g
Eccl. 7:4 (Quoniam; Wenzel, 1974, 363; Peraldus, SVV;
Petersen, 1901, p. 49; R; P; Wenzel, in B, 1987, n. 539).

540: . . . as seith the prophete David, "Irascimini et nolite
peccare."
g
Ps. 4:5(4); Eph. 4:26 (Quoniam; ibid., 363; Peraldus, SVV;
Petersen, 1901, p. 50; R; P; F; Wenzel, in B, 1987, n. 540).

561: . . . [Ire] stryveth eek alday agayn trouthe. . . .
Cp. James 1:20 (Quoniam; Wenzel, 1974, 363).

565: . . . as seith Seint John: "He that hateth his brother is an
homycide."
g
1 John 3:15 (Pennaforte, "De Homicidio"; Johnson, 1942, 53;
Peraldus, SVV; Petersen, 1901, p. 52; La, 1924, 95; cp.
Johnson, 1941, p. 106; R; P; F; Wenzel, in B, 1987, n. 565; cp.
Gower, CA 4.2325).

566: . . . of whiche bakbiteres seith Salomon that "they han
two swerdes with whiche they sleen hire neighebores."
g

Prov. 25:18 ? (S; R; P; F; Wenzel, in B, 1987, n. 566).
Prov. 30:14 (Johnson, 1942, 53).

568: Of whiche seith Salomon: "Leon rorynge and bere hongry
been like to the crueel lordshipes" in withholdynge or
abreggynge of the shepe . . . of povre folk.
   g
Prov. 28:15 (Patterson, 1978, 345, n. 39; R; P; F; Wenzel, in B,
   1987, n. 568).

569: For which the wise man seith, "Fedeth hym that almoost
dyeth for honger." . . .
   g
Prov. 25:21 ? (cp. Peraldus, *SVV*; Petersen, 1901, p. 52; cp.
   Johnson, 1941, pp. 106-07; R; P; F; Wenzel, in B, 1987, n.
   569).

574: Eek if a man, by caas or aventure, shete an arwe, or caste a
stoon with which he sleeth a man, he is homycide.
   Num. 35:17 (R; P).
   Prov. 26:18-19 (Johnson, 1942, 53-54).

575: Eek if a womman by necligence overlyeth hire child in hir
slepyng, it is homycide and deedly synne.
   Cp. *1 Kings 3:19*

582: . . . the mercy of God passeth alle his werkes; it is so greet,
and he so benigne.
   Cp. *Ps. 144(145):9* (R; P; Wenzel, in B, 1987, n. 582).

588: God seith, "Thow shalt nat take the name of thy Lord God
in veyn or in ydel."
   G
   Exod. 20:7, Deut. 5:11, etc. (Peraldus, *SVV*; Petersen, 1901,
   p. 53; R; P; F; Wenzel, in B, 1987, n. 588).

588-90: . . . Also oure Lord Jhesu Crist seith, by the word of Seint Mathew,/ "Ne wol ye nat swere in alle manere; neither by hevene, for it is Goddes trone; ne by erthe, for it is the bench of his feet; ne by Jerusalem, for it is the citee of a greet kyng; ne by thyn heed, for thou mayst nat make an heer whit ne blak./ But seyeth by youre word 'ye, ye,' and 'nay, nay'; and what that is moore, it is of yvel"—thus seith Crist.

§
Matt. 5:34-37 (Peraldus, *SVV*; Petersen, 1901, p. 53; cp. Johnson, 1941, pp. 98-99; Reiss, 1984, p. 61; R; P; F; Wenzel, in B, 1987, n. 589-90).

G

591: For Cristes sake, ne swereth nat so synfully in dismembrynge of Crist by soule, herte, bones, and body. For certes, it semeth that ye thynke that the cursede Jewes ne dismembred nat ynough the preciouse persone of Crist, but ye dismembre hym moore.

Cp. *James 5:12*
Cp. *Heb. 6:6* (R; cp. Wenzel, in B, 1987, n. 591).

592: . . . as seith Jeremye, *quarto capitulo:* Thou shalt kepe three condicions: thou shalt swere "in trouthe, in doom, and in rightwisnesse."

§
Jer. 4:2 (Peraldus, *SVV*; Petersen, 1901, p. 54; cp. Johnson, 1941, p. 107; Reiss, 1984, p. 61; S; R; P; F; Wenzel, in B, 1987, n. 592).

593: . . . for Crist is verray trouthe. And thynk wel this: that "every greet swerere, nat compelled lawefully to swere, the wounde shal nat departe from his hous" whil he useth swich unleveful swerying.

Cp. *John 14:6*
Ecclus. 23:12 (Peraldus, *SVV*; Petersen, 1901, p. 54; cp. Johnson, 1941, p. 112; R; P; F; Wenzel, in B, 1987, n. 593).

596: And therfore every man that taketh Goddes name in ydel, or falsly swereth with his mouth, or elles taketh on hym the name of Crist, to be called a Cristen man and lyveth agayns Cristes lyvynge and his techynge, alle they taken Goddes name in ydel.

Cp. *Exod. 20:7, Deut. 5:11; etc.*

597: Looke eek what seint Peter seith, *Actuum quarto, Non est aliud nomen sub celo, etc.,* "Ther nys noon oother name," seith Seint Peter, "under hevene yeven to men, in which they mowe be saved"; that is to seyn but the name of Jhesu Crist.

g
Acts 4:12 (R; P; F; Wenzel, in B, 1987, n. 597).

598: Take kep eek how precious is the name of Crist, as seith Seint Paul, *ad Philipenses secundo, In nomine Jhesus, etc.,* "That in the name of Jhesu every knee of hevenely creatures, or erthely, or of helle sholde bowe," for it is so heigh and so worshipful that the cursede feend in helle sholde tremblen to heeren it ynempned.

g
Phil. 2:9-10 (Peraldus, *SVV;* Petersen, 1901, p. 54; R; P; F; Wenzel, in B, 1987, n. 598).
Cp. *James 2:19*

599: Thanne semeth it that men that sweren so horribly by his blessed name, that they despise it moore booldely than dide the cursede Jewes, or elles the devel, that trembleth whan he heereth his name.

James 2:19 (R; P; Wenzel, in B, 1987, n. 599).

614: For sothe, Salomon seith that "Flaterie is wors than detraccioun." . . .

g
Cp. *Prov.16:19, 29* (Peraldus, *SVV;* Petersen, 1901, p. 55; S; R; cp. Wenzel, in B, 1987, n. 614).

616: . . . They been lyk to Judas that bitraysen a man to sellen
hym to his enemy; that is to the devel.
> Cp. *Matt. 10:4, etc.* (Peraldus, *SVV*; Petersen, 1901, p. 55).

617: . . . that syngen evere *Placebo.*
> *Ps. 114(116):9* (liturgy; S; R; P; *Roman de Fauvel* ?; Fleming,
> 1965; F; Wenzel, in B, 1987, n. 617).

619: . . . Swich cursynge bireveth man fro the regne of God, as
seith Seint Paul.
> *1 Cor. 6:10* (cp. Peraldus, *SVV*; Petersen, 1901, p. 56; cp.
> Johnson, 1941, pp. 111-12; R; P; F; Wenzel, in B, 1987, n.
> 619).
>
> g
> Cp. *Ecclus. 23:12*

620: And ofte tyme swich cursynge wrongfully retorneth agayn
to hym that curseth, as a bryd that retorneth agayn to his
owene nest.
> Cp. *Prov. 26:2* (Peraldus, *SVV*; Petersen, 1901, p. 56;
> Wenzel, in B, 1987, n. 620).

623: For certes, unnethes may a man pleynly been accorded with
hym that hath hym openly revyled and repreved and
disclaundred. This is a ful grisly synne, as Crist seith in the
gospel.
> *Matt. 5:22* (Peraldus, *SVV*; Petersen, 1901, p. 56; R; P; F;
> Wenzel, in B, 1987, n. 623).
>
> G

627: . . . For after the habundance of the herte speketh the
mouth ful ofte.
> *Matt. 12:34* (Peraldus, *SVV*; Petersen, 1901, p. 57; R; P; F;
> Wenzel, in B, 1987, n. 627).

629: For as seith Salomon, "The amyable tonge is the tree of
lyf"—that is to seyn, of lyf espiritueel—and soothly, a

deslavee tonge sleeth the spirites of hym that repreveth and
eek of hym that is repreved.

    g

    Prov. 15:4 (Peraldus, *SVV;* Petersen, 1901, p. 57; R; P; F;
    Wenzel, in B, 1987, n. 629).

630: . . . Seint Paul seith eek, "The servant of God bihoveth nat
to chide."

    g

    2 Tim. 2:24 (Peraldus, *SVV;* Petersen, 1901, p. 57; R; P; F;
    Wenzel, in B, 1987, n. 630).

631-32: . . . And therfore seith Salomon, "An hous that is
uncovered and droppynge and a chidynge wyf been lyke."/ . . .
So fareth it by a chydynge wyf; but she chide hym in o place,
she wol chide hym in another.

    g

    Prov. 19:13, 27:15 (Peraldus, *SVV;* Petersen, 1901, p. 58;
    Patterson, 1978, 345, n. 39; R; P; F; Wenzel, in B, 1987, n.
    631).

633: And therfore, "Bettre is a morsel of breed with joye than an
hous ful of delices with chidynge," seith Salomon.

    Prov.17:1 (Peraldus, *SVV;* Petersen, 1901, p. 58; R; P; F;
    Wenzel, in B, 1987, n. 633).

    g

634: Seint Paul seith, "O ye wommen, be ye subgetes to youre
housbondes as bihoveth in God, and ye men loveth youre
wyves." *Ad Colossenses tertio.*

    g

    Col. 3:18-19 (R; P; F; Wenzel, in B, 1987, n. 634).

639: Speke we now of wikked conseil, for he that wikked
conseil yeveth is a traytour. For he deceyveth hym that
trusteth in hym, *ut Achitofel ad Absolonem.* But nathelees, yet
is his wikked conseil first agayn hymself.

2 Kings 16-18 (R; P; F; Wenzel, in B, 1987, n. 639).
Ecclus. 27:30 (cp. Peraldus, *SVV;* Petersen, 1901, p. 59).

640: For, as seith the wise man, "Every fals lyvynge hath this propertee in hymself, that he that wole anoye another man, he anoyeth first hymself."
>g
>*Ecclus. 27:29-30; Prov. 26:27* (Peraldus, *SVV;* Petersen, 1901, p. 59; R; Wenzel, in B, 1987, n. 640).
>Cp. *Ps. 7:17(16)* (Johnson, 1941, p. 111).

642: Now comth the synne of hem that sowen and maken discord amonges folk, which is a synne that Crist hateth outrely. And no wonder is, for he deyde for to make concord.
>Cp. *Prov. 6:14-19; etc.* (cp. Peraldus, *SVV;* Petersen, 1901, p. 59; Wenzel, in B, 1987, n. 642).
>*Eph. 2:13-16* (R).

648: And al be it that ydel wordes been somtyme venial synne, yet sholde men douten hem, for we shul yeve rekenynge of hem bifore God.
>*Matt. 12:36* (Peraldus, *SVV;* Petersen, 1901, p. 60; R; P; F; Wenzel, in B, 1987, n. 648).

649: Now comth janglynge, that may nat been withoute synne. And, as seith Salomon, "It is a sygne of apert folye."
>g
>*Eccl. 5:2* (Peraldus, *SVV;* Petersen, 1901, p. 61; cp. Johnson, 1941, p. 108; R; P; F; Wenzel, in B, 1987, n. 649).

651: After this comth the synne of japeres, that been the develes apes. . . . Swiche japeres deffendeth Seint Paul.
>*Eph. 5:4* (Peraldus, *SVV;* Petersen, 1901, p. 61; cp. Rowland, 1971, p. 33; R; P; F; Wenzel, in B, 1987, n. 651).
>g

657: Seint Jerome seith thus of debonairetee, that "it dooth noon harm to no wight ne seith; ne for noon harm that men doon or seyn, he ne eschawfeth nat agayns his resoun."

> *1 Cor. 13:4-5* ? (cp. *Postquam* 7, 23; Wenzel, 1984, pp. 16-17; R; Wenzel, in B, 1987, n. 657).

661: This vertu maketh a man lyk to God, and maketh hym Goddes owene deere child, as seith Crist. . . .

> *Matt. 5:9* (*Postquam* 143; ibid., p. 17; R; P; F; Wenzel, in B, 1987, n. 661).
> G

663: The firste grevance is of wikkede wordes. Thilke suffrede Jhesu Crist withouten grucchyng, ful paciently, whan the Jewes despised and repreved hym ful ofte.

> Cp. *Matt. 26:63* (*Postquam* 287, 290; ibid.).

664: . . . for the wise man seith, "If thou stryve with a fool, though the fool be wrooth or though he laughe, algate thou shalt have no reste."

> g
> *Prov. 29:9* (*Postquam* 306; ibid.; R; P; F; Wenzel, in B, 1987, n. 664).

665: . . . Theragayns suffred Crist ful paciently, whan he was despoyled of al that he hadde in this lyf, and that nas but his clothes.

> Cp. *Matt. 27:35* (*Postquam* 391; ibid.; R; P; Wenzel, in B, 1987, n. 665).

666: The thridde grevance is a man to have harm in his body. That suffred Crist ful paciently in al his passioun.

> Cp. *Matt. 27:26-50* (*Postquam* 549; ibid.).

668: Heer-agayns suffred Crist ful paciently and taughte us pacience, whan he baar upon his blissed shulder the croys upon which he sholde suffren despitous deeth.

> Cp. *John 19:17* (*Postquam* 694; ibid., p. 18).

679: . . . it bynymeth the service that men oghte doon to Crist with alle diligence, as seith Salomon.
> Cp. *Eccl. 9:10* (cp. *Quoniam* 365; Wenzel, 1974, 365; R; P; F; cp. Wenzel, in B, 1987, n. 679).
> *g*

680: . . . for which the book seith, "Acursed be he that dooth the service of God necligently."
> G
> Cp. *Jer. 48:10* (Cp. *Quoniam* 365; ibid.; cp. Johnson, 1941, p. 123; R; P; Wenzel, in B, 1987, n. 680).

682-84: . . . th'estaat of innocence, as was th'estaat of Adam biforn that he fil into synne./ Another estaat is the estaat of synful men, in which estaat men been holden to laboure in preiynge to God for amendement of hire synnes. . . ./ Another estaat is th'estaat of grace, in which estaat he is holden to werkes of penitence. . . .
> Cp. *Rom. 5:12-21; 1 Cor. 15:21-34; etc.* (cp. Lawler, 1980, pp. 162-63).

686: . . . for they that been dampned been so bounde that they ne may neither wel do ne wel thynke.
> Cp. *Matt. 22:13* (*Quoniam* 365; ibid.; Wenzel, in B, 1987, n. 686).

687: Of Accidie comth first that a man is anoyed and encombred for to doon any goodnesse, and maketh that God hath abhomynacion of swich Accidie, as seith Seint John.
> *Apoc. 3:15-16* (*Quoniam* 365; ibid.; Peraldus, *SVV*; Petersen, 1901, p. 62; R; P; F; Wenzel, in B, 1987, n. 687).
> *g*

688: . . . For soothly, Slouthe is so tendre and so delicaat, as seith Salomon, that he wol nat suffre noon hardnesse ne penaunce, and therfore he shendeth al that he dooth.
> *g*

Prov. 18:9, etc. (*Quoniam* 365; ibid.; Peraldus, *SVV;* Petersen, 1901, p. 62; cp. Johnson, 1941, p. 109; R; P; F; Wenzel, in B, 1987, n. 688).

695: . . . it is cleped synnyng in the Hooly Goost.
Cp. *Matt. 12:32; etc.*

696: This horrible synne is so perilous . . . as shewed wel by Judas.
Matt. 27:3-5; etc. (Wenzel, in B, 1987, n. 696).

700: Allas, kan a man nat bithynke hym on the gospel of Seint Luc, 15, where as Crist seith that "as wel shal ther be joye in hevene upon a synful man that dooth penitence, as upon nynty and nyne rightful men that neden no penitence."
g
Luke 15:7, etc. (Peraldus, *SVV;* Petersen, 1901, p. 63; cp. Johnson, 1941, p. 104; R; P; F; Wenzel, in B, 1987, n. 700-03).

701: Looke forther, in the same gospel, the joye and the feeste of the goode man that hadde lost his sone, whan his sone with repentaunce was retourned to his fader.
g
Luke 15:11-32 (Peraldus, *SVV;* Petersen, 1901, p. 63; R; P; F; Wenzel, in B, 1987, n. 700-03).

702: Kan they nat remembren hem eek that, as seith Seint Luc, 23, how that the theef that was hanged bisyde Jhesu Crist, seyde, "Lord, remembre of me, whan thow comest into thy regnc"?
g
Luke 23:42 (Peraldus, *SVV;* Petersen, 1901, p. 63; R; P; F; Wenzel, in B, 1987, n. 700-03).

703: "For sothe," seyde Crist, "I seye to thee, to-day shaltow been with me in paradys."

Luke 23:43 (R; Wenzel, in B, 1987, n. 700-03).

704: Certes, ther is noon so horrible synne of man that it ne may in his lyf be destroyed by penitence, thurgh vertu of the passion and of the deeth of Crist.
Cp. *Rom. 5:8-9, Col. 1:20; etc.*

705: . . . Axe and have.
Cp. *Matt. 7:7, John 16:24; etc.* (R; P).

709: Lo, what seith Salomon: "Whoso wolde by the morwe awaken and seke me, he shal fynde."
g
Prov. 8:17 (cp. *Quoniam* 366; ibid.; cp. Peraldus, *SVV*; Petersen, 1901, p. 63; R; P; F; Wenzel, in B, 1987, n. 709).

712: . . . as seith the wise man, that "He that dredeth God, he spareth nat to doon that him oghte doon."
g
Eccl. 7:19 (*Quoniam* 366; ibid.; Peraldus, *SVV*; Petersen, 1901, p. 64; R; P; Wenzel, in B, 1987, n. 712).

716: Certes, the hevene is yeven to hem that wol labouren, and nat to ydel folk. Eek David seith that "they ne been nat in the labour of men, ne they shul nat been whipped with men"—that is to seyn, in purgatorie.
Matt. 11:12 ? (R; P; F).
g
Ps. 72(73):5 (*Quoniam* 364; ibid.; Peraldus, *SVV*; Petersen, 1901, pp. 64-65; R; P; F; Wenzel, in B, 1987, n. 716).

725: Thanne comth the synne of worldly sorwe, swich as is cleped *trisricia*, that sleeth man, as seith Seint Paul.
g
2 Cor. 7:10 (cp. Peraldus, *SVV*; Petersen, 1901, p. 66; cp. Johnson, 1941, pp. 104-05; R; P; Wenzel, in B, 1987, n. 725).

726: For certes, swich sorwe werketh to the deeth of the soule and of the body also; for therof comth that a man is anoyed of his owene lif.

Cp. *2 Cor. 7:10* (cp. Peraldus, *SVV*; Petersen, 1901, p. 66).

727: Wherfore swich sorwe shorteth ful ofte the lif of man, er that his tyme be come by wey of kynde.

Cp. *Ecclus. 30:24-26*

739: . . . of which synne seith Seint Paul that "the roote of alle harmes is Coveitise." *Ad Thimotheum Sexto.*

8
1 Tim. 6:10 (Peraldus, *SVV*; Petersen, 1901, p. 66; R; P; F; Wenzel, in B, 1987, n. 739).

745: Soothly, this Avarice is a synne that is ful dampnable, for al hooly writ curseth it and speketh agayns that vice, for it dooth wrong to Jhesu Crist.

G
Cp. *James 4:1-5* ? (cp. Peraldus, *SVV*; Petersen, 1901, p. 67).
Cp. *Isa. 5:8* (*Quoniam* 367; ibid.; cp. Peraldus, *SVV*; Petersen, 1901, p. 67).

748: And therfore seith Seint Paul *ad Ephesios quinto,* that an avaricious man is in the thraldom of ydolatrie.

8
Eph. 5:5 (*Quoniam* 367; ibid.; Peraldus, *SVV*; Petersen, 1901, p. 67; cp. Innocent III, *DMCH* 2.12; Köppel, 1890, 417; cp. Johnson, 1941, p. 105; R; P; F; Wenzel, in B, 1987, n. 748).

750-51: And certes, the synne of mawmettrie is the firste thyng that God deffended in the ten comaundementz, as bereth witnesse in *Exodi capitulo vicesimo:* / "Thou shalt have no false goddes bifore me, ne thou shalt make to thee no grave thyng." . . .

Exod. 20:1-17, Deut. 5:6-21

g

Exod. 20:3-4; etc. (cp. *Quoniam* 367; ibid.; cp. Johnson, 1941, pp. 99-100; Peraldus, *SVV*; Petersen, 1901, p. 67; cp. Dante, *Inf.* 19.112-14; Schless, 1984, pp. 218-19; R; P; F; Wenzel, in B, 1987, n. 750-51).

754-55: . . . *Augustinus, De Civitate libro nono.* / "Sooth is that the condicioun of thraldom and the firste cause of thraldom is for synne. *Genesis nono . . . .* "

Cp. *Gen. 9:24-27* (*Quoniam* 367; ibid.; P; F; R; Wenzel, in B, 1987, n. 754-56).

g

760: . . . for humble folk been Cristes freendes; they been contubernyal with the Lord.

Cp. *Matt. 11:19, James 4:6; etc.* (cp. Wenzel, in B, 1987, n. 760-62).

763: Every synful man is a cherl to synne. . . . lord, werke in swich wise with thy cherles that they rather love thee than drede.

Cp. *John 8:34; etc.*
Cp. *Deut. 6:2, 5; etc.*

766: This name of thraldom was nevere erst kowth til that Noe seyde that his sone Canaan sholde be thral to his bretheren for his synne.

Gen. 9:24-27 (R; P; F).

768-69: And, as seith Seint Augustyn, " They been the develes wolves that stranglen the sheep of Jhesu Crist," and doon worse than wolves./ For soothly, whan the wolf hath ful his wombe, he stynteth to strangle sheep. But soothly, the pilours and destroyours of the godes of hooly chirche ne do nat so, for they ne stynte nevere to pile.

Cp. *John 10:9-12; etc.* (cp. Wenzel, in B, 1987, n. 768).

770: . . . sith so is that synne was first cause of thraldom, thanne is it thus: that thilke tyme that al this world was in synne, thanne was al this world in thraldom and subjeccioun.

Cp. *Rom. 5:12, 6:17-18; etc.*

773-74: . . . but if God hadde ordeyned that som men hadde hyer degree and som men lower,/ therfore was sovereyntee ordeyned . . .

Cp. *Rom. 13:1, etc. (Quoniam* 368; ibid.; Wenzel, in B, 1987, n. 773).

775: . . . thilke lordes that been lyk wolves, that devouren the possessiouns or the catel of povre folk wrongfully . . .

Cp. *Acts 20:29; etc.* (cp. Peraldus, *SVV* ; Petersen, 1901, p. 68).

776: . . . they shul receyven by the same mesure that they han mesured to povre folk . . .

Cp. *Matt. 7:2, Mark 4:24, Luke 6:38* (Cp. *Quoniam*; ibid.; Peraldus, *SVV* ; Petersen, 1901, p. 68).

781: Espiritueel marchandise is proprely symonye. . . .

Cp. *Acts 8:9-24* (Peraldus, *SVV* ; Petersen, 1901, p. 68; R).

783: Certes symonye is cleped of Simon Magus, that wolde han boght for temporeel catel the yifte that God hadde yeven by the Hooly Goost to Seint Peter and to the apostles.

Acts 8:9-24 (Quoniam 368; ibid.; Peraldus, *SVV*; Petersen, 1901, p. 69; R; P; Wenzel, in B, 1987, n. 783).

789: . . . by hem that yeven chirches to hem that been nat digne.

Cp. *1 Cor. 3:17* (cp. *Quoniam* 373; ibid.).

792: They sellen the soules that lambes sholde kepen to the wolf that strangleth hem. And therfore shul they nevere han part of the pasture of lambes, that is the blisse of hevene.

Cp. *John 10:9-12* (cp. *Quoniam* 369; ibid.).

795: . . . And ye shul understonde that thise been grete synnes and expres agayn the comaundementz of God . . .
> *Exod. 20:15-16, Deut. 5:18-19; etc.* (Wenzel, in B, 1987, n. 795).

797: . . . for fals witnessyng was Susanna in ful gret sorwe and peyne, and many another mo.
> Cp. *Dan. 13:34-62* (R; P; F; Wenzel, in B, 1987, n. 797).

798: The synne of thefte is eek expres agayns Goddes heeste . . .
> Cp. *Exod. 20:15, Deut. 5:19; etc.* (*Quoniam* 369; ibid.).

819: This synne corrumped al this world, as is wel shewed in the synne of Adam and of Eve . . .
> *Gen. 3:6, 23-24* (*Quoniam* 370; ibid.; cp. Peraldus, *SVV*; Petersen, 1901, p. 70; Wenzel, in B, 1987, n. 819).

819-20: . . . Looke eek what seith Seint Paul of Glotonye:/ "Manye," seith Seint Paul, "goon, of whiche I have ofte seyd to yow, and now I seye it wepynge, that been the enemys of the croys of Crist; of whiche the ende is deeth, and of whiche hir wombe is hire god, and hire glorie in confusioun of hem that so savouren erthely thynges."
> g
> *Phil. 3:18-19* (*Quoniam* 370; ibid.; Peraldus, *SVV*; Petersen, 1901, p. 70; cp. Johnson, 1941, p. 99; Reiss, 1984, p. 60; R; P; F; Wenzel, in B, 1987, n. 820).

822: . . . and therfore, whan a man is dronken, he hath lost his resoun . . .
> Cp. *Prov. 20:1* (cp. *Quoniam* 370; ibid.; cp. Peraldus, *SVV*; Petersen, 1901, p. 70; cp. Wenzel, in B, 1987, n. 822).

837: . . . for he seyde hymself, "Do no lecherie." And therfore he putte grete peynes agayns this synne in the olde lawe.
> G

Exod. 20:14, etc. (Quoniam 371; ibid.; P; F; Wenzel, in B, 1987, n. 837).

Cp. *Lev. 19:20, 20:10-21; Deut. 22:21; etc. (Quoniam* 371; ibid.; P; F; Wenzel, in B, 1987, n. 837).

838: If womman thral were taken in this synne, she sholde be beten with staves to the deeth; and if she were a gentil womman, she sholde be slayn with stones; and if she were a bisshoppes doghter, she sholde been brent, by Goddes comandement.

Cp. *Deut. 22:21; Lev. 21:9* (cp. *Quoniam* 371; ibid.; P; Wenzel, in B, 1987, n. 838).

839: . . . by the synne of lecherie God dreynte al the world at the diluge. And after that he brente fyve citees with thonder-leyt, and sank hem into helle.

Cp. *Gen. 6:2-7; 7* (cp. *Quoniam* 371; ibid.; cp. Johnson, 1941, pp. 94-97; Wood, 1984, p. 43; P; F; Wenzel, in B, 1987, n. 839).

Cp. *Gen. 14:8; 19:4-9, 24-25* (cp. *Quoniam* 371; ibid.; cp. Johnson, 1941, pp. 94-97, 116-17; P; F; Wenzel, in B, 1987, n. 839).

Isa. 19:18 (R; P).

841: Seint John seith that avowtiers shullen been in helle, in a stank brennynge of fyr and of brymston . . .

8
Apoc. 21:8 (Quoniam 371; ibid.; R; P; F; Wenzel, in B, 1987, n. 841).

842: Certes, the brekynge of this sacrement is an horrible thyng. It was maked of God hymself in paradys, and confermed by Jhesu Crist, as witnesseth Seint Mathew in the gospel: "A man shal lete fader and mooder and taken hym to his wif, and they shullen be two in o flessh."

Gen. 2:24 (cp. Peraldus, *SVV;* Petersen, 1901, p. 72; R; P; F;
    Wenzel, in B, 1987, n. 842; Patterson, 1978, 343-44).
    g
    G
Matt. 19:5 (R; P; F; Wenzel, in B, 1987, n. 842).

843: This sacrement bitokneth the knyttynge togidre of Crist
and of hooly chirche.
    Cp. *Eph. 5:25* (R; P; Wenzel, in B, 1987, n. 843; Patterson,
    1978, 343-44).

844: . . . but eek he comanded that thou sholdest nat coveite thy
neighebores wyf.
    Exod. 20:17, Deut. 5:21; etc. (P; Wenzel, in B, 1987, n. 844).

845: . . . Lo, what seith Seint Mathew in the gospel, that
"whoso seeth a womman to coveitise of his lust, he hath doon
lecherie with hire in his herte."
    g
    Matt. 5:28 (S; R; P; F; Wenzel, in B, 1987, n. 845).

850: This synne, as seith the prophete, bireveth man and
womman hir goode fame and al hire honour, and it is ful
plesaunt to the devel, for therby wynneth he the mooste partie
of this world.
    Cp. *Ecclus. 9:10* (*Quoniam* 372; ibid.; Wenzel, in B, 1987, n.
    850).
    g
    Jer. 2:36 ? (*Quoniam* 372; ibid.; Wenzel, in B, 1987, n. 850).

854: . . . And therfore seith Salomon that "whoso toucheth and
handleth a womman, he fareth lyk hym that handleth the
scorpioun that styngeth and sodeynly sleeth thurgh his
envenymynge"; as whoso toucheth warm pych, it shent his
fyngres.
    g

Cp. *Ecclus. 13:1, 26:10* (*Quoniam* 372; ibid.; R; P; F; Wenzel, in B, 1987, n. 854).

863-64: . . . the feend . . . gripeth hym by the reynes for to throwen hym into the fourneys of helle,/ ther as they shul han the fyr and the wormes that evere shul lasten, and wepynge and wailynge, sharp hunger and thrust, [and] grymnesse of develes, that shullen al totrede hem withouten respit and withouten ende.

Cp. *Mark 9:42-45* (*Quoniam* 372-73; ibid.; R; P).

Cp. *Matt. 13:42* (*Quoniam* 372-73; ibid.).

Cp. *Job 20:25* (*Quoniam* 372-73; ibid.).

867: . . . for as muche as God forbad leccherie. And Seint Paul yeveth hem the regne that nys dewe to no wight but to hem that doon deedly synne.

G

Exod 20:14, Deut. 5:18, Matt. 5:27-28; etc. (Wenzel, in B, 1987, n. 867).

g

Gal. 5:19-21 (*Quoniam* 373; ibid.; R; P; F; Wenzel, in B, 1987, n. 867).

869: . . . and bireveth hire thilke precious fruyt that the book clepeth the hundred fruyt. I ne kan seye it noon ootherweyes in Englissh, but in Latyn it highte *Centesimus fructus*.

Matt. 13:8 (*Quoniam* 373; ibid.; Peraldus, *SVV*; Petersen, 1901, p. 72; R; F; Wenzel, in B, 1987, n. 869).

875: Of this synne, as seith the wise man, folwen manye harmes. First, brekynge of feith, and certes in feith is the keye of Cristendom.

g

Cp. *Ecclus. 23:32-33* (*Quoniam* 373; ibid.; Wenzel, in B, 1987, n. 875).

879: . . . for thise avowtiers breken the temple of God spiritually, and stelen the vessel of grace, that is the body and the soule, for which Crist shal destroyen hem, as seith Seint Paul.

> Cp. *1 Cor. 3:17* (*Quoniam* 373; ibid.; R; P; F; Wenzel, in B, 1987, n. 879).

8

880-81: Soothly, of this thefte douted gretly Joseph, whan that his lordes wyf preyed hym of vileynye, whan he seyde, "Lo, my lady, how my lord hath take to me under my warde al that he hath in this world, ne no thyng of his thynges is out of my power, but oonly ye, that been his wyf./ And how sholde I thanne do this wikkednesse, and synne so horribly agayns God and agayns my lord? God it forbeede!"

> *Gen. 39:8-9* (cp. Johnson, 1941, p. 123; R; P; F; Wenzel, in B, 1987, n. 880-81).

882: . . . thurgh which they breken the comandement of God, and defoulen the auctour of matrimoyne, that is Crist.

> Cp. *Ecclus. 23:33* (*Quoniam* 374; ibid.; Peraldus, *SVV*; Petersen, 1901, p. 73; Wenzel, in B, 1987, n. 875).
> Cp. *Heb. 2:10; etc.*

883: . . . for God made mariage in paradys, in the estaat of innocence, to multiplye mankynde to the service of God.

> *Gen. 1:28* (*Quoniam* 374; ibid.; Peraldus, *SVV*; Petersen, 1901, p. 73; R; P; Wenzel, in B, 1987, n. 883).
> *Gen. 2:24* (*Quoniam* 374; ibid.).

884: . . . of which brekynge comen false heires ofte tyme. . . . And therfore wol Crist putte hem out of the regne of hevene. . . .

> Cp. *Ecclus. 23:33* (*Quoniam* 374; ibid.; Peraldus, *SVV*; Petersen, 1901, p. 74; Wenzel, in B, 1987, n. 875).
> Cp. *Apoc. 21:8* (*Quoniam* 374; ibid.)

887: Understoond eek that Avowtrie is set gladly in the ten comandementz bitwixe thefte and manslaughtre . . .

> *Exod. 20:13-15; Deut. 5:17-19 (Quoniam* 374; ibid.; Peraldus, *SVV;* Petersen, 1901, p. 74; Wenzel, in B, 1987, n. 887).
> *Exod. 20:1-17, Deut. 5:6-21*

888: And it is lyk to homycide, for it kerveth atwo and breketh atwo hem that first were maked o flessh. And therfore, by the olde lawe of God, they sholde be slayn.

> Cp. *Gen. 2:28; Matt. 19:5-6; etc.* (cp. *Quoniam* 374; ibid.; Peraldus, *SVV;* Petersen, 1901, p. 74).
> *Lev. 20:10 (Quoniam* 374; ibid.; Peraldus, *SVV;* Petersen, 1901, p. 74; Wenzel, in B, 1987, n. 888).
> G (P).

889: But nathelees, by the lawe of Jhesu Crist, that is lawe of pitee, whan he seyde to the womman that was founden in avowtrie, and sholde han been slayn with stones, after the wyl of the Jewes, as was hir lawe, "Go," quod Jhesu Crist, "and have namoore wyl to synne," or, "wille namoore to do synne."

> G (P).
> *John 8:5, 11 (Quoniam* 374; ibid.; R; P; F; Wenzel, in B, 1987, n. 889).

890: Soothly the vengeaunce of Avowtrie is awarded to the peynes of helle. . . .

> Cp. *Apoc. 21:8 (Quoniam* 374; ibid.; cp. Peraldus, *SVV;* Petersen, 1901, p. 74; Wenzel, in B, 1987, n. 890).

895: . . . but for sothe, Seint Paul seith that Sathanas transformeth hym in an aungel of light.

> g
> *2 Cor. 11:14 (Quoniam* 374; ibid.; cp. Peraldus, *SVV;* Petersen, 1901, p. 75; R; P; Wenzel, in B, 1987, n. 895).

897: Swiche preestes been the sones of Helie, as sheweth in the Book of Kynges, that they weren the sones of Belial—that is, the devel.

> *g*
> 1 *Kings* 2:12 (*Quoniam* 374-75; ibid.; R; P; F; Wenzel, in B, 1987, n. 897).

898: Belial is to seyn, "withouten juge." And so faren they; hem thynketh they been free and han no juge, namoore than hath a free bole that taketh which cow that hym liketh in the town.

> *Judg.* 19:22 ? (*Quoniam* 374-75; ibid.; R; F; Wenzel, in B, 1987, n. 898).
> *Ps.* 67(68):31(30) ? (*Quoniam* 375; ibid.).

900: Thise preestes, as seith the book, ne konne nat the mysterie of preesthod to the peple, ne God ne knowe they nat. They ne helde hem nat apayd, as seith the book, of soden flessh that was to hem offred, but they tooke by force the flessh that is rawe.

> *G*
> 1 *Kings* 2:12-16 (*Quoniam* 375; ibid.; R; P; F; Wenzel, in B, 1987, n. 900).

902: . . . and preye for Cristene soules.

> Cp. 2 *Mach.* 12:42-46 (liturgy).

904-06: The thridde spece of avowtrie is somtyme bitwixe a man and his wyf, and that is whan they take no reward in hire assemblynge but oonly to hire flesshly delit, as seith Seint Jerome,/ and ne rekken of nothyng but that they been assembled; by cause that they been maried, al is good ynough, as thynketh to hem./ But in swich folk hath the devel power, as seyde the aungel Raphael to Thobie, for in hire assemblynge they putten Jhesu Crist out of hire herte and yeven hemself to alle ordure.

> *Tob.* 6:16-17 (*Quoniam* 375; ibid.; R; P; F; Wenzel, in B, 1987, nn. 904, 906; cp. Gower, *CA* 7.5307-65).

907: The fourthe spece is the assemblee of hem that been of hire kynrede, or of hem that been of oon affynytee, or elles with hem with whiche hire fadres or hir kynrede han deled in the synne of lecherie. . . .
    Cp. *Lev. 18:6-18* (*Quoniam* 375; ibid.).

910-11: The fifthe spece is thilke abhomynable synne, of which that no man unnethe oghte speke ne write; nathelees it is openly reherced in holy writ./ This cursednesse doon men and wommen in diverse entente and in diverse manere . . .
    Cp. *Gen. 19; Lev. 18:22-23; etc.* (*Quoniam* 376; ibid.).
    Rom. 1:26-27; etc. (R; P; F; Wenzel, in B, 1987, n. 910).

911: . . . but though that hooly writ speke of horrible synne, certes hooly writ may nat been defouled, namoore than the sonne that shyneth on the mixne.
    G (*Quoniam* 376; ibid.; Wenzel, in B, 1987, n. 911; see discussion in "Introduction," pp. 5-7, above).

917-18: Now shaltow understonde that matrimoyne is leefful assemblynge of man and of womman that receyven by vertu of the sacrement the boond thurgh which they may nat be departed in al hir lyf—that is to seyn, whil that they lyven bothe./ This, as seith the book, is a ful greet sacrement. God maked it, as I have seyd, in paradys, and wolde hymself be born in mariage.
    Eph. 5:31-32 (*Postquam* 21-27; ibid., p. 22; Peraldus, *SVV*; Petersen, 1901, p. 76; R; P; F; Wenzel, in B, 1987, n. 918).
    G
    Gen. 2:18, 21-24 (Peraldus, *SVV*; Petersen, 1901, p. 76; R; P; F).
    Matt. 1:16-25, etc. (*Postquam* 78; ibid., p. 23; Peraldus, *SVV*; Petersen, 1901, p. 76; R).

919: And for to halwen mariage he was at a weddynge, where as he turned water into wyn, which was the firste miracle that he wroghte in erthe biforn his disciples.

John 2:1-11 (cp. *Postquam* 27; ibid., p. 22; Peraldus, *SVV;* Petersen, 1901, p. 77; R; P; F; Wenzel, in B, 1987, n. 919).

921: This is verray mariage, that was establissed by God, er that synne bigan, whan natureel lawe was in his right poynt in paradys; and it was ordeyned that o man sholde have but o womman, and o womman but o man, as seith Seint Augustyn, by manye resouns.

> *Gen. 2:18* (cp. *Postquam* 45, 76; ibid., p. 23; Wenzel, in B, 1987, n. 921).
> Cp. *Gen. 2:21-24*

922: First, for mariage is figured bitwixe Crist and holy chirche. And that oother is for a man is heved of a womman; algate, by ordinaunce it sholde be so.

> *Eph. 5:23-25* (*Postquam* 77; ibid., p. 23; Peraldus, *SVV;* Petersen, 1901, p. 77; R; P; F; Wenzel, in B, 1987, n. 922).
> *1 Cor. 11:3* (*Postquam* 79; ibid., p. 23; R; P; F; Wenzel, in B, 1987, n. 922).

925-26: . . . as shewed Crist whan he made first womman./ For he made hire nat of the heved of Adam . . .

> *Gen. 2:18, 22* (*Postquam* 90-91, 93; ibid.; Wenzel, in B, 1987, n. 925-29).

928: Also, certes, God ne made nat womman of the foot of Adam, for she ne sholde nat been holden to lowe; for she kan nat paciently suffre. But God made womman of the ryb of Adam, for womman sholde be felawe unto man.

> *Gen. 2:18, 22* (*Postquam* 91, 93; ibid., pp. 23-24, 29; Wenzel, in B, 1987, n. 925-29).
> Cp. *1 Pet. 3[7]* (C. V. Kaske, 1975, p. 167).

929: Man sholde bere hym to his wyf in feith, in trouthe, and in love, as seith Seint Paul, that a man sholde loven his wyf as Crist loved hooly chirche, that loved it so wel that he deyde for it. . . .

Eph. 5:25 (*Postquam* 96; ibid., p. 24; R; P; F; Wenzel, in B, 1987, nn. 925-29, 929).

g

930: Now how that a womman sholde be subget to hire housbonde, that telleth Seint Peter. First, in obedience.
  1 Pet. 3:1 (*Postquam* 105; ibid.; R; P; F; Wenzel, in B, 1987, n. 930).

g

931: And eek, as seith the decree, a womman that is wyf, as longe as she is a wyf, she hath noon auctoritee to swere ne to bere witnesse withoute leve of hir housbonde. . . .
  G
  Num. 30:7-17 (cp. Wenzel, in B, 1987, n. 931).

932: She sholde eek serven hym in alle honestee, and been attempree of hire array. I woot wel that they sholde setten hire entente to plesen hir housbondes, but nat by hire queyntise of array.
  1 Pet. 3:3-5 (cp. *Postquam* 106, 109, 110, 111, 113; ibid.; R).

933: Seint Jerome seith that "wyves that been apparailled in silk and in precious purpre ne mowe nat clothen hem in Jhesu Crist." Loke what seith Seint John eek in thys matere?
  Apoc. 17:4, 18:16 ? (R; P; F; Wenzel, 1984, p. 29; Wenzel, in B, 1987, n. 933).

g

940: Another cause is to yelden everich of hem to oother the delte of hire bodies, for neither of hem hath power of his owene body. . . .
  1 Cor. 7:3-4 (*Postquam* 139, 44; ibid., pp. 25, 23; Peraldus, *SVV*; Petersen, 1901, p. 77; P; F; Patterson, 1978, 357).

947: . . . They been the vessel or the boyste of the blissed Magdalene, that fulfilleth hooly chirche of good odour.

Matt. 26:7; John 12:3 (Postquam 193; ibid., p. 25; cp. McCall, 1971; R; F; Wenzel, in B, 1987, n. 947).

948: . . . Thanne is she spouse to Jhesu Crist, and she is the lyf of angeles.
    Matt. 12:25 (Postquam 411, 429-30; ibid., p. 26; cp. Johnson, 1941, pp. 117-18; Sister Mary Immaculate, 1941, 65-66; R; cp. Wenzel, in B, 1987, n. 948).

950: Virginitee baar oure Lord Jhesu Crist. . . .
    Cp. *Luke 1:27, etc. (Postquam* 416; ibid.).

955: Ful ofte tyme I rede that no man truste in his owene perfeccioun, but he be stronger than Sampson, and hoolier than David, and wiser than Salomon.
    Cp. *Judg. 13-16* (Peraldus, *SVV;* Petersen, 1901, p. 78; Friend, 1948-49; R; cp. Wenzel, 1984, pp. 29-30).
    Cp. *1 Kings-3 Kings 2:11* (ibid.).
    Cp. *3 Kings 3, etc.* (ibid.; and cp. Gower, *CA* 7.3891-3912).

956: . . . I wolde telle yow the ten comandementz.
    Exod. 20:1-17, Deut. 5:6-21 (cp. Wenzel, in B, 1987, n. 956-57).

959: . . . agayn the lawe of Jhesu Crist . . .
    G (cp. Wenzel, in B, 1987, n. 959).

983: . . . as seyde the kyng Ezechias to God, "I wol remembre me alle the yeres of my lif in bitternesse of myn herte."
    Isa. 38:15 (R; P; F; Wenzel, in B, 1987, n. 983; cp. line 135, above).

986: Swich was the confessioun of the publican that wolde nat heven up his eyen to hevene, for he hadde offended God of hevene; for which shamefastnesse he hadde anon the mercy of God.

Luke 18:13-14 (Pennaforte, *SCP;* Petersen, 1901, p. 19; R; P;
F; Wenzel, in B, 1987, n. 986).

988: . . . of which seith Seint Peter, "Humbleth yow under the
myght of God." . . .
> g
1 Pet. 5:6 (Pennaforte, *SCP;* Petersen, 1901, p. 19; cp. Johnson,
1941, p. 112; R; P; F; Wenzel, in B, 1987, n. 988).

994: Swich was the confession of Seint Peter, for after that he
hadde forsake Jhesu Crist, he wente out and weep ful bitterly.
Matt. 26:75 (R; P; F; Wenzel, in B, 1987, n. 994).

996: Swich was the confessioun of the Magdalene, that ne
spared for no shame of hem that weren atte feeste, for to go to
oure Lord Jhesu Crist and biknowe to hym hire synne.
Luke 7:36-38, 47-48 (Pennaforte, *SCP;* Petersen, 1901, p. 19;
La, 1924, 94; cp. Johnson, 1941, pp. 103-04; cp. McCall,
1971; R; P; F; Wenzel, in B, 1987, n. 996).

997: . . . for certes, Jhesu Crist, for the giltes of o man, was
obedient to the deeth.
Cp. *Phil. 2:8* (cp. Pennaforte, *SCP;* Petersen, 1901, p. 20;
Wenzel, in B, 1987, n. 997).

1000-02: Certes, a man oghte hastily shewen his synnes for
manye causes; as for drede of deeth, that cometh ofte sodeynly,
and no certeyn what tyme it shal be, ne in what place. . . . and
eek the lenger that he tarieth, the ferther he is fro Crist. . . .
And for as muche as he ne hath nat in his lyf herkned Jhesu
Crist whanne he hath spoken, he shal crie to Jhesu Crist at his
laste day, and scarsly wol he herkne hym.
Cp. *Luke 12:45-46* (Pennaforte, *SCP;* Petersen, 1901, p. 20;
La; R; Wenzel, in B, 1987, n. 1000-02).

1007: For certes Jhesu Crist is entierly al good; in hym nys noon
imperfeccioun . . .

Cp. *Mark 10:18, 1 Pet. 1:19; etc.* (Pennaforte, *SCP;* Petersen, 1901, p. 21).

1015: . . . and that a man ne be nat despeired of the mercy of Jhesu Crist, as Caym or Judas.
Cp. *Gen. 4:14* (R; P; F; Wenzel, in B, 1987, n. 1014-15).
Cp. *Matt. 27:3-5; etc.* (R; P; F; Wenzel, in B, 1987, n. 1014-15).

1031: And tak kep that a man hath nede of thise thinges generally: he hath nede of foode, he hath nede of clothyng and herberwe, he hath nede of charitable conseil and visitynge in prisone and in maladie, and sepulture of his dede body.
Cp. *Matt. 25:35-36* (Wenzel, in B, 1987, n. 1031-33).

1033: Thise been general almesses or werkes of charitee of hem that han temporeel richesses or discrecioun in conseilynge. Of thise werkes shaltow heren at the day of doom.
Matt. 25:40, 46 (La; R; Wenzel, in B, 1987, nn. 1031-33, 1033).

1036-37: For, as witnesseth Seint Mathew, *capitulo quinto,* "A citee may nat been hyd that is set on a montayne, ne men lighte nat a lanterne and put it under a busshel, but men sette it on a candel-stikke to yeve light to the men in the hous./ Right so shal youre light lighten bifore men, that they may seen youre goode werkes, and glorifie youre fader that is in hevene."
8
Matt. 5:14-16 (R; P; F; Wenzel, in B, 1987, n. 1035-36).

1039: . . . of whiche orisouns, certes, in the orison of the *Pater noster* hath Jhesu Crist enclosed moost thynges.
Matt. 6:9-13; Luke 11:2-4 (cp. Pennaforte, *SCP;* Petersen, 1901, p. 28; Wenzel, in B, 1987, n. 1039).

1047: . . . for, as seith Seint Jerome, "By fastynge been saved the vices of the flessh, and by preyere the vices of the soule."

Cp. *Mark 9:28* (Pennaforte, *SCP;* Petersen, 1901, p. 29; cp. Wenzel, in B, 1987, n. 1047).

1048: . . . for Jhesu Crist seith, "Waketh and preyeth, that ye ne entre in wikked temptacioun."
   Matt. 26:41 (Pennaforte, *SCP;* Petersen, 1901, p. 29; Jerome, *EAJ* 2.3; Correale, 1964-65; R; P; F; Wenzel, in B, 1987, n. 1048).

1054: And therfore seith Seint Paul, "Clothe yow, as they that been chosen of God, in herte of misericorde, debonairetee, suffraunce, and swich manere of clothynge." . . .
   g
   Col. 3:12 (P; F; Wenzel, in B, 1987, n. 1054).

1062: A man sholde eek thynke that God seeth and woot alle his thoghtes and alle his werkes; to hym may no thyng been hyd ne covered.
   Heb. 4:13 (Pennaforte, *SCP;* Petersen, 1901, pp. 31-32). Cp. *Ps. 43(44):22(21);* etc.

1063-64: Men sholden eek remembren hem of the shame that is to come at the day of doom to hem that been nat penitent and shryven in this present lyf./ For alle the creatures in hevene, in erthe, and in helle shullen seen apertly al that they hyden in this world.
   Cp. *Rom. 2:16;* etc.

1068: . . . he shal thynke that oure lif is in no sikernesse, and eek that alle the richesses in this world ben in aventure and passen as a shadwe on the wal. . . .
   Cp. *James 4:15;* etc. (Pennaforte, *SCP;* Petersen, 1901, p. 32).
   Cp. *Job 27:19* ? (Pennaforte, *SCP;* Petersen, 1901, p. 32; R).
   Cp. *1 Par. 29:15; Wis. 2:5, 5:9; Job 8:9, 14:2;* etc. (cp. R; see *MerchT* 1315 and *ShipT* 9; cp. Wenzel, in B, 1987, n. 1068; Patterson, 1978, 357).

1073: . . . the mercy of Crist is alwey redy to receiven hym to mercy.
> Cp. *Ps. 102(103):17-18* (Pennaforte, *SCP*; Petersen, 1901, p. 33; R).

1080: This blisful regne may men purchace by poverte espiritueel, and the glorie by lowenesse, the plentee of joye by hunger and thurst, and the reste by travaille, and the lyf by deeth and mortificacion of synne.
> *Matt. 5:3-11* (Miller, 1977, p. 497; cp. Wenzel, in B, 1987, n. 1076-80).
> *Rom. 8:13*

Chaucer's Retraction, X (I), lines 1081-92:

1083: For oure book seith, "Al that is writen is writen for oure doctrine." . . .
> G
> Cp. *Rom. 15:4; 2 Tim. 3:16* (R; P; Wenzel, in B, 1987, n. 1083).

1091: . . . kyng of kynges . . . that boghte us with the precious blood of his herte . . .
> *1 Tim. 6:15; etc.*
> *Rom. 5:9; Col. 1:14; etc.*

1092: . . . so that I may been oon of hem at the day of doom that shulle be saved. *Qui cum Patre et Spiritu Sancto vivit et regnat Deus per omnia secula. Amen.*
> Cp. *Eph. 4:30; etc.* (liturgy).
> Cp. *Apoc. 1:18; etc.* (liturgy; F; Wenzel, in B, 1987, n. 1092).

THE BOOK OF THE DUCHESS

35-40: . . . but trewly, as I gesse,/ I holde hit be a sicknesse/ That I have suffred this eight yeer;/ And yet my boote is never the ner,/ For there is phisicien but oon/ That may me hele. . . .

Cp. *Acts 9:33-34* ? (Machaut, *RF* 1467-69; Windeatt, 1982, p. 64; cp. Machaut, *DL* 57; Windeatt, 1982, pp. 65-66; Huppé & Robertson, 1963, pp. 32-33; Wimsatt, 1981, pp. 113-15; cp. Wilcockson, in B, 1987, n. 30-43).
Cp. *Ps. 146(147):3; Matt. 9:12, Mark 2:17, Luke 5:31; etc.* ?

170-71: . . . as derk/ As helle-pit overal aboute.
Apoc. 9:1, etc. (cp. Wilcockson, in B, 1987, n. 171).

237: . . . For I ne knew never god but oon.
Mark 12:32 ? (La; R, pp. 720-21, n. 55).

280-82: . . . No, not Joseph, withoute drede,/ Of Egipte, he that redde so/ The kynges metynge Pharao . . .
Gen. 41 (Wilcockson, in B, 1987, nn. 280, 282).

294-320: . . . for I was waked/ With smale foules a gret hep. . . . .
. . . . . Was never herd so swete a steven/ But hyt had be a thyng of heven—/ . . . . They ne spared not her throtes.
Cp. *Ps. 32(33):3; Apoc. 14:3* ? (cp. Machaut, *JRB* 21; Wimsatt, 1981, pp. 120-21; cp. Wilcockson, in B, 1987, n. 291-343).

310: . . . for the toun of Tewnes . . .
Cp. *Cant., Eccl. 1:2; etc.* (Huppé and Robertson, 1963, p. 46; cp. Wimsatt, 1981, pp. 118-21; cp. Wilcockson, in B, 1987, n. 309-10).

333-34: . . . bothe text and glose,/ Of al the Romaunce of the Rose.
G ? (cp. Wilcockson, in B, 1987, n. 333-34).

345-46: Me thoght I herde an hunte blowe/ T'assay hys horn. . . .
Cp. *1 Cor. 15:51-55; etc.* ? (Delasanta, 1969, 250, et passim; cp. Wilcockson, in B, 1987, nn. 346-86, 346).

375-76: The mayster-hunte anoon, fot-hot,/ With a gret horn blew thre mot. . . .

> Cp. *1 Cor. 15:51-55; etc.* ? (Delasanta, 1969, 250, et passim; cp. Wilcockson, in B, 1987, nn. 346-86, 346).

378-80: Withynne a while the hert yfounde ys,/ Yhalowed, and rechased faste/ Longe tyme. . . .

> *Cant. 2:9; etc.* ? (Delasanta, 1969, 250-51, et passim; cp. Wilcockson, in B, 1987, nn. 346-86, 346).

398-447: . . . Doun by a floury grene wente/ Ful thikke of gras, ful softe and swete./ With floures fele, faire under fete,/ . . . . . .
. . . . so at the laste/ I was war of a man in blak,/ That sat and had yturned his bak/ To an ook, an huge tree.

> *Gen. 2:8-3:24* ? (cp. Machaut, *JRB* 33, et passim; Windeatt, 1982, pp. 3-4; cp. Machaut, *DL* 57, 107; Windeatt, 1982, pp. 65-66; Robertson, 1962, pp. 387-88; cp. Pearsall and Salter, 1973, pp. 76-101, et passim; cp. Wilcockson, in B, 1987, n. 402-33).

487-88: Whan he had mad thus his complaynte,/ Hys sorwful hert gan faste faynte. . . .

> *Cant. 2:9; etc.* ? (cp. Machaut, *JRB* 206; Windeatt, 1982, p. 6; Delasanta, 1969, 250-51, et passim).

583-86: The pure deth ys so ful my foo/ That I wolde deye, hyt wolde not soo;/ For whan I folwe hyt, hit wol flee;/ I wolde have hym, hyt nyl nat me.

> *Apoc. 9:6* ? (Wimsatt, 1981, p. 122; Wilcockson, in B, 1987, n. 583).

599-601: My song ys turned to pleynynge,/ And al my laughtre to wepynge,/ My glade thoghtes to hevynesse . . .

> Cp.*James 4:9; etc.* (cp. Machaut, *JRB* 206; Windeatt, 1982, p. 6; La; cp. Wilcockson, in B, 1987, n. 599-616).

738-39: And for Dalida died Sampson,/ That slough hymself with a piler.
> *Judg. 16* (F; cp. Wilcockson, in B, 1987, n. 738).

831: By God and by his halwes twelve . . .
> *Matt. 10:1-5; etc.* (F).

904-05: . . . that she/ Was whit, rody, fressh, and lyvely hewed. . . .
> Cp. *Cant. 5:10* (Machaut, *JRB* 358-61; Wimsatt, 1967, 35;
> ————, 1981, p. 121; cp. Wilcockson, in B, 1987, n. 905).

919-20: And which a goodly, softe speche/ Had that swete, my lyves leche!
> Cp. *Ps. 146(147):3; Matt. 9:12, Mark 2:17, Luke 5:31; etc.* ?
> (cp. Machaut, *RF* 217, 281; Windeatt, 1982, pp. 61-62).

939-46: But swich a fairnesse of a nekke/ Had that swete. . . .
Hyt was whit. . . . Hir throte, as I have now memoyre,/ Semed a round tour of yvoyre. . . .
> Cp. *Cant 7:4* (Machaut, *JRB* 352; Windeatt, 1982, pp. 8-9;
> Huppé & Robertson, 1963, p. 76; Wimsatt, 1967, 35;
> ————, 1981, p. 121; cp. Wilcockson, in B, 1987, n. 946).

948-51: And goode faire White she het;/ That was my lady name ryght./ She was bothe fair and bryght;/ She hadde not hir name wrong.
> *Wis. 7:26* ? (Wimsatt, 1967, 38-40; Wilcockson, in B, 1987, n. 946).

963-65: . . . That she was lyk to torche bryght/ That every man may take of lyght/ Ynogh, and hyt hath never the lesse.
> *Wis. 7:26* ? (Wimsatt, 1967, 38-40).

971-74: For I dar swere wel, yif that she/ Had among ten thousand be,/ She wolde have be, at the leste,/ A chef myrour of al the feste. . . .

Cant. 5:10 (Wimsatt, 1967, 35).
Cant. 6:7-8 ? (Wimsatt, 1981, p. 121).
Wis. 7:26 ? (Wimsatt, 1967, 38-40).

981-84: Trewly she was, to myn yë,/ The solcyn fenix of
Arabye,/ For ther livyth never but oon,/ Ne swich as she ne
knowe I noon.
    Cant. 6:7-8 ? (Wimsatt, 1967, 36; ———, 1981, p. 121; F; cp.
      Wilcockson, in B, 1987, nn. 946, 982).

985-88: To speke of godnesse, trewly she/ Had as moche
debonairte/ As ever had Hester in the Bible,/ And more, yif
more were possyble.
    Wis. 7:26 ? (Wimsatt, 1967, 38-40).
    Esth. 2:7, etc. (cp. Deschamps, *Mir.*; Lowes, 1910, 182; F;
      Wilcockson, in B, 1987, nn. 946, 987; Wimsatt, 1967, 37-
      38).
    G

1002-05: And I dar seyn and swere hyt wel—/ That Trouthe
hymself over al and al/ Had chose hys maner principal/ In hir
that was his restyng place.
    Prov. 9:1 ? (Wimsatt, 1967, 40).

1117-18: . . . Nay, certes, than were I wel/ Wers than was
Achitofel . . .
    2 Kings 14-18 (R; F; Wilcockson, in B, 1987, n. 1117-23).

1160-66: . . . Althogh I koude not make so wel/ Songes, ne knewe
the art al,/ As koude Lamekes sone Tubal,/ That found out first
the art of songe;/ For as hys brothres hamers ronge/ Upon hys
anvelt up and doun,/ Therof he took the firste soun . . .
    Gen. 4:21-22 (Peter Riga, *Aurora;* Young, 1937; R; F;
      Wilcockson, in B, 1987, n. 1162).

1205-07: . . . And eke, as helpe me God withal,/ I trowe hyt was
in the dismal,/ That was the ten woundes of Egipte . . .

Exod 7-12; etc. (F; cp. Wilcockson, in B, 1987, n. 1206-07).

1311-13: And with that word ryght anoon/ They gan to strake forth; al was doon,/ For that tyme, the hert-huntyng.
> *Cant. 2:9; etc.* ? (Delasanta, 1969, 250-51, et passim).
> Cp. *1 Cor. 15:51-55; etc.* ? (Delasanta, 1969, 250, et passim; cp. Wilcockson, in B, 1987, n. 1312).

1318-19: . . . A long castel with walles white,/ Be seynt Johan, on a ryche hil. . . .
> Cp. *Apoc. 21:10, etc.* ? (Huppé & Robertson, 1963, pp. 91-92; Wimsatt, 1981, p. 122; cp. Wilcockson, in B, 1987, n. 1314-29).

THE HOUSE OF FAME

59-63: For never sith that I was born,/ Ne no man elles me beforn,/ Mette, I trowe stedfastly,/ So wonderful a drem as I/ The tenthe day now of Decembre. . . .
> Cp. *Ezech. 40:1-2; 4 Kings 25:1* ? (Koonce, 1966, pp. 181-85; Jeffrey, 1984[d], pp. 220-22; cp. Fyler, in B, 1987, n. 63).

81-82: And he that mover ys of al,/ That is and was and ever shal . . .
> Cp. *Apoc. 4:8, 11:17; etc.* (liturgy, *Gloria Patri*; cp. Dante, *Par.* 1.1; La; cp. Henkin, 1941; cp. *TC* 1.245, below).

345: O wel-awey that I was born!
> Cp. *Job 3:3, Jer.20:14*

351: O, soth ys, every thing is wyst . . .
> Cp. *Luke 12:2; etc.* (Jeffrey, 1984[d], p. 227, n. 37; proverbial; Whi E167, S491; R; Fyler, in B, 1987, n. 351).

470: . . . "A, Lord!" thoughte I, "that madest us . . . "
> *Gen. 1:26-27, 2:7* (Bennett, 1968, pp. 46, 89-90).

492: "O Crist," thoughte I, "that art in blysse. . . . "
Mark 16:19; Luke 24:51; etc.

499-508: . . . Me thoughte I sawgh an egle sore,/ But that hit semed moche more/ Then I had any egle seyn. . . . Hyt was of gold. . . . And somwhat dounward gan hyt lyghte.
    Cp. *Ezech. 17:3-4* (cp. Dante, *Purg.* 9.19-24, 28-30, *Par.* 1.62-65; Schless, 1984, pp. 45-47; Fyler, in B, 1987, n. 499-508).

514-17: . . . That Isaye . . ./ Ne kyng Nabugodonosor,/ Pharoo . . . ne Elcanor,/ Ne mette such a drem as this.
    Isa. 6:1-13 (R; F; Fyler, in B, 1987, n. 514-17).
    Dan. 2, 4 (R; F; Fyler, in B, 1987, n. 514-17).
    Gen. 41 (R; F; Fyler, in B, 1987, n. 514-17).
    1 Kings 1:1 ? (cp. R; F; Fyler, in B, 1987, n. 514-17).

529-48: This egle, of which I have yow told . . . . Me, fleynge, in a swap he hente . . . For I cam up, y nyste how.
    Cp. *Ezech. 8:1-3, 17:3-4* ? (Jeffrey, 1984[d], p. 214, n. 12 and pp. 221-23, et passim; cp. Dante, *Purg.* 32.109-16; Schless, 1984, pp. 45-47; Fyler, in B, 1987, nn. 534-39, 543).
    Apoc. 21:10-11 ? (Rowland, 1971, p. 17).

555-57: Til at the laste he to me spak/ In mannes vois, and seyde, "Awak!/ And be not agast so, for shame!"
    Cp. *Eph. 5:14* ? (liturgy; Jeffrey[d], 1984, p. 215; cp. Fyler, in B, 1987, n. 557).

588: I neyther am Ennok, ne Elye . . .
    Gen. 5:24; Ecclus. 44:16, 49:16 (cp. Dante, *Inf.* 2.31-33; Schless, 1984, pp. 53-55; cp. Bennett, 1968, pp. 59-60; Fyler, 1979, pp. 43-49; La; R; F; Fyler, in B, 1987, n. 588-92).
    2 Kings 2:11 (R; F; Fyler, in B, 1987, n. 588-92).

747-49: And for this cause mayst thou see/ That every ryver to the see/ Enclyned ys to goo by kynde . . .
    Eccl. 1:7 ?

782-871: "Now hennesforth y wol the teche/ How every speche, or noyse, or soun,/ Thurgh hys multiplicacioun,/ Thogh hyt were piped of a mous,/ Mot nede come to Fames Hous. . . . .
. . . / How thinketh the my conclusyon?"
    Cp. *Matt. 12:34-37* ? (Jeffrey, 1984[d], p. 216; cp. Fyler, in B, 1987, n. 788-821).

949: . . . Which that in heven a sygne is yit.
    Cp. *Apoc. 15:1; etc.* (cp. Henkin, 1941).

970: "O God," quod I, "that made Adam . . . "
    Gen. 1:26-27, 2:7 (Bennett, 1968, pp. 46, 89-90).

979-82: Thoo gan y wexen in a were,/ And seyde, "Y wot wel y am here,/ But wher in body or in gost/ I not, ywys, but God, thou wost!"
    2 Cor. 12:2-4 (cp. Dante, *Inf.* 2.28-30, *Par.* 1.6, 73-75; Schless, 1984, pp. 64-65; Bennett, 1968, p. 92; cp. Watts, 1973, 91-92, 106-07; La; R; Fyler, in B, 1987, n. 981).
    Cp. *Apoc. 7:14-15* (cp. Henkin, 1941).

1034: "Peter . . . "
    Matt. 4:18; etc.

1084: "Yis," quod I tho, "by heven kyng!"
    Cp. *Dan. 4:34; etc.*

1113-16: . . . I wol yow al the shap devyse/ Of hous and site, and al the wyse/ How I gan to thys place aproche/ That stood upon so hygh a roche. . . .
    Cp. *Ezech. 8* ? (Jeffrey, 1984[d], pp. 221-22; cp. Fyler, in B, 1987, nn. 1116, 1116-17).

1216-17: . . . Many thousand tymes twelve,/ That maden lowde mynstralcies . . .
 Apoc. 7:5-10 ? (La; cp. Henkin, 1941).

1245: There herde I trumpe Joab also . . .
 2 *Kings 2:28, etc.* (R; F; Fyler, in B, 1987, n. 1245).

1261: . . . And Phitonesses . . .
 1 Kings 28:7, 1 Par. 10:13 (F; Fyler, in B, 1987, n. 1261; cp. Gower, *CA* 4.1935-62).

1274: . . . Limote, and eke Symon Magus.
 Acts 13:8 ? (S; F; Fyler, in B, 1987, n. 1274).
 Acts 8:9, etc. (F; Bennett, 1968, p. 125).

1334-35: . . . Men myghte make of hem a bible/ Twenty foot thykke, as y trowe.
 G (cp. Fyler, in B, 1987, n. 1329-35).

1374-75: . . . That with hir fet she erthe reighte,/ And with hir hed she touched hevene . . .
 Cp. *Gen. 28:12* ? (cp. Fyler, in B, 1987, n. 1368-92; cp. *Bo* 1.p.1.15-7).

1381-85: . . . For as feele eyen hadde she/ As fetheres upon foules be,/ Or weren on the bestes foure/ That Goddis trone gunne honoure,/ As John writ in th'Apocalips.
 Apoc. 4:6 (Henkin, 1941, 583; cp. Dante, *Purg.* 29.92-95; cp. Bennett, 1968, pp. 131-32; La; R; Fyler, in B, 1987, n. 1383-85).
 g

1654: . . . And hyt stank as the pit of helle.
 Cp. *Isa. 34:3; etc.* (cp. nn. to *ABC* 56 in: R; F; Gross, in B, 1987; cp. Spencer, 1927, 191-92).

1758: For Goddes love, that sit above . . .
    Cp. *Deut. 4:39; etc.*

2000: "Petre . . . "
    Matt. 4:18; etc. (F; Fyler, in B, 1987, n. 1034).

2126-27: O, many a thousand tymes twelve/ Saugh I eke of these pardoners . . .
    Apoc. 7:5-10 ? (La; cp. Henkin, 1941).

ANELIDA AND ARCITE

149-54: . . . for hit is kynde of man/ Sith Lamek was, that is so longe agoon,/ To ben in love as fals as evere he can;/ He was the firste fader that began/ To loven two, and was in bigamye,/ And he found tentes first, but yf men lye.
    Gen. 4:18-20 (S; F; cp. DiMarco, in B, 1987, n. 154).

262-63: . . . as wisly He/ That al wot . . .
    Cp. *Ps. 43(44):22(21), 1 John 3:20; etc.*

THE PARLIAMENT OF FOWLS

9: . . . Ne wot how that he quiteth folk here hyre . . .
    Cp. *Luke 10:7; etc.*

32-33: . . . of hevene and helle/ And erthe, and soules that therinne dwelle . . .
    Cp. *Matt. 5:19-22; etc.* (cp. Muscatine, in B, 1987, nn. 32, 33).

46-49: . . . what man, lered other lewed,/ That lovede commune profyt, wel ithewed,/ He shulde into a blysful place wende/ There as joye is that last withouten ende.
    Cp. *Matt. 5:19-22; etc.* (cp. Muscatine, in B, 1987, n. 47).
    Cp. *Eph. 3:21*

60-63: . . . And after that the melodye herde he/ That cometh of thilke speres thryes thre,/ That welle is of musik and melodye/ In this world here, and cause of armonye.

    Cp. *Job 38:37* (La; cp. Muscatine, in B, 1987, n. 59-63).

64-66: Than bad he hym, syn erthe was so lyte,/ And dissevable and ful of harde grace,/ That he ne shulde hym in the world delyte.

    Cp. *1 John 2:15-17; etc.*

73-84: . . . Know thyself first immortal,/ And loke ay besyly thow werche and wysse/ To commune profit, and thow shalt not mysse/ To comen swiftly to that place deere/ That ful of blysse is and of soules cleere./ But brekers of the lawe . . ./ And likerous folk, after that they ben dede,/ Shul whirle aboute th'erthe alwey in peyne,/ Tyl many a world be passed, out of drede,/ And than, foryeven al hir wikked dede,/ Than shul they come into this blysful place,/ To which to comen God the sende his grace.

    Cp. *Matt. 5:19-22; etc.* (cp. Bennett, 1957, pp. 41-42; cp.
    Muscatine, in B, 1987, n. 80-84).

173-74: . . . treës clad with leves that ay shal laste,/ Ech in his kynde . . .

    Cp. *Gen. 1:11* (Bennett, 1957, pp. 77-78).

183-210: A gardyn saw I ful of blosmy bowes/ Upon a ryver, in a grene mede . . . . was there joye more a thousandfold/ Than man can telle; ne nevere wolde it nyghte,/ But ay cler day to any mannes syghte.

    Cp. *Gen. 2:8-3:24* ? (Boccaccio, *Teseida* 51; Windeatt, 1982,
    p. 81; cp. Bennett, 1957, pp. 62-106; Robertson, 1962, pp.
    387-88; cp. Pearsall and Salter, 1973, pp. 94-101, et
    passim; Muscatine, in B, 1987, n. 183-294).

    Cp. *Cant. 4:12* ? (Huppé & Robertson, 1963, p. 110).

199: . . . That God, that makere is of al and lord,/ Ne herde nevere beter, as I gesse.

> *Gen.1* (cp. R, pp. 720-21, n. 55).
> Cp. *Apoc. 14:1-3, etc.*

209-10: . . . ne nevere wolde it nyghte,/ But ay cler day to any mannes syghte.

> Cp. *Apoc. 22:5* (cp. Muscatine, in B, 1987, n. 204-10).

231: . . . I saw a temple of bras ifounded stronge.

> *1 Cor. 13:1* ? (F).

316-22: And right as Aleyn, in the Pleynt of Kynde,/ Devyseth Nature of aray and face,/ In swich aray men myghte hire there fynde./ This noble emperesse, ful of grace,/ Bad every foul to take his owne place,/ As they were woned alwey fro yer to yeere,/ Seynt Valentynes day, to stonden theere.

> Cp. *Apoc. 19:17* ? (Huppé & Robertson, 1963, pp. 123-24; cp. Muscatine, in B, 1987, n. 316).

381: . . . by evene noumbres of acord . . .

> Cp. *Job 10:22; Apoc. 7:4-8; etc.* ? (Bennett, 1957, p. 133).

BOECE

1.p.1.1-42: In the mene while . . . I saw, stondynge aboven the heghte of myn heved, a womman of ful greet reverence. . . . The stature of hire was of a doutous jugement, for somtyme sche constreyned and schronk hirselven lik to the comunc mesure of men, and somtyme it semede that sche touchede the hevene with the heghte of here heved. . . . In the nethereste hem or bordure of thise clothes, men redden ywoven in a
Grekissch P . . . and aboven that lettre, in the heieste bordure, a Grekyssh T. . . . And for sothe this forseide womman bar smale bokis in hir right hand, and in hir left hand sche bar a ceptre.

Prov. 8:1-9:5; 1 Cor. 1:24; etc. ? (D'Alverny, 1956).
Cp. *Gen. 28:12*

1.p.1.53-57: Forsothe thise ben tho that with thornes and
prikkynges of talentz or affeccions, whiche that ne bien
nothyng fructifyenge nor profitable, destroyen the corn
plentyvous of fruytes of resoun.
   Cp. *Matt. 13:22* ? (De Vogel, 1972, 14).

1.p.5.8-25: But certes, al be thow fer fro thy cuntre, thou n'art
nat put out of it. . . . . but o lord and o kyng, and that is God,
that is lord of thi cuntre, whiche that rejoisseth hym of the
duellynge of his citezeens, and nat for to putten hem in exil; of
the whiche lord it is a sovereyn fredom to ben governed by the
brydel of hym and obeye to his justice.
   Cp. *Heb. 11:13-16* ? (cp. 5.p.1.12-15 and 5.m.5.9-25, below;
      cp. *Truth* 17-20 and *Rom* 5659; cp. Hanna and Lawler, in B,
      1987, n. 1.p.5.9-11; cp. Pearsall and Salter, 1973, pp. 125-
      27).
   Isa. 65:11-14 ? (Robertson, 1952, pp. 87-88; cp. Hanna and
      Lawler, in B, 1987, n. 1.p.5.20).

1.p.6.84-85: But I thanke the auctour and the makere of hele . . .
   Cp. *Heb. 2:10; etc.*

2.p.2.15-16: Whan that nature brought the foorth out of thi
modir wombe, I resceyved the nakid. . . .
   Cp. *Job 1:21* ? (De Vogel, 1972, 12-13).

2.p.7.123-40: Whilom ther was a man that hadde [assaillede]
with stryvynge wordes another man. . . . This feynede
philosophre took pacience a litel while; and whan he hadde
resceyved wordes of outrage, he, as in stryvynge ayen and
rejoysynge of hymself, seide at the laste ryght thus:
'[U]ndirstondistow nat that I am a philosophre?' The tother
man answerede ayen ful bytyngely and seyde: 'I hadde wel
undirstonden it yif thou haddest holde thi tonge stille.'

Cp. *Prov. 11:12, 17:28; Ecclus. 20:5-7; etc.* (cp. Hanna and Lawler, in B, 1987, n. 2.p.7.122ff.).

3.p.5.66-68: Certes swiche folk as weleful fortune maketh frendes, contraryous fortune maketh hem enemys.
   Cp. *Prov. 19:4; Ecclus. 6:8-10* (proverbial; Whi, F667; cp. *MkT* 2244-46; cp. Hanna and Lawler, in B, 1987, n. 3.p.5.66-68).

3.m.6.11-12: . . . God your auctour and yowr makere . . .
   Cp. *Heb. 2:10; etc.*

3.m.9.25-32: . . . the mene soule . . . gooth to torne ayen to hymself . . . and turneth the hevene by semblable ymage.
   Gen 1:26-27, Wis. 2:23 ? (De Vogel, 1972, 11-12).

3.m.9.32-38: Thow . . . enhauncest the soules and the lasse lyves. . . . And whan thei ben convertyd to the by thi benygne lawe, thow makest hem retourne ayen to the by ayen-ledynge fyer.
   Cp. *Phil. 3:14; etc.* (Lawler, 1980, pp. 28-30).

3.m.9.47-49: . . . thow thiself art bygynnynge, berere, ledere, path, and terme; to looke on the, that is our ende.
   Apoc. 1:8 ? (De Vogel, 1972, 7-17).
   John 14:6 ? (De Vogel, 1972, 7-17).

3.p.12.116-18: "Thanne is thilke the sovereyn good," quod sche, "that alle thinges governeth strongly and ordeyneth hem softly?"
   Cp. *Wis. 8:1* (Hanna and Lawler, in B, 1987, n. 3.p.12.117-18; cp. De Vogel, 1972, 13).

4.p.1.34: . . . God, that alle things woot . . .
   Cp. *Ps. 43(44):22(21), 1 John 3:20; etc.*

4.m.3.44-48: For vices ben so cruel that they percen and thurw-
passen the corage withinne; and, thoughe thei ne anoye nat the
body, yit vices woden to destroyen men by wounde of thought.
    Cp. *Matt. 10:28* ? (La).

4.p.6.51-56: . . . the whiche manere whan that men looken it in
thilke pure clennesse of the devyne intelligence, it is ycleped
purveaunce; but whanne thilke manere is referred by men to
thinges that it moeveth and disponyth, than of olde men it was
clepyd destyne.
    Cp. *Matt. 10:29-30* ? (cp. Dante, *Inf.* 7.67-96 ?; Schless, 1984,
        pp. 232-37; cp. R).

4.p.6.88-93: . . . ryght so God disponith in his purveaunce
singulerly . . . but he amynistreth in many maneris and in
diverse tymes by destyne thilke same thinges that he hath
disponyd.
    Cp. *Phil 3:14; etc.* (Lawler, 1980, pp. 28-30).

4.p.6.221: . . . God, that al knoweth . . .
    Cp. *Ps. 43(44):22(21), 1 John 3:20; etc.*

5.p.1.12-15: . . . I haste me to yelden and assoilen to the the
dette of my byheste, and to schewen and openen [the] the wey,
by whiche wey thou maist comen ayein to thi contre.
    Cp. *Heb 11:13-16* ? (cp. 1.p.5.8-25, above, and 5.m.5.9-25,
        below; see also *Truth* 17-20 and *Rom* 5659).

5.m.1.18-23: Right so fortune, that semeth as it fletith with
slakid or ungoverned bridles, it suffreth bridelis (that is to
seyn, to ben governed), and passeth by thilke lawe (that is to
seyn, by the devyne ordenaunce).
    Cp. *Matt. 10:29-30* ? (cp. Dante, *Inf.* 7.67-96 ?; Schless, 1984,
        pp. 232-37; cp. R).

5.m.3.12-17: . . . confownded and overthrowen by the derke
membres of the body, ne mai nat be fyr of his derked lookynge

(*that is to seyn, by the vigour of his insyghte while the soule is in the body*) knowen the thynne sutile knyttynges of thinges.
1 Tim. 6:16 ? (De Vogel, 1972, 5-6).

5.m.5.9-25: . . . and oothere beestes gladen hemself to diggen hir traas or hir steppys in the erthe. . . . Only the lynage of man heveth heyest his heie heved, and stondith light with his upryght body, and byholdeth the erthes undir hym. And, but yif thou, erthly man, waxest yvel out of thi wit, this figure amonesteth the, that axest the hevene with thi ryghte visage . . . syn that thi body is so heyghe areysed.
Cp. *Heb 11:13-16* ? (cp. Hanna and Lawler, in B, 1987, n. 5.m.9-19; cp. 1.p.5.8-25 and 5.p.1.12-15, above; see also *Truth* 17-20 and *Rom* 5659).

5.p.6.8-10: The comune jugement of alle creatures resonables thanne is this: that God is eterne.
Cp. *Rom. 1:20; etc.*

5.p.6.85-86: . . . for that it bereth a maner ymage or liknesse of the ai duellynge presence of God . . .
Cp. *Gen. 1:26-27* (Black, 1974, pp. 52-55).

5.p.6.134-35: . . . so seeth God alle thinges by his eterne present.
Cp. *Ps. 43(44):22(21), 1 John 3:20; etc.*

5.p.6.293-94: . . . and God, byholdere and forwytere of alle thingis, duelleth above . . .
Cp. *1 Pet. 1:2; etc.*
Cp. *Deut. 4:39; etc.*

TROILUS AND CRISEYDE

1.16 . . . Ne dar to love, for myn unliklynesse. . . .
Mark 1:7; Eph. 3:8 ? (cp. Dodd, 1913, pp. 191-96; Green, 1957, p. 62; cp. Barney, in B, 1987, n. 15-21).

1.29-51: And preieth for hem . . . And ek for me preieth . . . And biddeth ek for hem . . . For so hope I my sowle best avaunce . . . As though I were hire owne brother dere.
  Cp. *John 17:20; Heb. 13:18; etc.* (liturgy; cp. Boccaccio, *Fil.* 1.6; Wi; cp. Dodd, ibid; Barney, in B, 1987, n. 29-46).

1.31: . . . That Love hem brynge in hevene to solas. . . .
  Cp. *2 Cor. 5:1, 6-8; Apoc. 7:14-15; etc.* (cp. Dodd, ibid.).

1.36-37: And biddeth ek for hem that ben despeired/ In love that nevere nyl recovered be. . . .
  Mark 3:28-29 ? (Green, 1957, pp. 62-63; cp. Dodd, ibid.)

1.41: . . . So graunte hem soone owt of this world to pace . . .
  Cp. *2 Cor. 5:1, 6-8; Apoc. 7:14-15; etc.* (cp. Dodd, ibid.).

1.42: . . . That ben despeired out of Loves grace.
  Cp. *2 Cor. 13:13; etc.* (cp. Wi; cp. Dodd, ibid.).

1.44: . . . That God hem graunte ay good perseveraunce . . .
  Cp. *Eph. 3:16; etc.* (cp. Dodd, ibid.).

1.47: . . . For so hope I my sowle best avaunce . . .
  Cp. *Heb. 10:39; etc.* (cp. Dodd, ibid.).

1.49: . . . and lyve in charite . . .
  Cp. *1 Cor. 13:13; etc.* (cp. Dodd, ibid.).

1.50-51: . . . And for to have of hem compassioun,/ As though I were hire owne brother dere.
  Cp. *1 Pet. 3:8; etc.* (cp. Dodd, ibid.).

1.102-04: . . . So aungelik was hir natif beaute/ That lik a thing in-mortal semed she,/ As doth an hevenyssh perfit creature . . .
  Cp. *Matt. 22:30, Apoc. 10:1; etc.* (cp. Wi).

1.211: O blynde world . . .
>   Cp. *2 Cor. 4:4* ? (cp. Boccaccio, *Fil.* 1.25; Wi; Barney, in B, 1987, n. 211).

1.245: This was, and is, and yet men shal it see.
>   Cp. *Apoc. 4:8, 11:17; etc.* (liturgy, *Gloria Patri;* Wi; Barney, in B, 1987, n. 245; cp. *HF* 81-82).

1.271-77: And up-on cas bifel that thorugh a route/ His eye percede, and so depe it wente,/ Til on Criseyde it smote, and ther it stente./ And sodeynly he wax ther-with astoned,/ And gan hir bet biholde in thrifty wise./ "O mercy god," thoughte he, "wher hastow woned,/ That art so feyre and goodly to devise?"
>   *Ecclus. 9:7-9* ? (Robertson, 1952, rpt. in S&T, 2.97-98; cp. Wi; cp. Bishop, 1981, p. 63).

1.407-20: "And if that at myn owen lust I brenne,/ From whennes cometh my waillynge and my pleynte?/ . . . .
. . . / Allas, what is this wondre maladie?/ For hete of cold, for cold of hete, I dye."
>   *Ecclus 9:2* ? (cp. Petrarch, "S'amor non e"; Robertson, 1952, rpt. in S&T, 2.99; Barney, in B, 1987, n. 400-20).
>   *Gen. 3* ? (Robertson, 1952, rpt. in S&T, 2.104-05).

1.415-17: . . . thus possed to and fro,/ Al sterelees with-inne a boot am I/ Amydde the see, bitwixen wyndes two . . .
>   *Prov. 23:33-34* ? (Robertson, 1952, rpt. in S&T, 2.98; ———, 1962, p. 478; Wi; Barney, in B, 1987, nn. 416, 417; cp. Owst, 1961, pp. 63-76).

1.422-23: O lord, now youres is/ My spirit, which that oughte youres be.
>   *Luke 23:46* ? (cp. Boccaccio, *Fil.* 1.38; Rowe, 1976, p. 4; cp. Wi; cp. Dodd, 1913, pp. 196, 203-05).

1.432-33: For myn estat roial I here resigne/ In-to hire hond, and with ful humble chere/ Bicome hir man, as to my lady dere.
    Cp. *Ecclus. 9:2* ? (Robertson, 1952, rpt. in S&T, 2.99; cp. Wi).

1.436: . . . The fyre of love—the wherfro god me blesse. . . .
    Cp. *Ecclus. 9:7-9* ? (Robertson, 1952, rpt. in S&T, 2.97-98; cp. Root; Wi).

1.445-49: Forthi ful ofte, his hote fire to cesse,/ To sen hire goodly lok he gan to presse;/ For ther-by to ben esed wel he wende,/ And ay the ner he was, the more he brende./ For ay the ner the fire the hotter is. . . .
    Cp. *Ecclus. 9:7-9* ? (Robertson, 1952, rpt. in S&T, 2.97-98; cp. Root; Wi; Barney, in B, 1987, n. 449).

1.463-64: Alle other dredes weren from him fledde,/ Both of thassege and his savacioun. . . .
    Cp. *Heb. 2:3; etc.* ? (Boccaccio, *Fil.* 1.44.1-2; Wi; Barney, in B, 1987, n. 464).

1.490: . . . the hote fire of love hym brende. . . .
    Cp. *Ecclus. 9:7-9* ? (Robertson, 1952, rpt. in S&T, 2.97-98; cp. Wi).

1.625-30: . . . "Though I be nyce, it happeth often so/ That oon that excesse doth ful yvele fare/ By good counseil kan kepe his frend ther-fro./ I have myself ek seyn a blynd man goo/ Ther as he fel that couthe loken wide;/ A fool may ek a wis man ofte gide. . . . "
    Cp. *Matt. 15:14* ? (Robertson, 1952, rpt. in S&T, 2.99; proverbial; Whi F404; cp. Root; Wi; cp. Barney, in B, 1987, n. 628-30).

1.644: . . . and so the wyse it demeth.
    2 Kings 13:3; etc. ? (Robertson, 1952, rpt. in S&T, 2.99).

1.659-62: Phebus, that first fond art of medicyne . . . Yet to hym self his konnyng was ful bare . . .
>Cp. *Luke 4:23* ? (Green, 1957, p. 68; proverbial; Whi L171; cp. Root; Wi; Barney, in B, 1987, n. 659-65).

1.694-95: The wise seith, "wo hym that is allone,/ For, and he falle, he hath non helpe to ryse."
>*g*
>*Eccl. 4:10* (Root; Green, 1957, p. 68; Wi; Barney, in B, 1987, n. 694-95).

1.738-43: . . . For why to tellen nas nat his entente/ To nevere no man, for whom that he so ferde./ For it is seyd, "men maketh ofte a yerde/ With which the maker is hym self ybeten/ In sondry manere," as thise wyse treten;/ And namelich in his counseil tellynge . . .
>*Prov. 25:9-10* ? (proverbial; Whi S652; Root; Wi).
>*g*

1.780: . . . bendiste?
>*Dan. 3:57; etc.* (liturgy; Root; Wi; La; cp. *KtT* 1785, etc.).

1.841-47: Quod Pandarus, "Than blamestow Fortune/ For thow art wroth, ye, now at erst I see;/ Woost thow nat wel that Fortune is comune/ To everi manere wight in som degree?/ And yet thow hast this comfort, lo, perde,/ That as hire joies moten overgone,/ So mote hire sorwes passen everychone.
>*Isa. 65:11-14* ? (Robertson, 1952, rpt. in S&T, 2.87-88; cp. Root; Wi; cp. Barney, in B, 1987, nn. 843-44, 846-47).

1.857-58: For who-so list have helyng of his leche,/ To hym byhoveth first unwre his wownde.
>Cp. *Ps. 146(147):3; Matt. 9:12, Mark 2:17, Luke 5:31; etc.* (proverbial; Whi L173; Root; Wi; Barney, in B, 1987, n. 857-58; cp. *Bo* 1.p.4.3-6).

1.951: . . . And next the derke nyght the glade morwe . . .
   Ps. 29(30):6(5) ? (proverbial; Whi N108; cp. Alain de Lille,
   Liber Parabolarum; Root; Wi).

1.952: . . . And also joie is next the fyn of sorwe.
   Prov. 14:13 ? (cp. Alain de Lille, *Liber Parabolarum;* Root;
   Wi; Barney, in B, 1987, n. 948-52).
   Cp. *James 4:9; etc.*

1.969: . . . Stonde faste, for to good port hastow rowed. . . .
   1 Cor. 16:13 ? (Green, 1957, p. 69; cp. Boccaccio, *Fil.* 2.24;
   Root; Barney, in B, 1987, n. 969).

1.998-99: I thenke, sith that love of his goodnesse/ Hath the
converted out of wikkednesse . . .
   Cp. *James 5:19-20; etc.* (cp. Boccaccio, *Fil.* 2.28; Wi; cp.
   Dodd, 1913, pp. 202-03; cp. Barney, in B, 1987, n. 998-
   1008).

1.1000-01: . . . That thow shalt ben the beste post, I leve,/ Of al
his lay . . .
   Cp. *Gal. 2:9* (La; cp. Wi; cp. Dodd, 1913, pp. 202-03; Root;
   Barney, in B, 1987, n. 1000).

1.1065-69: For everi wight that hath an hous to founde/ Ne
renneth naught the werk for to bygynne/ With rakel hond, but
he wol bide a stounde,/ And sende his hertes line out fro with-
inne/ Aldirfirst his purpos forto wynne.
   Luke 14:28 ? (Green, 1957, p. 69; cp. Geoffrey of Vinsauf,
   Poetria Nova 43-45; Wi; cp. Root; Barney, in B, 1987, n.
   1065-71).

2.1: Owt of thise blake wawes forto saylle . . .
   Ps. 41(42):8(7) ? (Green, 1957, p. 70; cp. Dante, *Purg.* 1.1-3;
   Root; Wi).

2.201: He was hire deth, and sheld and lif for us. . . .
Cp. *Ps. 90(91):5(4-5)* ? (La; cp. Root).

2.393-99: "Thenk ek how elde wasteth every houre/ In ech of yow a partie of beautee;/ And therfore, er that age the devoure,/ Go love, for old, ther wol no wight of the;/ Lat this proverbe a loore un-to yow be:/ "To late ywar, quod beaute, whan it paste";/ And elde daunteth daunger at the laste.
Wis. 2:1-9 ? (Robertson, 1952, rpt. in S&T, 2.103; cp. Boccaccio, *Fil.* 2.54; Root; proverbial; Whi B155; cp. Wi).

2.500: . . . For his love which that us bothe made. . . .
Gen. 1:27 (cp. La, p. 122; cp. Wi).

2.508: In-with the paleis gardyn by a welle . . .
Gen. 2:8-3:24 ? (Robertson, 1962, p. 388; cp. Wi; cp. Pearsall and Salter, 1973, pp. 99, 76-101, et passim; Barney, in B, 1987, n. 508).

2.523: . . . lord have routhe up-on my peyne . . .
Cp. *Matt. 9:27; etc.* (cp. Boccaccio, *Fil.* 2.57.4-5; liturgy; Root; cp. Wi).

2.524: . . . Al have I ben rebell in myn entente . . .
Cp. *Num. 14:9; etc.* (liturgy).

2.525: Now *mea culpa* , lord, I me repente.
Cp. *Job 42:6; Matt. 11:25; etc.* (liturgy, *Confiteor;* Root; Wi; cp. Dodd, 1913, pp. 196-97; Barney, in B, 1987, n. 525; cp. *ParsT* 386).

2.526-28: O god that at thi disposicioun/ Ledest the fyn, by juste purveiaunce,/ Of every wight . . .
Cp. *Job 34:11-13; etc.* (cp. Root; Wi; cp. Dodd, 1913, pp. 196-97).

2.528-32: . . . my lowe confessioun/ Accepte in gree, and sende me
swich penaunce/ As liketh the, but from disesperaunce . . .
Thow be my sheld, for thi benignite.
> Cp. *Ps. 18(19):15(14)* (liturgy; cp. Root; Wi).
> Cp. *Ps. 117(118):18* (liturgy; cp. Root; Wi).
> Cp. *Ps. 90(91):5(4-5)* (liturgy; cp. Root; Wi).
> Cp. *Ps. 24(25):7* (liturgy; cp. Root; Wi).

2.570-71: . . . Ne nevere was to wight so depe i-sworn,/ Or he me
told who myghte ben his leche.
> Cp. *Ps. 146(147):3; Matt. 9:12, Mark 2:17, Luke 5:31; etc.* (cp.
> Wi).

2.577: And for the love of god that us hath wrought . . .
> Cp. *Rom. 5:5; etc.* (cp. Boccaccio, *Fil.* 2.64; Wi).
> *Gen. 1:26-27; 2:7* (cp. Boccaccio, *Fil.* 2.64; Wi).

2.583: . . . That han swich oon y-kaught with-outen net.
> Cp. *Ps. 123(124):7; Prov. 1:17; etc.* ? (Dante, *Purg.* 31:61-63 ?;
> Havely, 1984, pp. 57-59).
> *Eccl. 9:12* ? (proverbial; Whi N90; Wi).

2.827-30: "O love . . . to yow, lord, yeve ich al,/ For evere mo,
myn hertes lust to rente. . . . "
> Cp. *Deut. 6:5, 11:13; Matt. 22:37, Mark 12:30, Luke 10:27* ?
> (Dodd, 1913, pp. 198-99).

2.894-96: Men mosten axen at seyntes if it is/ Aught faire in
hevene—why? for they kan telle—/ And axen fendes is it foule
in helle.
> Cp. *Ps. 114(116):3; Matt. 5:22, 25:46; Apoc. 14:10-13; etc.*

2.972-73: . . . "O Venus deere,/ Thi myght, thi grace, y-heried
be it here."
> Cp. *Ps. 88(89):2(1), 144(145):8-13; etc.* (Cp. Boccaccio, *Fil.*
> 2.80-81; Wi).

2.975: . . . lord, al thyn be that I have . . .
Cp. *Luke 15:31* (liturgy; cp. Wi; cp. Green, 1957, p. 73).

2.976: . . . For I am hool, al brosten ben my bondes.
Cp. *Matt. 9:21-22; etc.* (cp. Green, 1957, p. 73).
Cp. *Ps. 106(107):14*
Cp. *Nah. 1:13* (cp. 3.1116, below; Wi).

2.989: . . . Quod Pandarus, "for every thing hath tyme. . . . "
Eccl. 3:1 (cp. Boccaccio, *Fil.* 90; proverbial; Whi T88; Wi;
Barney, in B, 1987, n. 989).

2.1066: . . . His hertes lif, his lust, his sorwes leche. . . .
Cp. *Ps. 146(147):3; Matt. 9:12, Mark 2:17, Luke 5:31; etc.* (cp.
Boccaccio, *Fil.* 96; Wi).

2.1272: . . . she hath now kaught a thorn . . .
2 Cor. 12:7 ? (F; cp. Root).

2.1384: . . . As don thise rokkes or thise milnestones . . .
Judg. 9:53 ?

2.1503: Thow shalt be saved by thi feyth in trouthe.
Cp. *Luke 8:48, 18:42; John 8:32; etc.* (Root; Wi; cp. Dodd,
1913, pp. 200-01; cp. Green, 1957, p. 73; Barney, in B, 1987,
n. 1503).

2.1513(-3.217): Thow shalt gon over nyght, and that bylyve,/
Unto Deiphebus hous as the to pleye,/ Thi maladie awey the
bet to dryve . . . . it joie was to here.
2 Kings 13:1-20 ? (Muscatine, 1948; Robertson, 1952, pp. 99,
105; Kaske, 1986; Barney, in B, 1987, n. 1394-1757).

2.1581-82: But ther sat oon, al list hire nought to teche,/ That
thoughte, "best koude I yet ben his leche."
Cp. *Ps. 146(147):3; Matt. 9:12, Mark 2:17, Luke 5:31; etc.* (cp.
Wi).

2.1681: This Pandarus gan newe his tong affile . . .
   Cp. *Ps. 63(64):4(3)* (proverbial; Whi T378; Wi; Barney, in
   B, 1987, n. 1681).

2.1733-36: . . . Nece, I conjure and heighly yow defende,/ On his
half which that soule us alle sende,/ And in the vertue of
corones tweyne,/ Sle naught this man that hath for yow this
peyne.
   Gen. 2:7
   Cant. 3:11 ? (William Durandus, *Rationale Divinorum
   Officiorum;* Kaske, 1986; cp. Root; Wi; Barney, in B, 1987,
   n. 1735).
   Exod. 20:13; etc. ? (Malarkey, 1963).
   Cp. *Prov. 4:9, 1 Cor. 9:25, 2 Tim. 4:8; etc.* (cp. *SecNT* 221).

3.1-49: O blisful light . . . . to Venus heryinge?/ To which
gladnesse who nede hath god hym brynge!
   Cp. *1 John 1:5; Ps. 42(43):3; etc.*
   Wis. 7:26; etc. (Boccaccio, *Fil.* 3.74-79; Root; Wi; cp. Dodd,
   1913, pp. 199-200; Barney, in B, 1987, n. 1-49; cp. *Bo* 2.m.8).

3.8-9: In hevene and helle, in erthe and salte see,/ Is felt thi
myght . . .
   Cp. *Ps. 71(72):19, 76(77):17(16); etc.* (liturgy; Boccaccio, *Fil.*
   3.75.1-2; Wi; cp. Dodd, 1913, pp. 205-08).

3.11: . . . The fele in tymes with vapour eterne.
   Cp. *Wis. 7:25* (Boccaccio, *Fil.* 3.75.5-6; Dante, *Purg.* 11.6;
   Root; R; Wi; Barney, in B, 1987, n. 11).

3.12: God loveth, and to love wol nought werne . . .
   Cp. *1 John 4:7-8; etc.* (cp. Wi).

3.35: . . . As whi this fissh, and naught that, comth to were.
   Eccl. 9:12 ? (Cp. Bishop, 1981, p. 33).

3.61: . . . And seyde, "god do boot on alle syke!"
  Cp. *Ps. 102(103):3; etc.*

3.168: Now beth al hool . . .
  Cp. *Luke 8:48; etc.*

3.178-79: . . . And I shal trewely with al my myght/ Youre
bittre tornen al in-to swetenesse.
  Cp. *Exod. 15:23-25, Ecclus. 38:5, Isa. 5:20* ? (cp. Green, 1957,
  p. 75).

3.185: Immortal god . . . that mayst nought deyen . . .
  Cp. *1 Tim. 1:17; etc.* (cp. Dodd, 1913, pp. 201-02, 205-06).

3.260: But god, that al woot . . .
  Cp. *Ps. 43(44):22(21), 1 John 3:20; etc.* (cp. Beauvau, *LRTC,*
  p. 175; Wi; cp. Dodd, 1913, pp. 205-06).

3.267-68: For wel thow woost, the name as yet of here/ Among
the peeple, as who seyth, halwed is . . .
  Cp. *Matt. 6:9, Luke 11:2* (liturgy; cp. Boccaccio, *Fil.* 3.8.1-2;
  Wi).

3.304: . . . weilaway the day that I was borne!
  Job 3:3, Jer. 20:14

3.332: . . . and be now of good cheere . . .
  Cp. *Acts 27:25; etc.*

3.372-73: . . . by that god . . . That as hym list may al this world
governe . . .
  Cp. *Ps. 21(22):29(28); etc.* (cp. Boccaccio, *Fil.* 15.1-2;
  Beauvau, *LRTC,* p. 177; Wi; cp. Dodd, 1913, pp. 205-06).

3.378: . . . For al the good that god made under sonne
  Cp. *Gen. 1:31*

3.380: ... As thynketh me, now stokked in prisoun ...
   Cp. *Acts 16:24* (S; La).

3.589-93: He swor hire yes, by stokkes and by stones,/ And by
the goddes that in hevene dwclle,/ Or elles were hym levere,
soule and bones,/ With Pluto kyng as depe ben in helle/ As
Tantalus ...
   Cp. *Jer. 2:27; etc.*
   Cp. *Deut. 4:39; etc.*
   Cp. *Matt. 5:29-30; etc.* (cp. Root; Wi; Barney, in B, 1987, n.
     593).

3.617-23: But O fortune, executrice of wyerdes,/ O influences of
thise hevenes hye,/ Soth is that under god ye ben oure
hierdes. ... But execut was al bisyde hire leve/ The goddes wil,
for which she moste bleve.
   Cp. *Matt. 10:29-30* ? (cp. Dante, *Inf.* 7.67-96 ?; cp. Schless,
     1984, pp. 232-37; cp. Root; R; Wi; Barney, in B, 1987, n.
     617-20).

3.757: ... benedicite?
   Dan. 3:57; etc. (liturgy; Howard, 1967, 451; Root; cp. *KtT*
     1785).

3.855: Nece, alle thyng hath tyme ...
   Eccl. 3:1 (proverbial; Whi T88; Root; Wi; Barney, in B,
     1987, n. 855; Howard, 1967, 451).

3.860: A, benedicite ...
   Dan. 3:57; etc. (liturgy; Root; cp. *KtT* 1785).

3.875: I bidde God ...
   Cp. *2 Cor. 13:7; etc.* (liturgy).

3.878: ... by that God above ...
   Cp. *Deut. 4:39; etc.*

3.1016-19: But O thow Jove, O auctour of nature,/ Is this an honour to thi deyte,/ That folk ungiltif suffren hire injure,/ And who that giltif is al quyt goth he?
Cp. *Gen. 1; Heb. 2:10; etc.*
Cp. *Eccl. 7:16; Job 9:22-24, 21:7; etc.* (Root; Wi; Barney, in B, 1987, n. 1016-19; cp. *KtT* 1313 and *Bo* 1.m.5.31ff.).

3.1027: . . . heighe god that sit a-bove . . .
Cp. *Deut. 4:39; etc.* (cp. Dodd, 1913, pp. 205-06).

3.1072-73: And in his mynde he gan the tyme acorse/ That he com there, and that he was born . . .
Cp. *Job 3:3, Jer. 20:14*

3.1103: . . . allas, that I was born.
Cp. *Job 3:3, Jer. 20:14*

3.1104-05: . . . wol ye pullen out the thorn/ That stiketh in his herte? . . .
2 Cor. 12:7; etc. ? (Howard, 1967, 453; cp. 2.1271-74, above; F).

3.1116-17: . . . And to deliveren hym fro bittre bondes,/ She ofte hym kiste . . .
Cp. *Ps. 106(107):14; Matt. 9:21-22; etc.* (cp. Boccaccio, *Fil.* 4.19; Wi).

3.1165: . . . by that god that bought us bothe two . . .
Cp. *1 Cor. 6:20, Rom. 5:9-10, Col. 1:20; etc.* (cp. Green, 1957, pp. 79-80; cp. Barney, in B, 1987, n. 1165).

3.1254: O Love, O Charite . . .
2 Pet. 1:7 ? (cp. Rowe, 1976, pp. 105-07, et passim).

3.1282: Here may men seen that mercy passeth right.
Cp. *Ps. 84(85):11(10)* (Root; Wi; Klinefelter, 1965; Barney, in B, 1987, n. 1282).

3.1290: . . . Syn god hath wrought me for I shall yow serve . . .
  Cp. *Deut. 6:13, Matt. 4:10; etc.*

3.1355: . . . Ye humble nettes of my lady deere.
  Cp. *Ps. 123(124):7; Prov. 1:17; etc.* ? (Dante, *Purg.* 31:61-63 ?;
    Havely, 1984, pp. 57-59).
  Eccl. 9:12 ? (proverbial; Whi N90; Wi).

3.1417: . . . And Lucyfer, the dayes messanger . . .
  Isa. 14:12-15 (cp. Root; Wi; Barney, in B, 1987, n. 1417-18).

3.1423: . . . That I was born, allas . . .
  Cp. *Job 3:3, Jer. 20:14* (cp. Wi; cp. Barney, in B, 1987, n. 1423).

3.1429-30: O blake nyght, as folk in bokes rede,/ That shapen
art by god this world to hide . . .
  Cp. *Gen. 1:4-5*

3.1437: . . . god, maker of kynde . . .
  Gen. 1

3.1458: . . . thyn be the peyne of helle!
  Cp. *Ps. 114(116):3; Matt. 5:22, 25:46; etc.*

3.1462: Go selle it hem that smale selys grave . . .
  Ecclus. 38:28 ? (Kaske, 1961, p. 177; Barney, in B, 1987, n.
    1462).

3.1490: . . . thise worldes tweyne . . .
  Cp. *Eph. 1:21; etc.* (cp. Boccaccio, *Fil.* 3.47.4; Wi; Barney, in
    B, 1987, n. 1490).

3.1499: Ye ben so depe in-with myn herte grave . . .
  Cant. 8:6-7 ? (Wetherbee, 1984, p. 203, n. 19; cp. 3.1462;
    Root; Barney, in B, 1987, n. 1499).

3.1501: . . . As wisly verray god my soule save . . .
  Cp. *James 1:21; etc.*

3.1503: And for the love of god that us hath wrought . . .
  Cp. *Rom. 5:5*
  Cp. *Gen. 1:26-27, 2:7*

3.1577: . . . god for-yaf his deth . . .
  Luke 23:34 ? (Root; Green, 1957, p. 81; proverbial; Whi G205; Wi; Besserman, 1984[b], p. 45; cp. Coghill, 1971, pp. 316-17; F; Barney, in B, 1987, n. 1577).

3.1595-96: . . . and gan the tyme blesse/ That he was born . . .
  Cp. *Job 3:3, Jer. 20:14*

3.1656-57: . . . he/ That ones may in hevene blisse be . . .
  Cp. *Matt. 10:28, Apoc. 14:10-13; etc.*

3.1733-34: . . . of al Criseydes nette;/ He was so narwe y-masked and y-knette . . .
  Cp. *Ps. 123(124):7; Prov. 1:17; etc.* ? (Dante, *Purg.* 31:61-63 ?; Havely, 1984, pp. 57-59).
  Eccl. 9:12 ? (proverbial; Whi N90; Wi).

3.1765: . . . god, that auctour is of kynde . . .
  Cp. *Gen 1; Heb. 2:10; etc.*

3.1804: . . . y-heried be his grace . . .
  Eph. 1:6; etc. (liturgy).

3.1813: . . . Ye heried ben for ay with-outen ende.
  Cp. *Ps. 60(61):9(8); etc.*

4.117-19: . . . the tyme is faste by/ That fire and flaumbe on al the town shal sprede,/ And thus shal Troie torne to asshen dede.
  Gen. 19:24, 28; Deut. 29:23 ?

4.194-96: " . . . O kyng Priam," quod they, "thus sygge we,/That al oure vois is to forgon Criseyde."/ And to deliveren Antenor they preyde.
> Luke 23:18 ? (Taylor, 1980).

4.251-52: Acorsed be that day which that nature/ Shop me to ben a lyves creature.
> Cp. Job 3:3, Jer. 20:14 (cp. Boccaccio, Fil. 4.28; Wi; Barney, in B, 1987, n. 251-52).

4.271: . . . wrecche of wrecches . . .
> Cp. Eccl. 1:2; Cant.; etc.

4.288-89: O verrey lord of love, O god, allas,/ That knowest best myn herte and al my thoughte . . .
> Cp. Ps. 138(139):23; etc. (cp. Dante, Convivio 2.51; cp. Beauvau, LRTC, p. 208; Wi).

4.319-21: . . . but whan myn herte dieth,/ My spirit, which that so unto yow hieth,/ Receyve in gree, for that shal ay yow serve;/ For-thi no fors is though the body sterve.
> Cp. Luke 23:46, Acts 7:58, etc.
> Cp. Rom. 8:10; etc.

4.333-34: O Calkas, which that wolt my bane be,/ In corsed tyme was thow born for me.
> Cp. Job 3:3, Jer. 20:14 (cp. Boccaccio, Fil. 4.38; Wi; cp. 4.250-52, above).

4.623: . . . And if thow deye a martyr, go to hevene.
> Cp. 2 Cor. 5:1, 6-8; Apoc. 7:14-15; etc. (liturgy; cp. Boccaccio, Fil. 4.76; cp. Beauvau, LRTC, p. 218; Wi; Barney, in B, 1987, n. 623; cp. R).

4.747-48: Wo worth, allas, that ilke dayes light/ On which I saugh hym first with eyen tweyne . . .
> Cp. Job 3:3, Jer. 20:14

4.762-63: O moder myn, that cleped were Argyve,/ Wo worth that day that thow me bere on lyve!
 Cp. *Job 3:3, Jer. 20:14*

4.785-87: Myn herte and ek the woful goost ther-inne/ Byquethe I with youre spirit to compleyne/ Eternaly for they shal nevere twynne . . .
 Cp. *Luke 23:46, Acts 7:58* (cp. Boccaccio, *Fil.* 4.91; Wi; Barney, in B, 1987, n. 785-87).
 Cp. *Matt. 25:46; etc.*

4.834-36: Endeth thanne love in wo? Ye, or men lieth,/ And alle worldly blisse as thynketh me:/ The ende of blisse ay sorwe it occupieth.
 Cp. *Prov. 14:13* (Root; Barney, in B, 1987, n. 836; proverbial; Whi E80; Wi).

4.839: . . . and ay my burthe a-corse . . .
 Cp. *Job 3:3, Jer. 20:14* (cp. Wi).

4.864: . . . lik of Paradys the ymage . . .
 Cp. *Gen. 2:8* (cp. Boccaccio, *Fil.* 4.100; Wi).

4.963: . . . Syn god seeth every thyng, out of doutaunce . . .
 Cp. *Ps. 93(94):9; etc.* (Cp. *Bo* 5.p.3; Root; Wi).

4.964-66: . . . And hem disponyth, thorugh his ordinaunce,/ In hire merites sothly for to be,/ As they shul comen by predestyne.
 Cp. *Eph. 1:11; etc.* (ibid.).

4.1137: . . . as is ligne aloes or galle.
 Cp. *Matt. 27:34; etc.* (proverbial; Whi G8; cp. Root; Wi; Barney, in B, 1987, n. 1135-41).

4.1174-75: . . . And pitously gan for the soule preye,/ And seyde, "O lord that set art in thi trone . . . "

Cp. *2 Mach. 12:42-46* (liturgy).
Cp. *Isa. 6:1; etc.* (cp. Boccaccio, *Fil.* 4.119; Root; Wi; Barney,
   in B, 1987, n. 1174).

4.1209-10: . . . O swete herte deere,/ Receyve now my spirit . . .
   Cp. *Luke 23:46, Acts 7:58* (cp. Boccaccio, *Fil.* 4.123; Wi).

4.1236: . . . For by that ilke lord that made me . . .
   Cp. *Gen. 1:26-27; 2:7, 22*

4.1251: . . . Bywaylinge ay the day that they were born . . .
   Cp. *Job 3:3, Jer. 20:14* (cp. Wi).

4.1337: . . . Or ellis se ich nevere Joves face.
   Cp. *Apoc. 22:4; etc.*

4.1364: . . . as wisly god my soule rede . . .
   Cp. *Ps. 118(119):81; etc.*

4.1370-71: . . . And I right now have founden al the gise,/ With-
outen net, wherwith I shal hym hente.
   Cp. *Ps. 123(124):7; Prov. 1:17; etc.* ? (Dante, *Purg.* 31:61-63 ?;
      Havely, 1984, pp. 57-59).
   Eccl. 9:12 ? (proverbial; Whi N90; Wi).

4.1409-10: . . . and that his coward herte/ Made hym amys the
goddes text to glose . . .
   G ?

4.1540: . . . Eternalich in Stix, the put of helle.
   Cp. *Ps. 114(116):3; Matt. 5:22, 25:46; etc.* (cp. Dante, *Inf.*
      7.106-07; Schless, 1984, pp. 136-37; cp. Root; Wi; Barney,
      in B, 1987, n. 1538-40).
   Cp. *Apoc. 9:1; etc.*

4.1554: . . . And I with body and soule synke in helle.
   Cp. *Matt. 10:28, Luke 12:5; etc.*

4.1585: . . . "who-so wole han lief, he lief moot lete."
 Matt. 10:39; etc. ? (Evans, 1959; cp. Baugh and Donaldson, 1961; proverbial; Whi L233; Root; Wi; Barney, in B, 1987, n. 1585).

4.1594: . . . as helpe me Juno, hevenes quene . . .
 Cp. *Jer. 7:18; 44:17, 25* (liturgy; cp. Boccaccio, *Fil.* 4.154; Root; Wi).

4.1636: . . . That of so good a confort and a cheere . . .
 Cp. *Phil. 2:19, Acts 27:25; etc.* (cp. Boccaccio, *Fil.* 4.160.4; Wi).

4.1654: Now god, to whom ther nys no cause y-wrye . . .
 Cp. *Ps. 93(94):9; Eph. 1:11; etc.* (cp. Boccaccio, *Fil.* 4.163; Wi).

4.1683-84: . . . But Juppiter that of his myght may do/ The sorwful to be glad, so yeve us grace . . .
 Cp. *James 4:6, 12; etc.* (cp. Boccaccio, *Fil.* 4.166; Wi).
 Cp. *John 16:20; etc.*

4.1695-96: . . . For mannes hed ymagynen ne kan,/ Nentendement considere, ne tonge telle/ The cruele peynes of this sorwful man,/ That passen every torment down in helle.
 Cp. *1 Cor. 2:9* (cp. Barney, in B, 1987, n. 1695-96).
 Cp. *Ps. 114(116):3; Matt. 5:22, 25:46; etc.*

5.208-09: He corseth . . . His burthe . . .
 Cp. *Job 3:3, Jer. 20:14* (Boccaccio, *Fil.* 5.17.5; Root; Wi).

5.212: . . . as doth he Ixion in helle.
 Cp. *Ps. 114(116):3; Matt. 5:22, 25:46; etc.* (cp. Root; Wi; Barney, in B, 1987, n. 212).

5.232: Who seth yow now, my righte lode sterre?
 Cp. *Wis. 14:3* ? (Robertson, 1952, rpt. in S&T, 2.116; cp. Wi).

5.540-53: Than seide he thus, "O paleys desolat . . . . far wel shryne, of which the seynt is oute."

> Cp. *Lam. 1:1, etc.* (cp. Boccaccio, *Fil.* "Proemio" and 5.53; Bloomfield, 1972; cp. Wood, 1984[b], p. 13; Besserman, forthcoming; cp. Root; Wi; Barney, in B, 1987, n. 540-53).

5.541: . . . O hous of houses . . .

> Cp. *Eccl. 1:2; Cant.; etc.*

5.543: O thow lanterne of which queynt is the light . . .

> *Matt. 25:1-13* ? (Adams, 1963; Gordon, 1970, pp. 133-34; cp. Frost, 1976-77; L. D. Benson, 1984; Barney, in B, 1987, n. 543).

5.593: . . . And lyve and dye I wole in thy byleve.

> Cp. *Rom. 14:8* (cp. Boccaccio, *Fil.* 5.57.3; Wi; Barney, in B, 1987, n. 589-93).

5.640-41: . . . That evere derk in torment nyght by nyght,/ Toward my deth with wynd in steere I saille . . .

> *Prov. 23:33-34* ? (cp. Boccaccio, *Fil.* 5.62-66; Wi; cp. 1.415-17, above; Barney, in B, 1987, n. 641; cp. Owst, 1961, pp. 63-76).

5.689-90: . . . "allas," she seyde,/ "That I was born! . . . "

> Cp. *Job 3:3, Jer. 20:14*

5.700: . . . That I was born, so weilaway the tide!

> Cp. *Job 3:3, Jer. 20:14*

5.732: . . . al torned in-to galle is . . .

> Cp. *Matt. 27:34; etc.* (cp. Wi; cp. 4.1137, above).

5.775-77: . . . In-to his net Criseydes herte bryng./ . . . To fisshen hire he leyde out hook and lyne.

> Cp. *Ps. 123(124):7, Prov. 1:17; etc.* ? (Dante, *Purg.* 31:61-63 ?; Havely, 1984, pp. 57-59).

Eccl. 9:12 ? (proverbial; Whi N90; Wi; cp. Bishop, 1981, p. 33).

Matt. 4:19; etc. ? (Barney, in B, 1987, n. 777).

5.817: . . . That Paradis stood formed in hire eyen.
Cp. *Gen. 2:8* (cp. Boccaccio, *Fil.* 4.100, etc.; Dante, *Par.* 18.21; Root; Wi; Barney, in B, 1987, n. 817; cp. Bishop, 1981, p. 29).

5.1004: . . . by God that sit above!
Cp. *Deut. 4:39; etc.*

5.1265: . . . That every word was gospel that ye seyde.
G (proverbial; Whi G401; cp. Boccaccio, *Fil.* 7.31.2; Wi; Barney, in B, 1987, n. 1265).
Cp. *Col. 1:5*

5.1275-76: . . . allas, the while/ That I was born!
Cp. *Job 3:3, Jer. 20:14* (cp. Boccaccio, *Fil.* 7.40; Wi).

5.1392: . . . For love of god, my righte lode sterre. . . .
Cp. *Wis. 14:3* ? (Robertson, 1952, rpt. in S&T, 2.116).

5.1532-33: . . . She ches for hym to dye and gon to helle,/ And starf anon as us the bokes telle.
Cp. *Rom. 5:9; etc.* (cp. Root; Wi; Barney, in B, 1987, n. 1527-33).
Cp. *Matt. 10:28; etc.* (cp. Root; Wi; Barney, in B, 1987, n. 1527-33).

5.1536-37: . . . And from his bedde al sodeynly he sterte,/ As though al hool hym hadde ymad a leche.
Cp. *Ps. 146(147):3; Matt. 9:12, Mark 2:17, Luke 5:31; etc.*

5.1541-45: Fortune--which that permutacioun/ Of thynges hath . . . as regnes shal be flitted/ Fro folk in folk or when they shal be smytted . . .

Cp. *Ecclus. 10:8; Dan. 2:21; etc.* (cp. Dante, *Inf.* 7.67-96;
Kellogg, 1954; cp. Schless, 1984, pp. 141-43; cp. Wi).
Cp. *Matt. 10:29-30* ? (cp. Dante, *Inf.* 7.67-96 ?; Schless, 1984,
pp. 232-37; cp. Root; R; Barney, in B, 1987, nn. 1541-47,
1545).

5.1639-40: But natheles men seyn that at the laste,/ For any
thyng men shal the soothe se. . . .
Cp. *Luke 12:2; etc.* (proverbial; Whi S491; Wi; Barney, in B,
1987, n. 1639-40).

5.1706-07: O god . . . that oughtest taken heede/ To fortheren
trouthe and wronges to punyce . . .
Cp. *Job 8:3, 20; etc.* (cp. Boccaccio, *Fil.* 8.17-18; Wi).

5.1787-88: . . . Ther god thi makere yet, er that he dye,/ So
sende myght . . . .
Cp. *Dan. 2:23; etc.* (cp. Barney, in B, 1987, n. 1787-88).

5.1818-19: . . . To respect of the pleyn felicite/ That is in hevene
above . . .
Cp. *Col. 1:5; etc.* (liturgy; cp. Boccaccio, *Teseida* 11.2.5-6;
Wi; cp. Barney, in B, 1987, n. 1818).

5.1821: And in hym self he lough. . . .
Cp. *Ps 2:4* ? (Black, 1974, pp. 74-75; cp. Lucan, *Pharsalia*
9.1-18; Wi).

5.1824-25: . . . The blynde lust, the which that may nat laste,/
And sholden al oure herte on heven caste.
Cp. *1 John 2:17* (Steadman, 1972, p. 166; liturgy; cp.
Boccaccio, *Teseida* 11.3; Wi; Barney, in B, 1987, n. 1824).
Cp. *Matt. 19:21; etc.*

5.1839-40: . . . To thilke god that after his ymage/ Yow
made . . .

Cp. *Gen. 1:26-27* (liturgy; Black, 1974, pp. 52-55; cp.
Boccaccio, *Fil.* 8.29.5-6; Root; Wi; cp. Bishop, 1981, p.
104).

5.1841: . . . This world that passeth soone as floures faire.
Cp. *Ps. 102(103):15; etc.* (liturgy; proverbial; Whi F326;
Root; Wi; Barney, in B, 1987, n. 1840-41).

5.1842-44: And loveth hym the which that right for love/
Upon a Crois oure soules forto beye,/ First starf and roos and sit
in hevene above. . . .
Cp. *1 Cor. 6:20, Rom. 5:9-10, Col. 1:20* (cp. Green, 1957, pp.
79-80; cp. Boccaccio, *Fil.* 8.29-33; Wi).
Cp. *Rom. 14:9, Eph. 6:24; etc.*
Cp. *Deut. 4:39; etc.*

5.1845-48: . . . For he nyl falsen no wight, dar I seye,/ That wol
his herte al holly on hym leye./ And syn he best to love is and
most meke,/ What nedeth feynede loves forto seke?
Cp. *James 1:17, Heb. 13:5; etc.* (Steadman, 1972, p. 167;
liturgy).
Cp. *1 John 4:16; etc.* (liturgy).
Cp. *1 John 2:15; etc.* (liturgy).

5.1860: . . . And to that sothfast Crist that starf on rode . . .
Col. 1:20; etc. (liturgy).

5.1861: . . . With al myn herte of mercy evere I preye . . .
Cp. *Ps. 4:2(1); etc.* (liturgy).

5.1863-64: Thow oon, and two, and thre, eterne on lyve,/ That
regnest ay in thre, and two, and oon . . .
Cp. *Matt. 28:19, 2 Cor. 13:13, 1 John 5:7; etc.* (cp. Dante, *Par.*
14.28-30; Root; liturgy; cp. Barney, in B, 1987, n. 1863-65).

5.1866-69: . . . Us from visible and in-visible foon/ Defende, and to thy mercye, everichon,/ So make us, Jhesus, for thi mercy digne,/ For loue of Mayde and moder thyn benigne. Amen.
> Cp. *Col. 1:16* (liturgy).
> Cp. *Ps. 58(59):2(1); etc.* (liturgy).
> Cp. *Ps. 6:5(4); etc.* (liturgy).
> *Luke 1:26-38* (liturgy).

THE LEGEND OF GOOD WOMEN

Prologue

F 1-2 (G 1-2): A thousand tymes have I herd men telle/ That ther ys joy in hevene and peyne in helle . . .
> Cp. *Matt. 10:28; etc.*

5-9 (G 5-9): . . . ther nis noon dwellyng in this contree/ That eyther hath in hevene or helle ybe,/ Ne may of hit noon other weyes witen/ But as he hath herd seyd or founde it writen;/ For by assay ther may no man it preve.
> Cp. *2 Cor. 12:1-4*
> Cp. *Wis. 2:1*

10-15 (G 10-15): But God forbede but men shulde leve/ Wel more thing then men han seen with ye!/ Men shal not wenen every thing a lye/ But yf himself yt seeth or elles dooth;/ For, God wot, thing is never the lasse sooth,/ Thogh every wight ne may it nat ysee.
> *Rom. 1:20*
> Cp. *1 Pet. 1:8; etc.*

17-39 (G 17-39): Than mote we to bokes that we fynde . . . That tellen of these olde appreved stories/ Of holynesse, of regnes, of victories. . . . Wel ought us thanne honouren and beleve/ These bokes, there we han noon other preve. . . . Farewel my bok and my devocioun!

G ? (cp. Shaner and Edwards, in B, 1987, n. 17-28).

53 (G 55): . . . of alle floures flour . . .
Cp. *Eccl. 1:2; Cant.; etc.* (cp. Shaner and Edwards, in B, 1987, n. 53-55).

73-77 (G 61-66): For wel I wot that ye han her-biforn/ Of makyng ropen, and lad awey the corn,/ And I come after, glenyng here and there,/ And am ful glad yf I may fynde an ere/ Of any goodly word that ye han left.
Cp. *Ruth 2:2, etc.* (cp. Ralph Higden, *Polychronicon;* R; Shaner and Edwards, in B, 1987, n. 74).

G 86: . . . The naked text in English to declare . . .
G ?

99-100: . . . men mosten more thyng beleve/ Then men may seen at eye, or elles preve . . .
Rom. 1:20 ?
Cp. *1 Pet. 1:8; etc.*

110-11: . . . at the resureccioun/ Of this flour . . .
Cp. *Matt. 27:53; etc.*

125-47 (G 113-33): Forgeten hadde the erthe his pore estat/ Of wynter. . . . The smale foules . . . yt did hem good/ To synge. . . . And some songen clere/ Layes of love. . . . And songen "Blessed be Seynt Valentyn,/ For on this day I chees yow to be myn,/ Withouten repentyng, myn herte swete!"
Cp. *Cant. 2:10-15, etc.* (Koonce, 1959, 184; cp. Shaner and Edwards, in B, 1987, n. 125-29).

130-31 (G 118-19): The smale foules, of the sesoun fayn,/ That from the panter and the net ben scaped . . .
Cp. *Jer. 5:26-27, Amos 3:5; etc. ?* (Koonce, 1959, 177).
Cp. *Ps. 123(124):7, Prov. 1:17; etc. ?* (Dante, *Purg.* 31:61-63 ?; Havely, 1984, pp. 57-59).

Eccl. 9:12 ? (proverbial; Whi N90).

138-39 (G 126-27): This was hire song: "The foweler we deffye,/ And al his craft."
> Cp. *Jer. 5:26-27, Amos 3:5; etc.* ? (Shaner and Edwards, in B, 1987, n. 138-39; cp. 130-31, above).

G 143: . . . I se his wynges sprede.
> Cp. *Apoc. 12:7, 14; etc.*

F 185: . . . and flour of floures alle.
> Cp. *Eccl. 1:2; Cant.; etc.*

G 189: . . . syn that God Adam [had] mad of erthe . . .
> *Gen. 2:7*

190 (G 74): . . . No more than of the corn agayn the sheef . . .
> *Matt. 3:12, Luke 3:17* ?
> *2 Cor. 3:6; Rom. 7:6* ?

203-09 (G 97-103): And in a litel herber that I have . . . I bad men sholde me my couche make;/ For deyntee of the newe someres sake,/ I bad hem strawen floures on my bed./ Whan I was leyd and had myn eyen hed,/ I fel on slepe within an houre or twoo.
> Cp. *Gen. 3* (cp. Pearsall and Salter, 1973, pp. 99, 76-101, et passim).
> Cp. *Cant. 5:1-2, 6:1, etc.*

213-22 (G 142-54): . . . and in his hand a quene,/ And she was clad in real habit grene./ A fret of gold she hadde next her heer,/ And upon that a whit corowne she beer/ With flourouns smale . . . ryght as a dayesye. . . . For of o perle fyn, oriental,/ Hire white coroune was ymaked al . . .
> *Apoc. 12:1* ? (cp. Root, 1904; cp. Dante, *Par.* 32.38ff.; Lowes, 1904, 668-69, n. 2; cp. Dodd, 1913, pp. 211-12).
> *Matt. 13:46* ?

229: The fresshest syn the world was first bygonne.
   Cp. *Gen. 1*

G 225-27 (cp. F 300-01): . . . Upon the softe and sote grene gras/
They setten hem ful softely adoun,/ By order alle in compas,
enveroun.
   Mark 6:39 ?

230-36 (cp. G 160-68): His gilte heer was corowned with a
sonne/ Instede of gold, for hevynesse and wyghte./ Therwith
me thoghte his face shoon so bryghte/ That wel unnethes
myghte I him beholde;/ And in his hand me thoghte I saugh
him holde/ Twoo firy dartes as the gledes rede,/ And
aungelyke hys wynges saugh I sprede.
   Cp. *Apoc. 12:1, 14:14* (cp. Dodd, 1913, pp. 211-12).
   Cp. *Exod. 33:20; etc.*
   Cp. *Apoc. 12:7, 14; etc.*

249 (G 203): Hyd, Absolon, thy gilte tresses clere . . .
   2 *Kings 14:25-26* (cp. *RR* 13870; R; F; Beichner, 1950; Shaner
   and Edwards, in B, 1987, n. 249).

250 (G 204): Ester, ley thou thy meknesse al adown . . .
   Cp. *Esth. 8, etc.* (cp. Deschamps, *Mir.;* Lowes, 1910, 182; F;
   cp. Shaner and Edwards, in B, 1987, n. 250-54).

251 (G 205): Hyd, Jonathas, al thy frendly manere . . .
   Cp. *1 Kings 19:1, 20:17, etc.* (F; Shaner and Edwards, in B,
   1987, n. 250-54).

255: My lady cometh, that al this may disteyne.
   Cant. 2:8 ?

262: My lady cometh, that al this may disteyne.
   Cant. 2:8 ?

269: My lady cometh, that al this may dysteyne.
   Cant. 2:8 ?

G 276-77: . . . Of sundry wemen, which lyf that they ladde,/
And evere an hundred goode ageyn oon badde. . . .
   Cp. *Eccl. 7:29* ? (cp. Allen, 1982, pp. 264-75).

282-301 (G 185-227): Behynde this god of Love, upon the grene,/
I saugh comyng of ladyes nyntene. . . . They setten hem ful
softely adoun.
   Apoc. 7 ? (Root, 1904; cp. Dante, *Par.* 32.38ff.; Lowes, 1904,
      668-69, n. 2).

286 (G 189): . . . That, syn that God Adam hadde mad of
erthe . . .
   Gen. 2:7

290-301: . . . And trewe of love thise women were echon. . . . Ful
sodeynly they stynten al attones,/ And kneled doun . . . And
songen with o vois, "Heel and honour/ To trouthe of
womanhede. . . . And with that word, a-compas enviroun,/
They setten hem ful softely adoun.
   Apoc. 14:1-5 ? (cp. Root, 1904).
   Mark 6:39 ?

G 311-12: But yit, I seye, what eyleth the to wryte/ The draf of
storyes, and forgete the corn?
   Matt. 3:12, Luke 3:17 ?
   2 Cor. 3:6; Rom. 7:6 ?

317-18 (G 243-44): Yt were better worthy, trewely,/ A worm to
neghen ner my flour than thow.
   Cp. *Ps. 21(22):7(6); etc.*

G 326: Al ne is nat gospel that is to yow pleyned.
   G (proverbial; Whi G401; Shaner and Edwards, in B, 1987,
      n. 326).

328 (G 254): . . . For in pleyn text, withouten nede of glose . . .
   G ?

428 (G 418): . . . Origenes upon the Maudeleyne.
   Cp. *John 20:11-18* (cp. pseudo-Origen, *De Maria Magdalena;*
   McCall, 1971; F; Shaner and Edwards, in B, 1987, n. 428).

445 (G 435): . . . That never yit syn that the world was newe . . .
   Gen. 1

456-59 (G 446-49): . . . the God above/ Foryelde yow that ye the
god of Love/ Han maked me his wrathe to foryive,/ And yeve
me grace so longe for to live . . .
   Cp. *Deut. 4:39; etc.*
   Cp. *1 Kings 24:20*

G 529: Let be the chaf, and writ wel of the corn.
   Matt. 3:12, Luke 3:17 ?
   2 Cor 3:6; Rom. 7:6 ?

539: . . . "Hyd, Absolon, thy tresses" . . .
   Cp. *2 Kings 14:25-26* (Beichner, 1950).

553: . . . Ne shal no trewe lover come in helle.
   Cp. *Matt. 23:33; etc.*

563-64: . . . I mot goon hom . . ./ To paradys, with al this
companye . . .
   Cp. *Gen. 2-3* (cp. Pearsall and Salter, 1973, pp. 99, 76-101, et
   passim).
   Cp. *Apoc. 14:10-13, etc.* (Root, 1904).

The Legend of Good Women

658: Allas . . . the day that I was born!
   Cp. *Job 3:3, Jer. 20:14*

706: At Babiloyne whylom fil it thus . . .
   Cp. *Apoc. 17:5; etc.* (cp. Shaner and Edwards, in B, 1987, n. 706).

718: . . . That estward in the world was tho dwellynge.
   Cp. *Gen. 13:11; etc.*

833: Allas . . . the day that I was born!
   Cp. *Job 3:3, Jer. 20:14*

924-25: Glorye and honour, Virgil Mantoan,/ Be to thy name! . . .
   Cp. *Apoc. 4:11; etc.*

1027: Allas, that I was born!
   Cp. *Job 3:3, Jer. 20:14*

1039-43: . . . That, if that God, that hevene and erthe made,/ Wolde han a love, for beaute and goodnesse,/ And womanhod, and trouthe, and semelynesse,/ Whom shulde he loven but this lady swete?/ Ther nys no woman to hym half so mete.
   Cp. *Gen. 1* (R; Shaner and Edwards, in B, 1987, n. 1039-43).
   Cp. *Luke 1:28-38; etc.* (liturgy).

1144-45: . . . but, as of that scripture,/ Be as be may, I take of it no cure.
   G ? (cp. McCall, 1979, p. 47).

1160: Now to th'effect, now to the fruyt of al . . .
   Matt. 3:12, Luke 3:17 ?
   2 Cor. 3:6; Rom. 7:6 ?

1308: That I was born, allas! What shal I do?
   Cp. *Job 3:3, Jer. 20:14*

1702-03: And lat us speke of wyves, that is best;/ Preyse every man his owene as hym lest . . .

Ecclus. 44-50 ?

1792: . . . By thilke God that formed man alyve . . .
  Gen. 1:26-27, 2:7

1805-11: "Ne wilt thow nat," quod he, this crewel man,/ "As wisly Jupiter my soule save,/ As I shal in the stable slen thy knave,/ And ley hym in thy bed, and loude crye/ That I the fynde in swich avouterye./ And thus thow shalt be ded and also lese/ Thy name, for thow shalt non other chese."
  Dan. 13:19-21 ?

1879-82: For wel I wot that Crist himselve telleth/ That in Israel, as wyd as is the lond,/ That so gret feyth in al that he ne fond/ As in a woman; and this is no lye.
  Cp. *Matt. 8:10, Luke 7:9* (cp. La, 1924, 100; LaHood, 1964; S; R; Shaner and Edwards, in B, 1987, n. 1881).
  Cp. *Matt. 15:22-28* (cp. La, 1924, 100; LaHood, 1964; S; R; Shaner and Edwards, in B, 1987, n. 1881).

1891: . . . the goddes of the heven above . . .
  Cp. *Deut. 4:39; etc.* (cp. Shaner and Edwards, in B, 1987, n. 1891-92).

2003-06: And we shul make hym balles ek also/ Of wex and tow, that whan he gapeth faste,/ Into the bestes throte he shal hem caste/ To slake his hunger and encombre his teth. . . .
  Cp. *Dan. 14:26-27* (R; Shaner and Edwards, in B, 1987, n. 2004).

2187: Allas . . . that evere I was wrought!
  Cp. *Job 3:3, Jer. 20:14*

2228-30: Thow yevere of the formes, that hast wrought/ This fayre world and bar it in thy thought/ Eternaly er thow thy werk began . . .

Cp. *Prov. 8:22-30* (cp. Shaner and Edwards, in B, 1987, n. 2228).

2395: ... wiked fruit cometh of a wiked tre ...
Cp. *Matt. 7:17* (proverbial; Whi F685; Shaner and Edwards, in B, 1987, n. 2395).

2579: ... That of the shef she sholde be the corn.
Matt. 3:12, Luke 3:17 ?
2 Cor. 3:6; Rom. 7:6 ?

THE SHORT POEMS

An ABC

4: ... of alle floures flour ...
Cp. *Eccl. 1:2; Cant.; etc.* (cp. Gross, in B, 1987, n. 4)

14: ... Haven of refut ...
Cp. *Ps. 45(46):2(1); etc.* (liturgy).

18-24: For loo, my sinne and my confusioun ... Han take on me a greevous accioun/ Of verrey right and desperacioun;/ And as bi right thei mighten wel susteene/ That I were wurthi my dampnacioun,/ Nere merci of you, blisful hevene queene.
Cp. *1 John 3:20-21; etc.* (La; R).
Cp. *Jer. 44:17, 25* (liturgy).

28-32: For certes, Crystes blisful mooder deere,/ Were now the bowe bent in swich maneere/ As it was first of justice and of ire,/ The rightful God nolde of no mercy heere;/ But thurgh thee han we grace as we desire.
Luke 1:28-38; etc.
Ps. 7:13(12) (R; F).
Ps. 84(85):11(10) ? (Klinefelter, 1965; Gross, in B, 1987, n. 25-32).

33: Evere hath myn hope of refut been in thee . . .
Cp. *Ps. 45(46):2(1); etc.*

36-37: . . . at the grete assyse/ Whan we shule come bifore the hye justyse.
2 Cor. 5:10; Rom. 14:10; etc. (F).

38-40: So litel fruit shal thanne in me be founde/ That, but thou er that day correcte [vice],/ Of verrey right my werk wol me confounde.
Cp. *Rom. 7:4; etc.* (La, 1924, 89; R; Gross, in B, 1987, n. 38).
Cp. *Heb.12:11; etc.*

41-42: Fleeinge, I flee for socour to thi tente/ Me for to hide from tempeste ful of drede . . .
Isa. 4:6 ?

43-44: . . . Biseeching yow that ye you not absente/ Though I be wikke. O, help yit at this neede!
Cp. *Isa. 26:10; etc.*
Cp. *Ps. 108(109):26; etc.*

45: Al have I ben a beste in wil and deede . . .
Cp. *Ps. 72(73):23(22)*

46: . . . Yit, ladi, thou me clothe with thi grace.
Cp. *Matt. 6:28; etc.*

47-48: Thin enemy and myn—ladi, tak heede—/ Unto my deth in poynt is me to chace!
Cp. *Ps. 142(143):3; etc.*

49-50: Glorious mayde and mooder, which that nevere/ Were bitter, neither in erthe nor in see. . . .
Cp. *Exod. 15:23; Ruth 1:20; etc.* (cp. S; R; Gross, in B, 1987, n. 50; cp. *SecNP* 58).

56: . . . To stink eterne he wole my gost exile.
  Cp. *Isa. 34:3; etc.* (R; F; Gross, in B, 1987, n. 56; Spencer, 1927, 191-92).

59-61: . . . And with his precious blood he wrot the bille/ Upon the crois as general acquitaunce/ To every penitent in ful creaunce . . .
  Cp. *Col. 2:13-14* (La, 1924, 89; R; Gross, in B, 1987, n. 59).

81-82: Ladi, thi sorwe kan I not portreye/ Under the cros, ne his greevous penaunce. . . .
  Cp. *John 19:25-30; etc.* (La; R).

89-94: Moises, that saugh the bush with flawnes rede/ Brenninge, of which ther never a stikke brende,/ Was signe of thin unwemmed maidenhede./ Thou art the bush on which ther gan descende/ The Holi Gost, the which that Moyses wende/ Had ben a-fyr, and this was in figure.
  Exod. 3:2 (La; R; F; Gross, in B, 1987, n. 88-89).

95-96: Now, ladi, from the fyr thou us defende/ Which that in helle eternalli shal dure.
  Cp. *Mark 9:42-43; etc.*

102-04: . . . Ne advocat noon that wole and dar so preye/ For us, and that for litel hire as yee/ That helpen for an Ave-Marie or tweye.
  Cp. *1 John 2:1*
  Luke 1:28 (liturgy).

105: O verrey light of eyen that ben blynde . . .
  Cp. *Rom. 2:19; etc.*

108: . . . Thee whom God ches to mooder for humblese!
  Cp. *Luke 1:26-38, 46-49; etc.*

109-10: From his ancille he made the maistresse/ Of hevene and erthe, oure bille up for to beede.

> *Luke 1:38, 48* (liturgy; La, 1924, 89; S; R; F; Gross, in B, 1987, n. 109).
> Cp. *Matt. 11:25, etc.*
> Cp. *Col. 2:13-14*

113-15: Purpos I have sum time for to enquere/ Wherfore and whi the Holi Gost thee soughte/ Whan Gabrielles vois cam to thin ere.

> Cp. *Luke 1:26-28* (Gross, in B, 1987, n. 114-15).
> *Ps. 84(85):11(10)* ? (Klinefelter, 1965).

116-17: He not to werre us swich a wonder wroughte,/ But for to save us that he sithen boughte.

> Cp. *Luke 1:68-72; etc.*
> Cp. *1 Cor. 6:20, Rom. 5:9, Col. 1:20; etc.*

118-20: Thanne needeth us no wepen us for to save,/ But oonly ther we dide not, as us oughte,/ Doo penitence, and merci axe and have.

> Cp. *Mark 1:4; etc.* (La).

126: . . . of pitee welle?

> Cp. *Zach. 13:1*

133-34: Mooder, of whom oure merci gan to springe,/ Beth ye my juge and eek my soules leche. . . .

> Cp. *Ps. 146(147):3; Matt. 9:12, Mark 2:17, Luke 5:31; etc.*

144: . . . He hath thee corowned in so rial wise.

> Cp. *Apoc. 12:1*

145: Temple devout, ther God hath his woninge . . .

> Cp. *1 Cor. 3:17* (La).

149-50: With thornes venymous, O hevene queen,/ For which
the eerthe acursed was ful yore . . .
> Cp. *Jer. 44:17, 25* (liturgy).
> *Gen. 3:18* (R; Gross, in B, 1987, n. 149-50).
> Cp. *Matt. 27:29; etc.*

161-65: Xristus, thi sone, that in this worlde alighte/ Upon the
cros to suffre his passioun,/ And eek that Longius his herte
pighte/ And made his herte blood to renne adoun,/ And al was
this for my salvacioun.
> Cp. *John 3:16; etc.*
> Cp. *John 19:34-35* (Gospel of Nicodemus; cp. Jacobus de
> Voragine, *Legenda Aurea*, p. 191; F; Gross, in B, 1987, nn.
> 161, 163).
> Cp. *Rom. 5:9, Col. 1:20; 1 John 4:9-10; etc.*

169-71: Ysaac was figure of his deeth, certeyn,/ That so fer
forth his fader wolde obeye/ That him ne roughte nothing to be
slayn.
> *Gen. 22:7-10, etc.* (R; F; Gross, in B, 1987, n. 169).
> Cp. *Heb. 11:17-19* (R; F; Gross, in B, 1987, n. 169).

172: Right soo thi Sone list as a lamb to deye.
> Cp. *John 19:34-35*
> Cp. *Isa. 53:7*

177-78: Zacharie yow clepeth the open welle/ To wasshe sinful
soule out of his gilt.
> 8
> Cp. *Zach. 13:1* (R; F; Gross, in B, 1987, n. 177).

182: . . . Ben to the seed of Adam merciable . . .
> Cp. *Rom. 5:14; etc.*

183-84: . . . Bring us to that palais that is bilt/ To penitentes
that ben to merci able. Amen.

Cp. *Heb. 11:16*
Cp. *Matt. 4:17; etc.*

The Complaint unto Pity

20: . . . And for the soule I shop me for to preye.
     Cp. *2 Mach. 12:42-46* (liturgy).

95: . . . That love and drede yow ever lenger the more.
     Cp. *Deut. 6:2, 5; etc.*

A Complaint to His Lady

42: . . . That wo is me that ever I was bore . . .
     Cp. *Job 3:3, Jer. 20:14*

78: For bothe I love and eek drede yow so sore . . .
     Cp. *Deut. 6:2, 5; etc.*

125: . . . And of your grace graunteth me som drope . . .
     Cp. *Rom. 1:5; etc.* (liturgy).

The Complaint of Mars

9-11: . . . and with seint John to borowe/ Apeseth sumwhat of your sorowes smerte./ Tyme cometh eft that cese shal your sorwe.
     8
     1 John 3:19-22 ? (F).

15: Yet sang this foul—I rede yow al awake. . . .
     Rom. 13:11-14 ? (Fleming, 1969, pp. 248-49; Wood, 1970, p. 145; cp. Bennett, 1971-72).

29: . . . the thridde hevenes lord above . . .
     Cp. *Deut. 4:39; etc.* (cp. Gross, in B, 1987, n. 29).

166: . . . Be him that lordeth ech intelligence . . .
Cp. *Ps 90(91):11, Matt. 4:6, Luke 4:10; etc.* (F; cp. Gross, in B, 1987, n. 166).

The Complaint of Venus

To Rosemounde

Womanly Noblesse

27: Auctour of norture . . .
Cp. *Heb. 2:10; etc.* ?

Adam Scriveyn

1-7: Adam scriveyn . . . al is thorugh thy negligence and rape.
Gen. 3 ? (Kaske, 1979).

The Former Age

50: The lambish peple, voyd of alle vyce . . .
John 1:29 ? (Levin, 1969, p. 6).

58-59: . . . ne Nembrot, desirous/ To regne, had nat maad his toures hye.
Cp. *Gen. 10:8-10, 11:4* (cp. Peter Comestor, *Historia Scholastica;* cp. Augustine, *De Civitate Dei* 16.4; Buermann, 1967, pp. 9-10; Flügel, 1897, 126-33; Schmidt, 1978; F; Gross, in B, 1987, n. 58).

Fortune

65-71: Lo, th'execucion of the majestee/ That al purveyeth of his rightwysnesse,/ That same thing "Fortune" clepen ye,/ Ye blinde bestes ful of lewednesse./ The hevene hath propretee of

sikernesse,/ This world hath ever resteles travayle;/ Thy laste day is ende of myn intresse. . . .
 Cp. *Matt. 10:29-30* ? (cp. Dante, *Inf.* 7.67-96 ?; Schless, 1984, pp. 232-37; cp. R; Gross, in B, 1987, nn. 65-67, 71).

Truth

5: Savour no more than thee bihove shal . . .
 Cp. *Rom. 12:3* (Gross, in B, 1987, n. 5).

7: . . . And trouthe thee shal delivere, it is no drede.
 Cp. *John 8:32; etc.* (Flügel, 1901, 215-16; Ames, 1984, pp. 22-23; F).

11: Be war therfore to sporne ayeyns an al.
 Cp. *Acts 9:5* (Pace & David, 1982, p. 62, n. 11; proverbial; Whi P377; F; Gross, in B, 1987, n. 11).

14: As in line 7, above.

17-20: Her is non hoom, her nis but wildernesse:/ Forth, pilgrim, forth! Forth, beste, out of thy stal!/ Know thy contree, look up, thank God of al;/ Hold the heye wey and lat thy gost thee lede . . .
 Cp. *Heb. 11:13-16; etc.* (cp. *Bo* 1.p.5.8-25, etc.; cp. Flügel, 1901, 216-17; F; cp. Gross, in B, 1987, nn. 17-18, 19, 20).
 Cp. *Jer. 31:21; etc.* (Flügel, 1901, 220-22).
 Cp. *Rom. 8:4, 1 Pet. 2:11; etc.* (cp. Flügel, 1901, 222).

21: As in line 7, above.

22: Therfore, thou Vache, leve thyn old wrecchednesse.
 1 Kings 6:12 ? (Gillmeister, 1980; cp. Gross, in B, 1987, n. 22).
 Amos 4:1 ? (Flügel, 1901, 223).

23: Unto the world leve now to be thral.
 Cp. *1 John 2:15; etc.*

24: Crye him mercy . . .
    Cp. *Ps.106(107):19; etc.*

24-25: . . . that of his hy goodnesse/ Made thee of noght . . .
    Gen. 1:26-27, 2:7

25-26: . . . and in especial/ Draw unto him.
    Cp. *James 4:8* (La; cp. Flügel, 1901, 224).

26-27: And pray in general/ For thee, and eek for other,
hevenlich mede.
    Cp. *James 5:16* (La).

28: As in line 7, above.

Gentilesse

1-4: The firste stok, fader of gentilesse—/ What man that
desireth gentil for to be/ Must folowe his trace, and alle his
wittes dresse/ Vertu to love and vyces for to flee.
    Cp. *John 1:1; etc.* (F; cp. Gross, in B, 1987, n. 1).
    Cp. *Matt. 23:8-10; etc.*
    Cp. *1 John 3:24; etc.*

8-13: This firste stok was ful of rightwisnesse,/ Trewe of his
word, sobre, pitous, and free,/ Clene of his gost, and loved
besinesse,/ Ayeinst the vyce of slouthe, in honestee;/ And, but
his heir love vertu, as dide he,/ He is noght gentil, thogh he
riche seme . . .
    Cp. *John 1:1; etc.* (cp. Gross, in B, 1987, n. 1).
    Cp. *Matt. 23:8-10; etc.*
    Cp. *1 Cor. 1:30; etc.* (La).
    Cp. *1 John 3:24; etc.*

18-20: . . . That is appropred unto no degree/ But to the firste
fader in magestee,/ That maketh hem his heyres that him
queme . . .

Cp. *Matt. 23:8-10; etc.* (cp. Dante, *Convivio* 4.20.47-57, et passim; Lowes, 1915-16, 25).
Cp. *Heb. 1:3; etc.*
Cp. *James 2:5; etc.*

Lak of Stedfastnesse

15-17: Trouthe is put doun, resoun is holden fable,/ Vertu hath now no dominacioun;/ Pitee exyled, no man is merciable . . .
Cp. *Isa. 59:14*

26: Shew forth thy swerd of castigacioun . . .
Cp. *Rom. 13:4*

27: Dred God, do law, love trouthe and worthinesse . . .
Cp. *Eccl. 12:13; etc.*

Lenvoy de Chaucer a Scogan

1-2: Tobroken been the statuz hye in hevene/ That creat were eternally to dure . . .
Cp. *Gen. 1:1; etc.* (cp. Gross, in B, 1987, n. 1-2).

8-10: By word eterne whilom was it shape/ That fro the fyfte sercle, in no manere,/ Ne myghte a drope of teeres doun escape.
Cp. *Gen. 1:6-8*

Lenvoy de Chaucer a Bukton

1-4: . . . whan of Crist our kyng/ Was axed what is trouthe or sothfastnesse,/ He nat a word answerde to that axing,/ As who saith, "No man is al trewe," I gesse.
Cp. *John 18:38* (F; Gross, in B, 1987, n. 2).

9-10: I wol nat seyn how that yt is the cheyne/ Of Sathanas, on which he gnaweth evere . . .
Cp. *2 Pet. 2:4, Apoc. 20:1-2; etc.* (Gross, in B, 1987, n. 9).

18: Bet ys to wedde than brenne in worse wise.
    1 Cor. 7:9 (F; Gross, in B, 1987, n. 18).

19-20: But thow shal have sorwe on thy flessh, thy lyf,/ And
ben thy wives thral, as seyn these wise.
    Cp. *Gen. 3:16* (cp. Gross, in B, 1987, n. 19-20).
    Cp. *1 Cor. 7:4, 28, 33*.
    g

21: And yf that hooly writ may nat suffyse . . .
    G

The Complaint of Chaucer to His Purse

15: . . . that ben to me my lyves lyght . . .
    Cp. *John 8:12; etc.*

16: . . . And saveour as doun in this world here . . .
    Cp. *1 John 4:14; etc.*

Proverbs

Against Women Unconstant

16: . . . Bet than Dalyda . . .
    Judg. 16 (F; Gross, in B, 1987, n. 15-17).

Complaynt D'Amours

Merciles Beaute

A Balade of Complaint

THE ROMAUNT OF THE ROSE

135-38: And whan I had a while goon,/ I saugh a gardyn right anoon,/ Ful long and brood, and everydell/ Enclosed was, and walled well. . . .
>Cp. *Gen. 2:8-3:24; etc.* ? (Robertson, 1962, pp. 386-88, et passim; Fleming, 1969, pp. 54-103; cp. David, in B, 1987, n. 71-131).
>Cp. *Cant. 4:12, etc.* ? (Fleming, 1969, pp. 54-103).

221: . . . As she were al with doggis torn. . .
>Cp. *3 Kings 21:19, 23; etc.* ?

431: A sauter held she fast in honde . . .
>*g* (liturgy).

432-34: . . . And bisily she gan to fonde/ To make many a feynt praiere/ To God and to his seyntis dere.
>Cp. *Rom. 15:30; etc.* (liturgy).

442-43: From hir the gate ay werned be/ Of paradys, that blisful place. . . .
>Cp. *Apoc. 2:7; etc.*
>*Gen. 2:8-3:24; etc.*

444-48: For sich folk maketh lene her face,/ As Crist seith in his evangile,/ To gete hem prys in toun a while;/ And for a litel glorie veine/ They lesen God and his reigne.
>*G*
>*Matt. 6:16* (La; R; David, in B, 1987, n. 446).

454: . . . For nakid as a worm was she.
>Cp. *Ps 21(22):7(6)* ?

468-69: Acursed may wel be that day/ That povre man conceyved is.
>Cp. *Job 3:3, Jer. 20:14* (R; David, in B, 1987, n. 468).

647-50: For wel wende I ful sikerly/ Have ben in paradys erthly./ So fair it was that, trusteth wel,/ It semede a place espirituel.

    Cp. *Gen. 2:8-3:24; etc.* (R; David, in B, 1987, n. 648).

652: . . . Ther is no place in paradys . . .

    Cp. *Gen. 2:8-3:24; etc.*

671-72: They songe her song as faire and wel/ As angels don espirituel.

    Cp. *Ps. 148:2; etc.*

741-42: For they were lyk, as to my sighte,/ To angels that ben fethered brighte.

    Cp. *Ezech. 1:6; etc.*

916-17: He semede as he were an aungell/ That doun were comen fro hevene cler.

    Cp. *Matt. 22:30; Apoc. 10:1; etc.* (cp. *TC* 1.102-04).

974: . . . Were also blak as fend in helle.

    Cp. *Joel 2:6; etc.*

1471: . . . And in his net gan hym so strayne . . .

    Cp. *Ps. 123(124):7; Prov. 1:17; etc.* ? (cp. Dante, *Purg.* 31:61-
       63; Havely, 1984, pp. 57-59).
    Eccl. 9:12 ? (proverbial; Whi N90).

1623-24: Love will noon other bridde[s] cacche,/ Though he sette either net or lacche.

    Cp. *Ps. 123(124):7; Prov. 1:17; etc.* ? (cp. Dante, *Purg.* 31:61-
       63; Havely, 1984, pp. 57-59).
    Eccl. 9:12 ? (proverbial; Whi N90).

1715-18: The God of Love, with bowe bent . . . Was stondyng by a fige-tree.

    Cp. *Matt. 21:19; etc.* ?

1757-58: I nyste what to seye or do,/ Ne gete a leche my woundis to. . . .
  Cp. *Ps. 146(147):3; Matt. 9:12, Mark 2:17, Luke 5:31; etc.* ?

1965-66: The helthe of love mot be founde/ Where as they token first her wounde.
  Cp. *Ps. 146(147):3; Matt. 9:12, Mark 2:17, Luke 5:31; etc.* ?
  (cp. David, in B, 1987, n. 1965).

2825-26: 'The secounde shal be Swete-Speche,/ That hath to many oon be leche,/ To bringe hem out of woo and wer. . . .
  Cp. *Ps. 146(147):3; Matt. 9:12, Mark 2:17, Luke 5:31; etc.* ?

2944: . . . Of all thyne harmes thei shall be leche. . . .
  Cp. *Ps. 146(147):3; Matt. 9:12, Mark 2:17, Luke 5:31; etc.* ?

3190-3216: . . . Til that me saugh so mad and mat/ The lady of the highe ward,/ Which from hir tour lokide thiderward./ Resoun men clepe that lady,/ Which from hir tour delyverly/ Com doun to me, withouten mor. . . . Whoso wole trowe hir lore,/ Ne may offenden nevermore.
  Cp. *Prov. 8:1-9:5; Wis. 6-8; 1 Cor. 1:24; etc.* ? (Fleming, 1969, pp. 98-120, et passim; Badel, 1970; Fleming, 1984, pp. 25-30, et passim; cp. Hill, 1985; cp. David, in B, 1987, n. 3191).

3205-06: Hir goodly semblaunt, by devys,/ I trowe were maad in paradys. . . .
  Cp. *Gen. 2:8-3:24; etc.* (R; cp. David, in B, 1987, n. 3205-11).

3209: . . . but if the letter ly . . .
  G

3210-11: . . . God hymsilf, that is so high,/ Made hir aftir his ymage . . .
  Cp. *Ps. 112(113):4-5; etc.*
  Cp. *Gen. 1:26-27* (Black, 1974, pp. 52-55).

3265-68: Thou delest with angry folk, ywis;/ Wherfore to thee bettir is/ From these folk awey to fare,/ For they wole make thee lyve in care.
> *Prov. 22:24-25* ? (Burnley, 1986, pp. 211-13).

3463-66: By sufferaunce and wordis softe/ A man may overcome ofte/ Hym that aforn he hadde in drede,/ In bookis sothly as I rede.
> Cp. *Prov. 15:1* (R; David, in B, 1987, n. 3463; proverbial; cp.
> Whi W615).
> G

4617: . . . And I not where to fynde a leche. . . .
> Cp. *Ps. 146(147):3; Matt. 9:12, Mark 2:17, Luke 5:31; etc.* ?

4879-82: For of ech synne it is the rote,/ Unlefull lust, though it be sote,/ And of all yvell the racyne,/ As Tulius can determyne. . . .
> *1 Tim. 6:10* (Fleming, 1969, p. 120).

4989-95: 'Where Elde abit I wol thee telle . . . For thidir byhoveth thee to goo./ If Deth in youthe thee not sloo,/ Of this journey thou maist not faile./ With hir Labour and Travaile/ Logged ben, with Sorwe and Woo. . . .
> Cp. *Ps. 89(90):10; Ecclus 18:8* ? (La).

5097: . . . Withoute more (what shulde I glose?) . . .
> G ?

5453: . . . And trowe hem as the Evangile. . . .
> G (F).

5513-20: But sothfast freendis, what so bitide,/ In every fortune wolen abide;/ Thei han her hertis in such noblesse/ That they nyl love for no richesse,/ Nor for that Fortune may hem sende/ Thei wolen hem socoure and defende,/ And chaunge for softe ne for sore;/ For who is freend, loveth evermore.

Cp. *Prov. 17:17; etc.* (S; La; R; cp. David, in B, 1987, n. 5513-14).

5521-32: Though men drawe swerd his freend to slo,/ He may not hewe her love a-two./ But, in cas that I shall sey,/ For pride and ire lese it he may,/ And for reprove by nycete,/ And discovering of privite,/ With tonge woundyng, as feloun,/ Thurgh venemous detraccioun./ Frend in this cas wole gon his way,/ For nothyng greve hym more ne may;/ And for nought ellis wole he fle,/ If that he love in stabilite.
    Ecclus. 22:26-27 (La; R; David, in B, 1987, n. 5521-29).

5533-34: And certeyn, he is wel bigon,/ Among a thousand that fyndith oon.
    Cp. *Eccl. 7:29* ? (David, in B, 1987, n. 5534).

5659: 'In erthe is nat oure countre. . . . '
    Cp. *Heb. 11:13-16* (La; cp. R; David, in B, 1987, n. 5659-60; cp. *Bo* 1.p.5.8-25, 5.p.1.12-15 and *Truth* 17-20).

5887-88: For who that dredith sire ne dame,/ Shal it abye in body or name.
    Cp. *Deut. 21:18-21* (La).

6251-52: . . . Whanne they resseyved martirdom,/ And wonnen hevene unto her hom.
    Cp. *2 Cor. 5:1, 6-8; Apoc. 7:14-15; etc.*

6354: . . . I take the strawe, and lete the corn.
    Cp. *Matt. 3:12, Luke 3:17* ? (cp. Dahlberg, 1983, p. 394, n. 11216).
    2 Cor. 3:6; Rom. 7:6 ?

6452-54: And this ageyns holy scripture,/ That biddith every heerde honest/ Have verry knowing of his beest.
    G

Prov. 27:23; *John* 10:14; *etc.* (La; R; David, in B, 1987, n. 6453-54).

6529-43: For Salamon, full wel I wot,/ In his Parablis us wrot,/ As it is knowe to many a wight,/ In his thrittene chapitre right,/ 'God thou me kepe . . . . Unnethe that he nys a mycher/ Forsworn, or ellis God is lyer.'/Thus seith Salamones sawes.
   Prov. 30:8-9 (La; R; F; David, in B, 1987, n. 6532; cp.
      Dahlberg, 1983, pp. 395-96, nn. 11277-90, 11293 ff.).

6544-50: Ne we fynde writen in no lawis . . . That Crist, ne his apostlis dere . . . Were never seen her bred beggyng,/ For they nolden beggen for nothing.
   Cp. *Mark* 1:16; *etc.* (La; cp. William of St. Amour, *De Periculis* 12; David, in B, 1987, n. 6547-50).

6556: . . . The nakid text, and lete the glose . . .
   G (David, in B, 1987, n. 6556).

6561-62: For they weren Goddis herdis deere,/ And cure of soules hadden heere. . . .
   Cp. *John* 10:11; *etc.* (La).

6563-67: They nolde nothing begge her fode;/ For aftir Crist was don on rode,/ With ther propre hondis they wrought,/ And with travel, and ellis nought,/ They wonnen all her sustenaunce. . . .
   Cp. *John* 21:3 ? (La).

6568-72: And lyveden forth in her penaunce,/ And the remenaunt yave awey/ To other pore folkis alwey./ They neither bilden tour ne halle,/ But ley in houses smale withalle.
   Cp. *Acts* 2:44-47 ? (La).

6595-98: Yit shulde he selle all his substaunce,/ And with his swynk have sustenaunce,/ If he be parfit in bounte./ Thus han tho bookes told me.

Cp. *Matt. 19:20-21; Luke 18:22* (R; William of St. Amour, *De Periculis* 12; David, in B, 1987, n. 6595-96; cp. lines 6653-60, below).
G

6636-44: But I trowe that the book seith wel,/ Who that takith almessis that be/ Dewe to folk that men may se/ Lame, feble, wery, and bare . . . He etith his owne dampnyng,/ But if he lye, that made al thing.
G
Matt. 23:14 (R; cp. William of St. Amour, *De Periculis* 12; David, in B, 1987, n. 6636).
Titus 1:2
Gen. 1

6653-60: And witeth wel that [ther] God bad/ The good-man selle al that he had,/ And folowe hym, and to pore it yive,/ He wolde not therfore that he lyve/ To serven hym in mendience . . . But he bad wirken whanne that neede is,/ And folwe hym in goode dedis.
Matt. 19:20-21; Luke 18:22 (La; R; William of St. Amour, *De Periculis* 12; David, in B, 1987, n. 6653-58; cp. lines 6595-96, above).

6661-65: Seynt Poul . . . bad th'appostles for to wirche,/ And wynnen her lyflode in that wise,/ And hem defended truandise,/ And seide, 'Wirketh with youre honden.'
8
1 Thess. 4:11; Eph. 4:28 (cp. William of St. Amour, *De Periculis* 12; cp. David, in B, 1987, n. 6661-65; R; I.a).

6668: . . . Ne sellen gospel . . .
G

6679-84: The goode folk, that Poul to preched,/ Profred hym ofte, whan he hem teched,/ Som of her good in charite./ But

therof right nothing tok he;/ But of his hondwerk wolde he gete/ Clothes to wryen hym, and his mete.
> Cp. *Acts 20:33-35* (cp. William of St. Amour, *De Periculis* 12; David, in B, 1987, n. 6679-84; La; R).

6775-76: . . . Al shulde I dye, and be putt doun,/ As was Seynt Poul, in derk prisoun. . . .
> Cp. *Acts 16:23-24* (La).

6885-922: I wole you seyn, withouten drede,/ What men may in the gospel rede/ Of Seynt Mathew, the gospelere,/ That seith, as I shal you sey heere:/ 'Uppon the chaire of Moyses' . . . . The gospel is ther-ageyns, I gesse,/ That shewith wel her wikkidnesse.
>   8
> Cp. *Matt. 23:1-8, 13-15* (cp. Innocent III, *DMCH* 2.23; La; R; F; David, in B, 1987, n. 6887).
>   G

6963-64: We ben the folk, without lesyng,/ That all thyng have without havyng.
> Cp. *2 Cor. 6:10* (cp. Innocent III, *DMCH* 2.15; La).

6995-7000: I love noon hermitage more./ All desertes and holtes hore,/ And grete wodes everichon,/ I lete hem to the Baptist John./ I quethe hym quyt and hym relesse/ Of Egipt all the wildirnesse.
> Cp. *Matt. 3:1; Mark 1:4; Luke 3:2-3; John 1:23* (La; R; F; cp. David, in B, 1987, n. 6998).

7009-12: Of Antecristes men am I,/ Of whiche that Crist seith openly,/ They have abit of hoolynesse,/ And lyven in such wikkednesse.
> Cp. *Matt. 7:15; 1 John 2:18* (La; R).

7013-16: Outward, lambren semen we,/ Fulle of goodnesse and of pitee,/ And inward we, withouten fable,/ Ben gredy wolves ravysable.
Cp. *Matt. 7:15* (La).

7017: We enviroune bothe lond and se. . . .
Cp. *Matt. 23:15* (La; R; cp. David, in B, 1987, n. 7017).

7145: . . . By exposicioun ne glose . . .
G ?

7155-56: Thus Antecrist abiden we,/ For we ben alle of his meyne. . . .
Cp. *1 John 2:18; etc.*

7165-7207: Thus mych wole oure book signifie,/ That while Petre hath maistrie,/ May never John shewe well his myght. . . . . But I wole stynt of this matere. . . .
Cp. *Acts 1:1-2; etc.* (cp. William of St. Amour, *De Periculis* 8; R, p. 882, n. 7096; F; cp. David, in B, 1987, n. 7166-70).

7191-92: And all with Antecrist they holden,/ As men may in the book biholden.
Cp. *1 John 2:18*
g

7285-86: He is the hound, shame is to seyn,/ That to his castyng goth ageyn.
Prov. 26:11; 2 Pet. 2:22 (cp. Jerome, *EAJ;* La; R; David, in B, 1987, n. 7285-86).

7369: . . . but she forgat not hir sawter . . .
g (liturgy; F).

7389-96: That false traytouresse untrewe/ Was lyk that salowe hors of hewe,/ That in the Apocalips is shewed. . . . For on that hors no colour is,/ But only deed and pale, ywis.

Cp. *Apoc. 6:8* (R; David, in B, 1987, n. 7391).

7412: About his necke he bar a byble. . . .
    G

7490-91: To fysshen synful men we go,/ For other fysshynge ne
fysshe we.
    Cp. *Matt. 4:19; Luke 5:10* (La; R; David, in B, 1987, n. 7490-
    91).

INDEX II:
SCRIPTURAL REFERENCES

[A Note to Index II: Index II comprises a "reverse" index of all the biblical allusions noted in Index I. Listed first are all of the "general references" to the Bible, Holy Writ, the Gospel, Old Testament or "olde lawe," etc., which were identified in Index I by a "G ." Listed next, by biblical chapter and verse and opposite the abbreviated titles of the works and line-numbers in Chaucer where they occur, or purportedly occur, are all the remaining allusions in Index I. Line references to the *Legend of Good Women Prologue* are to the "F" Version, unless marked "G." All references to a specific biblical book or to the author of a specific book (e.g., "Ecclesiaste," "Solomon," "Job," "Paul," etc.) are placed at the head of the listing for that book and identified, as in Index I, by a "*g*." Chaucer's erroneous references to specific authors or books are listed with a "*g*" under the erroneous biblical work when that work is remote from the one Chaucer cites (e.g., *ParsT* 134, attributed by Chaucer to Job but actually from Proverbs, is listed under Job), or—more often—under the heading of the work from which Chaucer apparently thought he was quoting (thus *Mel* 1003, 1159-60, and 1161 and *ParsT* 854, all attributed by Chaucer to Solomon but actually from Ecclesiasticus, by Jesus the son of Sirach, are listed under Proverbs, to which Chaucer refers repeatedly in both *Melibee* and the *Parson's Tale*). A list of the references in Index I to extra-canonical sources follows the entries for The Apocalypse of St. John. Passages in Chaucer that were related in Index I to more than one biblical verse (e.g., to parallel passages in two or three of the Gospels) are listed more than once.

Throughout Index II the notations "cp.," "?," and "etc.," which were used in Index I, have been omitted; hence all verses cited in Index I as comparable with or only doubtfully connected to Chaucer's words are here listed alongside more certain references—the reader must therefore refer back to Index I in order to eliminate references which are problematic. Index II makes it possible for the reader to examine Chaucer's various uses of the same biblical texts synoptically and to discover which books of the Bible and which scenes or sayings within those books he favored in his own compositions.]

General References

Canterbury Tales:	
GP	435-38, 481, 496-98, 709, 739
RvP	3902
MLT	666-67
MLE	1180
WBP	26-29, 59-68, 129-30, 346-47, 650, 687
WBT	1208-10
FrT	1647
SumT	1789-93, 1794, 1844-45, 1885-90, 1904-05, 1919-24, 1935-36
MerchT	2300-02
PardT	483-84, 573-78, 583-87, 742-44
ShipT	91(*1281), 131(*1321)
Thop-MelL	943-52(*2133-42)
Mel	1079-80(*2269-70), 1144-45(*2334-35), 1162(*2352), 1164(*2354), 1177(*2367),

		1197(*2387), 1459-60(*2649-50), 1583(*2773)
	NPT	3127-29(*4317-19)
	SecNT	122-23, 201-16
	CYT	857-58
	ParsT	115, 116, 191, 195, 208, 289-90, 291, 294, 313, 323, 355-56, 392, 413, 517, 522-23, 526-30, 588, 588-90, 623, 661, 680, 745, 754-55, 837, 842, 867, 888, 889, 900, 911, 917-18, 931, 959
	Ret	1083
	BD	333-34, 985-88
	HF	1334-35
	TC	4.1409-10; 5.1265
	LGWP	17-39(G17-39), G86, G326, 328(G254)
	LGW	1144-45
	Buk	21
	Rom	444-48, 3209, 3463-66, 5097, 5453, 6452-54, 6556, 6595-98, 6636-44, 6668, 6885-922, 7145, 7412

Genesis

1	*GP*	1-18
1	*SumT*	1972-73
1-3	*MkT*	2007-14(*3197-3204)
1	*NPT*	3187-88(*4377-78)
1	*PF*	199
1	*TC*	3.1016-19, 1437, 1765
1	*LGWP*	229, 445(G435)
1	*LGW*	1039-43
1	*Rom*	6636-44
1:1	*GP*	253-55

1:1	*NPT*	3163(*4353)
1:1	*Scog*	1-2
1:4-5	*TC*	3.1429-30
1:6-8	*Scog*	8-10
1:11	*PF*	173-74
1:26-27	*FrT*	1642-43
1:26-27	*SqT*	552
1:26-27	*FranklT*	879-80
1:26-27	*PardT*	901
1:26-27	*Mel*	1103-04(*2293-94)
1:26-27	*HF*	470, 970
1:26-27	*Bo*	3.m.9.25-32, 5.p.6.85-86
1:26-27	*TC*	2.577; 3.1503; 4.1236; 5.1839-40
1:26-27	*LGW*	1792
1:26-27	*Truth*	24-25
1:26-27	*Rom*	3210-11
1:26-31	*NPT*	3341(*4531)
1:27	*Mel*	1626-27(*2816-17)
1:27	*TC*	2.500, 2.577
1:28	*WBP*	26-29
1:28	*MerchT*	1448-49
1:28	*ParsT*	883
1:29	*MkT*	2007-14(*3197-3204)
1:31	*TC*	3.378
2-3	*LGWP*	563-64
2:3-8	*MerchT*	2134-36
2:7	*GP*	5-6
2:7	*SqT*	552
2:7	*FranklT*	983
2:7	*Mel*	1103-04(*2293-94)
2:7	*MkT*	2007-14(*3197-3204)
2:7	*HF*	470, 970
2:7	*TC*	2.577, 1733-36; 3.1503; 4.1236
2:7	*LGWP*	286(G189)
2:7	*LGW*	1792

2:7	*Truth*	24-25
2:7, 21-22	*PardT*	901
2:8	*TC*	4.864, 5.817
2:8-3:24	*MerchT*	1264-65, 1325-32, 1822, 1964, 2134-36, 2143, 2335-36
2:8-3:24	*FranklT*	911-12
2:8-3:24	*BD*	398-447
2:8-3:24	*PF*	183-210
2:8-3:24	*TC*	2.508
2:8-3:24	*Rom*	135-38, 442-43, 647-50, 652, 3205-06
2:16-17	*MkT*	2007-14(*3197-3204)
2:18	*Mel*	1103-04(*2293-94)
2:18	*ParsT*	921
2:18, 21-22	*MerchT*	1325-32
2:18, 22	*ParsT*	925-26, 928
2:18, 21-24	*ParsT*	917-18, 921
2:18, 23-24	*MerchT*	1334-36
2:21-24	*ParsT*	921
2:22	*TC*	4.1236
2:24	*WBP*	30-31
2:24	*MerchT*	1261-62
2:24	*ParsT*	842, 883
2:25	*MerchT*	1325-32
2:25	*ParsT*	325
2:28	*ParsT*	888
3	*KtT*	1051
3	*MLT*	368
3	*PardT*	505-11
3	*NPT*	3257-59(*4447-49)
3	*TC*	1.407-20
3	*LGWP*	203-09(G97-103)
3	*Adam*	1-7
3:1	*MLT*	360
3:1	*PrT*	558(*1748), 560-64(*1750-54)

3:1	ParsT	326
3:1-6	ParsT	331-32
3:1-7	ParsT	325
3:1-16	WBP	713-20
3:2-3	ParsT	327
3:4-5	ParsT	328
3:6	ParsT	329, 819
3:6-24	SumT	1915-17
3:6-24	PardT	498-511
3:7	ParsT	330
3:16	MLT	286-87
3:16	Buk	19-20
3:18	ABC	149-50
3:23-24	PardT	505-11
3:23-24	MkT	2007-14(*3197-3204)
3:23-24	ParsT	819
4:1	ParsT	461-62, 516
4:10	PrT	578(*1768)
4:14	ParsT	1015
4:18-20	Anel	149-54
4:18-24	WBP	53-54
4:19-23	SqT	550-51
4:21-22	BD	1160-66
5:3	WBP	696
5:24	HF	588
6:2-7	ParsT	839
6:5-7	MLT	811-12
6-9	MilT	3517-82
6:17	MilT	3519-21
6:17-19	MilT	3534-36
7	ParsT	839
7:7	MilT	3539-40

7:10-24	*MilT*	3616, 3818, 3834
7:11-24	*GP*	1-18
8:1	*GP*	5-6
8:1	*FranklT*	888
8:16	*MilT*	3560-61, 3581-82
8:21	*MilT*	3612
9:2-3	*MilT*	3581-82
9:15	*MilT*	3834
9:24-27	*ParsT*	754-55, 766
10:8-9	*GP*	177-78
10:8-10	*Form Age*	58-59
11	*MerchT*	1704-05
11:4	*Form Age*	58-59
13:11	*LGW*	718
14:8	*ParsT*	839
16:2-3	*WBP*	55-57
19	*ParsT*	910-11
19:4-9, 24-25	*ParsT*	839
19:24, 28	*TC*	4.117-19
19:29-38	*PardT*	485-87
22	*ClT*	351-54, 362-63, 456-58, 493-94
22:1	*ClT*	451-52, 619-20, 706-07, 735, 786
22:1-14	*MLT*	837-38
22:3-5	*FranklT*	1487-92
22:7-10	*ABC*	169-71
22:9	*ClT*	704
22:12	*ClT*	1056

24	*MerchT*	1704-05
24:15-67	*ClT*	274-76
25:1	*WBP*	55-57
25:20	*FrT*	1573
27:5-29	*MerchT*	1362-65
27:5-29	*Mel*	1098(*2288)
28:12	*HF*	1374-75
28:12	*Bo*	1.p.1.1-42
29:1-12	*ClT*	274-76
29:32-35	*SecNP*	96-98
30:1-13	*WBP*	55-57
30:16-21	*SecNP*	96-98
30:27, 30	*ParsT*	443
30:31-43	*PardP*	351, 364
37	*NPT*	3130-32(*4320-22)
39:8-9	*ParsT*	880-81
40	*NPT*	3130-32(*4320-22), 3134-35(*4324-25)
41	*NPT*	3130-32(*4320-22), 3133(*4323)
41	*BD*	280-82
41	*HF*	514-17
41:47-49, 53-57	*ParsT*	443

Exodus

| *g* | *Pars T* | 750-51 |

3:2	*PrP*	468(*1658)
3:2	*ABC*	89-94
4	*GP*	673-74
7-12	*BD*	1205-07
7:10-11	*SqT*	249-51
10:16	*Mel*	1420(*2610)
14:21-31	*MLT*	488-90
15:9	*ParsT*	355-56
15:23	*SecNP*	58
15:23	*ABC*	49-50
15:23-25	*TC*	3.178-79
20:1-17	*ParsT*	750-51, 887, 956
20:3-4	*ParsT*	750-51
20:7	*PardT*	472-75, 639-47
20:7	*ParsT*	588, 596
20:13	*TC*	2.1733-36
20:13-15	*ParsT*	887
20:14	*ParsT*	837, 867
20:15	*ParsT*	798
20:15-16	*ParsT*	795
20:17	*ParsT*	521, 844
23:19	*SumT*	2275-77, 2284
31:18	*SumT*	1740-45
32:1-6	*PardT*	906-09
32:6	*PardT*	467-68
33:20	*LGWP*	230-36(cp. G160-68)

34:7	*Mel*	1458(*2648)
34:26	*SumT*	2275-77, 2284
34:28	*SumT*	1885-90

Leviticus

10:8-9	*SumT*	1894-1901
18:6-18	*ParsT*	907
18:22-23	*ParsT*	910-11
19:13	*ParsT*	520
19:20	*ParsT*	837
19:32	*WBT*	1208-10
19:32	*PardT*	742-44
20:10	*ParsT*	888
20:10-21	*ParsT*	837
21:9	*ParsT*	838
23:10	*SumT*	2275-77, 2284
23:20	*SumT*	2284

Numbers

5:11-31	*PardP*	366-71
6:1-5	*KtT*	2414-18
6:2-5	*MkT*	2055-57(*3245-47)
6:3-4	*PardT*	554-55
7:13-20	*PardP*	364
11:5	*GP*	634
14:9	*TC*	2.524

18:26	*SumT*	2275-77, 2284
30:7-17	*ParsT*	931
34:6-7	*GP*	59
35:17	*MilT*	3712
35:17	*ParsT*	574

Deuteronomy

4:39	*KtT*	1599, 1800, 2249, 2439, 2987-3035
4:39	*WBP*	207
4:39	*MerchT*	1449, 1974
4:39	*FranklT*	989, 1321
4:39	*NPT*	2909(*4099), 2917(*4107)
4:39	*HF*	1758
4:39	*Bo*	5.p.6.293-94
4:39	*TC*	3.589-93, 878, 1027; 5.1004, 1842-44
4:39	*LGWP*	456-59(G446-49)
4:39	*LGW*	1891
4:39	*Mars*	29
5:6-21	*ParsT*	750-51, 887, 956
5:11	*PardT*	639-47
5:11	*ParsT*	588, 596
5:17-19	*ParsT*	887
5:18	*ParsT*	867
5:18-19	*ParsT*	795
5:19	*ParsT*	798
5:21	*ParsT*	521, 844
6:2, 5	*SecNT*	125
6:2, 5	*ParsT*	763
6:2, 5	*Pity*	95

6:2, 5	*Lady*	78
6:4	*MerchT*	2291
6:5	*TC*	2.827-30
6:13	*TC*	3.1290
8:3	*SumT*	1844-45
11:1	*Mel*	1626-27(*2816-17)
11:13	*TC*	2.827-30
18:3	*PardP*	351
21:18-21	*Rom*	5887-88
22:21	*ParsT*	837, 838
24:17	*FrT*	1614-15
29:23	*TC*	4.117-19
32:24, 33	*ParsT*	195

Josue

1:4	*GP*	59
9:21, 23, 27	*KtT*	1422

Judges

g	*MkT*	2015-46(*3205-36), 2039-46(*3229-36)
4:21	*KtT*	2007
4:21	*WBP*	769-70

6:36-40	*PardP*	351
9:53	*TC*	2.1384
11:34	*PhysT*	5-6
11:34-39	*PhysT*	231-55
11:35	*PhysT*	221-26
13:3-5	*MkT*	2015-17(*3205-07)
13:5, 7, 14	*MkT*	2055-57(*3245-47)
13:7, 14	*PardT*	554-55
13-16	*Mel-MkL*	1951-53(*3141-43)
13-16	*MkT*	2015-46(*3205-36),
13-16	*ParsT*	955
14-16	*MkT*	2019-20(*3209-10)
14	*MkT*	2062(*3252)
14:5-7	*MkT*	2023-26(*3213-16)
14:16-17, 20	*MkT*	2027-30(*3217-20)
14:17	*MkT*	2021(*3211), 2053(*3243), 2091-94(*3281-84)
15:4-5	*MkT*	2031-36(*3221-26)
15:15	*MkT*	2037-38(*3227-28)
15:18-19	*MkT*	2039-46(*3229-36)
15:20	*MkT*	2059-60(*3249-50)
16	*MkT*	2062(*3252)
16	*BD*	738-39
16	*Wom Unc*	16
16:1, 3	*MkT*	2047-51(*3237-41)
16:4-30	*MkT*	2022(*3212)
16:6, 10, 13, 17	*MkT*	2071-72(*3261-62)
16:17	*KtT*	2414-18
16:17	*MkT*	2021(*3211), 2053(*3243), 2058(*3248)

16:17-21	*WBP*	721-23
16:17-21	*MkT*	2063-70(*3253-60), 2091-94(*3281-84)
16:21	*MkT*	2073-74(*3263-64)
16:23-30	*MkT*	2079-86(*3269-76)
16:27, 30	*MkT*	2087-89(*3277-79)
16:29-30	*KtT*	2466
16:29-30	*MLT*	201-02
19:22	*ParsT*	898
20:26	*PardT*	573-78

Ruth

1:9	*MerchT*	1258-60
1:20	*SecNP*	58
1:20	*ABC*	49-50
2:2	*LGWP*	73-77(G61-66)

1-4 Kings

1.*g*	*ParsT*	897
1-3.2:11	*ParsT*	955
1.1:1	*HF*	514-17
1.1:20	*PardT*	583-87
1.2:12	*ParsT*	897
1.2:12-16	*ParsT*	900
1.2:30	*ParsT*	189
1.3:19	*ParsT*	575
1.6:12	*Truth*	22

1.17:4	*GP*	560
1.17:4-51	*MLT*	934-38
1.17:40-50	*Thop*	827-32(*2017-22)
1.19:1	*LGWP*	251(G205)
1.20:17	*LGWP*	251(G205)
1.24:20	*LGWP*	456-59(G446-49)
1.25:2-35	*MerchT*	1369-71
1.25:2-35	*Mel*	1100(*2290)
1.25:22, 34	*WBP*	534
1.28:7	*HF*	1261
1.28:7-25	*FrT*	1507-12
2.g	*Mel*	1668-69(*2858-59)
2.2:11	*HF*	588
2.2:28	*MerchT*	1719
2.2:28	*HF*	1245
2.11:25	*Mel*	1668-69(*2858-59)
2.13:1-20	*TC*	2.1513(-3.217)
2.13:3	*TC*	1.644
2.14-18	*BD*	1117-18
2.14:25-26	*MilT*	3312-17
2.14:25-26	*LGWP*	249(G203), 539
2.16-18	*ParsT*	639
3.3	*ParsT*	955
3.3:12	*CYT*	960-61

3.3:13	*MerchT*	2294

3.6	*MerchT*	2292-93

3.11	*KtT*	1942
3.11:1-4	*MerchT*	2298-99
3.11:3	*WBP*	35-43
3.11:7-8	*MerchT*	2295-96
3.11:11-12	*MerchT*	2300-02

3.18:19-20	*SumT*	2116-17

3.19:4-9	*SumT*	1890-93

3.21:19	*MerchT*	1438
3.21:19, 23	*Rom*	221

4.2:2	*SumT*	2116-17

4.9:30-37	*MerchT*	1438

4.24:11-16	*MkT*	2147-48(*3337-38)

4.25:1	*HF*	59-63
4.25:1-9	*MkT*	2147-48(*3337-38)

1-2 Paralipomenon

1.10:13	*FrT*	1507-12
1.10:13	*HF*	1261

1.29:15	*MerchT*	1315
1.29:15	*ShipT*	9(*1199)
1.29:15	*ParsT*	1068

2.24:20	*CYT*	1476-78

2.30:9	*Mel*	1418-19(*2608-09)

2.36:6-20	*MkT*	2147-48(*3337-38)

1-2 Esdras

Tobias

g	*MerchT*	1288-92

4:19	*Mel*	1162(*2352)
4:20	*Mel*	1117-18(*2307-08)

6:16-17	*ParsT*	904-06

11	*MerchT*	2355-67

Judith

2-3	*MkT*	2551-57(*3741-47)
2-13	*MkT*	2550a(*3740a)

3:1-13	*MkT*	2559-64(*3749-54)

4:5	*MkT*	2565-66(*3755-56)

6:10	*MkT*	2565-66(*3755-56)

8-13	*Mel*	1099(*2289)

13:1-10	*MLT*	939-42
13:1-10	*MerchT*	1366-68
13:1-12	*MkT*	2567-74(*3757-64)
13:10	*MkT*	2558(*3748)

Esther

2	*MerchT*	1744-45
2:7	*MerchT*	1781-82
2:7	*BD*	985-88
5-7	*Merch*	1744-45
7	*Mel*	1101(*2291)
7-8	*MerchT*	1371-74
8	*LGWP*	250
14:15-16	*MerchT*	1744-45
15:8, 10	*MerchT*	1744-45

Job

g	*KtT*	1307-12
g	*MLT*	813-16
g	*WBP*	436
g	*ClT*	1155-62
g	*ParsT*	134, 176-78, 181-86, 211, 217, 223
1-2	*Mel*	999-1000(*2189-90)
1:12	*FrT*	1489-91
1:12	*PardT*	847-48
1:21	*ClT*	654-55, 871-72, 1150-51
1:21	*Mel*	999-1000(*2189-90)
1:21	*MancP*	99
1:21	*Bo*	2.p.2.15-16
2:1-6	*ClT*	785-91
2:3	*ClT*	456-58, 1056
2:6	*FrT*	1489-91

2:6	*PardT*	847-48
3:3	*KtT*	1073, 1542
3:3	*ClT*	901-03
3:3	*SqT*	499
3:3	*FranklT*	1558
3:3	*PhysT*	215
3:3	*MancT*	273
3:3	*HF*	345
3.3	*TC*	3.304, 1072-73, 1103, 1423, 1595-96; 4.251-52, 333-34, 747-48, 762-63, 839, 1251; 5.208-09, 689-90, 700, 1275-76
3:3	*LGW*	658, 833, 1027, 1308, 2187
3:3	*Lady*	42
3:3	*Rom*	468-69
7:9	*ParsT*	225
8:3, 20	*TC*	5.1706-07
8:9	*ParsT*	1068
9:22-24	*TC*	3.1016-19
10:20-22	*ParsT*	176-78
10:21-22	*ParsT*	181-86
10:22	*ParsT*	211, 217, 223
10:22	*PF*	381
12:12	*Mel*	1164(*2354)
13:15	*SecNT*	420
14:2	*MerchT*	1315
14:2	*ShipT*	9(*1199)

14:2	*ParsT*	1068
20:25	*ParsT*	191, 863-64
21:7	*TC*	3.1016-19
21:12-15	*MLT*	1135-38
23:10	*ClT*	1167-69
23:12	*SumT*	1844-45
27:19	*ParsT*	1068
34:11-13	*TC*	2.526-28
38:37	*PF*	60-63
39:33-35	*ClT*	932
41:5-22	*MancP*	37-38
42:1-6	*ClT*	932
42:6	*ParsT*	143, 386
42:6	*TC*	2.525
42:7	*ClT*	1056
42:10-16	*ClT*	1121-37

Psalms

8	*SumT*	1933-34
8	*Mel*	1198(*2388), 1303-04(*2493-94), 1630-31(*2820-21), 1692-93(*2882-83), 1735(*2925)
8	*MancT*	345
8	*ParsT*	125, 193, 204, 220, 307, 309, 442, 540, 716
8	*Rom*	431, 7369

1:1	*Mel*	1198(*2388)
2:4	*TC*	5.1821
4:2(1)	*TC*	5.1861
4:5(4)	*ParsT*	540
6:5(4)	*TC*	5.1866-69
7:13(12)	*ABC*	28-32
7:17(16)	*ParsT*	640
8:2(1)	*PrP*	Headnote
8:2-3(1-2)	*PrP*	453-59(*1643-49)
8:3(2)	*PrT*	607-08(*1797-98)
10(11):6(5)	*ParsT*	204
10:8-9(*Hebrew*)	*FrT*	1657-58
10:8-9(*Hebrew*)	*ParsT*	512
11(12):4(3)	*MancT*	339-42
18(19):15(14)	*TC*	2.528-32
20(21):4(3)	*Mel*	1735(*2925)
21(22):7(6)	*ClT*	880
21(22):7(6)	*LGWP*	317-18(G243-44)
21(22):7(6)	*Rom*	454
21(22):24(23)	*SumT*	1866
21(22):29(28)	*TC*	3.372-73
23(24):8, 10	*MerchT*	1267
24(25):7	*TC*	2.528-32

29(30):4(3)	*MerchT*	1400-01
29(30):6(5)	*TC*	1.951
30(31)15-16(15)	*MLT*	762-63
31(32):5	*ParsT*	309
32(33):3	*BD*	294-320
33(34):15(14)	*Mel*	1692-93(*2882-83)
33(34):14(13)	*MancT*	314-15
34(35):4, 10	*SecNT*	135-37
36(37):1, 7	*ParsT*	500-01
36(37):16	*Mel*	1630-31(*2820-21)
36(37):28	*ParsT*	500-01
39(40)	*PrT*	571(*1761)
39(40):15(14)	*SecNT*	135-37
41(42):8(7)	*TC*	2.1
42(43):3	*TC*	3.1-49
43(44):22(21)	*ShipT*	113(*1303)
43(44):22(21)	*ParsT*	1062
43(44):22(21)	*Bo*	4.p.1.34, 4.p.6.221, 5.p.6.134-35
43(44):22(21)	*TC*	3.260
43(44):22(21)	*Anel*	262-63
44(45):2(1)	*SumT*	1933-34
44(45):8(7)	*ParsT*	121
45(46):2(1)	*MLT*	852
45(46):2(1)	*SecNP*	75-76

45(46):2(1)	*ABC*	14, 33
49(50):20-21	*MLT*	674-76
51(52):4(2)	*MancT*	339-42
54(55):16(15)	*MLT*	783-84
54(55):16(15)	*ParsT*	442
56(57):5(4)	*MancT*	339-42
58(59):2(1)	*TC*	5.1866-69
60(61):9(8)	*TC*	3.1813
63(64):4(3)	*TC*	2.1681
63(64):4-9(3-8)	*MancT*	339-42
67(68):31(30)	*ParsT*	898
68(69):5(4)	*ParsT*	273
71(72):19	*TC*	3.8-9
72(73):5	*ParsT*	716
72(73):23(22)	*ABC*	45
75(76):6(5)	*ParsT*	193
76(77):17(16)	*TC*	3.8-9
84(85):11(10)	*KtT*	3089
84(85):11(10)	*TC*	3.1282
84(85):11(10)	*ABC*	28-32, 113-15
88(89):2(1)	*TC*	2.972-73

88(89):47(46)	*SumT*	1981-82
89(90):10	*Rom*	4989-95
90(91):5(4-5)	*TC*	2.201, 528-32
90(91):11	*SecNT*	152-55
90(91):11	*Mars*	166
90(91):12	*RvT*	4280
93(94):2-6	*MLT*	813-16
93(94):9	*TC*	4.963, 1654
96(97):3-4	*ParsT*	174
96(97):10	*ParsT*	307
102(103):1-5	*WBT*	1251
102(103):3	*TC*	3.61
102(103):15	*TC*	5.1841
102(103):17-18	*ParsT*	1073
103(104):15	*MancP*	96-98
106(107):14	*TC*	2.976, 3.1116-17
106(107):19	*Truth*	24
106(107):33-34	*ParsT*	220
108(109):26	*ABC*	43-44
112(113):4-5	*Rom*	3210-11
113(115):6	*GP*	446
114(116):3	*TC*	2.894-96; 3.1458; 4.1540, 1695-96; 5.212
114(116):9	*SumT*	2075
114(116):9	*MerchT*	1476, 1478, 1520, 1571, 1617

114(116):9	*ParsT*	617
117(118):18	*TC*	2.528-32
118(119):81	*TC*	4.1364
118(119):113	*ParsT*	125
123(124):7	*TC*	2.583; 3.1355, 1733-34; 4.1370-71; 5.775-77
123(124):7	*LGWP*	130-31(G118-19)
123(124):7	*Rom*	1471, 1623-24
126(127):1	*Mel*	1303-04(*2493-94)
138(139):23	*TC*	4.288-89
139(140):4(3)	*GP*	712
139(140):4(3)	*PardP*	413
142(143):3	*ABC*	47-48
144(145):8-13	*TC*	2.972-73
144(145):9	*ParsT*	582
146(147):3	*SumT*	1892, 1956
146(147):3	*PardT*	916
146(147):3	*SecNP*	56
146(147):3	*BD*	35-40, 919-20
146(147):3	*TC*	1.857-58; 2.570-71, 1066, 1581-82; 5.1536-37
146(147):3	*ABC*	133-34
146(147):3	*Rom*	1757-58, 1965-66, 2825-26, 2944, 4617
148-50	*MilT*	3305-06
148:2	*Rom*	671-72

| 149:5 | *MilT* | 3213-15 |

Proverbs

g	*MLP*	117-18
g	*WBP*	368-69, 679
g	*Mel*	997(*2187), 1003(*2193), 1047(*2237), 1060(*2250), 1087(*2277), 1113(*2303), 1158(*2348), 1159-60(*2349-50), 1161(*2351), 1167(*2357), 1171(*2361), 1173(*2363), 1178(*2368), 1179(*2369), 1186(*2376), 1194(*2384), 1317-18(*2507-08), 1416-17(*2606-07), 1485(*2675), 1512(*2702), 1513(*2703), 1514(*2704), 1515-16(*2705-06), 1539(*2729), 1542-44(*2732-34), 1571(*2761), 1572(*2762), 1578(*2768), 1579-80(*2769-70), 1589(*2779), 1590-91(*2780-81), 1628-29(*2818-19), 1638(*2828), 1639-40(*2829-30), 1671(*2861), 1696(*2886), 1704-05(*2894-95), 1719-20(*2909-10), 1739-40(*2929-30), 1754-58(*2944-48)
g	*MancT*	314-15, 343-44
g	*ParsT*	119, 127, 155-57, 168, 227, 566, 568, 569, 614, 629, 631-32, 633, 664, 688, 709, 854
g	*TC*	1.738-43
1:17	*TC*	2.583; 3.1355, 1733-34; 4.1370-71; 5.775-77
1:17	*LGWP*	130-31(G118-19)

1:17	*Rom*	1471, 1623-24
1:28	*ParsT*	168
2:1	*MancT*	318, 319, 321, 322, 325, 329, 335, 346, 351, 359
2:2	*Mel*	1501(*2691)
2:14	*ParsT*	492
3:1	*MancT*	318, 319, 321, 322, 325, 329, 335, 346, 351, 359
3:11-12	*ClT*	1152, 1155-62
3:13-20	*Mel*	967(*2157)
3:18	*ParsT*	127
4:9	*SecNT*	221
4:9	*TC*	2.1733-36
5:1	*MancT*	318, 319, 321, 322, 325, 329, 335, 346, 351, 359
6:1, 20	*MancT*	318, 319, 321, 322, 325, 329, 335, 346, 351, 359
6:14-19	*ParsT*	642
6:16-17	*MancT*	343-44
6:34-35	*ParsT*	168
7:1	*MancT*	318, 319, 321, 322, 325, 329, 335, 346, 351, 359
8:1-9:5	*Bo*	1.p.1.1-42
8:1-9:5	*Rom*	3190-3216
8:17	*ParsT*	709
8:22-30	*LGW*	2228-30
9:1	*BD*	1002-05

10:19	MancT	335-38
10:26	Mel	1086(*2276)
11:7	ParsT	227
11:12	Bo	2.p.7.123-40
11:14	Mel	1171(*2361)
11:22	WBP	784-85
11:22	ParsT	155-57
12:4	ParsT	134
12:5	Mel	1197(*2387)
12:11	Mel	1590-91(*2780-81)
13:7	GP	478-79
13:11	Mel	1579-80(*2769-70)
13:24	PhysT	93-100
14:13	MLT	421-23, 424, 1132-33
14:13	MerchT	2055
14:13	NPT	3205(*4395)
14:13	TC	1.952; 4.834-36
14:20	MLP	115
14:29	Mel	1513(*2703)
15:1	Rom	3463-66
15:4	ParsT	629
15:15	MLP	117-18
15:16	Mel	1628-29(*2818-19)
15:18	Mel	1514(*2704)
15:22	Mel	1171(*2361)
16:6	ParsT	119
16:7	Mel	1719-20(*2909-10)
16:19, 29	ParsT	614
16:24	Mel	1113(*2303)
16:32	Mel	1515-16(*2705-06)

17:1	*ParsT*	633
17:14	*Mel*	1039(*2229)
17:17	*Rom*	5513-20
17:22	*Mel*	995(*2185)
17:28	*Bo*	2.p.7.123-40
18:9	*ParsT*	688
19:4	*MkT*	2244-46(*3434-36)
19:4	*Bo*	3.p.5.66-68
19:6-7	*Mel*	1558-60(*2748-50)
19:7	*MLP*	120-21
19:11	*Mel*	1512(*2702)
19:13	*WBP*	278-80
19:13	*MerchT*	2307
19:13	*Mel*	1086(*2276)
19:13	*ParsT*	631-32
19:14	*MerchT*	1264-65, 1311
19:19	*Mel*	1539(*2729)
20:1	*PardT*	549-50
20:1	*ParsT*	822
20:3	*Mel*	1485(*2675)
20:4	*Mel*	1593(*2783)
21:9	*WBP*	778-79
21:9	*Mel*	1087(*2277)
21:19	*WBP*	778-79
21:23	*MancT*	314-15
22:1	*Mel*	1638(*2828)
22:17	*Mel*	1162(*2352)
22:24-25	*SumT*	2085-88
22:24-25	*PardT*	958-59
22:24-25	*Rom*	3265-68

23:13-14	*PhysT*	93-100
23:15, 19, 26	*MancT*	318, 319, 321, 322, 325, 329, 335, 346, 351, 359
23:31-33	*GP*	635-36
23:33-34	*TC*	1.415-17; 5.640-41
25:9-10	*TC*	1.738-43
25:10	*Mel*	1639-40(*2829-30)
25:16	*Mel*	1416-17(*2606-07)
25:18	*ParsT*	566
25:20	*WBP*	376-77
25:20	*Mel*	997(*2187)
25:21	*ParsT*	569
25:24	*WBP*	778-79
25:24	*Mel*	1087(*2277)
26:2	*ParsT*	620
26:11	*Rom*	7285-86
26:17	*Mel*	1542-44(*2732-34)
26:18-19	*ParsT*	574
26:27	*ParsT*	640
27:6	*NPT*	3329(*4519)
27:9	*Mel*	1158(*2348)
27:15	*WBP*	278-80
27:15	*MerchT*	2307
27:15	*Mel*	1086(*2276)
27:15	*ParsT*	631-32
27:20	*Mel*	1617-18(*2807-08)
27:23	*Rom*	6452-54
28:13	*ParsT*	127
28:14	*Mel*	1317-18(*2507-08), 1696(*2886)
28:15	*ParsT*	568
28:19	*Mel*	1590-91(*2780-81)
28:20	*Mel*	1578(*2768)

28:23	*Mel*	1177(*2367), 1704-05(*2894-95)
29:5	*Mel*	1178(*2368), 1179(*2369)
29:5	*NPT*	3329(*4519)
29:9	*ParsT*	664
30:8-9	*Rom*	6529-43
30:14	*ParsT*	566
30:16	*WBP*	371-75
30:21-23	*WBP*	362-67
30:29-32	*NPT*	3179-84(*4369-74)
31:4	*MLT*	776-77
31:4	*PardT*	560-61
31:4	*Mel*	1194(*2384)
31:4-5	*PardT*	583-87
31:10	*ClT*	1164-65
31:10	*Mel*	967(*2157)
31:10-31	*GP*	445-76
31:10-31	*WBP*	688-89
31:10-31	*ClT*	211-31, 428-29, 1177-1212
31:10-31	*ShipT*	3-7(*1193-97)
31:13	*WBP*	401-02
31:17	*SecNT*	437
31:22	*GP*	453-55

Ecclesiastes

g	*WBP*	651-53
g	*ClP*	6
g	*MerchT*	2242-49, 2276-79, 2287-90
g	*Mel*	1057(*2247), 1076-79(*2266-69), 1550(*2740), 1653(*2843), 1664-67(*2854-57), 1707-08(*2897-98), 1709-10(*2899-2900)
g	*NPT*	3329(*4519)

g	*ParsT*	229, 539, 649, 679, 712
g	*TC*	1.694-95
1:2	*CYT*	1447
1:2	*BD*	310
1:2	*TC*	4.271; 5.541
1:2	*LGWP*	53(G55), 185
1:2	*ABC*	4
1:7	*HF*	747-49
1:18	*ParsT*	229
3:1	*FrT*	1475
3:1	*ClP*	6
3:1	*MerchT*	1972
3:1	*TC*	2.989; 3.855
3:18-19	*KtT*	1307-12
4:9-12	*PardT*	825
4:10	*TC*	1.694-95
5:2	*ParsT*	649
5:10	*Mel*	1653(*2843)
7:1	*KtT*	2847-48
7:4	*Mel*	1709-10(*2899-2900)
7:4	*ParsT*	539
7:6	*Mel*	1707-08(*2897-98)
7:16	*TC*	3.1016-19
7:19	*ParsT*	712
7:29	*MilP*	3154-55
7:29	*MerchT*	2242-49, 2276-79, 2287-90
7:29	*Mel*	1057(*2247), 1076-79(*2266-69)
7:29	*LGWP*	G276-77
7:29	*Rom*	5533-34
9:1	*Mel*	1664(*2854)

9:10	*ParsT*	679
9:12	*TC*	2.583; 3.35, 1355, 1733-34; 4.1370-71; 5.775-77
9:12	*LGWP*	130-31(G118-19)
9:12	*Rom*	1471, 1623-24
9:13-15	*Mel*	1664-67(*2854-57)
10:19	*Mel*	1550(*2740)
12:13	*Sted*	27

Canticle of Canticles

title; KJ 1:1	*CYT*	1447
title; KJ 1:1	*BD*	310
title; KJ 1:1	*TC*	4.271; 5.541
title; KJ 1:1	*LGWP*	53(G55), 185
title; KJ 1:1	*ABC*	4
1:1	*MilT*	3734
1:14	*MerchT*	2141
2:2	*PrP*	461-62(*1651-52)
2:5	*MilT*	3705-06
2:7	*MilT*	3712
2:8	*LGWP*	255, 262, 269
2:9	*BD*	378-80, 487-88, 1311-13
2:10	*GP*	672
2:10-12	*MerchT*	2138-40
2:10-15	*LGWP*	125-47(G113-33)
2:12	*MilT*	3705-06
2:13	*MerchT*	2141
2:13-14	*MilT*	3700
2:13-14	*MerchT*	2147-48
3:5	*MilT*	3712

3:11	*TC*	2.1733-36
4:4	*MilT*	3265-66
4:7	*MerchT*	2146
4:7-8	*GP*	672
4:8-9	*MerchT*	2144-45
4:9-12	*NPT*	2867(*4057)
4:10	*MerchT*	2142
4:11, 14	*MilT*	3698-99
4:12, 16	*MerchT*	2143
4:12	*NPT*	2847-48(*4037-38)
4:12	*PF*	183-210
4:12	*Rom*	135-38
4:12-13	*MerchT*	2134-36
5:1	*MerchT*	2134-36, 2147-48
5:1-2	*LGWP*	203-09(G97-103)
5:2	*MilT*	3702
5:5	*MilT*	3708
5:8	*MilT*	3705-06
5:10	*BD*	904-05, 971-74
5:10-12	*MilT*	3312-17
5:13, 16	*MilT*	3690-93
6:1	*LGWP*	203-09(G97-103)
6:7-8	*BD*	971-74, 981-84
7:1	*MilT*	3259, 3263, 3267
7:4	*BD*	939-46
7:8-9	*MilT*	3261-62
8:4	*MilT*	3712
8:6	*ClT*	666-67
8:6-7	*TC*	3.1499

Wisdom

1:1	*PhysT*	154
2:1-9	*TC*	2.393-99
2:1	*LGWP*	5-9(G5-9)
2:5	*MerchT*	1315
2:5	*ShipT*	9(*1199)
2:5	*ParsT*	1068
2:23	*Bo*	3.m.9.25-32
2:24	*MLT*	365-66
5:9	*ShipT*	9(*1199)
5:9	*MerchT*	1315
5:9	*ParsT*	1068
6-8	*Rom*	3190-3216
7:25	*TC*	3.11
7:26	*BD*	948-51, 963-65, 971-74, 985-88
7:26	*TC*	3.1-49
8:1	*Bo*	3.p.12.116-18
14:3	*TC*	5.232, 1392

Ecclesiasticus

g	*MilT*	3529-30
g	*CkP*	4330-32
g	*MLP*	113-14
g	*SumT*	1988-90
g	*MerchT*	1483-87, 2250-51
g	*Mel*	995(*2185), 996(*2186), 1045(*2235), 1059(*2249), 1141-42(*2331-32), 1635(*2825)

8	*ParsT*	640, 875
1:17-18	*ParsT*	229
2:1	*FrT*	1659-60
3:27	*Mel*	1671(*2861)
4:35	*SumT*	1988-90
6:5	*Mel*	1739-40(*2929-30)
6:6	*Mel*	1167(*2357)
6:8-10	*MkT*	2244-46(*3434-36)
6:8-10	*Bo*	3.p.5.66-68
6:14	*Mel*	1161(*2351)
6:15	*Mel*	1159-60(*2349-50)
8:7	*PardT*	745-47
8:20	*Mel*	1173(*2363)
8:22	*Mel*	1144-45(*2334-35)
9:2	*TC*	1.407-20, 432-33
9:7-9	*TC*	1.271-77, 436, 445-49, 490
9:10	*ParsT*	850
10:8	*TC*	5.1541-45
10:15	*ParsT*	388
11:27	*MLT*	425-27
11:27	*MerchT*	2055
11:27	*NPT*	3205(*4395), 3206(*4396)
11:28	*MLP*	113-14
11:31	*CkP*	4330-32
12:10	*Mel*	1186(*2376)
12:10-16	*NPT*	3329(*4519)

12:11-12	*Mel*	1187-88(*2377-78)
13:1	*ParsT*	854
13:30	*Mel*	1583(*2773), 1635(*2825)
18:8	*Rom*	4989-95
18:25	*Mercht*	2055
18:26	*MLT*	1133-34
19:8-9	*Mel*	1141-42(*2331-32)
20:5-7	*Bo*	2.p.7.123-40
22:6	*Mel*	1045(*2235)
22:26-27	*Rom*	5521-32
23:12	*PardT*	648-50
23:12	*ParsT*	593, 619
23:32-33	*ParsT*	875
23:33	*ParsT*	882, 884
25:17-26	*MerchT*	2250-51
25:21-23	*SumT*	2001-04
25:23	*WBP*	775-77
25:30	*WBP*	780-81
25:30	*Mel*	1059(*2249)
25:34	*WBP*	651-53
26:1-3	*MerchT*	1311
26:10	*ParsT*	854
26:14	*MerchT*	1311
27:29-30	*ParsT*	640
27:30	*ParsT*	639
28:11	*SumT*	1991

30:17	*Mel*	1572(*2762)
30:24-26	*ParsT*	727
30:25	*Mel*	996(*2186)
32:6	*Mel*	1047(*2237)
32:6	*NPP*	2800-02(*3990-02)
32:24	*MilT*	3529-30
32:24	*MerchT*	1483-87
32:24	*Mel*	1003(*2193)
33:19-20	*Mel*	1754-58(*2944-48)
33:20-22	*Mel*	1060(*2250)
33:29	*Mel*	1589(*2779)
36:27	*MerchT*	1277-80, 1381-82
37:32-34	*PardT*	512-16
38:5	*TC*	3.178-79
38:28	*TC*	3.1462
40:1	*PardT*	729
40:4	*MLT*	1135-38
40:29	*MLP*	113-14
40:29	*Mel*	1571(*2761)
41:15	*Mel*	1639-40(*2829-30)
44:16	*HF*	588
44-50	*LGW*	1702-03
49:16	*HF*	588

Isaias

| *g* | *ParsT* | 198, 209, 210, 281 |

1:3	*ClT*	206-07, 291
1:8	*ClT*	398
2:4	*MilT*	3785
4:6	*ABC*	41-42
5:8	*ParsT*	745
5:11, 14	*MancP*	37-38
5:20	*TC*	3.178-79
6:1	*TC*	4.1174-75
6:1-13	*HF*	514-17
11:1	*ParsT*	288
14:11	*ParsT*	198
14:12-15	*MkT*	1999-2006(*3189-96)
14:12-15	*TC*	3.1417
14:13-14	*FrT*	1413
19:18	*ParsT*	839
24:9	*ParsT*	209
26:10	*ABC*	43-44
34:3	*HF*	1654
34:3	*ABC*	56
38:15	*ParsT*	135, 983
53:5	*ParsT*	281
53:7	*MLT*	617-18
53:7	*ClT*	538-39
53:7	*ABC*	172

59:7	*ParsT*	140-41
59:14	*Sted*	15-17
65:11-14	*Bo*	1.p.5.8-25
65:11-14	*TC*	1.841-47
66:24	*ParsT*	210

Jeremias

g	*PardT*	635-37
g	*ParsT*	76-78, 592, 850
1:6, 9	*PrT*	662-63(*1852-53)
2:27	*TC*	3.58?-93
2:36	*ParsT*	140-41, 850
4:2	*PardT*	635-37
4:2	*ParsT*	592
5:26-27	*LGWP*	130-31(G118-19)
5:26-27	*LGWP*	138-39(G126-27)
6:16	*ParsT*	Headnote, 76-78
7:18	*TC*	4.1594
20:14	*KtT*	1073, 1542
20:14	*SqT*	499
20:14	*FranklT*	1558
20:14	*PhysT*	215
20:14	*MancT*	273
20:14	*HF*	345
20:14	*TC*	3.304, 1072-73, 1103, 1423, 1595-96;

		4.251-52, 333-34, 747-48, 762-63, 839, 1251; 5.208-09, 689-90, 700, 1275-76
20:14	*LGW*	658, 833, 1027, 1308, 2187
20:14	*Lady*	42
20:14	*Rom*	468-69
31:21	*Truth*	17-20
33:6	*MLT*	479
44:17, 25	*CYT*	1089
44:17, 25	*TC*	4.1594
44:17, 25	*ABC*	18-24, 149-50
48:10	*ParsT*	680

Lamentations

1:1	*TC*	5.540-53
4:1	*GP*	500

Baruch

Ezechiel

8	*ParsT*	135, 140-41, 143, 236
1:6	*Rom*	741-42
3:20	*ParsT*	237
8	*HF*	1113-16
8:1-3	*HF*	529-48

10:2	GP	624
17:3-4	HF	499-508, 529-48
18:23, 32	ParsT	75
18:24	ParsT	236
20:43	ParsT	140-41, 143
33:11	ParsT	75
40:1-2	HF	59-63

Daniel

g	ParsT	126
1-4	MkT	2142a(*3332a)
1-5	MkT	2143-2238(*3333-3428)
1:1-2	MkT	2149-50(*3339-40)
1:2	MkT	2147-48(*3337-38)
1:3-5	MkT	2151-53(*3341-43)
1:6	MkT	2154(*3344)
1:17	MkT	2155(*3345)
1:17	NPT	3127-29(*4317-19)
2	MkT	2156-58(*3346-48)
2	NPT	3127-29(*4317-19)
2	HF	514-17
2:21	TC	5.1541-45
2:23	TC	5.1787-88
2:37	MkT	2167(*3357)
3:1	MkT	2159-60(*3349-50)
3:4-6	MkT	2161-64(*3351-54)
3:18	MkT	2165-66(*3355-56)

3:57	*KtT*	1785, 2115
3:57	*MilT*	3768
3:57	*MLE*	1170
3:57	*WBP*	280
3:57	*FrT*	1456
3:57	*SumT*	2170
3:57	*Thop*	784(*1974)
3:57	*NPT*	3393(*4583)
3:57	*SecN-CYL*	628
3:57	*TC*	1.780; 3.757, 860
4	*NPT*	3127-29(*4317-19)
4	*HF*	514-17
4:7-24	*ParsT*	126
4:27-34	*MkT*	2167-82(*3357-72)
4:34	*MilT*	3464
4:34	*ShipT*	393(*1583)
4:34	*PrT*	618(*1808)
4:34	*NPP*	2796(*3986)
4:34	*HF*	1084
5	*MkT*	2156-58(*3346-48)
5:1	*MkT*	2183a(*3372a)
5:1-6	*MkT*	2194-2204(*3381-94)
5:8	*MkT*	2207-08(*3397-98)
5:17-23	*MkT*	2209-30(*3399-3420)
5:22-31	*MkT*	2183-90(*3373-80)
5:24-25	*MkT*	2205-06(*3395-96), 2231-32(*3421-22)
5:26-27	*MkT*	2233(*3423)
5:27	*ParsP*	11
5:28	*MkT*	2234-35(*3424-25)
5:30-31	*MkT*	2236-37(*3426-27)
6:16-24	*MLT*	473-76

7-9	*NPT*	3127-29(*4317-19)
7:18	*NPT*	3446(*4636)
10	*NPT*	3127-29(*4317-19)
13:19-21	*LGW*	1805-11
13:20	*MerchT*	2134-36, 2143
13:34-62	*ParsT*	797
13:43-44	*MLT*	639-40
14:26-27	*LGW*	2003-06
14:30-42	*MLT*	473-76

Osee

7	*ParsT*	159

Joel

2:6	*Rom*	974

Amos

3:5	*LGWP*	130-31(G118-19)
3:5	*LGWP*	138-39(G126-27)
4:1	*Truth*	22
5:15	*ParsT*	307

Abdias

Jonas

2:1, 11	*MLT*	486-87

2:8	*ParsT*	304
3:2	*MLT*	486-87

Micheas

g	*ParsT*	201
7:6	*ParsT*	201

Nahum

1:13	*TC*	2.976

Habacuc

Sophonias

Aggeus

Zacharias

g	*ParsT*	434
g	*ABC*	177-78
9:9-10	*ParsT*	434
10:5	*ParsT*	434
12:4	*ParsT*	434
13:1	*PrT*	656(*1846)
13:1	*ABC*	126, 177-78

Malachias

1-2 Machabee

1.g	*MkT*	2655(*3845)
1.1:1	*MkT*	2656-57(*3846-47)
1.1:3	*MkT*	2631-41(*3821-31)
1.1:8	*MkT*	2655(*3845)
1.3:18-19	*Mel*	1656-57(*2846-47), 1658-63(*2848-53)
2.g	*MkT*	2575-82(*3765-72)
2.8-9	*MkT*	2574a(*3764a)
2.8:24, 30	*MkT*	2591-92(*3781-82)
2.9	*MkT*	2575-82(*3765-72)
2.9:3	*MkT*	2591-92(*3781-82)
2.9:4	*MkT*	2588-90(*3778-80), 2593-97(*3783-87)
2.9:5-6	*MkT*	2598-606(*3788-96)
2.9:7, 11	*MkT*	2607-09(*3797-99)
2.9:7-8	*MkT*	2610-14(*3800-04)
2.9:8, 10	*MkT*	2583-87(*3773-77)
2.9:9-13	*MkT*	2615-22(*3805-12)
2.9:9-11, 28	*MkT*	2626-30(*3816-20)
2.9:10, 12	*MkT*	2623-25(*3813-15)
2.10:32-37	*MkT*	2591-92(*3781-82)
2.12:42-46	*GP*	301
2.12:42-46	*ParsT*	902
2.12:42-46	*TC*	4.1174-75
2.12:42-46	*Pity*	20

Matthew

g	WBP	107-11
g	PardT	633-34
g	Thop-MelL	943-52(*2133-42)
g	ParsT	588-90, 842, 845, 1036-37
g	Rom	6885-922
1:16-25	ParsT	917-18
1:19-25	MerchT	2355-67
1:21	ParsT	285, 286
2	MilT	3384
2:16	PrP	484(*1674)
2:16	PrT	574(*1764)
2:18	PrT	627(*1817)
3:1	Rom	6995-7000
3:8	ParsT	115, 291
3:12	MLT	701-02
3:12	NPT	3443(*4633)
3:12	ParsP	35-36
3:12	LGWP	190(G74), G311-12, G529
3:12	LGW	1160, 2579
3:12	Rom	6354
4:1-11	ParsT	256-59
4:2	SumT	1879-80, 1904-05
4:4	GP	435-38
4:4	SumT	1844-45
4:6	SecNT	152-55
4:6	Mars	166
4:10	ClT	365, 1051
4:10	TC	3.1290
4:17	ABC	183-84
4:18	MilT	3486

4:18	*WBP*	446
4:18	*FrT*	1332
4:18	*ShipT*	214(*1404)
4:18	*SecN-CYL*	665
4:18	*HF*	1034, 2000
4:19	*SumT*	1820
4:19	*TC*	5.775-77
4:19	*Rom*	7490-91
5:3	*SumT*	1919-24
5:3-4	*SumT*	1935-36
5:3-11	*ParsT*	1080
5:9	*Mel*	1679-80(*2869-70)
5:9	*ParsT*	661
5:10	*SumT*	1909
5:13	*SumT*	2196
5:14-16	*ParsT*	1036-37
5:19	*GP*	496-98, 527-28
5:19-22	*PF*	32-33, 46-49, 73-84
5:22	*ParsT*	158, 623
5:22	*TC*	2.894-96; 3.1458; 4.1540, 1695-96; 5.212
5:23-24	*GP*	449-52
5:27-28	*ParsT*	867
5:28	*ParsT*	845
5:29-30	*TC*	3.589-93
5:34	*PardT*	633-34
5:34-37	*ParsT*	588-90
5:37	*SecNT*	212
5:44	*ParsT*	522-23, 526-30
6:6	*ShipT*	85-87(*1275-77)
6:9	*ParsT*	516
6:9	*TC*	3.267-68
6:9-13	*MilT*	3485, 3638
6:9-13	*ParsT*	508, 1039

6:14-15	*Mel*	1881-84(*3071-74)
6:16	*Rom*	444-48
6:24	*FrT*	1352
6:28	*ABC*	46
7:2	*ParsT*	776
7:3	*RvP*	3919-20
7:7	*ParsT*	705
7:15	*Rom*	7009-12, 7013-16
7:17	*LGW*	2395
7:20	*ParsT*	116
8:10	*LGW*	1879-82
8:12	*ParsT*	208
9:12	*SumT*	1892, 1956
9:12	*PardT*	916
9:12	*SecNP*	56
9:12	*BD*	35-40, 919-20
9:12	*TC*	1.857-58; 2.570-71, 1066, 1581-82; 5.1536-37
9:12	*ABC*	133-34
9:12	*Rom*	1757-58, 1965-66, 2825-26, 2944, 4617
9:15	*MilT*	3710-11, 3716-17
9:21-22	*TC*	2.976, 3.1116-17
9:27	*TC*	2.523
9:34	*ParsT*	256-59
10:1	*MLT*	460
10:1-5	*BD*	831
10:4	*CYT*	1001-05, 1007
10:4	*ParsT*	616
10:8	*GP*	240-45
10:8	*SumT*	1832-33, 1851-68
10:8-14	*SumT*	1765-71

10:9-10	*SumT*	1737
10:10	*SumT*	1972-73
10:28	*ParsT*	118, 132
10:28	*Bo*	4.m.3.44-48
10:28	*TC*	3.1656-57; 4.1554; 5.1532-33
10:28	*LGWP*	1-2(G1-2)
10:29-30	*KtT*	1663-73, 2987-3035
10:29-30	*Bo*	4.p.6.51-56, 5.m.1.18-23
10:29-30	*TC*	3.617-23; 5.1541-45
10:29-30	*Fort*	65-71
10:39	*TC*	4.1585
11:12	*ParsT*	716
11:19	*ParsT*	760
11:16-17	*RvP*	3876
11:25	*ParsT*	386
11:25	*TC*	2.525
11:25	*ABC*	109-10
12:25	*ParsT*	948
12:32	*ParsT*	485, 695
12:33	*ParsT*	115
12:34	*ParsT*	627
12:34-37	*HF*	782-871
12:36	*ParsT*	166, 648
12:48-50	*FrT*	1626
13	*PrT*	662-63(*1852-53)
13:8	*ParsT*	869
13:9-16	*GP*	446
13:10-13	*GP*	739
13:22	*Bo*	1.p.1.53-57
13:25	*MLE*	1183
13:41-43	*ParsT*	221-22
13:42	*ParsT*	208, 863-64
13:46	*LGWP*	213-22(G142-54)

13:55	*MilP*	3141-42
13:55	*MilT*	3189
14:6-11	*PardT*	488-91
14:13-21	*MLT*	502-04
14:29-31	*GP*	696-98
15:14	*TC*	1.625-30
15:22-28	*SecNP*	59-61
15:22-28	*LGW*	1879-82
15:26-28	*GP*	142-50
16:21	*ShipT*	75(*1265)
16:26	*GP*	187
17:2	*KtT*	1104-05
17:20	*SumT*	1879-80, 1883-84, 1904-05
17:22	*ShipT*	75(*1265)
18:11	*ClT*	440-41
18:15	*GP*	521-23
18:22	*NPE*	3454(*4644)
18:23	*ShipT*	76-79(*1266-69)
18:23-34	*FrT*	1390-91
19:5	*WBP*	30-31
19:5	*MerchT*	1334-36
19:5	*ParsT*	842
19:5-6	*ParsT*	888
19:11-12	*WBP*	77-78
19:12	*GP*	689-91
19:12	*PardT*	952-55
19:17	*Mel*	1079-80(*2269-70)
19:17	*MerchT*	2287-90
19:20-21	*Rom*	6595-98, 6653-60
19:21	*WBP*	107-11

19:21	*TC*	5.1824-25
20:11	*ParsT*	506
21:7	*ParsT*	435
21:9, 15	*MLT*	640-42
21:9, 15	*SecNP*	69-70
21:15-17	*PrP*	453-59(*1643-49)
21:19	*Rom*	1715-18
21:33-41	*GP*	256
21:33-41	*SumT*	1821-22
22:13	*ParsT*	686
22:30	*TC*	1.102-04
22:30	*Rom*	916-17
22:37	*TC*	2.827-30
22:37-39	*GP*	533-35
22:37-39	*ParsT*	515
22:39	*ParsT*	517, 519
23:1-8, 13-15	*Rom*	6885-922
23:6-10	*SumT*	2185-88
23:8-10	*WBT*	1117-18, 1129-31, 1162-63
23:8-10	*Gent*	1-4, 8-13, 18-20
23:9	*WBT*	1211-12
23:10	*GP*	261
23:10	*FrP*	1300
23:10	*SumT*	1781, 2185-88
23:14	*Rom*	6636-44
23:15	*MLP*	127
23:15	*Rom*	7017
23:25-26	*GP*	133-35
23:27	*SqT*	518-20
23:33	*SqT*	512-13
23:33	*LGWP*	553

25:1-13	*TC*	5.543
25:14-30	*Mel*	1609(*2799)
25:30	*ParsT*	208
25:35-36	*ParsT*	1031
25:36, 43	*ParsT*	376
25:40, 46	*ParsT*	1033
25:41	*PardT*	946
25:46	*Mel*	1888(*3078)
25:46	*TC*	2.894-96; 3.1458; 4.785-87, 1540, 1695-96; 5.212
26:7	*ParsT*	947
26:14-16	*NPT*	3227(*4417)
26:34	*RvT*	4233
26:34	*NPT*	2849(*4039), 3015(*4205)
26:36-46	*ParsT*	256-59
26:39, 42	*NPT*	3444-45(*4634-35)
26:41	*FrT*	1653-55
26:41	*ParsT*	1048
26:47-49	*NPT*	3227(*4417)
26:48-49, 67-68	*ParsT*	277-80
26:63	*ParsT*	663
26:67	*ParsT*	256-59, 270
26:75	*ParsT*	994
27:2	*MilP*	3124
27:2, 26, 35-50	*MilT*	3478
27:2, 26, 35-50	*RvT*	4084
27:2, 26, 35-50	*CkP*	4327
27:2, 26, 35-50	*Thop-MelL*	943-52(*2133-42)
27:2, 26, 35-50	*ParsT*	277-80
27:3-5	*ParsT*	696, 1015
27:26-50	*ParsT*	666
27:29	*ABC*	149-50
27:34	*TC*	4.1137; 5.732
27:35-50	*ParsT*	272

27:35	ParsT	665
27:50	MLT	456-58
27:50	ParsT	256-59
27:53	LGWP	110-11
28:18-20	PrT	652-53(*1842-43)
28:19	TC	5.1863-64

Mark

g	WBP	145-46
g	Thop-MelL	943-52(*2133-42)
1:4	ABC	118-20
1:4	Rom	6995-7000
1:7	SqT	555
1:7	TC	1.16
1:16	Rom	6544-50
1:17	SumT	1820
2:17	SumT	1892, 1956
2:17	PardT	916
2:17	SecNP	56
2:17	BD	35-40, 919-20
2:17	TC	1.857-58; 2.570-71, 1066, 1581-82; 5.1536-37
2:17	ABC	133-34
2:17	Rom	1757-58, 1965-66, 2825-26, 2944, 4617
2:22	PardT	871, 876-77
3:28-29	TC	1.36-37
4:24	ParsT	776
5:13	SumT	2185-88

6:7-10	*PardP*	444-48
6:21-28	*PardT*	488-91
6:30-44	*MLT*	502-04
6:34-42	*WBP*	145-46
6:39	*LGWP*	G225-27(cp. 300-01), 290-301
8:36	*GP*	187
9:1	*KtT*	1104-05
9:28	*SumT*	1883-84
9:28	*ParsT*	1047
9:42-43	*ABC*	95-96
9:42-45	*ParsT*	863-64
10:18	*MerchT*	2287-90
10:18	*Mel*	1079-80(*2269-70)
10:18	*ParsT*	301, 1007
11:9	*MLT*	640-42
11:9	*SecNP*	69-70
12:29	*MerchT*	2291
12:30-31	*GP*	533-35
12:30-31	*ParsT*	515
12:30	*TC*	2.827-30
12:32	*BD*	237
12:33	*ParsT*	518
12:38-39	*SumT*	2185-88
12:42	*GP*	253-55
14:38	*FrT*	1653-55
16:9	*Mel*	1075(*2265)
16:15	*PrT*	652-53(*1842-43)
16:19	*HF*	492

Luke

g	*Thop-MelL*	943-52(*2133-42)
g	*ParsT*	700, 701, 702
1-2	*Thop*	784(*1974)
1-2	*Mel*	1074(*2264)
1-2	*SecNP*	29-77
1:26-28	*ABC*	113-15
1:26-38	*MilP*	3141-42
1:26-38	*MilT*	3216
1:26-38	*TC*	5.1866-69
1:26-38, 46-49	*ABC*	108
1:27	*ParsT*	950
1:28	*SecNP*	67
1:28	*ABC*	102-04
1:28-38	*LGW*	1039-43
1:28-38	*ABC*	28-32
1:28, 42	*PrT*	506(*1696), 508(*1698), 510(*1700)
1:35, 48	*PrP*	467-71(*1657-61)
1:38, 48	*ABC*	109-10
1:38	*ClT*	361
1:39-45	*MerchT*	2414
1:68-72	*ABC*	116-17
2:7	*ClT*	206-07, 291, 398
2:7	*NPT*	2987-97(*4177-87), 3004(*4194)
2:13-14	*MLT*	640-42
2:13-14	*SecNP*	69-70
2:36	*FrT*	1613
2:37	*SumT*	1883-84
3:2-3	*Rom*	6995-7000
3:17	*MLT*	701-02
3:17	*NPT*	3443(*4633)

3:17	*ParsP*	35-36
3:17	*LGWP*	190(G74), G311-12, G529
3:17	*LGW*	1160, 2579
3:17	*Rom*	6354
4:4	*SumT*	1844-45
4:10	*SecNT*	152-55
4:10	*Mars*	166
4:13	*CIT*	365, 1051
4:23	*TC*	1.659-62
5:10	*SumT*	1820
5:10	*Rom*	7490-91
5:31	*SumT*	1892, 1956
5:31	*PardT*	916
5:31	*SecNP*	56
5:31	*BD*	35-40, 919-20
5:31	*TC*	1.857-58; 2.570-71, 1066, 1581-82; 5.1536-37
5:31	*ABC*	133-34
5:31	*Rom*	1757-58, 1965-66, 2825-26, 2944, 4617
6:32-35	*ParsT*	522-23, 526-30
6:38	*ParsT*	776
7	*ShipT*	76-79(*1266-69)
7:9	*LGW*	1879-82
7:31-32	*RvP*	3876
7:36-38, 47-48	*ParsT*	996
7:39-40	*ParsT*	504
8:48	*TC*	2.1503; 3.168
9:1	*FrT*	1503
9:3	*SumT*	1737

9:10-17	*MLT*	502-04
9:29	*KtT*	1104-05
10:1	*SumT*	1740-45
10:4	*SumT*	1737
10:7	*SumT*	1972-73
10:7	*PF*	9
10:7-8	*SumT*	1836-45
10:17-19	*FrT*	1503
10:18	*MkT*	1999-2006(*3189-96)
10:27	*TC*	2.827-30
11:2	*ParsT*	516
11:2	*TC*	3.267-68
11:2-4	*MilT*	3485, 3638
11:2-4	*ParsT*	508, 1039
11:43	*SumT*	2185-88
12:2	*HF*	351
12:2	*TC*	5.1639-40
12:5	*TC*	4.1554
12:22-23	*ParsT*	413
12:45-46	*ParsT*	1000-02
13	*ShipT*	76-79(*1266-69)
13:31-32	*NPT*	3215(*4405)
14:28	*TC*	1.1065-69
15:7	*ParsT*	291, 700
15:11-32	*ParsT*	701
15:31	*TC*	2.975
16:2	*ParsT*	253-54
16:13	*FrT*	1352
16:19	*ParsT*	413

16:19-26	*MLP*	110-12
16:19-31	*SumT*	1877-78
16:20	*GP*	240-45
18:1	*SecNT*	139-40
18:13-14	*ParsT*	986
18:19	*MerchT*	2287-90
18:19	*Mel*	1079-80(*2269-70)
18:22	*Rom*	6595-98, 6653-60
18:42	*TC*	2.1503; 3.168
19:10	*ClT*	440-41
19:12-27	*Mel*	1609(*2799)
19:35-36	*ParsT*	413
20:46	*SumT*	2185-88
21:18	*ParsT*	253-54
23:9	*ClT*	897-900
23:18	*TC*	4.194-96
23:27	*ClT*	897-900
23:34	*TC*	3.1577
23:41	*Mel*	1495-96(*2685-86)
23:42	*ParsT*	702
23:43	*FrT*	1636
23:43	*ParsT*	703
23:46	*RvT*	4287
23:46	*ClT*	559
23:46	*TC*	1.422-23; 4.319-21, 785-87, 1209-10
24:39	*NPT*	3015(*4205)
24:51	*HF*	492

John

g	*WBP*	164
g	*FrT*	1647
g	*SqT*	596
g	*Thop-MelL*	943-52(*2133-42)
1:1	*Gent*	1-4, 8-13
1:1(-14)	*GP*	253-55
1:1(-14)	*NPT*	3163(*4353)
1:23	*Rom*	6995-7000
1:29	*MLT*	451-53
1:29	*Form Age*	50
2:1-2	*WBP*	10-11
2:1-11	*ParsT*	919
3:4	*PardT*	729
3:16	*ABC*	161-65
4:5-19	*GP*	460
4:5-19	*WBP*	14-23
4:7	*ClT*	274-76
4:17-18	*WBP*	6-7, 44
4:28	*ClT*	290
4:34	*SumT*	1844-45
6:1-13	*MLT*	502-04
6:3-11	*WBP*	145-46
6:20	*MLT*	1109
8:3-8	*Mel*	1033(*2223)
8:3-11	*MilT*	3712
8:5, 11	*ParsT*	889
8:12	*Purse*	15
8:32	*TC*	2.1503

8:32	*Truth*	7, 14, 21, 28
8:34	*ParsT*	142, 149, 463, 763
10:1-30	*GP*	503-14
10:9-12	*ParsT*	768-69, 792
10:11	*Rom*	6561-62
10:11-12	*PhysT*	101-02
10:14	*Rom*	6452-54
11:35	*Mel*	987(*2177)
11:35	*ParsT*	256-59
12:3	*ParsT*	947
12:3-6	*ParsT*	502
12:6	*GP*	686-87
12:6	*FrT*	1350-51
12:13	*MLT*	640-42
12:13	*SecNP*	69-70
12:24	*PardT*	859-64
12:35-36	*ParsP*	70-71
13:27	*MLT*	783-84
13:37-38	*ClT*	560
14:6	*ParsT*	76-78, 593
14:6	*Bo*	3.m.9.47-49
14:15	*ParsT*	125
14:18	*PrT*	669(*1859)
15:12-13	*PardT*	721-24
16:20	*TC*	4.1683-84
16:24	*ParsT*	705
16:25	*ParsP*	31-34
17:20	*TC*	1.29-51

| 18:33-38 | *SecNT* | 421-512 |
| 18:38 | *Buk* | 1-4 |

19:9-11	*SecNT*	421-512
19:17	*ParsT*	668
19:19	*ParsT*	284, 288
19:25	*MLT*	844-48
19:25	*ClT*	554-60
19:25-30	*NPT*	3341(*4531)
19:25-30	*ABC*	81-82
19:34-35	*ABC*	161-65, 172

20:1-15	*ShipT*	178-79(*1368-69)
20:1-18	*GP*	410
20:11-18	*LGWP*	428(G418)
20:14	*Mel*	1075(*2265)
20:22-23	*SumT*	2262-74
20:25	*ParsT*	256-59
20:26-30	*SumT*	1978-80, 2119-49

| 21:3 | *Rom* | 6563-67 |

Acts

| *g* | *ParsT* | 597 |

1:1	*GP*	527-28
1:1-2	*Rom*	7165-7207
1:7	*MilT*	3451-54

2:1-4	*SumT*	2262-74
2:1-13	*SumT*	2119-49
2:1-15	*GP*	637-38
2:13	*MancP*	60
2:44-47	*Rom*	6568-72

4:12	*ParsT*	287, 597
4:24	*KtT*	2561-62
7:22	*SqT*	249-51
7:58	*TC*	4.319-21, 785-87, 1209-10
8:9	*HF*	1274
8:9-24	*FrT*	1309
8:9-24	*ParsT*	781, 783
8:18	*RvT*	3941
9:5	*Truth*	11
9:11	*KtT*	2160
9:33-34	*BD*	35-40
13:8	*HF*	1274
13:23	*ParsT*	285
16:23-24	*Rom*	6775-76
16:24	*TC*	3.380
18:3	*PardP*	444-48
19:12	*PardP*	348
19:15	*FrT*	1503
20:29	*ParsT*	775
20:33-35	*PardP*	444-48
20:33-35	*Rom*	6679-84
27:25	*TC*	3.332, 4.1636
27:30	*WBP*	399

Romans

| *8* | *FrT* | 1647 |

g	*SumT*	1819
g	*Mel*	989(*2179), 1290-94(*2480-84), 1406-07(*2596-97), 1440-41(*2630-31),
g	*NPT*	3441-42(*4631-32)
g	*ParsT*	162-63, 322, 344
1:5	*Lady*	125
1:20	*Bo*	5.p.6.8-10
1:20	*LGWP*	10-15(G10-15), 99-100
1:26-27	*ParsT*	910-11
2:16	*ParsT*	1063-64
2:19	*ABC*	105
3:7-8	*PardP*	429-31
3:13-14	*PardP*	413
3:13-14	*PardT*	558
3:16	*ParsT*	140-41
3:23	*FranklT*	779-80
3:25	*WBP*	717-18
4:25	*ParsT*	256-59
5:5	*TC*	2.577; 3.1503
5:8-9	*SecNT*	138
5:8-9	*ParsT*	255, 256-59, 277-80, 704
5:9	*MLT*	633
5:9	*ClT*	556-58, 560, 1062
5:9	*PardT*	501, 658, 766, 902
5:9	*ShipT*	178-79(*1368-69)
5:9	*NPP*	2796(*3986)
5:9	*ParsT*	132
5:9	*Ret*	1091
5:9	*ABC*	116-17, 161-65
5:9	*TC*	5.1532-33

5:9-10	*TC*	3.1165; 5.1842-44
5:10	*ParsT*	528
5:11	*ClT*	440-41
5:12	*ParsT*	322, 324, 333, 334, 770
5:12-21	*ParsT*	682-84
5:14	*ParsT*	323
5:14	*ABC*	182
5:15-19	*ParsT*	333, 334
6:1-6	*PardT*	713
6:17-18	*ParsT*	770
7:2-3	*WBP*	47-50
7:4	*ABC*	38-40
7:6	*MLT*	701-02
7:6	*MLE*	1183
7:6	*SumT*	1794
7:6	*NPT*	3443(*4633)
7:6	*LGWP*	190(G74), G311-12, G529
7:6	*LGW*	1160, 2579
7:6	*Rom*	6354
7:24	*PardT*	727-28
7:24	*SecNP*	72-74
7:24	*ParsT*	344
8:4	*Truth*	17-20
8:6	*PardT*	547-48
8:10	*TC*	4.319-21
8:13	*ParsT*	1080
8:13-17	*SecNP*	62
8:26	*KtT*	1260
8:28	*FrT*	1496
8:28	*FranklT*	885-86
11:33	*Mel*	1406-07(*2596-97)

12:3	*Truth*	5
12:9	*ParsT*	307
12:10	*ParsT*	482
12:15	*Mel*	989(*2179)
12:17	*PrT*	561(*1751)
12:17	*Mel*	1290-94(*2480-84)
12:19	*Mel*	1459-60(*2649-50)

13:1	*ParsT*	773-74
13:1-6	*ClT*	1145-47
13:4	*Mel*	1440-41(*2630-31)
13:4	*Sted*	26
13:11-14	*Mars*	15
13:12	*SecNT*	384-85

14:8	*TC*	5.593
14:9	*TC*	5.1842-44
14:10	*ABC*	36-37
14:10-12	*ParsT*	162-63

15:4	*MLE*	1183
15:4	*NPT*	3441-42(*4631-32)
15:4	*Ret*	1083
15:30	*Rom*	432-34

1 Corinthians

g	*WBP*	47-50, 51, 59-68, 73-74, 79-81, 91-92, 158-60, 161-62
g	*PardT*	521-23
g	*Mel*	1290-94(*2480-84), 1406-07(*2596-97)
g	*ParsT*	619, 879
g	*Buk*	19-20
1:2	*PardT*	748

1:24	*PrP*	472(*1662)
1:24	*Bo*	1.p.1.1-42
1:24	*Rom*	3190-3216
1:30	*Gent*	8-13
2:9	*TC*	4.1695-96
3:17	*ParsT*	789, 879
3:17	*ABC*	145
4:5	*Mel*	1406-07(*2596-97)
4:12	*Mel*	1290-94(*2480-84)
6:10	*ParsT*	619
6:13	*PardT*	521-23
6:18	*MLT*	925-27
6:20	*PardT*	501, 766, 902
6:20	*ParsT*	132
6:20	*TC*	3.1165; 5.1842-44
6:20	*ABC*	116-17
7:1	*WBP*	87
7:2	*MerchT*	1446-47
7:2-3	*MerchT*	1451-52
7:3	*MerchT*	2048
7:3	*WBP*	129-30, 153, 154-55, 161-62
7:3	*ShipT*	375-76(*1565-66), 397-98(*1587-88), 413-17(*1603-07), 423-24(*1613-14)
7:3	*ParsT*	375
7:3-4	*ParsT*	940
7:4	*WBP*	158-60, 313-14
7:4	*Buk*	19-20
7:6	*WBP*	83-84
7:7	*WBP*	39, 79-81, 102-04
7:8-9	*WBP*	91-92

7:9	*WBP*	46, 52
7:9	*Buk*	18
7:20	*WBP*	147-48
7:25	*WBP*	73-74, 82
7:25-26	*WBP*	59-68
7:28	*WBP*	51, 156-57, 167
7:28, 33	*Buk*	19-20
7:32	*WBP*	274-75
7:39	*WBP*	47-50, 84-86
9:24	*WBP*	75-76
9:25	*SecNT*	221
9:25	*TC*	2.1733-36
9:26-27	*NPT*	3322-24(*4512-14)
10:7	*PardT*	467-68
10:13	*FrT*	1661-62
10:20-21	*PardT*	469-71
11:3-10	*GP*	453-55, 680-83
11:3	*ParsT*	922
11:14	*GP*	675-79
13:1	*PF*	231
13:3	*SecNP*	118
13:4	*ClT*	1155-62
13:4	*FranklT*	777
13:4-5	*ParsT*	657
13:13	*GP*	162
13:13	*TC*	1.49
15:21-22	*WBP*	717-18
15:21-34	*ParsT*	682-84
15:26	*PardT*	710
15:45-50	*ParsT*	461-62
15:51-55	*BD*	345-46, 375-76, 1311-13

15:52	*MancP*	37-38
16:13	*TC*	1.969

2 Corinthians

g	*Mel*	1509-10(*2699-700), 1634(*2824)
g	*ParsT*	343, 725, 895
1:12	*Mel*	1634(*2824)
2:14-16	*SecNT*	246-47
3:2	*PhysT*	107-09
3:3	*SumT*	1740-45
3:6	*MLT*	701-02
3:6	*MLE*	1183
3:6	*SumT*	1794
3:6	*NPT*	3443(*4633)
3:6	*LGWP*	F190(G74), G311-12, G529
3:6	*LGW*	1160, 2579
3:6	*Rom*	6354
4:4	*TC*	1.211
4:17	*Mel*	1509-10(*2699-2700)
5:1, 6-8	*KtT*	2809-10
5:1, 6-8	*MerchT*	2282-83
5:1, 6-8	*TC*	1.31, 41; 4.623
5:1, 6-8	*Rom*	6251-52
5:10	*ABC*	36-37
6:5	*SecNT*	139-40
6:10	*Rom*	6963-64
7:10	*ParsT*	725, 726

8:9	*WBT*	1178-79
11:14	*FrT*	1465
11:14	*ParsT*	895
11:25-27	*ParsT*	343
12:1-4	*LGWP*	5-9
12:2-4	*HF*	979-82
12:4	*SumP*	1675-79
12:7	*RvP*	3877
12:7	*TC*	2.1272, 3.1104-05
13:7	*TC*	3.875
13:13	*TC*	1.42, 5.1863-64

Galatians

g	*ParsT*	342, 867
2:9	*GP*	214
2:9	*TC*	1.1000-01
3:26	*ParsT*	461-62
3:28	*MerchT*	2287-90
4:22	*WBP*	801
4:22	*ClT*	1170-71
5:13-14	*ParsT*	519
5:17	*ParsT*	342, 459
5:19-21	*ParsT*	867
5:22-23	*SumT*	2275-77

Ephesians

g	*WBP*	161-62

g	*ParsT*	651, 748, 929
g	*Rom*	6661-65
1:6	*TC*	3.1804
1:7	*ParsT*	285
1:11	*TC*	4.964-66, 1654
1:21	*TC*	3.1490
2:3	*ParsT*	313, 335
2:13-16	*ParsT*	642
3:8	*TC*	1.16
3:16	*TC*	1.44
3:21	*Mel*	1888(*3078)
3:21	*PF*	46-49
4:5-6	*SecNT*	201-16
4:17-24	*PardT*	713
4:26	*ParsT*	540
4:28	*Rom*	6661-65
4:30	*SumT*	1734
4:30	*Ret*	1092
4:31	*SumT*	1834
5:4	*ParsT*	651
5:5	*ParsT*	748
5:14	*HF*	555-57
5:18	*PardT*	483-84
5:23-25	*ParsT*	922
5:25	*WBP*	161-62
5:25	*ParsT*	843, 929
5:25, 28, 29	*MerchT*	1384-88
5:31-32	*ParsT*	917-18
5:32	*MerchT*	1319
5:32	*WBP*	30-31

| 6:24 | *TC* | 5.1842-44 |

Philippians

| *g* | *PardT* | 521-23, 529-33 |
| *g* | *ParsT* | 598, 819-20 |

| 1:15 | *PardP* | 407-08 |

2:5-6	*SecNT*	417-18
2:8	*ParsT*	997
2:9-10	*ParsT*	598
2:19	*TC*	4.1636

3:14	*Bo*	3.m.9.32-38, 4.p.6.88-93
3:18-19	*PardT*	521-23, 529-33
3:18-19	*ParsT*	819-20

Colossians

| *g* | *WBP* | 161-62 |
| *g* | *ParsT* | 634, 1054 |

1:5	*TC*	5.1265, 1818-19
1:14	*Ret*	1091
1:16	*TC*	5.1866-69
1:20	*MLT*	633
1:20	*CIT*	556-58, 560, 1062
1:20	*PardT*	501, 658, 766, 902
1:20	*ShipT*	178-79(*1368-69)
1:20	*NPP*	2796(*3986)
1:20	*SecNT*	138
1:20	*ParsT*	132, 255, 256-59, 277-80, 704
1:20	*TC*	3.1165; 5.1842-44, 1860
1:20	*ABC*	116-17, 161-65
1:25	*SumT*	1821-22

2:13-14	*ABC*	59-61, 109-10

3:1-10	*PardT*	713
3:5	*PardT*	469-71
3:12	*ParsT*	1054
3:18-19	*ParsT*	634
3:19	*WBP*	161-62

1-2 Thessalonians

1.*g*	*Mel*	1290-94(*2480-84)
1.*g*	*Rom*	6661-65

1.4:3	*NPT*	3444-45(*4634-35)
1.4:11	*Rom*	6661-65

1.5:2-8	*MilT*	3790-91
1.5:15	*Mel*	1290-94(*2480-84)
1.5:23	*SecNT*	135-37

2.2	*CYT*	916-18

1 Timothy

g	*WBP*	341-45
g	*SumT*	1881-82
g	*Mel*	1130(*2320), 1840(*3030)
g	*ParsP*	31-34
g	*ParsT*	739

1:4	*NPT*	3438(*4628)
1:4	*ParsP*	31-34
1:5	*SecNT*	434
1:17	*TC*	3.185

2:4	*ParsT*	75

2:9	WBP	341-45
2:13-14	ParsT	461-62
2:14	MLT	842-43

| 3:8 | PrT | 491(*1681) |

4:4	Mel	1553(*2743)
4:7	NPT	3438(*4628)
4:7	ParsP	31-34

| 5:6 | PardT | 547-48, 558 |
| 5:18 | SumT | 1972-73 |

6:6, 8	WBP	326-27
6:8	SumT	1881-82
6:10	MLT	358
6:10	PardP	Headnote, 333-34, 425-26
6:10	Mel	1130(*2320), 1840(*3030)
6:10	ParsT	739
6:10	Rom	4879-82
6:15	Ret	1091
6:16	Bo	5.m.3.12-17

2 Timothy

| g | ParsP | 31-34 |
| g | ParsT | 630 |

2:3-4	SecNT	383
2:6	SumT	2275-77
2:20	WBP	99-101
2:22	WBP	469-70
2:24	ParsT	630

| 3:16 | Ret | 1083 |

4:4	*NPT*	3438(*4628)
4:4	*ParsP*	31-34
4:7-8	*SecNT*	386-90
4:8	*SecNT*	221
4:8	*TC*	2.1733-36

Titus

1:2	*ParsT*	120, 124
1:2	*Rom*	6636-44

Philemon

Hebrews

1:3	*WBP*	1162-63
1:3	*Gent*	18-20
1:9	*ParsT*	121
2:3	*TC*	1.463-64
2:10	*ParsT*	882
2:10	*Bo*	1.p.6.84-85, 3.m.6.11-12
2:10	*TC*	3.1016-19, 1765
2:10	*Wom Nob*	27
4:13	*ParsT*	1062
6:6	*PardT*	472-75, 708-09
6:6	*ParsT*	591
10:39	*TC*	1.47
11:13	*GP*	1-18
11:13-16	*GP*	26
11:13-16	*KtT*	2847-48
11:13-16	*ParsP*	48-50

11:13-16	*Bo*	1.p.5.8-25, 5.p.1.12-15, 5.m.5.9-25
11:13-16	*Truth*	17-20
11:13-16	*Rom*	5659
11:16	*ABC*	183-84
11:17-19	*ABC*	169-71
12:5-7	*ClT*	967-70
12:11	*ABC*	38-40
13	*ParsP*	61-66
13:5	*PrT*	669(*1859)
13:5	*TC*	5.1845-48
13:18	*TC*	1.29-51

James

g	*ClT*	1153-54
g	*Mel*	1119(*2309), 1517(*2707), 1676-77(*2866-67), 1869(*3059)
g	*ParsT*	348
1:4	*Mel*	1517(*2707)
1:5	*Mel*	1119(*2309)
1:12	*FrT*	1497-98
1:12	*ClT*	1152, 1155-62
1:13	*ClT*	1153-54
1:14	*ParsT*	348
1:17	*TC*	5.1845-48
1:20	*ParsT*	561
1:21	*TC*	3.1501
1:22	*SumT*	1937
2:5	*WBP*	1162-63
2:5	*Gent*	18-20
2:8	*ParsT*	519

2:13	*Mel*	1867-68(*3057-58), 1869(*3059), 1881-84(*3071-74)
2:17, 20	*SecNP*	64
2:19	*ParsT*	598, 599
3:1	*GP*	261
3:1	*FrP*	1300
3:1	*SumT*	1781, 2185-88
3:3-10	*MancT*	319-24, 329-34, 339-42, 355-60
3:16-18	*Mel*	1676-77(*2866-67)
4:1-5	*ParsT*	745
4:6	*ParsT*	760
4:6	*TC*	4.1683-84
4:8	*Truth*	25-26
4:9	*TC*	1.952
4:9	*BD*	599-601
4:12	*TC*	4.1683-84
4:14-15	*ClT*	120-26
4:15	*ParsT*	1068
5:3	*ClT*	1167-69
5:7	*ClT*	1150-51
5:11	*WBP*	436
5:11	*ClT*	932
5:12	*PardT*	633-34
5:12	*ParsT*	591
5:16	*Truth*	26-27
5:19-20	*TC*	1.998-99
5:20	*ClT*	1064

1 Peter

g	*SumT*	1819
g	*Mel*	1290-94(*2480-84), 1501-04(*2691-94)

g	*ParsT*	287, 930, 988

1:2	*Bo*	5.p.6.293-94
1:8	*LGWP*	10-15(G10-15), 99-100
1:19	*ParsT*	1007
1:23	*ParsT*	117

2:11	*KtT*	2847-48
2:11	*ParsP*	48-50
2:11	*Truth*	17-20
2:13-14	*ParsT*	483
2:13-16	*ClT*	1145-47
2:21-23	*Mel*	1501-04(*2691-94)

3:1	*ParsT*	930
3:3-5	*ParsT*	932
3:7	*ParsT*	928
3:8	*TC*	1.50-51
3:9	*Mel*	1290-94(*2480-84)
3:18	*ParsT*	273
3:21	*ParsT*	335

5:6	*ParsT*	988
5:8	*MLT*	582
5:8	*FrT*	1657-58
5:8	*ParsT*	132, 492, 512

2 Peter

g	*ParsT*	142

1:7	*GP*	162
1:7	*TC*	3.1254

2:4	*MLT*	361, 634
2:4	*Buk*	9-10

2:19	*ParsT*	142
2:22	*ParsT*	138
2:22	*Rom*	7285-86
3:9	*ParsT*	75

1-3 John

g	*ParsT*	349, 565
g	*Mars*	9-11
g	*Rom*	7191-92
1.1:5	*TC*	3.1-49
1.1:8	*ParsT*	349
1.1:9	*Mel*	1885-87(*3075-77)
1.2:1	*SecNP*	68
1.2:1	*ABC*	102-04
1.2:15	*SumT*	1876
1.2:15	*TC*	5.1845-48
1.2:15	*Truth*	23
1.2.15-17	*PF*	64-66
1.2:16	*Mel*	970(*2160), 1421-24(*2611-14)
1.2:16	*ParsT*	186, 336
1.2:17	*TC*	5.1824-25
1.2:18	*Rom*	7009-12, 7155-56, 7191-92
1.3:15	*ParsT*	565
1.3:19-22	*Mars*	9-11
1.3:20	*ShipT*	113(*1303)
1.3:20	*Anel*	262-63
1.3:20	*Bo*	4.p.1.34, 4.p.6.221, 5.p.6.134-35
1.3:20	*TC*	3.260
1.3:20-21	*ABC*	18-24
1.3:24	*Gent*	1-4, 8-13

1.4:7-8	*TC*	3.12
1.4:9-10	*ABC*	161-65
1.4:14	*Purse*	16
1.4:16	*TC*	5.1845-48
1.5.7	*TC*	5.1863-64
2.7	*CYT*	916-18

Jude

| 6 | *MLT* | 361, 634 |

Apocalypse

g	*PrT*	579-85(*1769-75)
g	*ParsT*	136, 216, 687, 841, 933
g	*HF*	1381-85
1:8	*Bo*	3.m.9.47-49
1:10	*ParsT*	160-61
1:18	*SumT*	1734
1:18	*Ret*	1092
2:5	*ParsT*	136
2:7	*Rom*	442-43
2:14-15	*MilT*	3199
2:22	*MerchT*	1435-36
3:15-16	*ParsT*	687
3:17	*WBT*	1185-90
3:20	*SecNT*	239-41
3:20	*ParsT*	289-90
4:6	*HF*	1381-85
4:8	*HF*	81-82

4:8	*TC*	1.245
4:11	*LGW*	924-25
5:6	*MLT*	459
5:11	*KtT*	1055
6:8	*Rom*	7389-96
6:9-17	*ParsT*	169-73
7	*LGWP*	282-301(G185-227)
7:1-3	*MLT*	491-94
7:4-8	*PF*	381
7:5-10	*HF*	1216-17, 2126-27
7:12	*MancP*	101
7:14-15	*MerchT*	2282-83
7:14-15	*HF*	979-82
7:14-15	*TC*	1.31, 41; 4.623
7:14-15	*Rom*	6251-52
9:1	*BD*	170-71
9:1	*TC*	4.1540
9:6	*PardT*	727-28
9:6	*ParsT*	216
9:6	*BD*	583-86
9:10	*MerchT*	2058-60
10:1	*TC*	1.102-04
10:1	*Rom*	916-17
11:17	*HF*	81-82
11:17	*TC*	1.245
12:1	*CIT*	1117-19
12:1	*LGWP*	213-22(G142-54), 230-36(cp. G160-68)
12:1	*ABC*	144

12:1-12	*KtT*	2075-86
12:7, 14	*LGWP*	G143, 230-36(cp. G160-68)
12:7-9	*MkT*	1999-2006(*3189-96)
12:10	*ParsT*	512
14:1-3	*PF*	199
14:1-5	*WPB*	105
14:1-5	*LGWP*	290-301
14:3	*BD*	294-320
14:3-4	*PrT*	579-85(*1769-75)
14:4	*WBP*	77-78
14:7	*ParsT*	159
14:10-11	*FrT*	1652
14:10-13	*ParsT*	118, 132
14:10-13	*LGWP*	563-64
14:10-13	*TC*	2.894-96; 3.1656-57
14:14	*LGWP*	230-36(cp. G160-68)
15:1	*HF*	949
17:4	*ParsT*	933
17:5	*LGW*	706
18:16	*ParsT*	933
19:7, 9	*ClT*	1117-19
19:9	*SecNT*	239-41
19:17	*PF*	316-22
20:1-3	*MLT*	361, 634
20:1-2	*Buk*	9-10
20:2	*FrT*	1651
20:2-3	*MancP*	37-38
20:12	*ParsT*	160-61
21:2	*ParsP*	51

21:4	*KtT*	2470, 2478
21:8	*ParsT*	841, 884, 890
21:10	*BD*	1318-19
21:10-11	*HF*	529-48
22:4	*TC*	4.1337
22:5	*PF*	209-10
22:16	*MLT*	852

Apocryphal Gospels and other Extra-canonical Sources

Protevangelium of James	*MilP*	3141-42
	MLT	640-42
	MerchT	1461-66
Gospel of Pseudo-Matthew	*ClT*	206-07, 211-31, 291, 398
	MerchT	2335-36, 2355-67
Gospel of Nicodemus	*MilT*	3512
	MLT	361, 634
	SumT	2107
	MancP	37-38
	ABC	161-65
Acts of Peter	*RvT*	3941

Vernacular Biblical Drama, Saint's Lives, and other Popular Sources (excluding proverbs and the liturgy)		
	GP	253-55
	MilP	3124
	MilT	3384, 3485, 3486, 3512
		3539-40
	MLT	361, 634, 640-42, 837-38
	FrT	1613

SumT	1978-80, 2107, 2119-49
ClT	*351-54*
MerchT	1461-66, 2335-36, 2355-67, 2414
NPT	3163(*4353)
SecNP	69-70, 96-98
SecNT	122-23, 135-37, 152-55, 201-16, 212, 239-41, 246-47, 383, 384-85, 386-90, 420, 434
MancP	37-38
ABC	161-65

BIBLIOGRAPHY

[Note: Most of the titles listed below are referred to either in the critical review of scholarship on Chaucer and the Bible (pp. 15-37, above) or in the annotations to Index I (pp. 55-304). A few titles that are not referred to in either of the latter sections of the book are listed nevertheless because they have helped me find relevant items for the Bibliography or are otherwise important for the study of Chaucer's poetry and the Bible; I have also included a very small number of titles that sound relevant but which I was not able to examine (these are identified as "not seen"). The standard concordances to the Vulgate and various English Bibles are not listed. Titles of journals are abbreviated according to the usage of the Modern Language Association of America's annual bibliography.]

Primary Sources

Editions of Chaucer's Works:
Baker, Donald C., ed. *The Manciple's Tale.* In *A Variorum Edition of the Works of Geoffrey Chaucer. Vol. II. Part Ten. The Canterbury Tales.* Norman, Okla.: Univ. of Oklahoma Press, 1984.

Benson, Larry D., gen. ed. *The Riverside Chaucer.* 3rd ed. Boston: Houghton Mifflin, 1987.

Coghill, Nevill, ed. and trans. *Geoffrey Chaucer: Troilus and Criseyde.* Harmondsworth, England: Penguin Books, 1971.

Fisher, John H., ed. *The Complete Poetry and Prose of Geoffrey Chaucer.* New York: Holt, Rinehart and Winston, 1977.

Manly, John M., ed. *The Canterbury Tales*. New York: Henry Holt and Co., 1928.

Pace, George B., and Alfred David, eds. *The Minor Poems, Part One*. In *A Variorum Edition of the Works of Geoffrey Chaucer. Vol. V*. Norman, Okla.: Univ. of Oklahoma Press, 1982.

Pearsall, Derek, ed. *The Nun's Priest's Tale*. In *A Variorum Edition of the Works of Geoffrey Chaucer. Vol. II. Part Nine. The Canterbury Tales*. Norman, Okla.: Univ. of Oklahoma Press, 1983.

Pratt, Robert A., ed. *The Tales of Canterbury*. Boston: Houghton Mifflin, 1974.

Robinson, F. N., ed. *The Works of Geoffrey Chaucer*. 2nd ed. Boston: Houghton Mifflin, 1957.

Root, Robert K., ed. *The Book of* Troilus and Criseyde. Princeton: Princeton Univ. Press, 1926.

Ross, Thomas W., ed. *The Miller's Tale*. In *A Variorum Edition of the Works of Geoffrey Chaucer. Vol. II. Part Three. The Canterbury Tales*. Norman, Okla.: Univ. of Oklahoma Press, 1983.

Skeat, Walter W., ed. *The Complete Works of Geoffrey Chaucer*. 6 vols. Oxford: Clarendon Press, 1894.

Spearing, A. C., ed. *The Pardoner's Prologue and Tale*. Cambridge: Cambridge Univ. Press, 1965.

Sutherland, Ronald. *The Romaunt of the Rose and Le Roman de la Rose: A Parallel-Text Edition*. Oxford: Blackwell; Berkeley and Los Angeles: Univ. of California Press, 1968.

Windeatt, B. A., ed. *Geoffrey Chaucer: Troilus & Criseyde, A new edition of 'The Book of Troilus.'* London and New York: Longman, 1984.

Editions of the Bible and Apocrypha:

Biblia Sacra iuxta Vulgatam Clementinam. 4th ed. A. Colunga and L. Turrado, eds. Madrid: Biblioteca de Autores Cristianos, 1965.

[The "Wycliffite" Bible]. *The Holy Bible . . . made from the Latin Vulgate by John Wycliffe and his Followers.* Josiah Forshall and Frederic Madden, eds. 4 vols. Oxford: Oxford Univ. Press, 1850.

——. *The Middle English Bible: Prefatory Epistles of Jerome.* Conrad Linberg, ed. Oslo: Universitetsforlaget, 1978.

The Holy Bible [Douay-Rheims Version], Translated from the Latin Vulgate. Rockford, Ill.: Tan Books and Publishers, 1971 (rpt. of 1899 ed.; first publ., 1582 [New Testament] and 1609 [Old Testament]).

The Holy Bible . . . The Authorized, King James Version. Cleveland and New York: World Publishing Co., n.d. (first publ., 1611).

Hennecke, Edgar, and Wilhelm Schneemelcher, eds. *New Testament Apocrypha.* 2 vols. English trans. ed. by R. McL. Wilson. Philadelphia: The Westminster Press, 1963, 1965.

Other Primary Sources:

Aelred of Rievaulx's De Institutione Inclusarum: Two English Versions. John Ayto and Alexandra Barratt, eds. (EETS O.S. 287.) London and New York: Oxford Univ. Press, 1984.

Augustine of Hippo. *On Christian Doctrine [De Doctrina Christiana].* D. W. Robertson, Jr., trans. Indianapolis: Bobbs Merrill, 1958.

Benedict of Nursia. *The Rule of Saint Benedict.* Anthony C. Meisel and M. L. del Matro, eds. and trans. Garden City, N.Y.: Doubleday-Image Books, 1975.

Boccaccio, Giovanni. *The Decameron: A New Translation, 21 Novelle, Contemporary Reactions, Modern Criticism.* Mark Musa and Peter Bondanella, eds. and trans. New York and London: W. W. Norton & Co., 1977.

Boethius. *De Consolatione Philosophiae.* Ludwig Bieler, ed. (Corpus Christianorum, Series Latina, 94.) Brussels: Turnholt, 1957.

Breviarum ad usum insignis ecclesiae Sarum. Francis Procter and Christopher Wordsworth, eds. 3 vols. Cambridge: Cambridge Univ. Press, 1879-86 (rpt. Farnborough, Hants., England: Gregg International, 1970).

Bryan, W. F., and Germaine Dempster, eds. *Sources and Analogues of Chaucer's Canterbury Tales.* New York: The Humanities Press, 1958 (first publ., 1941).

Gower, John. *The Complete Works of John Gower.* 4 vols. G. C. Macaulay, ed. Oxford: Clarendon Press, 1899-1902.

————. *The Major Latin Works of John Gower: The Voice of One Crying, and the Tripartite Chronicle.* Eric W. Stockton, ed. and trans. Seattle: Univ. of Washington Press, 1962.

Havely, N. R., ed. and trans. *Chaucer's Boccaccio: Sources of* Troilus *and the* Knight's *and* Franklin's Tales. (Chaucer Studies 5.) Woodbridge, Suffolk: Boydell & Brewer; Totowa, N. J.: Rowman & Littlefield, 1980.

Innocent III. Lothario Dei Segni (Pope Innocent III). *On the Misery of the Human Condition.* Donald R. Howard, ed. Margaret Mary Dietz, trans. Indianapolis and New York: Bobbs-Merrill—the Library of Liberal Arts, 1969.

————. *Lotario dei Segni (Pope Innocent III) De Miseria Condicionis Humane.* Robert E. Lewis, ed. Athens, Ga.: Univ. of Georgia Press—The Chaucer Library, 1978.

Jacobus de Voragine. *The Golden Legend [Legenda Aurea].* Trans. and adapted by Granger Ryan and Helmut Ripperger. New York, London, Toronto: Longmans, Green and Co., 1941; rpt. Salem, N.H.: Ayer, 1967.

Lorris, Guillaume de, and Jean de Meun. *Le Roman de la Rose.* 3 vols. Félix Lecoy, ed. (Les Classiques Français du Moyen Age, 92, 95, 98.) Paris: Champion, 1965-82.

————. *The Romance of the Rose.* Charles Dahlberg, ed. and trans. Hanover, N. H., and London: Univ. Press of New England, 1983 (first publ., 1971).

Plimpton, George. *The Education of Chaucer Illustrated from the Schoolbooks in Use in his Time.* London and New York: Oxford Univ. Press, 1935.

[Sarum Missal] *Missale ad Usum Insignis et Praeclarae Ecclesiae Sarum.* Francis H. Dickinson, ed. Oxford and London: J. Parker, 1861-83.

The Sarum Missal. J. Wickham Legg, ed. Oxford: Clarendon Press, 1916.

Summa Virtutum de Remediis Anime. Siegfried Wenzel, ed. Athens, Ga.: Univ. of Georgia Press-The Chaucer Library, 1984.

Walther, Hans. *Proverbia Sententiaeque Latinitatis Medii Aevi: Lateinisch Sprichworter des Mittelalters in alphabetischer Anordnung.* Carmina Medii Aevi Posterioris Latina, II/5. 9 vols. (Vols. 7-9 ed. Paul Gerhard Schmidt.) Göttingen: Vanderschoeck and Ruprecht, 1963-69.

Whiting, Bartlett Jere. *Chaucer's Use of Proverbs.* (Harvard Studies in Comparative Literature, 11.) Cambridge, Mass.: Harvard Univ. Press, 1934.

Whiting, Bartlett Jere, and Helen Wescott Whiting. *Proverbs, Sentences, and Proverbial Phrases, From English Writings Mainly Before 1500.* Cambridge, Mass.: Harvard Univ. Press, 1968.

Windeatt, B. A., ed. and trans. *Chaucer's Dream Poetry: Sources and Analogues.* (Chaucer Studies 7.) Woodbridge, Suffolk: Boydell and Brewer; Totowa, N. J.: Rowman and Littlefield, 1982.

Wyclif. *The English Works of Wyclif Hitherto Unprinted.* 2nd rev. ed. F. D. Matthew, ed. (EETS O.S. 74.) London: Kegan Paul, 1902 (rpt. Millwood, N. Y.: Kraus, 1978).

————. *Selections from English Wycliffite Writings.* Anne Hudson, ed. Cambridge: Cambridge Univ. Press, 1978.

————. *English Wycliffite Sermons.* Volume I. Anne Hudson, ed. New York: Oxford Univ. Press, 1983.

Secondary Sources

Adams, George R., and Bernard S. Levy. "Good and Bad Fridays and May 3 in Chaucer." *ELN*, 3 (1965-66), 245-48.
———. "Chauntecleer's Paradise Lost and Regained." *MS*, 29 (1967), 178-92.
Adams, John F. "The Structure of Irony in *The Summoner's Tale*." *EIC*, 12 (1962), 126-32.
———. "Irony in Troilus' Apostrophe to the Vacant House of Criseyde." *MLQ*, 24 (1963), 61-65.
Adams, Robert. "The Concept of Debt in *The Shipman's Tale*." *SAC*, 6 (1984), 85-102.
Aiken, Pauline. "Vincent of Beauvais and Chaucer's *Monk's Tale*." *Speculum*, 17 (1942), 56-68.
Alford, John A. "Scriptural Testament in *The Canterbury Tales*: The Letter Takes Its Revenge." In Jeffrey, ed., *Chaucer and Scriptural Tradition*, 1984[a]. Pp. 197-203.
Allen, Judson Boyce. "The Ironic Fruyt: Chauntecleer as Figura." *SP*, 66 (1969), 25-35.
———. *The Friar as Critic: Literary Attitudes in the Later Middle Ages.* Nashville, Tenn.: Vanderbilt Univ. Press, 1971.
———. "The Old Way and The Parson's Way: An Ironic Reading of the Parson's Tale." *JMRS*, 3 (1973), 255-71.
———. *The Ethical Poetic of the Later Middle Ages: A Decorum of Convenient Distinction.* Toronto, Buffalo, London: Univ. of Toronto Press, 1982.
———. "Reading and Looking Things Up in Chaucer's England." *Chaucer Newsletter*, 7 (1985[a]), 1-2.
———. Letter to the author. 30 April 1985[b].
———, and Patrick Gallacher. "Alisoun through the Looking Glass: Or Every Man His Own Midas." *ChauR*, 4 (1969-70), 99-105.
———, and Theresa Anne Moritz. *A Distinction of Stories: The Medieval Unity of Chaucer's Fair Chain of Narratives for Canterbury.* Columbus, Ohio: Ohio State Univ. Press, 1980.

Ames, Ruth M. "Prototype and Parody in Chaucerian Exegesis." In Szarmach and Levy, eds., *The Fourteenth Century*, 1977. Pp. 87-105.

———. "Religious Implications of Chaucer's Biblical Parody." Paper read at the New Chaucer Society conference in San Francisco, April, 1982.

———. *God's Plenty: Chaucer's Christian Humanism.* Chicago: Loyola Univ. Press, 1984.

Andrew, Malcolm. "Chaucer's 'General Prologue' to the *Canterbury Tales.*" *Expl*, 43 (1984), 5-6.

Annunziata, Anthony. "Tree Paradigms in the Merchant's Tale." In Szarmach and Levy, eds., *The Fourteenth Century*, 1977. Pp. 125-35.

Arrathoon, Leigh A., ed. *Chaucer and the Craft of Fiction.* Rochester, Mich.: Solaris Press, 1986.

Badel, P. "Raison 'Fille de Dieu' et le Rationalisme de Jean de Meun." In *Mélanges de langue et de littérature du Moyen Age et de la Renaissance offerts à Jean Frappier.* 2 vols. Geneva: Droz, 1970. I:41-52.

Baldwin, Ralph. *The Unity of the* Canterbury Tales. (Anglistica, V.) Copenhagen: Rosenkilde & Bagger, 1955.

Barney, Stephen A. "Explanatory Notes to *Troilus and Criseyde.*" In Larry D. Benson, gen. ed., *The Riverside Chaucer*, 1987. Pp. 1020-58.

Battenhouse, Roy W. *Shakespearean Tragedy: Its Art and Its Christian Premises.* Bloomington and London: Indiana Univ. Press, 1969.

Baugh, Albert C., and E. T. Donaldson. "Chaucer's *Troilus* iv.1585: A Biblical Allusion?" *MLN*, 76 (1961), 1-5.

Beichner, Paul E., C. S. C. "Absolon's Hair." *MS*, 12 (1950), 222-33.

———. "Non Alleluia Ructare." *MS*, 18 (1956), 135-44.

Beidler, Peter G. "Noah and the Old Man in the *Pardoner's Tale.*" *ChauR*, 15 (1980-81), 250-54.

Bennett, J. A. W. *The Parlement of Foules: An Interpretation.* Oxford: Clarendon Press, 1957.

———. *Chaucer's Book of Fame: An Exposition of 'The House of Fame.'* Oxford: Clarendon Press, 1968.

———. Rev. of *Chaucer and the Country of the Stars,* by Chauncey Wood. *UTQ,* 41 (1971-72), 174-75.

Benson, C. David. "Explanatory Notes to *The General Prologue* and *The Physician's Tale.* " In Larry D. Benson, gen. ed., *The Riverside Chaucer,* 1987. Pp. 815-17, 901-04.

Benson, Larry D. "The 'Queynte' Punnings of Chaucer's Critics." *SAC Proceedings,* 1 (1984), 23-47.

Berger, Samuel. *Histoire de la Vulgate pendant les premières siècles du Moyen Age.* Paris: Hachette, 1893.

Besserman, Lawrence. "Chaucer and the Bible: The Case of the Merchant's Tale." *HUSL,* 6 (1978), 10-31.

———. *The Legend of Job in the Middle Ages.* Cambridge, Mass.: Harvard Univ. Press, 1979.

———. "Chaucer's Pardoner." [Letter to *PMLA* "Forum," in reply to Storm (1982).] *PMLA,* 98 (1983), 405-06.

———. *"Glosynge is a Glorious Thyng:* Chaucer's Biblical Exegesis." In Jeffrey, ed. *Chaucer and Scriptural Tradition,* 1984[a]. Pp. 65-73.

———. "Chaucer and the Bible: Parody and Authority in the *Pardoner's Tale.*" In *Biblical Patterns in Modern Literature.* (Brown Judaic Studies, no. 77.) Ed. David Hirsch and Nehama Aschkenasy. Chico, Calif.: Scholar's Press, 1984[b]. Pp. 43-50.

———. "On the Sources of *Troilus and Criseyde* 5.540-63." In press, *ChauR.*

Bestul, Thomas A. "True and False Cheere in Chaucer's *Clerk's Tale.*" *JEGP,* 82 (1983), 500-14.

La Bibbia Nell'Alto Medioevo. (Settimane di Studio del Centro Italiano di Studi sull' Alto Medioevo, 10.) Spoleto: Presso La Sede del Centro, 1963.

Biggins, D. "Chaucer's *General Prologue,* A 696-698." *N&Q,* N.S. 7 (1960), 93-95.

Birney, Earle. "'After his ymage': The Central Ironies of the 'Friar's Tale.'" *MS*, 21 (1959), 17-35.

Bishop, Ian. *Chaucer's 'Troilus and Criseyde': A Critical Study*. Bristol: Univ. of Bristol Press, 1981.

———. Rev. of *The Elements of Chaucer's* Troilus, by Chauncey Wood. *SAC*, 7 (1985), 270-72.

Black, Robert R. "Sacral and Biblical Parody in Chaucer's Canterbury Tales." Diss. Princeton, 1974.

Bleeth, Kenneth A. "The Image of Paradise in the *Merchant's Tale*." In *The Learned and the Lewed: Studies in Chaucer and Medieval Literature*. (Harvard English Studies 5.) Larry D. Benson, ed. Cambridge, Mass.: Harvard Univ. Press, 1974. Pp. 45-60.

———. "Joseph's Doubting of Mary and the Conclusion of the *Merchant's Tale*." *ChauR*, 21 (1986), 58-66.

Block, Edward A. "Originality, Controlling Purpose, and Craftsmanship in Chaucer's *Man of Law's Tale*." *PMLA*, 68 (1953), 572-616.

Bloomfield, Morton W. *The Seven Deadly Sins: An Introduction to the History of A Religious Concept, with Special Reference to Medieval English Literature*. East Lansing: Michigan State College Press, 1952.

———. "Chaucer's Sense of History." *JEGP*, 51 (1952), 301-13; rpt. in Bloomfield, *Essays and Explorations*, 1970. Pp. 13-26.

———. "The Magic of *In Principio*." *MLN*, 70 (1955), 559-65.

———. *Essays and Explorations: Studies in Ideas, Language, and Literature*. Cambridge, Mass.: Harvard Univ. Press, 1970.

———. "Troilus' Paraclausithyron and Its Setting: *Troilus and Criseyde* V, 519-602." *NM*, 73 (1972), 15-24.

———. "Fourteenth-Century England: Realism and Rationalism in Wyclif and Chaucer." *ESA*, 16 (1973), 59-70.

———. "The Canterbury Tales as Framed Narratives." In Derek Pearsall, ed., *LeedsSE*, 1983. Pp. 44-56.

Bode, Edward L. "The Source of Chaucer's 'Rusted Gold.'" *MS*, 24 (1962), 369-70.

Boitani, Piero, ed. *Chaucer and the Italian Trecento.* Cambridge and New York: Cambridge Univ. Press, 1983.

Bolton, W. F. "*The Miller's Tale:* An Interpretation." *MS*, 24 (1962), 83-94.

Boren, James L. "Alysoun of Bath and the Vulgate 'Perfect Wife.'" *NM*, 76 (1975), 247-56.

Boyd, Beverly. *Chaucer and the Liturgy.* Philadelphia, Pa.: Dorrance and Co., 1967.

———. *Chaucer and the Medieval Book.* San Marino, Calif.: Henry E. Huntington Library, 1973.

Boyle, Leonard E. "Innocent III and Vernacular Versions of Scripture." In Walsh and Wood, eds., *The Bible in the Medieval World*, 1985. Pp. 97-107.

Brennan, John P. "Reflections on a Gloss to the *Prioress's Tale* from Jerome's *Adversus Jovinianum.*" *SP*, 70 (1973), 243-51.

Brewer, Derek S. *Chaucer.* 3rd ed. London: Longman, 1973; rpt. 1977.

———, ed. *Writers and their Background: Geoffrey Chaucer.* London: G. Bell and Sons, 1974; Athens, Ohio: Ohio Univ. Press, 1975.

———. "The Reconstruction of Chaucer." *SAC Proceedings*, 1 (1984), 3-19.

Brooke, Rosalind, and Christopher Brooke. *Popular Religion in the Middle Ages: Western Europe 1000-1300.* London and New York: Thames and Hudson, 1984.

Brown, Carleton F. "Chaucer's 'Litel Clergeoun.'" *MP*, 3 (1905-06), 467-91.

———. "The Prologue of Chaucer's 'Lyf of Seint Cecile.'" *MP*, 9 (1911-12), 1-16.

———. "Chaucer and the Hours of the Blessed Virgin." *MLN*, 30 (1915), 231-32.

Brown, Emerson, Jr. "The Merchant's Tale: Why is May Called 'Mayus'?" *ChauR*, 2 (1967-68), 273-77.

————. "Hortus Inconclusus: The Significance of Priapus, and Pyramus and Thisbe in the *Merchant's Tale*." *ChauR*, 4 (1970), 31-40.

————. "*The Merchant's Tale:* Why Was Januarie Born of Pavye?" *NM*, 71 (1970), 654-58.

————. "*The Merchant's Tale:* January's 'Unlikely Elde.'" *NM*, 74 (1973), 92-106.

————. "Biblical Women in the *Merchant's Tale*: Feminism, Antifeminism, and Beyond." *Viator*, 5 (1974), 387-412.

————. "Of Mice and Women: Thoughts on Chaucerian Allusion." In Arrathoon, ed., *Chaucer and the Craft of Fiction*, 1986. Pp. 63-84.

Brown, William J. "Chaucer's Double Apology for *The Miller's Tale*." *University of Colorado Studies: Series in Language and Literature*, 10 (1966), 15-22.

Brusendorff, Aage. *The Chaucer Tradition.* Copenhagen: Branner; London: Oxford Univ. Press, 1925.

Buermann, Theodore B. "Chaucer's 'Book of Genesis' in *The Canterbury Tales:* The Biblical Schema of the First Fragment." Diss. Univ. of Illinois, 1967.

Bugge, John. "Tell-Tale Context: Two Notes on Biblical Quotation in *The Canterbury Tales*." *AN&Q*, 14 (1975-76), 82-85.

Bühler, Curt F. "Wirk Alle Thyng by Conseil." *Speculum*, 24 (1949), 410-12.

Burchmore, David W. "Januarie's 'Blosmy Tree' and the Designation of Joseph." Paper read at the New Chaucer Society conference in San Francisco, April, 1982.

Burnley, J. D. "Chaucer's Host and Harry Bailly." In Arrathoon, ed. *Chaucer and the Craft of Fiction*, 1986. Pp. 195-218.

Burrow, J. A. "Irony in the *Merchant's Tale*." *Anglia*, 75 (1957), 199-208 (rpt. in Burrow's *Essays on Medieval Literature* [Oxford: Clarendon Press, 1984], pp. 49-59).

———. "Explanatory Notes to *The Prologue* and *Tale of Sir Thopas.*" In Larry D. Benson, gen. ed., *The Riverside Chaucer*, 1987. Pp. 917-23.

———, and V. J. Scattergood. "Explanatory Notes to *The General Prologue.*" In Larry D. Benson, gen. ed., *The Riverside Chaucer*, 1987. Pp. 815-17.

Cahn, Walter. *Romanesque Bible Illumination.* Ithaca, N. Y.: Cornell Univ. Press, 1982.

Caie, Graham D. "The Significance of the Early Chaucer Manuscript Glosses (with Special Reference to the *Wife of Bath's Prologue*)." *ChauR*, 10 (1975-76), 350-60.

———. "The Significance of Marginal Glosses in the Earliest Manuscripts of *The Canterbury Tales.*" In Jeffrey, ed., *Chaucer and Scriptural Tradition*, 1984[a]. Pp. 75-88.

Carruthers, Mary. "Letter and Gloss in the Friar's and Summoner's Tales." *JNT*, 2 (1972), 208-14.

———, and Elizabeth D. Kirk, eds. *Acts of Interpretation, The Text In Its Context: Essays on Medieval and Renaissance Literature in Honor of E. Talbot Donaldson.* Norman, Okla.: Pilgrim Books, 1982.

Cavanaugh, Susan. "Explanatory Notes to *The General Prologue, The Monk's Prologue* and *Tale*, and *The Nun's Priest's Prologue* and *Tale.*" In Larry D. Benson, gen. ed., *The Riverside Chaucer*, 1987. Pp. 806-07, 928-41.

Cawley, A. C., ed. *Chaucer's Mind and Art.* Edinburgh: Oliver and Boyd; New York: Barnes and Noble, 1969.

Chamberlain, David. "Musical Signs and Symbols in Chaucer." In Hermann and Burke, eds., *Signs and Symbols*, 1981. Pp. 43-80.

Chesterton, G. K. *Chaucer.* London: Faber and Faber, 1932. Pp. 20-22.

Clark, Roy Peter. "Wit and Witsunday in Chaucer's *Summoner's Tale.*" *AnM*, 17 (1976), 48-57.

———. "Doubting Thomas in Chaucer's *Summoner's Tale.*" *ChauR*, 11 (1976-77), 164-78.

Clark, S. L., and Julian N. Wasserman. "Echoes of Leviathan and the Harrowing of Hell in Chaucer's *Man of Law's Tale*." *SCB*, 38, no. 4 (1978), 140-42.

Coghill, Nevill. *The Poet Chaucer.* 2nd ed. London, Oxford, New York: Oxford Univ. Press, 1967.

Coleman, Janet. *English Literature in History: 1350-1400, Medieval Readers and Writers.* London: Hutchinson, 1981.

———. "English Culture in the Fourteenth Century." In Boitani, ed. *Chaucer and the Italian Trecento*, 1983. Pp. 33-63.

Coletti, Theresa. "The Meeting at the Gate: Comic Hagiography and Symbol in the *Shipman's Tale*." *SIcon*, 3 (1977), 47-56.

———. "The Pardoner's Vernicle and the Image of Man in the *Pardoner's Tale*." *Chaucer Newsletter*, 1, no. 1 (1979), 10-12.

———. "The *Mulier Fortis* and Chaucer's *Shipman's Tale*." *ChauR*, 15 (1980-81), 236-49 (rpt. in Jeffrey, ed., *Chaucer and Scriptural Tradition*, 1984[a], pp. 171-82).

Conley, John. "The Peculiar Name *Thopas*." *SP*, 73 (1976), 42-61.

Cook, Albert S. "Chaucer's Griselda and Homer's Arete." *AJP*, 39 (1918), 75-78.

Cook, Robert. "Another Biblical Echo in the Wife of Bath's Prologue?" *ES*, 59 (1978), 390-94.

Correale, Robert M. "St. Jerome and the Conclusion of the *Friar's Tale*." *ELN*, 2 (1964-65), 171-74.

———. "Chaucer's Parody of Compline in the *Reeve's Tale*." *ChauR*, 1 (1966-67), 161-66.

———. "Chaucer's *Nun's Priest's Tale*, VII, 3444-46." *Expl*, 39 (1980), 43-45.

———. "Nicholas of Clairvaux and the Quotation from 'Seint Bernard' in Chaucer's *The Parson's Tale*, 130-32." *AN&Q*, 20 (1981), 2-3.

———. "The Sources of Some Patristic Quotations in Chaucer's *The Parson's Tale*." *ELN*, 19 (1981-82), 95-98.

Cottino-Jones, Marga. "Fabula vs. Figura: Another Interpretation of the Griselda Story." *Italica*, 50 (1973), 38-52 (rpt. in Musa and Bondanella, eds., Boccaccio, *The Decameron: A New Translation . . . Modern Criticism*, 1977. Pp. 295-305).

Cowgill, Bruce Kent. "'By *Corpus Dominus*': Harry Bailey as False Spiritual Guide." *JMRS*, 15 (1985), 157-81.

Cummings, Hubertis M. *The Indebtedness of Chaucer's Works to the Italian Works of Boccaccio (A Review and Summary)*. New York: Haskell House, 1965 (first publ., 1916).

Cunningham, J. V. "Ideal Fiction: The *Clerk's Tale*." *Shenandoah*, 19 (1968), 38-41.

Dahlberg, C. R. "Chaucer's Cock and Fox." *JEGP*, 53 (1954), 277-90.

D'Alverny, M. T. "Le symbolisme de la Sagesse et le Christ de Saint Dunstan." *BLR*, 5 (1956), 232-44.

David, Alfred. *The Strumpet Muse: Art and Morals in Chaucer's Poetry*. Bloomington and London: Indiana Univ. Press, 1976.

―――. "An ABC to the Style of the Prioress." In Carruthers and Kirk, eds., *Acts of Interpretation*, 1982. Pp. 147-57.

―――. "Explanatory Notes to *The Romaunt of the Rose*." In Larry D. Benson, gen. ed., *The Riverside Chaucer*, 1987. Pp. 1103-16.

Dean, James. "Dismantling the Canterbury Book." *PMLA*, 100 (1985), 746-62.

Deanesly, Margaret. *The Lollard Bible and Other Medieval Biblical Versions*. Cambridge: Cambridge Univ. Press, 1920.

―――. *The Significance of the Lollard Bible*. (The Ethel M. Wood Lecture delivered before the University of London on 13 March, 1951.) London: Univ. of London—The Athlone Press, 1951.

De Hamel, C. F. R. *Glossed Books of the Bible and the Origins of the Paris Booktrade.* Woodbridge, Suffolk: D. S. Brewer, 1984.

Delany, Sheila. *Chaucer's* House of Fame: *The Poetics of Skeptical Fideism.* Chicago and London: Univ. of Chicago Press, 1972.

―――. "Doer of the Word: The Epistle of St. James as a Source for Chaucer's *Manciple's Tale.*" *ChauR*, 17 (1982-83), 250-54.

Delasanta, Rodney. "The Horsemen of the *Canterbury Tales.*" *ChauR*, 3 (1968-69), 29-36.

―――. "Christian Affirmation in *The Book of the Duchess.*" *PMLA*, 84 (1969), 245-51.

―――. "The Theme of Judgment in the *Canterbury Tales.*" *MLQ*, 31 (1970), 298-307.

―――. "And of Great Reverence: Chaucer's Man of Law." *ChauR*, 5 (1970-71), 288-310.

―――. "Alisoun and the Saved Harlot: A Cozening of Our Expectation." *ChauR*, 12 (1977-78), 218-35.

―――. "Penance and Poetry in the *Canterbury Tales.*" *PMLA*, 93 (1978), 240-47.

DeLong, Sharon Hiltz. "Explanatory Notes to *The Prologue* and *Tale of Melibee.*" In Larry D. Benson, gen. ed., *The Riverside Chaucer*, 1987. Pp. 923-28.

De Lubac, Henri. *Exégèse Médiévale: Les Quatre Sens de l'Ecriture.* 4 vols. (Etudes Publiées sous la Direction de la Faculté de Théologie S. J. de Lyon-Fournière, tomes 41 [vols. 1-2], 42 [vol. 3], 59 [vol. 4].) Paris: Aubier, 1959-64.

Dempster, Germaine. "The Merchant's Tale." In Bryan and Dempster, eds., *Sources and Analogues*, 1941[a]. Pp. 333-56.

―――. "The Parson's Tale." In Bryan and Dempster, eds., *Sources and Analogues*, 1941[b]. Pp. 723-60.

De Vogel, C. J. "Boethiana." *Vivarium*, 10 (1972), 1-40.

Dillon, Bert. *A Chaucer Dictionary: Proper Names and Allusions, Excluding Place Names.* Boston: G. K. Hall, 1974.

DiMarco, Vincent J. "Explanatory Notes to *The Knight's Tale, The Squire's Prologue* and *Tale*, and *Anelida and Arcite*." In Larry D. Benson, gen. ed., *The Riverside Chaucer*, 1987. Pp. 826-41, 890-94, 991-93.

Disbrow, Sarah. "The Wife of Bath's Old Wives' Tale." *SAC*, 8 (1986), 59-71.

Dodd, William George. *Courtly Love in Chaucer and Gower*. (Harvard Studies in English, vol. 1.) Boston and London: Ginn and Co., 1913.

Dolan, T. P. Rev. of *Summa Virtutum de Remediis Anime*, by Siegfried Wenzel, ed. *SAC*, 8 (1986), 260-63.

Donaldson, E. Talbot. "Patristic Exegesis in the Criticism of Medieval Literature: The Opposition." In Dorothy Bethurum, ed., *Critical Approaches to Medieval Literature: Selected Papers from the English Institute, 1958-59*. New York and London: Columbia Univ. Press, 1967 (first publ., 1960). Pp. 1-26.

Donovan, Mortimer J. "The *Moralite* of the Nun's Priest's Sermon." *JEGP*, 52 (1953), 498-508.

Dronke, Peter. "Chaucer and the Medieval Latin Poets: Part A." In Derek Brewer, ed., *Writers and their Background*, 1975. Pp. 154-72.

Eberle, Patricia J. "Explanatory Notes to *The Man of Law's Tale*." In Larry D. Benson, gen. ed., *The Riverside Chaucer*, 1987. Pp. 854-63.

Economou, George, ed. *Geoffrey Chaucer: A Collection of Original Articles*. New York: McGraw-Hill, 1975.

Ehrhart, Margaret J. "Machaut's *Jugement dou roy de Navarre* and the Book of Ecclesiastes." *NM*, 81 (1980), 318-25.

Evans, G. R. *The Language and Logic of the Bible: The Earlier Middle Ages*. Cambridge: Cambridge Univ. Press, 1984.

Evans, Lawrence Gove. "A Biblical Allusion in *Troilus and Criseyde*." *MLN*, 74 (1959), 584-87.

Farrell, Robert T. "Chaucer's Use of the Theme of the Help of God in the *Man of Law's Tale*." *NM*, 71 (1970), 239-43.

Ferster, Judith. *Chaucer on Interpretation.* Cambridge: Cambridge Univ. Press, 1985.

Fichte, Joerg O. "*The Clerk's Tale:* An Obituary to *Gentilesse*." In W. C. Johnson, Jr., and Lauren C. Gruber, eds., *New Views on Chaucer*, 1973. Pp. 9-16.

Fleming, John V. "Chaucer's 'Syngeth Placebo' and the 'Roman de Fauvel.'" *N&Q*, 210 (1965), 17-18.

——. "The Antifraternalism of the *Summoner's Tale*." *JEGP*, 65 (1966), 688-700.

——. *The Roman de la Rose: A Study in Allegory and Iconography.* Princeton, N. J.: Princeton Univ. Press, 1969.

——. "Chaucer's Ascetical Images." *C&L*, 28 (1978-79), 19-26.

——. *An Introduction to the Franciscan Literature of the Middle Ages.* Chicago: Franciscan Herald Press, 1977.

——. "Chaucer and the Visual Arts of His Time." In Rose, ed., *New Perspectives*, 1981. Pp. 121-36.

——. "Gospel Asceticism: Some Chaucerian Images of Perfection." In Jeffrey, ed., *Chaucer and Scriptural Tradition*, 1984[a]. Pp. 183-95.

——. *Reason and the Lover.* Princeton, N. J.: Princeton Univ. Press, 1984.

——. "Chaucer and Erasmus on the Pilgrimage to Canterbury: An Iconographical Speculation." In Thomas J. Heffernan, ed., *The Popular Literature of Medieval England.* (Tennessee Studies in Literature, vol. 28.) Knoxville: Univ. of Tennessee Press, 1985. Pp. 148-66.

Flügel, Ewald. "Some Notes on Chaucer's Prologue." *JEGP*, 1 (1897), 118-35.

——. "Chaucers Kleinere Gedichte(II)." *Anglia*, 23 (1901), 195-224.

Fowler, David C. *The Bible in Early English Literture.* Seattle and London: Univ. of Washington Press, 1976.

———. *The Bible in Middle English Literature*. Seattle and London: Univ. of Washington Press, 1984.

Frese, Dolores Warwick. "Chaucer's *Clerk's Tale:* The Monsters and the Critics Reconsidered." *ChauR*, 8 (1973-74), 133-46.

Friend, Albert C. "Sampson, David, and Solomon in the Parson's Tale." *MP*, 46 (1948-49), 117-21.

Fyler, John M. *Chaucer and Ovid*. New Haven and London: Yale Univ. Press, 1979.

———. "Explanatory Notes to *The House of Fame*." In Larry D. Benson, gen. ed., *The Riverside Chaucer*, 1987. Pp. 977-90.

Gardner, William B. "Chaucer's 'Unworthy Sone of Eve.'" In *Studies in English*. Austin: Univ. of Texas Press, 1947. Pp. 77-83.

Gates, Barbara T. "'A Temple of Fals Goddis': Cupidity and Mercantile Values in Chaucer's Fruit-Tree Episode." *NM*, 77 (1976), 369-75.

Gellrich, Jesse M. "The Parody of Medieval Music in the *Miller's Tale*." *JEGP*, 73 (1974), 176-88.

———. *The Idea of the Book in the Middle Ages: Language Theory, Mythology, and Fiction*. Ithaca and London: Cornell Univ. Press, 1985.

Gerould, Gordon Hall. "The Second Nun's Prologue and Tale." In Bryan and Dempster, eds., *Sources and Analogues*, 1941. Pp. 664-84.

———. *Chaucerian Essays*. Princeton, N. J.: Princeton Univ. Press, 1952.

Gibson, Gail McMurray. "Resurrection as Dramatic Icon in *The Shipman's Tale*." In Hermann and Burke, eds., *Signs and Symbols*, 1981. Pp. 102-12.

Gillmeister, Heiner. *Discrecioun: Chaucer und die Via Regia*. Bonn: Bouvier Verlag Herbert Grundmann, 1972.

———. "The Whole Truth About *Vache*." *Chaucer Newsletter*, 2 (1980), 13-14.

Ginsberg, Warren S. "Explanatory Notes to *The General Prologue* and *The Clerk's Prologue* and *Tale.*" In Larry D. Benson, gen. ed., *The Riverside Chaucer*, 1987. Pp. 810-11, 879-84.

Glunz, Hans H. *History of the Vulgate in England from Alcuin to Roger Bacon.* Cambridge: Cambridge Univ. Press, 1933.

Gordon, Ida L. *The Double Sorrow of Troilus: A Study of Ambiguities in Troilus and Criseyde.* Oxford: Clarendon Press, 1970.

Gray, Douglas. "Explanatory Notes to *The General Prologue, The Miller's Prologue* and *Tale, The Reeve's Prologue* and *Tale,* and *The Cook's Prologue* and *Tale.*" In Larry D. Benson, gen. ed., *The Riverside Chaucer*, 1987. Pp. 820-22, 841-53.

Green, Marion N. "Christian Implications of Knighthood in Chaucer's *Troilus.*" *Delaware Notes*, 30 (1957), 57-92.

Grennen, Joseph E. "'Sampsoun' in the *Canterbury Tales:* Chaucer Adapting a Source." *NM*, 67 (1966), 117-22.

Gross, Laila Z. "Explanatory Notes to the Short Poems." In Larry D. Benson, gen. ed., *The Riverside Chaucer*, 1987. Pp. 1076-91.

Hamilton, Marie P. "The Summoner's 'Psalm of Davit.'" *MLN*, 57 (1942), 655-57.

Hammond, Eleanor Prescott. *Chaucer: A Bibliographical Manual.* New York: Macmillan, 1908.

Hanna III, Ralph. "Textual Notes to *The Canterbury Tales.*" In Larry D. Benson, gen. ed., *The Riverside Chaucer*, 1987. Pp. 1118-35.

———, and Traugott Lawler. "Explanatory Notes to *Boece.*" In Larry D. Benson, gen. ed., *The Riverside Chaucer*, 1987. Pp. 1003-19.

Harder, Kelsie B. "Chaucer's Use of the Mystery Plays in the *Miller's Tale.*" *MLQ*, 17 (1956), 193-98.

Hargreaves, Henry. "The Marginal Glosses to the Wycliffite New Testament." *SN*, 33 (1961), 285-300.

————. "From Bede to Wyclif: Medieval English Bible Translations." *BJRL*, 48 (1965-66), 118-40.

Harty, Kevin J. "The Reputation of Queen Esther in the Middle Ages: *The Merchant's Tale* IV (E). 1742-45." *BSUF*, 19, iii (1978), 65-68. [Not seen.]

Harwood, Britton J. "The Wife of Bath and the Dream of Innocence." *MLQ*, 33 (1972), 257-73.

Hatton, Tom. "Chaucer's Friar's 'Old Rebekke.'" *JEGP*, 67 (1968), 266-71.

Havely, Nicholas. "Tearing or Breathing? Dante's Influence on *Filostrato* and *Troilus*." *SAC Proceedings*, 1 (1984), 51-59.

Hawkins, Sherman. "Chaucer's Prioress and the Sacrifice of Praise." *JEGP*, 63 (1964), 599-624.

Henkin, Leo J. "Jacob and the Hooly Jew." *MLN*, 55 (1940), 254-59.

————. "The Apocrypha and Chaucer's *House of Fame*." *MLN*, 56 (1941), 583-88.

Henninger, S. K., Jr. "The Concept of Order in Chaucer's *Clerk's Tale*." *JEGP*, 56 (1957), 382-95.

Hermann, John P., and John J. Burke, eds. *Signs and Symbols in Chaucer's Poetry*. University, Alabama: Univ. of Alabama Press, 1981.

Herz, Judith Scherer. "Chaucer's Elegaic Knight." *Criticism*, 6 (1964), 212-24.

Herzman, Ronald B. "The *Reeve's Tale*, Symkyn, and Simon the Magician." *ABR*, 33 (1982), 325-33.

Higdon, David Leon. "The Wife of Bath and Refreshment Sunday." *PLL*, 8 (1972), 199-201.

Hilary, Christine Ryan. "Explanatory Notes to *The General Prologue, The Wife of Bath's Prologue* and *Tale*, and *The Pardoner's Introduction, Prologue,* and *Tale*." In Larry D. Benson, gen. ed., *The Riverside Chaucer*, 1987. Pp. 817-19, 823-25, 864-74, 904-10.

Hill, Thomas D. Rev. of *Reason and the Lover*, by John V. Fleming. *Speculum*, 60 (1985), 973-77.

Hinckley, Henry Barrett. "Chauceriana: *The Canterbury Tales.*" *MP,* 14 (1916-17), 317-18.

Hoffman, Richard L. "Two Notes on Chaucer's Arcite." *ELN,* 4 (1966-67), 172-75.

———. "Jephthah's Daughter and Chaucer's Virginia." *ChauR,* 2 (1967-68), 20-31.

———. "Ovid and the Wife of Bath's Tale of Midas." *N&Q,* N.S., 13 (1968), 48-50.

———. "The Wife of Bath's Uncharitable Offerings." *ELN,* 11 (1973-74), 165-67.

Howard, Donald R. *The Three Temptations: Medieval Man in Search of the World.* Princeton, N. J.: Princeton Univ. Press, 1966.

———. "Literature and Sexuality: Book III of Chaucer's *Troilus.*" *MR,* 8 (1967), 442-56.

———. *The Idea of the Canterbury Tales.* Berkeley and London: Univ. of California Press, 1976.

Hudson, Anne. "The Debate on Bible Translation, Oxford 1401." *English Historical Review,* 90 (1975), 1-18.

Hulbert, James R. "The Nun's Priest's Tale." In Bryan and Dempster, eds., *Sources and Analogues,* 1941. Pp. 645-63.

Huppé, Bernard F. *A Reading of the Canterbury Tales.* Rev. ed. Albany, N. Y.: State Univ. of New York Press, 1967.

———. "The Unlikely Narrator: The Narrative Strategy of the *Troilus.*" In Hermann and Burke, eds., *Signs and Symbols,* 1981. Pp. 179-94.

———, and D. W. Robertson, Jr. *Fruyt and Chaff: Studies in Chaucer's Allegories.* Princeton, N. J.: Princeton Univ. Press, 1963.

Jacobs, Edward Craney. "Further Biblical Allusions for Chaucer's Prioress." *ChauR,* 15 (1980-81), 151-54.

Jacobs, Edward C., and Robert E. Jungman. "His Mother's Curse: Kinship in *The Friar's Tale.*" *PQ,* 64 (1985), 256-59.

Jeffrey, David L. "The Friar's Rent." *JEGP,* 70 (1971), 600-06.

——, ed. *Chaucer and Scriptural Tradition.* In *Revue de l'Université d'Ottawa/University of Ottawa Quarterly,* 53 (1983), 255-490 (rpt. by the Univ. of Ottawa Press, with corrections and indexes, 1984[a]).

——. "Introduction." In Jeffrey, ed., *Chaucer and Scriptural Tradition,* 1984[b]. Pp. XIII-XVI.

——. "Chaucer and Wyclif: Biblical Hermeneutic and Literary Theory in the XIVth Century." In Jeffrey, ed., *Chaucer and Scriptural Tradition,* 1984[c]. Pp. 109-40.

——. "Sacred and Secular Scripture: Authority and Interpretation in *The House of Fame.*" In Jeffrey, ed., *Chaucer and Scriptural Tradition,* 1984[d]. Pp. 207-28.

Johnson, Dudley R. "Chaucer and the Bible." Diss. Yale, 1941.

——. "'Homicide' in the Parson's Tale." *PMLA,* 57 (1942), 51-56.

——. "The Biblical Characters of Chaucer's Monk." *PMLA,* 66 (1951), 827-43.

Johnson, Lynn Staley. "The Prince and His People: A Study of the Two Covenants in the *Clerk's Tale.*" *ChauR,* 10 (1975-76), 17-29.

Johnson, William C., Jr. "*The Man of Law's Tale:* Aesthetics and Christianity in Chaucer." *ChauR,* 16 (1981-82), 201-21.

Jungman, Robert E. "The Pardoner's Quarrel with the Host." *PQ,* 55 (1976), 279-81.

Justman, Stewart. "Literal and Symbolic in the *Canterbury Tales.*" *ChauR,* 14 (1979-1980), 199-214.

Kadish, Emilie P. "The Proem of Petrarch's *Griselda.*" *Mediaevalia,* 2 (1976), 189-206.

——. "Petrarch's Griselda: An English Translation." *Mediaevalia,* 3 (1977), 1-24.

Kaminsky, Alice R. *Chaucer's* Troilus and Criseyde *and the Critics.* Athens, Ohio: Ohio Univ. Press, 1980.

Kane, George. "Langland and Chaucer: An Obligatory Conjunction." In Rose, ed., *New Perspectives,* 1981. Pp. 5-19.

Kaske, Carol V. "Getting Around the Parson's Tale." In Rossell Hope Robbins, ed., *Chaucer at Albany.* New York: Burt Franklin and Co., 1975. Pp. 147-77.

Kaske, Robert E. "The Summoner's Garleek, Oynons, and eek Lekes." *MLN,* 74 (1959), 481-84.

———. "An Aube in the *Reeve's Tale.*" *ELH,* 26 (1959), 295-310.

———. "Patristic Exegesis in the Criticism of Medieval Literature: the Defense." In Dorothy Bethurum, ed., *Critical Approaches to Medieval Literature: Selected Papers from the English Institute, 1958-59.* New York and London: Columbia Univ. Press, 1967 (first publ., 1960). Pp. 27-60.

———. "January's 'Aube.'" *MLN,* 75 (1960), 1-4.

———. "The Aube in Chaucer's *Troilus.*" In Schoeck and Taylor, eds., *Chaucer Criticism,* 1961. Pp. 167-79.

———. "The *Canticum Canticorum* in the *Miller's Tale.*" *SP,* 59 (1962), 479-500.

———. "Chaucer and Medieval Allegory." *ELH,* 30 (1963), 175-92.

———. "Horn and Ivory in the *Summoner's Tale.*" *NM,* 73 (1972), 122-26.

———. "Chaucer's Marriage Group." In Mitchell and Provost, eds., *Chaucer the Love Poet,* 1973. Pp. 45-65.

———. Comments in "Panel Discussion," in Mitchell and Provost, eds., *Chaucer the Love Poet,* 1973. Pp. 95-96.

———. "*Clericus Adam* and Chaucer's *Adam Scriveyn.*" In Vasta and Thundy, eds. *Chaucerian Problems,* 1979. Pp. 114-18.

———. "Chaucer and Biblical Exegesis." Paper presented at the Third International Congress of the New Chaucer Society, San Francisco, April 16, 1982.

———. "Pandarus's 'Vertue of Corones Tweyne.'" *ChauR,* 21 (1986), 226-33. (*A Volume of Essays in Memory of Judson Boyce Allen [1932-85],* Collected by R. A. Shoaf.)

412 Bibliography

————. *Medieval Christian Imagery: A Guide to Interpretation.* Toronto: Univ. of Toronto Press, forthcoming.

Kean, Patricia M. *Chaucer and the Making of English Poetry.* 2 vols. London: Routledge & Kegan Paul, 1972.

Kee, Kenneth. "Two Chaucerian Gardens." *MS,* 23 (1961), 154-62.

Keenan, Hugh T. "The *General Prologue* to the *Canterbury Tales,* Lines 345-346: The Franklin's Feast and Eucharistic Shadows." *NM,* 79 (1978), 36-40.

Kellogg, Alfred L. "An Augustinian Interpretation of Chaucer's Pardoner." In Kellogg, *Essays,* 1972. Pp. 245-68 (rpt. from *Speculum,* 26 [1951], 465-81).

————. "Chaucer's Satire of the Pardoner." In Kellogg, *Essays,* 1972. Pp. 212-44 (rpt. with revisions from *PMLA,* 66 [1951], 251-77).

————. "St. Augustine and the Parson's Tale." *Traditio,* 8 (1952), 424-30.

————. "The Fraternal Kiss in the 'Summoner's Tale.'" In Kellogg, *Essays,* 1972. Pp. 273-75 (rpt. from *Scriptorium,* 7 [1953], 115).

————. "Seith Moses by the Devel: A Problem in Chaucer's Parson's Tale." In Kellogg, *Essays,* 1972. Pp. 339-42 (rpt. from *RBPH,* 31 [1953], 61-64).

————. "A Reading of the 'Friar's Tale,' Line 1314." In Kellogg, *Essays,* 1972. Pp. 269-72 (rpt. from *N&Q,* 204 [1959], 190-92).

————. "Susannah and the 'Merchant's Tale.'" In Kellogg, *Essays,* 1972. Pp. 330-38 (rpt. from *Speculum,* 35 [1960], 275-79).

————. "Chaucer's Self-Portrait and Dante's." In Kellogg, *Essays,* 1972. Pp. 353-55 (rpt. from *MAE,* 229 [1960], 119-20).

————. *Chaucer, Langland, Arthur: Essays in Middle English Literature.* New Brunswick, N. J.: Rutgers Univ. Press, 1972.

————. "Chaucer's May 3 and Its Contexts." In Kellogg, *Essays,* 1972. Pp. 155-98.

————. "The Evolution of the 'Clerk's Tale': A Study in Connotation." In Kellogg, *Essays*, 1972. Pp. 276-329.

Kirk, Elizabeth D. "'Paradis Stood Formed in Hire Yen': Courtly Love and Chaucer's Re-Vision of Dante." In Carruthers and Kirk, eds., *Acts of Interpretation*, 1982. Pp. 257-77.

Kittredge, George L. "Chaucer and the *Roman de Carite*." *MLN*, 12 (1897), 113-15.

Klaeber, Frederick. "Traces of the *Canticum* and of Boethius' 'De Consolatione Philosophiae' in Chaucer's 'Book of the Duchess.'" *MLN*, 12 (1897), 189-90.

Klinefelter, Ralph A. "Chaucer's *An ABC*, 25-32." *Expl*, 24 (1965), no. 5.

Knoepflmacher, U. C. "Irony Through Scriptural Allusion: A Note on Chaucer's Prioress." *ChauR*, 4 (1970), 180-83.

Köppel, Emil. "Chaucer und Innocenz des Dritten Traktat *De Contemptu Mundi sive De Miseria Conditionis Humanae*." *Archiv*, 84 (1890), 405-18.

————. "Chaucer und Albertanus Brixiensis." *Archiv*, 86 (1891[a]), 29-46.

————. "Über das Verhältnis von Chaucers Prosawerken zu seinen Dichtungen und die Echtheit der 'Parson's Tale.'" *Archiv*, 87 (1891[b]), 33-54.

————. "Chauceriana." *Anglia*, 13 (1891[c]), 174-86.

Kolve, V. A. "Chaucer's *Second Nun's Tale* and the Iconography of Saint Cecilia." In Rose, ed., *New Perspectives*, 1981, pp. 137-74.

————. *Chaucer and the Imagery of Narrative: The First Five Canterbury Tales*. Stanford, Calif.: Stanford Univ. Press, 1984.

Koonce, B. G. "Satan the Fowler." *MS*, 21 (1959), 176-84.

Kreuzer, James R. "A Note on Chaucer's *Tale of Melibee*." *MLN*, 63 (1948), 53-54.

Kugel, James. "The Bible as Literature in Late Antiquity and the Middle Ages." *HUSLA*, 11 (1983), 20-70.

414 *Bibliography*

LaHood, Marvin J. "Chaucer's 'The Legend of Lucrece.'" *PQ*, 43 (1964), 274-76.

Lampe, G. W. H., ed. *The Cambridge History of the Bible.* vol. 2. *The West from the Fathers to the Reformation.* Cambridge: Cambridge Univ. Press, 1969.

Lancashire, Anne. "Chaucer and the Sacrifice of Isaac." *ChauR*, 9 (1974-75), 320-26.

Landrum, Grace Warren. "Chaucer's Use of the Vulgate." Diss. Radcliffe College, 1921.

———. "Chaucer's Use of the Vulgate." *PMLA*, 39 (1924), 75-100.

Lanham, Richard A. "Chaucer's *Clerk's Tale:* The Poem Not the Myth." *L&P*, 16 (1966), 157-65.

Law, Robert Adger. "*In Principio.*" *PMLA*, 37 (1922), 208-15.

Lawler, Traugott. *The One and the Many in the Canterbury Tales.* Hamden, Conn.: The Shoe String Press-Archon, 1980.

———. "The Chaucer Library: 'Jankyn's Book of Wikked Wyves.'" *Chaucer Newsletter*, 7 (1985), 1-4.

———. "Chaucer." In A. S. G. Edwards, ed., *Middle English Prose: A Critical Guide to Major Authors and Genres.* New Brunswick, N. J.: Rutgers Univ. Press, 1984. Pp. 296-99.

Leclercq, Jean. *L'Amour des Lettres et le Désir de Dieu: Initiation aux Auteurs Monastiques du Moyen Age.* Paris: Editions du Cerf, 1957.

Leff, Gordon. *The Dissolution of the Medieval Outlook: An Essay on Intellectual and Spiritual Change in the Fourteenth Century.* New York: New York Univ. Press, 1976.

Leicester, H. Marshall, Jr. "'Synne Horrible': The Pardoner's Exegesis of His Tale, and Chaucer's." In Carruthers and Kirk, eds., *Acts of Interpretation*, 1982. Pp. 25-50.

Levin, Harry. *The Myth of The Golden Age in the Renaissance.* Bloomington and London: Indiana Univ. Press, 1969.

Levitan, Alan. "The Parody of Pentecost in Chaucer's *Summoner's Tale.*" *UTQ*, 40 (1971), 236-46.

Levy, Bernard S. "Chaucer's Wife of Bath, The Loathly Lady, and Dante's Siren." *Symposium,* 19 (1965), 359-73.

―――. "Biblical Parody in the Summoner's Tale." *TSL,* 11 (1966), 45-60.

―――. "The Wife of Bath's *Queynte Fantasye.*" *ChauR.* 4 (1970), 106-22.

―――, and George R. Adams. "Chauntecleer's Paradise Lost and Regained." *MS,* 29 (1967), 178-92.

Levy, M. L. "As Myn Auctor Seyth." *MAE,* 12 (1943), 25-39.

Lewis, Robert E. "Glosses to the *Man of Law's Tale* from Pope Innocent III's *De Miseria Humanae Conditionis.*" *SP,* 64 (1967), 1-16.

―――. "Chaucer's Artistic Uses of Innocent III's *De Miseria Humanae Conditionis* in the Man of Law's Prologue and Tale." *PMLA,* 81 (1966), 485-92.

Loewe, Raphael. "The Medieval History of the Latin Vulgate." In Lampe, ed., *Cambridge History of the Bible,* 1969. Pp. 102-54.

Loomis, L. H. "Sir Thopas and David and Goliath." *MLN,* 51 (1936), 311-13.

Loomis, Roger Sherman. "Was Chaucer a Laodicean?" In Schoeck & Taylor, eds., *Chaucer Criticism,* 1960. I:291-310 (rpt. from *Essays and Studies in Honor of Carleton Brown.* New York: New York Univ. Press, 1940. Pp. 129-48).

―――, ed. *Arthurian Literature in the Middle Ages: A Collaborative History.* Oxford: Clarendon Press, 1967 (first publ., 1959).

―――. "Was Chaucer a Free Thinker?" In MacEdward Leach, ed., *Studies in Medieval Literature In Honor of Albert Croll Baugh.* Philadelphia: Univ. of Pennsylvania Press, 1961. Pp. 21-42.

Lounsbury, Thomas R. *Studies in Chaucer.* 3 vols. New York: Harper and Brothers, 1892.

Lourdaux, W., and D. Verhelst, eds. *The Bible and Medieval Culture.* (Mediaevalia Lovaniensia, Series I, Studia VII.) Louvain: Louvain Univ. Press, 1979.

Lowes, John Livingston. "The Prologue to the *Legend of Good Women* as Related to the French *Marguerite* Poems, and the *Filostrato*." *PMLA*, 19 (1904), 593-683.

———. "Chaucer and the *Miroir de Mariage* (I), (II)." *MP*, 8 (1910-11), 165-86, 305-52.

———. "Chaucer and Dante's *Convivio*." *MP*, 13 (1915-16), 19-33.

Ludlum, Chas. D. "Heavenly Word-Play in Chaucer's 'Complaint to His Purse.'" *N&Q*, N. S. 23 (1976), 391-92.

Luengo, A. "Audience and Exempla in the *Pardoner's Prologue* and *Tale*." *ChauR*, 11 (1976-77), 1-10.

MacDonald, Donald. "Proverbs, *Sententiae*, and *Exempla* in Chaucer's Comic Tales: The Function of Comic Misapplication." *Speculum*, 41 (1966), 453-65.

Madeleva, Sister. *Chaucer's Nuns and other Essays*. New York and London: D. Appleton and Co., 1925.

Magoun, Francis P., Jr. *A Chaucer Gazeteer*. Chicago: Univ. of Chicago Press, 1961.

Makarewicz, Sister Mary R. *The Patristic Influence on Chaucer*. Washington, D. C.: The Catholic Univ. of America Press, 1953.

Malarkey, Stoddard. "The 'Corones Tweyne': An Interpretation." *Speculum*, 38 (1963), 473-78.

Maltman, Sister Nicholas, O. P. "The Divine Granary, Or the End of the Prioress's 'Greyn.'" *ChauR*, 17 (1982-83), 163-70.

Mann, Jill. "Chaucer and the Medieval Latin Poets: Part B." In Derek Brewer, ed., *Writers and their Background*, 1975. Pp. 172-83.

Mariella, Sister. "The Parson's Tale and the Marriage Group." *MLN*, 53 (1938), 251-56.

Mary Immaculate, Sister, C. S. C. "'Sixty' as a Conventional Number and Other Chauceriana." *MLQ*, 2 (1941), 59-66.

———. "Fiends as 'Servant Unto Man' in the *Friar's Tale*." *PQ*, 21 (1942), 240-44.

McCall, John P. "The *Clerk's Tale* and the Theme of Obedience." *MLQ,* 27 (1966), 260-69.

———. "Chaucer and the Pseudo Origen *De Maria Magdalena:* A Preliminary Study." *Speculum,* 46 (1971), 491-509.

———. *Chaucer Among the Gods: The Poetics of Classical Myth.* University Park and London: Penn State Univ. Press, 1979.

McGrady, Donald. "Chaucer and the *Decameron* Reconsidered." *ChauR,* 12 (1977-78), 1-26.

McNally, Robert E., S. J. *The Bible in the Early Middle Ages.* (Woodstock Papers: Occasional Essays for Theology, No. 4.) Westminster, Md.: The Newman Press, 1959.

McNamara, John. "Chaucer's Use of the Epistle of St. James in the *Clerk's Tale.*" *ChauR,* 7 (1972-73), 184-93.

Middleton, Anne. "The *Physician's Tale* and Love's Martyrs: 'Ensamples mo than ten' as a Method in the *Canterbury Tales.*" *ChauR,* 8 (1973-74), 9-31.

———. "The Clerk and His Tale: Some Literary Contexts." *SAC,* 2 (1980), 121-50.

Miller, Clarence H., and Roberta Bux Bosse. "Chaucer's Pardoner and the Mass." *ChauR,* 6 (1971-72), 171-84.

Miller, Robert P. "Chaucer's Pardoner, the Scriptural Eunuch, and the *Pardoner's Tale.*" In Schoeck and Taylor, eds., *Chaucer Criticism,* 1960. 1.221-44 (rpt. from *Speculum,* 30 [1955], 180-99).

———, ed. *Chaucer: Sources and Backgrounds.* New York: Oxford Univ. Press, 1977.

Minnis, Alastair J. "'Authorial Intention' and 'Literal Sense' in the Exegetical Theories of Richard Fitzralph and John Wyclif." *Proceedings of the Royal Irish Academy,* 75, sec. C (1975), 1-31.

———. "'Authorial Role' and 'Literary Form' in Late-Medieval Scriptural Exegesis." *BGDSL,* 99 (1977), 37-65.

———. "A Note on Chaucer and the *Ovide Moralisé.*" *MAE,* 48 (1979), 254-57.

————. "Literary Theory in Discussions of *Formae Tractandi* by Medieval Theologians." *NLH*, 11 (1979-80), 133-45.

————. "Chaucer and Comparative Literary Theory." In Rose, ed., *New Perspectives*, 1981. Pp. 53-69.

————. "The Influence of Academic Prologues on the Prologues and Literary Attitudes of Late-Medieval English Writers." *MS*, 43 (1981), 342-83.

————. *Chaucer and Pagan Antiquity*. (Chaucer Studies 8.) Cambridge, England: D. S. Brewer; Totowa, N. J.: Rowman and Littlefield, 1982.

————. *Medieval Theory of Authorship: Scholastic Literary Attitudes in the Later Middle Ages*. London: Scolar Press, 1984.

Miskimin, Alice S. *The Renaissance Chaucer*. New Haven and London: Yale Univ. Press, 1975.

Mitchell, Jerome, and William Provost, eds. *Chaucer the Love Poet*. Athens, Ga.: Univ. of Georgia Press, 1973.

Morris, Lynn King. *Chaucer Source and Analogue Criticism*. New York and London: Garland Publishing, 1985.

Morse, Charlotte. "The Exemplary Griselda." *SAC*, 7 (1985), 51-86.

Morse, J. Mitchell. "The Philosophy of the Clerk of Oxenford." *MLQ*, 19 (1956), 3-20.

Mossé, Fernand. "Chaucer et la liturgie." *Revue Germanique*, 14 (1923), 283-89.

Muir, Lawrence. "Translations and Paraphrases of the Bible, and Commentaries." In J. Burke Severs, ed., *A Manual of the Writings in Middle English 1050-1500*. Hamden, Conn.: Archon Books, 1970. Pp. 381-409, 534-552.

Muscatine, Charles. "The Feigned Illness in Chaucer's *Troilus and Criseyde*." *MLN*, 63 (1948), 372-77.

————. *Chaucer and the French Tradition: A Study in Style and Meaning*. Berkeley and Los Angeles: Univ. of California Press, 1957.

———. "Explanatory Notes to *The Parliament of Fowls.*" In Larry D. Benson, gen. ed., *The Riverside Chaucer,* 1987. Pp. 994-1002.

Nicholson, Lewis E. "Chaucer's 'Com Pa Me': A Famous Crux Reexamined." *ELN,* 19 (1981-82), 98-102.

Nitzsche, J. C. "Creation in Genesis and Nature in Chaucer's *General Prologue* 1-18." *PLL,* 14 (1978), 459-64.

Noble, Charles. "The Bible in Chaucer." In *The Faculty Corner: Papers Contributed to 'The Unit' by Members of the Faculty of Iowa College* (Grinnell, Iowa, 1901). Pp. 157-67.

Nolan, Barbara. "The Art of Expropriation: Chaucer's Narrator in *The Book of the Duchess.*" In Rose, ed., *New Perspectives,* 1981. Pp. 203-22.

Noll, Dolores L. "The Serpent and the Sting in the *Pardoner's Prologue* and *Tale.*" *ChauR,* 17 (1982-83), 159-62.

Oberman, Heiko A. *Archbishop Thomas Bradwardine, A Fourteenth-Century Augustinian: A Study of His Theology in Its Historical Context.* Utrecht: Kemink & Zoon, 1957.

Olson, Glending. "A Reading of the *Thopas-Melibee* Link." *ChauR,* 10 (1975-76), 147-53.

———. "Rhetorical Circumstances and the Canterbury Storytelling." *SAC,* Proceedings 1 (1984), pp. 211-18.

Olson, Paul A. "Chaucer's Merchant and January's 'Hevene in Erthe Heere.'" *ELH,* 28 (1961), 203-14.

———. "The *Reeve's Tale:* Chaucer's *Measure for Measure.*" *SP,* 59 (1962), 1-17.

———. "Poetic Justice in the *Miller's Tale.*" *MLQ,* 24 (1963), 227-36.

Otten, Charlotte F. "Proserpine: *Liberatrix Suae Gentis.*" *ChauR,* 5 (1970-71), 277-87.

Owen, Charles A., Jr. "The *Tale of Melibee.*" *ChauR,* 7 (1972-73), 267-80.

Owst, G. R. *Literature and Pulpit in Medieval England: A Neglected Chapter in the History of English Letters and of the English People*. 2nd rev. ed. Oxford: Basil Blackwell, 1961 (first publ., 1933).

Pace, George B. "Adam's Hell." *PMLA*, 78 (1963), 25-35.
———. "The Scorpion of Chaucer's *Merchant's Tale*." *MLQ*, 26 (1965), 369-74.
Palomo, Dolores. "What Chaucer Really Did to *Le Livre de Melibee*." *PQ*, 53 (1974), 304-20.
Pantin, W. A. *The English Church in the Fourteenth Century*. Cambridge: Cambridge Univ. Press, 1955.
Parr, Johnstone. "*Life is a Pilgrimage* in Chaucer's *Knight's Tale* 2847-49." *MLN*, 67 (1952), 340-41.
Patch, Howard R. *The Tradition of Boethius: A Study of His Importance in Medieval Culture*. New York: Oxford Univ. Press, 1935.
Patterson, Lee W. "Chaucerian Confession: Penitential Literature and the Pardoner." *M&H*, N.S. 7 (1976), 153-73.
———. "The *Parson's Tale* and the Quitting of the *Canterbury Tales*." *Traditio*, 34 (1978), 331-80.
———. "Ambiguity and Interpretation: A Fifteenth-Century Reading of *Troilus and Criseyde*." *Speculum*, 54 (1979), 297-330.
———. "'For the Wyves love of Bath': Feminine Rhetoric and Poetic Resolution in the *Roman de la Rose* and the *Canterbury Tales*." *Speculum*, 58 (1983), 656-95.
Paues, Anna C., ed. *A Fourteenth-Century Middle English Biblical Version*. Cambridge: Cambridge Univ. Press, 1902; rev. ed., 1904.
Pearcy, Roy J. "Does the Manciple's Prologue Contain a Reference to Hell's Mouth?" *ELN*, 11 (1973-74), 167-75.
Pearsall, Derek, ed. *LeedsSE*, N.S. 14 (1983) [special issue of "Essays in Memory of Elizabeth Salter"].
———. *The Canterbury Tales*. London and Boston: G. Allen & Unwin, 1985.
———. "Chaucer's Poetry and Its Modern Commentators: The Necessity of History." In David Aers, ed., *Medieval*

Literature: Criticism, Ideology and History. Brighton, Sussex: The Harvester Press, 1986. Pp. 123-47.

———, and Elizabeth Salter. *Landscapes and Seasons of the Medieval World.* London: Paul Elek; Toronto and Buffalo: Univ. of Toronto Press, 1973.

Peck, Russell A. "Public Dreams and Private Myths: Perspective in Middle English Literature." *PMLA,* 90 (1975), 461-68.

———. "Chaucer and the Nominalist Questions." *Speculum,* 53 (1978), 745-60.

———. "Biblical Interpretation: St. Paul and *The Canterbury Tales.*" In Jeffrey, ed., *Chaucer and Scriptural Tradition,* 1984[a]. Pp. 143-70.

Petersen, Kate Oelzner. *On the Sources of the Nonne Prestes Tale.* New York: Haskell House, 1966 (first publ., 1898).

———. *The Sources of the Parson's Tale.* (Radcliffe College Monographs, No. 12.) Boston: Ginn & Co.—The Atheneum Press, 1901.

Popkin, Richard H. *The History of Scepticism from Erasmus to Descartes.* Rev. ed. New York, Evanston, and London: Harper and Row—Harper Torchbooks, 1968 (first publ., 1964).

Pratt, Robert A. "Jankyn's Book of Wikked Wyves: Medieval Anti-matrimonial Propaganda and the Universities." *AnM,* 3 (1962), 5-27.

———. "Chaucer and the Hand that Fed Him." *Speculum,* 41 (1966), 619-42.

———. "Three Old French Sources of The Nonnes Preestes Tale (Parts I & II)." *Speculum,* 47 (1972), 422-44; 646-68.

———. "Chaucer's Title: 'The tales of Caunterbury.'" *PQ,* 54 (1975), 19-25.

———. "Some Latin Sources of the Nonnes Preest on Dreams." *Speculum,* 52 (1977), 538-70.

Quinn, Esther C. "Religion in Chaucer's *Canterbury Tales:* A Study in Language and Structure." In George Economou, ed. *Geoffrey Chaucer,* 1975. Pp. 55-73.

Ramsay, J. H. "Chaucer and Wycliffe's Bible." *Academy,* 2 (1882), 435-36.

Reidy, John. "Explanatory Notes to *The Canon's Yeoman's Prologue* and *Tale.*" In Larry D. Benson, gen. ed., *The Riverside Chaucer,* 1987. Pp. 946-51.

Reiman, Donald H. "The Real Clerk's Tale; or, Patient Griselda Exposed." *TSLL,* 5 (1963), 356-73.

Reiss, Edmund. "Daun Gerveys in the Miller's Tale." *PLL,* 6 (1970), 122-23.

———. "Chaucer and Medieval Irony." *SAC,* 1 (1979), pp. 67-82.

———. "Chaucer and his Audience." *ChauR,* 14 (1979-80), 390-402.

———. "Biblical Parody : Chaucer's 'Distortions' of Scripture." In Jeffrey, ed., *Chaucer and Scriptural Tradition,* 1984[a]. Pp. 47-61.

Rice, Joanne. "Explanatory Notes to *The Franklin's Prologue* and *Tale.*" In Larry D. Benson, gen. ed., *The Riverside Chaucer,* 1987. Pp. 895-901.

Richardson, Janette. "Hunter and Prey: Functional Imagery in the Friar's Tale." *English Miscellany,* 12 (1961), 9-20 (rpt. in A. C. Cawley, ed., *Chaucer's Mind and Art,* 1969. Pp. 155-65).

———. "Explanatory Notes to *The General Prologue, The Friar's Prologue* and *Tale,* and *The Summoner's Prologue* and *Tale.*" In Larry D. Benson, gen. ed., *The Riverside Chaucer,* 1987. Pp. 807-09, 822-23, 874-79.

Riché, Pierre, and Guy Lobrichon, eds. *Le Moyen Age et la Bible.* (Bible de Tous les Temps, 4.) Paris: Beauchesne, 1984.

Ridley, Florence H. "Explanatory Notes to *The General Prologue, The Prioress's Prologue* and *Tale,* and *The Second*

Nun's Prologue and *Tale*." In Larry D. Benson, gen. ed., *The Riverside Chaucer*, 1987. Pp. 803-06, 913-16, 942-46.

Robertson, D. W., Jr. "Historical Criticism." In *English Institute Essays 1950*. New York: Columbia Univ. Press, 1951. Pp. 3-31 (rpt. in Robertson, [1980], pp. 3-20)

———. "The Doctrine of Charity in Medieval Literary Gardens: A Topical Approach Through Symbolism and Allegory." *Speculum*, 26 (1951), 24-49 (rpt. in Robertson, [1980], pp. 21-50).

———. "Chaucerian Tragedy." *ELH*, 19 (1952), 1-37 (rpt. in Schoeck & Taylor, *Chaucer Criticism*, 1961, 2.86-121).

———. *A Preface to Chaucer: Studies in Medieval Perspectives.* Princeton, N. J.: Princeton Univ. Press, 1962.

———. "The Medieval Bible." In Robertson, *The Literature of Medieval England.* New York: McGraw-Hill, 1970. Pp. 24-27.

———. "'And for my land thus hastow mordred me?': Land Tenure, the Cloth Industry, and the Wife of Bath." *ChauR*, 14 (1979-80), 403-20.

———. *Essays in Medieval Culture.* Princeton, N. J.: Princeton Univ. Press, 1980.

———. "Chaucer and Christian Tradition." In Jeffrey, ed., *Chaucer and Scriptural Tradition*, 1984[a]. Pp. 3-32.

Rogers, William E. "The Raven and the Writing Desk: The Theoretical Limits of Patristic Criticism," *ChauR*, 14 (1979-80), 260-77.

Root, Robert K. "Chaucer and the Bible." *The Nation*, Oct. 20, Vol. 79 (1904), no. 2051, p. 315.

———. "Chaucer and the *Decameron*." *Englische Studien*, 44 (1912), 1-7.

———. "The Monk's Tale." In Bryan and Dempster, eds., *Sources and Analogues*, 1941. Pp. 615-44.

Rose, Donald M., ed. *New Perspectives in Chaucer Criticism.* Norman, Okla.: Pilgrim Books, 1981.

Rosenberg, Bruce. "Swindling Alchemist, Antichrist." *CentR*, 6 (1962), 566-80.

————. "The 'Cherry-Tree Carol' and the *Merchant's Tale*." *ChauR*, 5 (1970-71), 246-76.

Ross, Thomas W. "Notes on Chaucer's Miller's Tale, A 3216 and 3320." *ELN*, 13 (1976), 256-58.

Rost, Hans. *Die Bibel im Mittelalter: Beiträge zur Geschichte und Bibliographie der Bibel.* Augsburg: M. Seitz, 1939.

Rothman, Irving N. "Humility and Obedience in the *Clerk's Tale*, with the Envoy Considered as an Ironic Affirmation." *PLL*, 9 (1973), 115-27.

Rouse, Richard H., and Mary A. Rouse. "Biblical *distinctiones* in the Thirteenth Century." *Archives d'Histoire Doctrinale et Littéraire du Moyen Age*, 41 (1974[a]), 27-37.

————. "The Verbal Concordance to the Scriptures." *Archivum Fratrum Praedicatorum*, 44 (1974[b]), 5-30.

————. "*Statim invenire:* Schools, Preachers, and New Attitudes to the Page." In Robert L. Benson and Giles Constable, eds., with Carol D. Lanham, *Renaissance and Renewal in the Twelfth Century.* Cambridge, Mass.: Harvard Univ. Press, 1982. Pp. 201-25.

Rowe, Donald W. *O Love O Charite! Contraries Harmonized in Chaucer's Troilus.* Carbondale and Edwardsville, Ill.: Southern Illinois Univ. Press, 1976.

Rowland, Beryl. "The Play of the *Miller's Tale:* A Game Within a Game." *ChauR*, 5 (1970-71), 140-46.

————. *Blind Beasts: Chaucer's Animal World.* Kent, Ohio: Kent State Univ. Press, 1971.

————, ed. *Chaucer and Middle English Studies: In Honor of Rossell Hope Robbins.* London: George Allen & Unwin, 1974.

————. "Chaucer's Blasphemous Churl: A New Interpretation of the *Miller's Tale*." In Beryl Rowland, ed., *Chaucer and Middle English Studies*, 1974. Pp. 43-55.

————, ed. *Companion to Chaucer Studies.* Rev. ed. New York and Oxford: Oxford Univ. Press, 1979.

Rudat, Wolfgang E. H. "Heresy and Springtime Ritual: Biblical and Classical Allusion in the *Canterbury Tales*." *RBPH*, 54 (1976), 823-36.

Rutter, G. M. "An Holy Jewes Shepe." *MLN*, 43 (1928), 536.

Salter, Elizabeth. *Chaucer: The Knight's Tale and the Clerk's Tale*. London: Arnold, 1962.

———. *Nicholas Love's 'Myrrour of the Blessed Lyf of Jesu Christ.'* (Analecta Cartusiana, 10.) Salzburg: Universität Salzburg, 1974.

Scattergood, V. J. "Explanatory Notes to *The Manciple's Prologue* and *Tale*." In Larry D. Benson, gen. ed., *The Riverside Chaucer*, 1987. Pp. 952-54.

Scheps, Walter. "Chaucer's Numismatic Pardoner and the Personification of Avarice." In Szarmach and Levy, eds., *The Fourteenth Century*, 1977. Pp. 107-23.

Schinnerl, Hubert. "Die Belesenheit Chaucers in der Bibel und der antiken Literatur." Diss. Munich, 1921. [Not seen.]

Schlauch, Margaret. "Constantine, Jonah, and the *Gesta Romanorum*." *Kwartalnik Neofilologiczny*, 20 (1973), 305-06.

Schless, Howard H. *Chaucer and Dante: A Revaluation*. Norman, Okla.: Pilgrim Books, 1984.

Schmidt, A. V. C. "Chaucer's *Nembrot*: A Note on *The Former Age*." *MAE*, 47 (1978), 304-07.

Schoeck, Richard J., and Jerome Taylor, eds. *Chaucer Criticism, Vol. I: The Canterbury Tales*. Notre Dame, Ind., and London: Univ. of Notre Dame Press, 1960.

———. *Chaucer Criticism, Vol. 2: Troilus and Criseyde & the Minor Poems*. Notre Dame, Ind., and London: Univ. of Notre Dame Press, 1961.

Severs, J. Burke. "The Job Passage in the *Clerk's Tale*." *MLN*, 49 (1934), 461-62.

———. "The Source of Chaucer's *Melibeus*." *PMLA*, 50 (1935), 92-99.

————. *The Literary Relationships of Chaucer's Clerk's Tale.* (Yale Studies in English, 96.) Hamden, Conn.: Archon, 1972 (first publ., 1942).

————. "The Clerk's Tale." In Bryan and Dempster, eds., *Sources and Analogues,* 1941[a]. Pp. 288-331.

————. "The Tale of Melibeus." In Bryan and Dempster, eds. *Sources and Analogues,* 1941[b]. Pp. 560-614.

————. "The *Summoner's Tale* D 2184-88." *Expl,* 23 (1964-65), Item 20.

Shaner, M. C. E., and A. S. G. Edwards. "Explanatory Notes to *The Legend of Good Women.*" In Larry D. Benson, gen. ed., *The Riverside Chaucer,* 1987. Pp. 1059-75.

Shannon, Edgar F. "The Physician's Tale." In Bryan and Dempster, eds., *Sources and Analogues,* 1941. Pp. 398-408.

Shepherd, Geoffrey. "Religion and Philosophy in Chaucer." In Derek Brewer, ed., *Writers and Their Background,* 1975. Pp. 262-89.

Silvia, Daniel S., Jr. "Glosses to the *Canterbury Tales* from St. Jerome's *Epistola Adversus Jovinianum.*" *SP,* 62 (1965), 28-39.

Sledd, James. "The *Clerk's Tale:* The Monsters and the Critics." *MP,* 51 (1953-54), 73-82 (rpt. in Schoeck and Taylor, eds., *Chaucer Criticism,* 1960, I:160-74).

Smalley, Beryl. *Studies in Medieval Thought and Learning: From Abelard to Wyclif.* London: Hambledon Press, 1981.

————. *The Study of the Bible in the Middle Ages.* 3rd ed. revised. Oxford: Blackwell, 1983 (first publ., 1952).

————. *The Gospels in the Schools c.1100-c.1280.* London and Ronceverte, W. Va.: Hambledon Press, 1985.

————. *Medieval Exegesis of Wisdom Literature: Essays by Beryl Smalley.* Roland E. Murphy, ed. Atlanta: Scholars Press, 1986.

Smith, R. M. "Three Obscure English Proverbs." *MLN,* 65 (1950), 441-47.

Spargo, John Webster. "The Canon's Yeoman's Prologue and Tale." In Bryan and Dempster, eds., *Sources and Analogues,* 1941. Pp. 685-98.

Spencer, Theodore. "Chaucer's Hell: A Study in Mediaeval Convention." *Speculum,* 2 (1927), 177-200.

Spiers, Edward Howard. "Chaucer's References to Old Testament Personages, Including Textual Comparison with the Vulgate." Master's Thesis, Univ. of Washington, 1950. [Not seen.]

Spisak, James. "Anti-Feminism Bridled: Two Rhetorical Contexts." *NM,* 81 (1980), 150-60.

Stapleton, Christopher R. "Chaucer the Catholic." *Catholic World,* 127 (1928), 186-93.

Stegmüller, Friedrich. *Repertorium Biblicum Medii Aevi.* 11 vols. Madrid: Instituto Francisco Suárez, 1950-80.

Stepsis, Robert. "*Potentia Absoluta* and the *Clerk's Tale.*" *ChauR,* 10 (1975-76), 129-46.

Stevens, John. "Angelus ad virginem: The History of a Medieval Song." In *Medieval Studies for J. A. W. Bennett, Aetatis Suae LXX.* Ed. P. L. Hegworth. Oxford: Clarendon Press, 1981. Pp. 297-328.

Stock, Lorraine K. "The Reenacted Fall in Chaucer's *Shipman's Tale.*" *SIcon,* 7-8 (1981-82), 134-45.

Stockton, Eric W. "The Deadliest Sin in the *Pardoner's Tale.*" *TSL,* 6 (1961), 47-59.

Storm, Melvin. "The Pardoner's Invitation: Quaestor's Bag or Beckett's Shrine?" *PMLA,* 97 (1982), 810-18.

Strachan, James. *Early Bible Illustrations.* Cambridge: Cambridge Univ. Press, 1957.

Strohm, Paul. "The Allegory of the *Tale of Melibee.*" *ChauR,* 2 (1967-68), 32-42.

Sutherland, R. C. "A Note on Lines D 1645-1662 of Chaucer's *Friar's Tale.*" *PQ,* 31 (1952), 436-39.

Szarmach, P. E., and B. S. Levy, eds. *The Fourteenth Century* (Acta 4). Binghampton: SUNY, Binghampton, Center for Medieval and Renaissance Studies, 1977.

Szittya, Penn R. "The Friar as False Apostle: Antifraternal Exegesis and the *Summoner's Tale*." *SP*, 71 (1974), 19-46.

——. "The Antifraternal Tradition in Middle English Literature." *Speculum*, 52 (1977), 287-313.

Taitt, Peter. "In Defense of Lot." *N&Q*, N.S. 18 (1971), 284-85.

Talbert, Ernest W. and S. Harrison Thomson. "Wyclyf and His Followers." In J. Burke Severs, ed., *A Manual of the Writings in Middle English 1050-1500*. Hamden, Conn.: Archon Books, 1970. Pp. 354-80, 517-33.

Tatlock, J. S. P. *The Development and Chronolgy of Chaucer's Works*. (Chaucer Society Publications, Second Series, 37.) London: Kegan Paul, 1907.

——. "Chaucer and Wyclif." *MP*, 14 (1916), 257-68.

——. "The Canterbury Tales in 1400." *PMLA*, 50 (1935), 100-39.

——, and Arthur G. Kennedy. *A Concordance to the Complete Works of Geoffrey Chaucer and to the Romaunt of the Rose*. Gloucester, Mass.: Peter Smith, 1963 (first publ., 1927).

Tavormina, M. Teresa. "Explanatory Notes to *The Merchant's Prologue* and *Tale*." In Larry D. Benson, gen. ed., *The Riverside Chaucer*, 1987. Pp. 884-90.

Taylor, Ann M. "A Scriptural Echo in the Trojan Parliament of *Troilus and Criseyde*." *NMS*, 24 (1980), 51-56.

Taylor, Paul B. "The Alchemy of Spring in Chaucer's *General Prologue*." *ChauR*, 17 (1982-83), 1-4.

Thomas, Mary Edith. *Medieval Skepticism and Chaucer*. New York: William Frederick, 1950.

Thompson, W. Meredith. "Chaucer's Translation of the Bible." In Norman Davis and C. L. Wrenn, eds., *English and Medieval Studies Presented to J. R. R. Tolkien*. London: Allen & Unwin, 1962. Pp. 183-99.

Thundy, Zacharias P. "Matheolus, Chaucer, and the Wife of Bath." In Vasta and Thundy, eds., *Chaucerian Problems and Perspectives*, 1979. Pp. 24-58.

Trinkaus, Charles. *The Scope of Renaissance Humanism.* Ann Arbor: Univ. of Michigan Press, 1983.

——, and Heiko Oberman, eds. *The Pursuit of Holiness in Late Medieval and Renaissance Religion.* Leiden: E. J. Brill, 1974.

Tuck, J. Anthony. "Carthusian Monks and Lollard Knights: Religious Attitudes at the Court of Richard II." In *SAC,* Proceedings, 1 (1984), pp. 149-61.

Tupper, Frederick. "Chaucer's Bed's Head." *MLN,* 30 (1915), 5-12.

Turner, W. Arthur. "Biblical Women in *The Merchant's Tale* and *The Tale of Melibee.*" *ELN,* 3 (1965), 92-95.

Ussery, Huling E. "How Old is Chaucer's Clerk?" *TSE,* 15 (1967), 1-18.

——. "Fourteenth-Century English Logicians: Possible Models for Chaucer's Clerk." *TSE,* 18 (1970), 1-15.

Utley, Francis Lee, ed. *The Forward Movement of the Fourteenth Century.* Columbus: Ohio State Univ. Press, 1961.

——. "Chaucer and Patristic Exegesis." In A. C. Cawley, ed., *Chaucer's Mind and Art,* 1969. Pp. 69-85.

——. "Five Genres in the *Clerk's Tale.*" *ChauR,* 6 (1971-72), 198-228.

——. "Chaucer's Troilus and St. Paul's Charity." In Beryl Rowland, ed., *Chaucer and Middle English Studies,* 1974. Pp. 272-87.

Vasta, Edward, and Zacharias P. Thundy, eds. *Chaucerian Problems and Perspectives: Essays Presented to Paul E. Beichner C.S.C.* Notre Dame, Ind., and London: Univ. of Notre Dame Press, 1979.

Vaughan, M. F. "Chaucer's Imaginative One-Day Flood." *PQ,* 60 (1981), 117-23.

Vawter, Bruce, C. M. *The Bible in the Church.* New York: Sheed & Ward, 1959. [Not seen.]

Wallace, David. *Chaucer and the Early Writings of Boccaccio.*
(Chaucer Studies 12.) Woodbridge, Suffolk: D. S. Brewer,
1985.

Walsh, Katherine, and Diana Wood, eds. *The Bible in the
Medieval World: Essays in Memory of Beryl Smalley.*
(Studies in Church History, Subsidia, 4.) Oxford:
Blackwell, 1985.

Watts, Ann C. "'*Amor gloriae*' in Chaucer's *House of Fame.*"
JMRS, 3 (1973), 87-113.

Weissman, Hope Phyllis. "Antifeminism and Chaucer's
Characterization of Women." In George Economou, ed.,
Geoffrey Chaucer, 1975. Pp. 93-110.

———. "The Pardoner's Vernicle, the Wife's Coverchiefs, and
Saint Paul." *Chaucer Newsletter*, 1, no. 2 (1979), 10-12.

Wenk, J. C. "On the Sources of *The Prioress's Tale.*" *MS*, 17
(1955), 214-19.

Wenzel, Siegfried. "The Sources of the 'Remedia' of the
Parson's Tale." *Traditio*, 27 (1971), 433-53.

———. "The Pilgimage of Life as a Late Medieval Genre."
MS, 35 (1973), 370-88.

———. "The Source of Chaucer's Seven Deadly Sins."
Traditio, 30 (1974), 351-78.

———. "Chaucer and the Language of Contemporary
Preaching." *SP*, 73 (1976), 138-61.

———. "Notes on *The Parson's Tale.*" *ChauR*, 16 (1981-82),
237-56.

———. Letter to the author. 28 April 1985.

———. "Explanatory Notes to *The General Prologue, The
Parson's Prologue* and *Tale*, and *Chaucer's Retraction.*" In
Larry D. Benson, gen. ed., *The Riverside Chaucer*, 1987. Pp.
819, 954-65.

Wetherbee, Winthrop. "Convention and Authority: A
Comment on Some Recent Critical Approaches to Chaucer."
In Rose, ed., *New Perspectives*, 1981. Pp. 71-81.

———. *Chaucer and the Poets: An Essay on* Troilus and
Criseyde. Ithaca and London: Cornell Univ. Press, 1984.

Whitlark, James S. "Chaucer and the Pagan Gods." *AnM*, 18 (1977), 65-75.

Wilcockson, Colin. "Explanatory Notes to *The Book of the Duchess*." In Larry D. Benson, gen. ed., *The Riverside Chaucer*, 1987. Pp. 966-76.

Willard, Rudolph. "Chaucer's 'Text that Seith that Hunters Ben Nat Hooly Men.'" *Studies in English*. Austin: Univ. of Texas Press, 1947. Pp. 209-51.

Williams, Arnold. "Chaucer and the Friars." *Speculum*, 28 (1953), 499-513.

Wimsatt, James I. "The Apotheosis of Blanche in *The Book of the Duchess*." *JEGP*, 66 (1967), 26-44.

————. *Chaucer and the French Love Poets*. Chapel Hill, N. C.: Univ. of North Carolina Press, 1968.

————. "Chaucer and the Canticle of Canticles." In Jerome Mitchell and William Provost, eds., *Chaucer the Love Poet*, 1973. Pp. 66-90.

————. "Medieval and Modern in Chaucer's *Troilus and Criseyde*." *PMLA*, 92 (1977), 203-16.

————. "*The Book of the Duchess*: Secular Elegy or Religious Vision?" In Hermann and Burke, eds., *Signs and Symbols*, 1981. Pp. 113-29.

Witlieb, Bernard. "Jupiter and Nimrod in *The Former Age*." *Chaucer Newsletter*, 2 (1980), 12-13.

Wood, Chauncey. "Chaucer's Man of Law as Interpreter." *Traditio*, 23 (1967), 149-90.

————. *Chaucer and the Country of the Stars: Poetic Uses of Astrological Imagery*. Princeton, N. J.: Princeton Univ. Press, 1970.

————. "The Sources of Chaucer's Summoner's 'Garleek, Onyons, and eek Lekes.'" *ChauR*, 5 (1970-71), 20-44.

————. "Chaucer's Use of Signs in His Portrait of the Prioress." In Hermann and Burke, eds., *Signs and Symbols*, 1981. Pp. 81-101.

————. Letter to the author. 10 February 1984[a].

————. *The Elements of Chaucer's* Troilus. Durham, N. C.: Duke Univ. Press, 1984[b].

————. "Artistic Intention and Chaucer's Uses of Scriptural Allusion." In Jeffrey, ed., *Chaucer and Scriptural Tradition,* 1984[a]. Pp. 35-46.

Work, James A. "The Manciple's Tale." In Bryan and Dempster, eds., *Sources and Analogues,* 1941. Pp. 699-722.

Wormald, Francis. "Bible Illustration in Medieval Manuscripts." In Lampe, ed., *The Cambridge History of the Bible,* 1969. Pp. 309-37.

Wurtele, Douglas. "Marian Overtones in Chaucer's *Merchant's Tale.*" *Proceedings of the Symposium of Ottawa-Carleton Medieval-Renaissance Club,* 1 (1976), 56-74.

————. "The Figure of Solomon in Chaucer's Merchant's Tale." *RUO,* 47 (1977), 478-87.

————. "Ironical Resonance in the *Merchant's Tale.*" *ChauR,* 13 (1978-79), 66-79.

————. "The Blasphemy of Chaucer's Merchant." *AnM,* 21 (1981), 91-110.

————. "Chaucer's *Canterbury Tales* and Nicholas of Lyre's *Postillae litteralis et moralis super totam Bibliam.*" In Jeffrey, ed., *Chaucer and Scriptural Tradition,* 1984[a]. Pp. 89-107.

Yots, Michael. "Chaucer's Shipman's Tale." *Expl,* 36 (1978), 23-24.

Young, Karl. "Chaucer and Peter Riga." *Speculum,* 12 (1937), 299-303.

Yunck, John A. "Religious Elements in Chaucer's *Man of Law's Tale.*" *ELH,* 27 (1960), 249-61.